International Perspectives on Reminiscence, Life Review and Life Story Work

by the same author

Reminiscence and Life Story Work
A Practice Guide
Faith Gibson
ISBN 978 1 84905 151 4
eISBN 978 0 85700 338 6

of related interest

Life Story Work with People with Dementia
Ordinary Lives, Extraordinary People
Edited by Polly Kaiser and Ruth Eley
ISBN 978 1 84905 505 5
eISBN 978 0 85700 914 2

Remembering Yesterday, Caring Today
Reminiscence in Dementia Care: A Guide to Good Practice
Pam Schweitzer and Errollyn Bruce
ISBN 978 1 84310 649 4
eISBN 978 1 84642 804 3

Facilitating Spiritual Reminiscence for People with Dementia
A Learning Guide
Elizabeth MacKinlay and Corinne Trevitt
ISBN 978 1 84905 573 4
eISBN 978 1 78450 018 4

INTERNATIONAL PERSPECTIVES ON REMINISCENCE, LIFE REVIEW AND LIFE STORY WORK

EDITED BY FAITH GIBSON

Foreword by Barbara Haight

Jessica Kingsley *Publishers*
London and Philadelphia

First published in 2019
by Jessica Kingsley Publishers
73 Collier Street
London N1 9BE, UK
and
400 Market Street, Suite 400
Philadelphia, PA 19106, USA

www.jkp.com

Copyright © Jessica Kingsley Publishers 2019
Foreword copyright © Barbara Haight 2019

Front cover image source: iStockphoto®.

All rights reserved. No part of this publication may be reproduced in any material form (including photocopying, storing in any medium by electronic means or transmitting) without the written permission of the copyright owner except in accordance with the provisions of the law or under terms of a licence issued in the UK by the Copyright Licensing Agency Ltd. www.cla.co.uk or in overseas territories by the relevant reproduction rights organisation, for details see www.ifrro.org. Applications for the copyright owner's written permission to reproduce any part of this publication should be addressed to the publisher.

Warning: The doing of an unauthorised act in relation to a copyright work may result in both a civil claim for damages and criminal prosecution.

Library of Congress Cataloging in Publication Data
Names: Gibson, Faith, editor.
Title: International perspectives on reminiscence, life review and life story work / edited by Faith Gibson.
Description: Philadelphia : Jessica Kingsley Publishers, [2019]
Identifiers: LCCN 2018020643 | ISBN 9781785923920
Subjects: LCSH: Reminiscing in old age. | Reminiscing. | Aging.
Classification: LCC HD58.9 .I58 2019 | DDC 153.1/2--dc23
LC record available at https://lccn.loc.gov/2018020643

British Library Cataloguing in Publication Data
A CIP catalogue record for this book is available from the British Library

ISBN 978 1 78592 392 0
eISBN 978 1 78450 744 2

Printed and bound in Great Britain

To Peter Coleman, who introduced me to gerontology and intrigued me about reminiscence

Contents

Foreword by Barbara Haight   11

Acknowledgements   14

Part 1: Recent and Contemporary Research

1. Introduction   17
   Faith Gibson, Ulster University, Northern Ireland, UK

2. Recent Progress in Reminiscence Research   38
   Thomas W. Pierce, Radford University, Virginia, USA, and
   Ann N. Elliott, Radford University, Virginia, USA

3. Reminiscence Work with People with Dementia:
   Making Sense of the Evidence Base   60
   Bob Woods, Bangor University, Wales, UK

Part 2: Age and Cultural Variations and Applications

4. Reminiscence and Life Review in Later Life:
   The Southampton Longitudinal Study   86
   Peter G. Coleman, University of Southampton, UK, Christine
   Ivani-Chalian, University of Southampton, UK, and
   Maureen Robinson, University of Southampton, UK

5. Developmental Foundations of Lifelong Reminiscing   109
   Robyn Fivush, Emory University, Atlanta, Georgia, USA, and
   Jordan A. Booker, Emory University, Atlanta, Georgia, USA

6. Reminiscence and Life Review Work in Taiwan   125
   TsuAnn Kuo, Chung Shan Medical University, Taiwan

7. Spiritual Reminiscence in Later Life   145
   Elizabeth MacKinlay, Charles Sturt University, Canberra, Australia

8. The Loss of a Loved One: Remembering
   the Life and the Dying Days — 162
   *Emily L. Mroz, University of Florida, USA, and
   Susan Bluck, University of Florida, USA*

9. Guided Autobiography: Scope, Implementation
   and International Applications — 180
   Cheryl Svensson and Brian de Vries

10. Reminiscence, Narrative and the
    Presence of Meaning in Life — 200
    Jeffrey Dean Webster

Part 3: Implications of Reminiscence, Life Review and Life Story Work for Health and Wellbeing

11. The Narrative Self in the Lived Experience of Dementia — 212
    Christine Bryden, Charles Sturt University, Canberra, Australia

12. Self Reminiscences of Clinically Depressed Older Adults
    and the Tripartite Functional Model Revisited — 225
    Philippe Cappeliez, University of Ottawa, Ontario, Canada

13. Reminiscence, Self and Meaningful Connections:
    A Case Example of Bill — 244
    *Kate de Medeiros, Miami University, Oxford, Ohio, USA, and
    Sara Stemen, Miami University, Oxford, Ohio, USA*

14. Sharing Memories Building Communities through
    an Arts-Based Reminiscence Project — 263
    *Marian Ferguson, Reminiscence Network Northern Ireland, UK, and
    Geraldine Gallagher, Reminiscence Network Northern Ireland, UK*

15. Reminiscence Arts: Creative Exploration of the
    Past in the Present — 281
    *Pam Schweitzer, European Reminiscence Network
    and University of Greenwich, UK*

16. The Structured Life Review — 304
    *Juliette Shellman, University of Connecticut, USA, and
    Julia McNeil, University of Connecticut, USA*

17. Life Review: Lifespan Development, Meaning Processes
    and Interventions 312
    Gerben J. Westerhof

Part 4: Technology in Reminiscence Practice, Training and Development

18. Memoir Writing: The Challenge of Leaving a Legacy 328
    Mary O'Brien Tyrrell, Memoirs LLC, Osterville, Massachusetts, USA

19. The Contribution of Information Technology to
    Reminiscence, Life Review and Life Story Work:
    The Perspective of People Living with Dementia and
    their Families 341
    Assumpta Ryan, Ulster University, Northern Ireland, UK

20. Increasing the Use of Reminiscence and Life Review:
    Experiences with the Development, Implementation, and
    Evaluation of an Online International Certificate Course 359
    Juliette Shellman, University of Connecticut, USA,
    Loriena Yancura, University of Hawaii, USA, and
    Esther Gieschen, University of Wisconsin, USA

21. Afterword 372
    Faith Gibson, Ulster University, Northern Ireland, UK

    References 381

    List of Contributors 417

    Subject Index 423

    Author Index 429

Foreword

Faith Gibson has made another significant contribution to the field of reminiscing with this timely collection. Faith provides an international perspective on reminiscence work, having started her social work career in her home country of Australia, becoming a Fulbright Scholar at the School of Social Service Administration, University of Chicago, then moving on as a social worker and academic to Northern Ireland, and finally continuing her story as a dementia expert both in Northern Ireland and in her birth country of Australia, where she currently resides. Faith is one of the foremost experts on the use of reminiscence with those who have dementia. She is the recipient of an OBE, a millennium medal of the British Geriatrics Society, a lifetime achievement award from the British Association of Social Workers and has an honorary doctorate from the University of Stirling. She is the author of numerous publications, training manuals, chapters and books, and as such she is widely respected. From this background and expertise, Faith presents a global view of reminiscing.

This new book, *International Perspectives on Reminiscence, Life Review and Life Story Work*, is the most comprehensive review of the field in several years. The book combines the analysis of experienced authors with the questions and ideas of new scholars. This global combination of authors, working at various levels of academic and practice expertise, should stimulate further progressive thinking as the contributors present ideas on related issues from diverse parts of the world. For example, some authors focus on the ways of reminiscing through memoir writing, or autobiography, or the arts. Although these writers explore the common topic of reminiscing, each one investigates the process differently. They hold different viewpoints, use different techniques, and report different outcomes. This book will inform readers of the accomplishments and achievements of the last 16 years and inspire them to develop new ideas that will continue to advance reminiscence work. To this end, the book is divided into four parts:

Recent and Contemporary Research; Age and Cultural Variations and Applications; Implications of Reminiscence, Life Review and Life Story Work for Health and Wellbeing; and Technology in Reminiscence Practice, Training and Development.

Part 1 on reminiscence research contains a comprehensive critical analysis of recent research by American and British writers. A report on an updated Cochrane Review provides a timely, systematic evaluation of research on reminiscence in healthcare with people who have dementia. The research section will inform researchers of the latest developments in the field and provide a road map for their future work.

Part 2 is rich with ideas revealing the diversity of reminiscing as an intervention with people of different ages and from different cultures. We see the importance of reminiscing over time and with people at different stages of the life cycle, and the part played by reminiscence in people's search for meaning in various cultures. Here we find that, surprisingly, children use reminiscing as much or more than older people. For many who reminiscence, the story — the end product — is the most important outcome, but for others it is the therapeutic process of revisiting and reconsidering memories which is more important.

Part 3 talks about gaining insight through sharing other people's memories as we live the experience of dementia through a contributor writing her own life story. The health and wellbeing gains for people with depression and anxiety and the inherent power of being heard receive attention from several contributors. From these examples, the reader can see that each author defines the use and application of reminiscence for themselves and uses the experience in their own way while drawing from the established understanding of the various purposes served by reminiscence. Here there are accounts of practical projects drawn from different countries and using a wide variety of creative arts to stimulate recall of the past as a means of enriching the present, decreasing isolation, increasing self-understanding and sustaining relationships.

Part 4 shows how many older people use reminiscence as a way to establish themselves and their place in history. Some do this by hiring a writer to help them compile their memoirs. Others may join various types of groups in which they share in the process of reminiscing, writing and reading their stories. Not only is the reminiscing enjoyed by the one recalling the past, but also the resulting memoirs are enjoyed by all. Such tangible records can then be looked at many times, alone or shared with others, as people continue to reminisce and stimulate others to do the same, and by doing so family legacies may be created.

Part 4 also reports on the growing use of technology in the work of reminiscing. One chapter describes the foundation and delivery of an online Certificate in Reminiscence and Life Story Work, a program provided by the Center for Continuing Education at the University of Wisconsin–Superior (UWS-CCE). The International Institute for Reminiscence and Life Review (IIRLR) and the Association of Personal Historians contributed to the development of this Certificate program. This series of classes provides certification for individuals to learn about and use reminiscing and life review. Earlier chapters describe the formation of leaders of guided autobiographical writing groups and a European apprenticeship training and development model to develop skills for reminiscing with people with dementia and their carers. Another describes the use of the internet to deliver interactive classes. The internet can also be a tool for running an autobiography group, allowing people from various locations to share their stories with one another. Faith's book demonstrates how far we've come, but future work in the field could be even more impressive with increased knowledge and use of information technology, artificial intelligence and neuroscience.

Reminiscence now has an international journal that provides legitimacy to the work that is being done. The International Institute for Reminiscence and Life Review sponsors an international meeting every two years to discuss work in progress, and the European Reminiscence Network continues to pursue its reminiscence project work, primarily concerned with dementia. There is no doubt that this book will move us forwards again, hastening further growth. Faith Gibson will always be associated with reminiscence work and many of us in the international reminiscence community will always be grateful and indebted to her for continuing to lead the way. I personally am honoured to write the foreword for this book.

Barbara Haight DRPH FAAN FGSA
Professor Emeritus, College of Nursing
Medical University of South Carolina, Charleston, USA

Acknowledgements

A great many people have contributed to the writing and production of this book. I have appreciated the unfailing advice and assistance of Sarah Hamlin, Hannah Snetsinger and other Jessica Kingsley staff. My warmest thanks to Barbara Haight for her friendship and support over many years and for writing the book's foreword. All the contributing authors, with their willingness to contribute and their patience and promptness in dealing with my queries, have made editing the book a great pleasure. I am much indebted to the late Craig Garrett, a West Point graduate, physician and poet who died last year, for his permission to use his unpublished poem *Unremembered* about his great aunt Stella May who died in Iowa in 1872. I also appreciate Margaret McClintock's willingness to have her poem *Mum Now* included, which is about her mother Patricia Norman, who has dementia. I am so glad that Mary O'Brien Tyrrell and Lorna Buining introduced me to these poems, which capture so well the joys and sorrows of remembering and forgetting, and the riches as well as the fallibility of memory that to a greater or lesser extent we all share.

Benny, Patrick and Robert's computer assistance and Linda's cheerfulness helped along the way, and without Kathryn's loving care and encouragement it is unlikely this book would ever have been commenced, let alone completed.

My thanks to you all.

Faith Gibson

Part 1

RECENT AND CONTEMPORARY RESEARCH

Chapter 1

INTRODUCTION

Faith Gibson

This book has many worthy forbears. Over a number of years, numerous books and journal papers have reported and reviewed literature concerned with reminiscence, life review and life story work research and practice; they identified current issues and concerns and suggested various areas for further research and exploration. Risking ignoring or neglecting some of these pivotal international milestone publications, by placing this book within its wider historical intellectual lineage may assist contemporary readers, and especially those new to reminiscence and other narrative methods, to appreciate the rich foundations on which this book builds and the intellectual, practice and clinical debts we present authors owe to our predecessors. In the main, the works cited in this introductory chapter refer to major milestone publications that have personally influenced me during my 40 years or so of preoccupation with studying memory and seeking to understand how memories and their recall influence thinking and behaviour in the present. This introduction does not pretend to be a comprehensive history of the burgeoning growth of interest in reminiscence and reminiscence work, that sometimes − not always helpfully, in my view − is referred to as reminiscence therapy (Gibson 1994, 2004; Haight and Burnside 1993). Rather, it refers to writing and other developments that have intrigued and excited me, informed my own research, teaching and practice, and helped me to make fruitful connections between personal experience and academic pursuits.

Heeding Pear's view (1922) that the mind never photographs but rather paints pictures, and conscious of many classical and literary references to the interplay of memory and imagination so eloquently explored by writers like Proust (1981) and Warnock (1987) among others, I note that it is customary to attribute the beginnings of the modern reminiscence movement, almost exclusively focused at first on older people, and situated within a life cycle developmental perspective (Erikson 1959, 1978), to Butler's (1963a, 1963b) seminal paper. A psychiatrist by profession, he recognised the positive significance reminiscence plays in the lives of people as they age, contrary to earlier views about its negative impact on mental health, a theme further explored by Lewis (1971) and Butler and Lewis (1977). Almost all the contributors to this book have cited Butler's work as well, and a substantial number also refer to the influence of Erikson's ideas on their own research and practice.

Frankl's book, *Man's Search for Meaning* (1984), also cited by several chapter authors, helped me to understand the influence of past experience on the present and to appreciate that in varying degrees, and in different ways, to live is to suffer, to survive is to find meaning in the suffering; and it's important to live in hope rather than despair. Or put another way by an anonymous writer: 'Man is made for good and ill/ If this you know/Safely through the world you go.' McMahon and Rhudick (1964) focused attention on the value of veterans reviewing and recounting their wartime experiences and Pincus (1970) wrote about the social work treatment implications and applications of undertaking reminiscence with aged people.

Johnson (1976), a British gerontologist, began to alert clinicians and service providers to the value of reminiscence as a way into understanding an older person's past. He regarded such understanding of the past as an essential gateway to recognising, assessing and responding to a person's present health and social care needs. In 1978, Burnside, a nurse educator, first published her widely influential book *Working with Older Adults: Group Processes and Techniques*, and her subsequent revisions written with Schmidt, a social worker, (1986, 1994) all contained important chapters on reminiscence and guided autobiographical writing. The fourth memorial edition honoring her extensive work that was edited by Haight and Gibson (2005) again included germane chapters on these topics.

An architect in the United Kingdom's Department of Health, Kemp (1978) led a reminiscence aids project aimed at stimulating frail elderly people and enlivening their boredom-inducing residential care homes by using photographs of familiar places, people and events to encourage conversation and social interaction. This project was subsequently developed by an international voluntary organisation, Help the Aged, which in 1981 prompted a near avalanche of interest in practical reminiscence and life story work with the publication of three tape/slide audio-visual programmes known as *Recall* that featured largely London-based images and sounds. *Recall* spawned many similar more localised publications of trigger materials and training packages (Gibson 1989, 2000; Price 1992).

Raised in rural Australia and familiar with School of the Air, the Royal Flying Doctor Service and images of vast space and isolation where 'the nearest woman's face may be a hundred miles away' (Evans 1906), I thought I knew about distance. Relocating after marriage to Northern Ireland where a 'stranger' meant someone from the next village, or sometimes even from the next street, let alone from another Christian denomination, I was quick to develop a new perspective on 'distance' and learn anew about the significance of 'place'. It was from these personal influences from childhood and young adulthood as well as practising social work in psychiatric settings, where to know a person's history was pivotal in establishing relationships in the present, that I came to realise the impact of memories and began to understand the therapeutic potential of reminiscing. Although reminiscences may often be related to universal experiences, I was also learning that memories are intensely personal, embedded in particular times and contexts and related to an individual's lived experiences of people, places and events.

Merriam (1980, 1993) and Merriam and Cross (1982) reviewed the early literature, raised issues about the occurrence of reminiscence at different stages of the lifespan and the different functions it fulfils. Dobrof (1984), referring back to Butler's work, wrote of reminiscence being a liberation that freed old people to remember, to regret, and to look reflectively at the past as they sought to understand their lives. Importantly, Dobrof wrote that the health and care staff who worked with such frail elderly people were likewise liberated because now they were permitted to listen and respect both the rememberers and their reminiscences without thinking that talking about the past was a sign of mental ill-health.

Kaminsky (1984a, 1984b) reflected on the uses of reminiscence while describing storytelling as a sort of spadework that was likely to turn up precious metals. Molinari and Reichlin (1985) published an extensive review of the literature concerned with life review with elderly people. Disch (1988) wrote about the close relationship between reminiscence and oral history. He also perceived the therapeutic potential inherent in bearing testimony through sharing personal history across the generations. Moody, writing in the same book, *Twenty Five Years of the Life Review: Theoretical and Practical Considerations*, was interested in two questions: 'Where did we come from?' and 'Where are we going?' Such questions concerning our search for meaning through life review are still contemporary and pervade many of the chapters in this book.

Coleman (1986a) in his seminal book, *Ageing and Reminiscence Processes: Social and Clinical Implications*, identified different types of reminiscers and stressed that reminiscence isn't necessarily a universal process nor is it universally helpful for all people as they age – a position reinforced in his chapter in this book (Chapter 4) and further confirmed by Cappeliez in Chapter 12 and Westerhof in Chapter 17.

Bornat, an oral historian who was involved in the publication of *Recall* (Help the Aged 1981) and who edited *Reminiscence Reviewed: Perspectives, Evaluations and Achievements* (1994), explored whether reminiscence and oral history are 'parallel universes or shared endeavours', a debate that continues to the present day as oral history seemingly grows more abstruse compared with the usually freer, less structured, more individualistically responsive and often therapeutically oriented approaches commonly found in reminiscence work (Bornat 2001; Thompson with Bornat 2017).

For me, McConkey (1996) and Warnock (1987) were writers with different but extremely relevant perspectives on our urge and need to establish a sense of personal identity and to seek self-assurance and stability over time. McConkey wrote of how both are vitally important and of his belief in how 'memory searches for connections among present and past experiences in its desire to know, to evaluate, to make sense of life' (p.447). Warnock (1987), a philosopher, was also interested in exploring the importance of links between the past and present in establishing a sense of personal identity:

> Who we presently perceive ourselves to be is indisputably connected to who we perceive ourselves to have been in the past and will be in the future. Although we realize there have been changes over time, we are still the person we always were in core ways and shall be hereafter, for change and continuity go hand in hand. (p.100)

Webster, a psychologist (1993, 1997), introduced a taxonomy of reminiscence and wrote about its therapeutic implications. His validated Reminiscence Functions Scale (RFS), consisting of 43 items grouped into eight factors or functions served by reminiscence, has been replicated and used in various countries throughout the world. The RFS focused sharper attention on the differential nature and complexity of reminiscence. (Webster's eight reminiscence functions are listed by Cappeliez in Chapter 12.) Cappeliez and O'Rourke (2006) and Cappeliez, Guindon and Robitaille (2008) regrouped these factors into three distinct types of reminiscence when considering therapies for older people with depression. Drawing on both cognitive therapy and reminiscence theories, they distinguished between integrative, instrumental and prosocial reminiscence, a discussion revisited and further developed by Cappeliez in Chapter 12.

Integrative functions encourage a constructive reappraisal of past self-defining events and their associated emotions, and instrumental recollection of evidence of past effective coping provides understanding and reassurance for developing present coping. The third category of prosocial reminiscence involves sharing recall of the past to teach and inform others. To what extent cultural factors may influence the type and content of reminiscence has been explored by Shellman, Mokel and Hewitt (2009), who researched the effects of integrative reminiscence on depressive symptoms in older African Americans. They introduced ideas about the possible role of cultural influences on frequency, content and consequences of recall research questions, some of which were also explored by Nile and van Bergen (2015) and are considered in Chapter 10 by Webster.

Bluck (2003; Bluck and Alea 2011; Bluck and Levine 1998) and later publications have increased understanding about the range, purposes and processes of reminiscence. Bohlmeijer *et al.* (2007) from the Netherlands provided a persuasive meta-analysis concerned with the relevance of reminiscence engagement to ameliorating depression in later life. Having been trained and then practised as a psychiatric social worker with children and adults, I found this review and associated writing by Bohlmeijer *et al.* (2005) and O'Rourke, Cappeliez and Claxton (2011) particularly helpful. MacKinlay, whose writing with Trevitt (2012) distinguished between simple and spiritual reminiscence, emphasised the importance of life review in assisting people with and without dementia to articulate their lifetime values and to make meaning in their lives. This is also a theme explored in several other chapters and especially by Christine Bryden in Chapter 11, who writes from the viewpoint of a person who has dementia.

Haight and Webster's *The Art and Science of Reminiscence* (1995) and a second volume, Webster and Haight (2002) *Critical Advances in Reminiscence Work: From Theory to Application* were landmark volumes that made accessible the work of many international researchers, practitioners and clinicians. Each of these books contained extensive literature reviews by Haight and Hendrix (1995) and Hendrix and Haight (2002) and reports of a growing number of empirical studies and applied projects from North America, the UK and Japan, together with a smaller number from other parts of the world. These two publications were the first to make a determined effort to document within single comprehensive books the growing international interest in reminiscence, life review and life story work research and practice.

The second volume arranged under the headings of conceptual work, developmental work and sociocultural issues, special populations and clinical applications reflected the increasing diversity of types of narrative interventions and the people engaged in them. Along with this diversity has also come a growing interest in studying differential outcomes of reminiscence work undertaken with specific populations drawn from various age groups, cultural backgrounds and states of health. Sharing in research with Haight in a Northern Ireland study increased my knowledge of one particular systematised intervention – the structured life review using Haight's life review form (Haight 1998a, 1998b; Haight, Michel and Hendrix 1998). This study highlighted the issue of the relative value of structured chronological life review versus opportunistic, spontaneous, simple reminiscence (Haight, Gibson and Michel 2006). Shellman in Chapter 16 reviews more recent studies concerned with using structured life review.

Fivush (2007) broadened my understanding of the importance of reminiscence with age groups other than older people and, with Booker, she writes further about this in Chapter 5. The long-term influence of parent–child reminiscing on identity development, from infancy onwards through adolescence and into adult life has been a significant contribution. Except for intergenerational oral-history-type projects (for examples see Chapter 15 by Schweitzer), reminiscence seen as primarily the province of old people is being replaced by an appreciation of its relevance at other stages of the life cycle.

In the 16 years since Webster and Haight (2002, p.xvi) noted that 'researchers and practitioners have struggled over the past forty years to strike an empirically grounded balance between unbridled enthusiasm and mainstream neglect of reminiscence', a number of systematic reviews and meta-analyses have been published. Some have been general reviews, others have focused on specific groups, especially people with dementia and people who are depressed. The earlier Cochrane Library Reviews of reminiscence with people with dementia have been periodically updated, and in Chapter 3 Woods writes about the most recently released review of research concerned with reminiscence and dementia (Woods *et al.* 2018). Webster, Bohlmeijer and Westerhof's (2010) 'Mapping the future of reminiscence: A conceptual guide for research and practice' describes a comprehensive, multifaceted conceptual model that still has considerable relevance for guiding future research and practice, as does Westerhof, Bohlmeijer and Webster's review (2010) 'Reminiscence and mental health: A review of recent progress in theory, research and interventions.' The continuing work on the role of reminiscence in mental health being undertaken by Bohlmeijer, Westerhof and colleagues in the Netherlands and Cappeliez, O'Rourke and colleagues in Canada and further afield has done much to focus attention on clinical applications of reminiscence.

Reading the thoughts of Birren and colleagues on guided autobiographical writing, and hearing Birren speak, took me on a journey of personal exploration that greatly influenced my reminiscence practice with both individuals and small groups (Birren and Deutchman 1991; Birren and Cochran 2001).[1] The focus on significant points of transition throughout our lifetime has the potential for moving our personal recollections beyond simple reminiscence towards evaluative and integrative reminiscence and life review. Developing the courage to put our life experience outside ourselves, as it were, not just in verbal recall but in tangible external writing or other medium, has proved richly rewarding in my own ongoing journey of exploration but also for the people I have encountered in such groups. See Chapter 9 on guided autobiographical groups by Svensson and de Vries.

In *Transformational Reminiscence: Life Story Work*, Kunz and Soltys (2007) provided further evidence of expanded applications of

---

1   For an appreciation of the far-reaching influence of James Birren see the special issue of the *International Journal of Reminiscence and Life Review*, accessed on 23/06/2018 at http://143.95.253.101/~radfordojs/index.php/IJRLR/issue/current

reminiscence work with people contending with very varied life challenges, including end-of-life care. This is an area of growing interest that involves assisting terminally ill people, and frequently their family members, in preparing legacy documents, letters, audio recordings or some other type of record emanating from engagement in life review. Mroz and Bluck in Chapter 8 write on reminiscence and the significance of the dying days. The article by Subramaniam and Woods (2012), 'The impact of individual reminiscence therapy for people with dementia: A systematic review', and Westerhof and Bohlmeijer's (2014) 'Celebrating fifty years of research and applications in reminiscence and life review: State of the art and new directions' both reviewed contemporary studies and stressed the need for further critical research.

It is not only by reading and attending conferences and courses that my knowledge has grown. Since facilitating a considerable number of reminiscence groups and undertaking life story work with many individuals, with and without dementia, I have slowly learned about (and I hope acquired) empathetic listening skills that encourage the teller to relate his or her story at their own pace. It is this rich and diverse practice experience that never fails to fascinate me. The work of Age Exchange in Blackheath, London and the enthusiasm of its founding artistic director, Pam Schweitzer (2006), have played a very influential role in the development of reminiscence practice in the UK and beyond. Pam highlights aspects of this influential work in Chapter 15. The European Reminiscence Network and its use of reminiscence linked to creative activities, especially in dementia care, has provided a rich and varied European perspective. The newsletters of the International Institute for Reminiscence and Life Review, the published papers from its biennial conferences and its online journal (see Chapter 20 by Shellman, Yancura and Gieschen) have kept me up to date with wide-ranging scholarship and practice developments. The National Center for Creative Aging (NCCA) and its predecessors exercise a worldwide arts influence. The NCCA is dedicated to fostering an understanding of the vital relationship between creative expression and healthy ageing, and to developing programmes that build on this understanding; in my experience, reminiscence is frequently the way into creative arts for many people.

An invaluable contribution to the development of reminiscence practice has been made by innumerable actors, visual artists, poets, photographers, film makers, clinicians with artistic interests and art, dance, drama and music therapists and the many arts organisations, museums and libraries which use myriad artistic formats to portray and preserve people's recalled memories. It is invidious to single out individuals but Basting and Killick (2003), Cohen (2005, 2006, 2009), Killick and Craig (2012), Miller, Cohen and Barker (2016), and Patterson and Perlstein (2011) dramatically transformed my thinking about the arts and dementia. Chapters 6 by Kuo, 13 by de Medeiros, 14 by Ferguson and Gallagher and 18 by O'Brien Tyrrell provide examples of varied artistic methods as does the NCCA website.[2]

Another transformative experience occurred for me in the early 1990s when colleagues and I linked together the widely occurring urge to write a legacy life story with the power of word processing. We found that the possibility of writing a life story wonderfully motivated hitherto computer-illiterate, very physically frail older nursing home residents to acquire word processing skills (James *et al.* 1995). By employing 'the methodology of the worst case' – by demonstrating that seemingly the most unlikely very frail, very old people could master word processing and use their new skills to produce a desk-top published life story was amazingly exciting and rewarding; without doubt this work of 'teaching older dogs to learn new tricks' has been my most enjoyable work experience. Ryan, in Chapter 19, writes about the relevance of using contemporary computer technology to locate personally significant reminiscence triggers to stimulate reminiscence, and Pierce and Elliott, Woods, and Westerhof also refer to its considerable potential in their chapters.

In the course of my long personal and professional life, witnessing examples of the sterility and boredom-inducing ethos of many residential care regimes has encouraged me to work for change. Miller and Gwynne (1972) described such care in relation to physically handicapped and young chronic sick people as 'warehousing'. This term is equally applicable to many health and social care facilities for physically and cognitively frail older people. They distinguished between 'warehousing' and 'horticultural' models of care. Though sadly still too common, 'warehousing' institutions never were, and still are, unacceptable. The reminiscence movement – and the training and

---

2   National Center for Creative Aging (NCCA): www.creativeaging.org, accessed on 21/12/2017

research it has spawned in many countries – has been influential in supporting a 'horticultural model' that is founded on a knowledge of each individual care recipient's personal values, ethnic and cultural needs and their idiosyncratic life story, rather than just on their clinical history (Shadden, Hagstrom and Koski 2008). Such a philosophy challenges the pre-eminence of task-focused rather than person-in-relationship-focused care. The philosophy of care and type of activities described in this book seeks to generate life-enhancing growth for all concerned, be they residents, patients, families, friends or formal staff carers.

The International Institute for Reminiscence and Life Review (IIRLR) (see Chapter 20 by Shellman, Yancura and Gieschen), Age Exchange, the European Reminiscence Network (see Chapter 15 by Schweitzer) and the Reminiscence Network Northern Ireland – regrettably now defunct – (see Chapter 14 by Ferguson and Gallagher), and many other organisations, small and large, have provided a focus, periodic conferences, trans-national networking opportunities and fruitful national and international opportunities for research collaboration, professional exchanges and personal friendship. These organisations and the publications they inspired have played a significant role in developing productive, cooperative international scholarship. They have influenced policy and practice developments concerned with artistic and non-pharmacological interventions for certain health conditions, most particularly dementia and depression, and provided education and training in what has become a trans-national, inter-disciplinary and multi-professional movement. The relevance of this field of study to people of all ages, and who may or may not be contending with life crises, physical and mental ill health, cognitive deficits or adverse social conditions and circumstances is now well recognised. The establishment in 2013 of the IIRLR's open access electronic journal (International Journal of Reminiscence and Life Review) under the editorship of Tom Pierce (see Chapters 2 and 20) heralded another major milestone in disseminating knowledge and promoting the development of new research.[3]

Many people (by no means all are mentioned here), and their writing, and countless reminiscers of all ages, reminiscence trainees, students and experienced practitioners have served as stepping stones in

---

3   See http://reminiscenceandlifereview.org/online-journal, accessed on 20/12/2017

my lengthy path towards understanding something about the intricacies of memory, recall and the riches reminiscence makes, more or less freely available, to help many of us understand ourselves in the present and our relationships with other people, other places and other times.

In seeking to provide a contemporary account of international reminiscence, life review and life story work, it is inevitable that it is somewhat incomplete. A much larger publication would have been necessary to include all significant authors. It does, however, demonstrate the progress made in recent years in productively holding together the undoubted tensions that have been apparent in this field of scholarship and practice since its beginnings. Two orientations repeatedly surface throughout the book. One group works to advance understanding of the complexities inherent in the apparently not-so-simple bio/neuro/psycho/social processes involved in reminiscence, life review and life story work. Mostly these researchers are committed to using quantitative methodology. The other group, which includes many reminiscence practitioners, think that qualitative approaches more accurately capture the subtle inter and intra-personal connections generated by reminiscing. Here, an impressive number of long-established researchers and practitioners, many of whom combine both roles, and other younger, newer researchers write about their current understandings and the outcomes of these narrative-based interventions and activities undertaken in partnership with people of all ages from varied cultural, linguistic and geographic backgrounds.

This book is concerned with making connections. What does this mean? It means people making connections between their past and their present, and their present and an envisioned future (see Chapter 17 by Westerhof). It means people making connections with others, mediated through sharing stories of their mutual pasts, refracted through their recollections in the present about the past. It means individuals coming to see that their life, with all its ups and downs, its problems, opportunities, failures and triumphs, is a life worth remembering. In recalling and recording our lifetime memories in a myriad of different ways, we may come not only to understand them better but accept and celebrate our lives. For we, the seemingly most ordinary of people, have lived the most extraordinary lives in historically dramatically changing times, which, in the process of remembering, we come to see, to see again and understand a little better. We open our hearts to ourselves and to other people.

> In reminiscence work we are seeking to explore where we started and where we have arrived, and through the partial reconstruction of our memories, to paraphrase T.S. Eliot, we come to know the place as if for the first time or in a different way. (Gibson 2004, p.xv)

So why is this important, and why bother to devote a whole book to this most ordinary, yet extraordinary aspect of cognition and its linked emotions? The exploration of this question lies at the very heart of each chapter. Each contributor has provided a pathway into a rich, still relatively unexplored goldmine of such potential to assist us better to understand both separateness or individuality and our connections to other people, other places and other times. For it is in remembering that we are connected both to ourselves and to others. In understanding ourselves better, we may understand others better, and possibly even have them join us as fellow travelers in undertaking similarly fruitful journeys of exploration and enlarged understanding.

It is important to recognise from the outset that the terms reminiscence, life review and life story work are not always precisely and consistently used, whether by the same person at different times or by different people at the same time. Each is a loose, somewhat fluid term. The book is divided into four parts. The allocation of authors to sections is somewhat arbitrary and many could justifiably have been placed within a different section. Within each section the chapters are arranged alphabetically by author.

Most of the authors are long-established and well-known through their extensive published work on various aspects of reminiscence. They share a common interest and commitment to the task of studying the significance of memory for individuals, families and communities, its intricacies, its multiple functions and the outcomes it achieves. Together with the willing cooperation of these luminaries, there are contributions by newer, less well-known co-researchers, graduate students and practitioners, whose shared chapters affirm the continuing liveliness, importance and relevance of these research interests. Their contributions have enriched the book immensely.

Here there is an eclectic mix of academic research and applied approaches involving health and social care staff and various clinical professionals from around the world, responsible for providing direct care for many people with physical, cognitive and mental health disabilities. The strident demand, arising largely from the biological sciences, is to prove effectiveness of interventions by providing evidence from 'gold standard' double-blind quantitative randomised controlled trials. The numerous complexities involved in undertaking this kind of rigorous research in a field such as reminiscence and life review are discussed by Pierce and Elliott and Woods in Part 1.

Direct care practitioners either already know, or have been helped to discover, the intense pleasure that talking about days gone by gives to most, although not all, people, and not necessarily only older people. They understand because they see daily the way such conversations encourage meaningful communication and empathetic connections, change perceptions and enrich relationships. Professionals socialised into a rigorous psycho-bio-medical paradigm are not easily persuaded by such so called 'soft evidence', too often dismissed as 'only anecdotal'. They tend to be less interested in process and more interested in measureable outcomes and do not always remember that while it may be possible to demonstrate association, this does not necessarily mean causality. We may ask how is it that one type of evidence has become more privileged than another, especially when such privilege tends to bring funding, publication, peer and public esteem.

Such tensions about the nature of evidence are reflected in this collection of writings where a considerable peer-reviewed published literature is cited concerning accounts of carefully constructed 'experiments' using varied intervention and control groups. Then there are other accounts of projects, many involving reminiscence linked with creative arts used as both vehicles to encourage recall and reconstruction of memories but also as a means of preserving the memories evoked in diverse written and artistic forms. One group of researchers seeks to impose a pre-determined research methodology, the second seeks novel ways of capturing the processes and outcomes from planned and/or spontaneous multi-sensory stimulation used to evoke and interpret whatever interactions and outcomes emerge, as the work of Shik *et al.* (2009), Young, Camic and Tischler (2016) and Zeilig, Killick and Fox (2014) illustrates.

There are examples described here and many others cited in references in which quantitative and qualitative methods are not juxtaposed but rather combined in order to appreciate both process and outcomes, using both statistical and ethnographic evidence in ways which more fully demonstrate the effectiveness of such interventions.

While acknowledging that gold standard randomised controlled trials have not yet produced indubitable evidence of effectiveness, qualitative studies, as well as the daily experience of many participants, family and paid carers testify to pleasurable, personally significant results, albeit somewhat transitory, from a growing variety of interventions.

Perhaps a book such as this will assist the growth of mutual understanding of and respect for the need for varied methodologies as although it presents evidence of a 'softer' sort, it also shows evidence of randomised controlled trials, frequently relatively small, because of the nature of the interventions being implemented and the problems associated with blinding, but nonetheless promising and/or indicative. The present state of knowledge concerning narrative methods is still incomplete, with many questions not yet addressed, and the nature of what constitutes 'evidence' requires considerable clarification. To explore such issues about theories of knowledge and the nature of evidence in detail is beyond the scope of this book but they are very relevant to the future development of reminiscence research and practice.

Types of work loosely falling under the intellectual banner of 'narrative psychology' or 'narrative methods' or 'narrative therapy' are both numerous and varied. The scope of this book is limited to reminiscence, life review and life story work, with each having both generic and specific aspects, some more rigorously delineated than others. The contributors, despite differences of geographic location, academic discipline and professional socialization, are all committed to critical and rigorous intellectual examination of the processes involved when people set out to construct, deconstruct, reconstruct and record, in innumerable ways, their life stories. 'Telling the stories of life' knows few limits and is an endlessly fascinating process of trying to make our lives, however they are turning out, to be more acceptable to ourselves and more interesting to other people (Tarman 1988).

The chapters that follow illustrate the relevance and dynamism of a range of interventions as well as provide extensive discussions about outcome effectiveness. Some seek to elucidate generic or near universal experiences from across the lifespan; others are more narrowly focused on a particular group who may share a common developmental stage or age, health problem or life challenge across the whole of the lifespan. Some chapters relate to single individuals and the changes they experienced when engaging in reminiscence.

Part 1, Recent and Contemporary Research, contains two extensive key literature review chapters. Tom Pierce, Editor of the *International Journal of Reminiscence and Life Review* and colleague Ann Elliott review recent research progress and demonstrate that reminiscence, life review and life story work all have both basic and applied dimensions that may be productively held together by research. They review highlights of recent progress, including the use of technology within these active fields of inquiry, and identify the research designs and data analytic techniques that have the greatest potential for expanding basic and applied as well as generic and specific knowledge about these interventions.

Bob Woods updates the earlier Cochrane Reviews of reminiscence therapy for dementia undertaken by himself and colleagues by summarising the findings of the 2018 Review as well as discussing and illustrating the inherent difficulties of using randomised controlled trials to assess evidence of effectiveness of psychosocial interventions such as reminiscence.

Part 2, Age and Cultural Variations and Applications, has chapters that represent the extensive range and reach of reminiscence work in terms of the age of persons engaged, the relevance of cultural and geographic characteristics of people and the influence of these variations on a number of practical projects involving participants drawn from across the lifespan, the northern and southern hemispheres and the types of practical and artistic applications that have been utilised.

Peter Coleman and colleagues Christine Ivani-Chalian and Maureen Robinson present a series of 21 case studies of now very elderly people who were interviewed at intervals spanning some 25 years in the UK's Southampton Longitudinal Study between 1977 and 2002. The vivid case studies illustrate gender variations in the styles and content of reminiscence, the functions it served at different times in the lives of these people and the enduring value and relevance, and in some cases, irrelevance, of recalled memories.

Robyn Fivush and Jordan Booker write about the importance of developing a capacity for self-narration early in life. They discuss the contribution to identity development from infancy onwards of shared reminiscence between children and their parents. Such conversations make for positive emotional bonding, personal growth and development and building shared values across the generations. The exchanges involved in sharing family and individual stories, they maintain, are mutually beneficial to both older and younger family members who reminiscence together because both become the co-constructors of the individual and family histories.

TsuAnn Kuo from Taiwan writes about developing and evaluating a modified culturally appropriate version of Birren's guided autobiographical writing approach and the training program she developed for leaders of guided autobiography groups for older people. Case studies illustrate the effectiveness of the versatile verbal, written and artistic methods she developed to enable both well- and less well-educated older people to review their lives. She poignantly writes that 'the world has begun to move too quickly for those deemed too slow to keep up and too fast for the young to slow down and listen.'

Elizabeth MacKinlay debates the importance of reminiscence in the lives of older Australians whom she engaged in individual interviews to explore with them their search for meaning in life. She views this as a process in which lifetime values can be consolidated at a time of life when old certainties, hitherto mostly taken for granted, such as reasonable health, financial security and established significant relationships, may be threatened by changing circumstances and advancing age. She names her approach 'spiritual reminiscence' and stresses the need to create safe spaces for listening and encouraging people, either in one-to-one meetings or in small groups, to situate their present lives within the overarching experiences of a lifetime, in order to clarify their personal values and in doing so to value themselves.

Emily Mroz and Susan Bluck discuss the significance of the context in which dying people spend their last days and the consequences of the recall of 'last words' for how surviving relatives, most frequently a spouse, negotiate the memory of their significant other. They explore how this recalled memory of last words may assist or impede the grieving process as the survivor negotiates their own new social status with its changed roles, responsibilities and their perceived value as seen by other people.

Cheryl Svensson and Brian de Vries summarise the major characteristics of guided autobiographical writing – the widely known methodology first introduced and tested by Jim Birren, his colleagues and students, and further adapted for use in various countries around the world. This internationally used approach combines both individual and group participation, most often in two-hour meetings over ten weeks, a format which involves both private and public reflection. Participants write privately on a series of pre-set themes or life turning points and then share their writing by reading it aloud to the group, whose members provide positive feedback and engage in supportive discussion. International examples illustrate the method's wide applicability.

Jeff Webster reports results from a preliminary study that used questionnaires to explore possible inter-relationships between reminiscence, narrative structure and meaning-making in people of various ages drawn from three different cultural groups – Caucasian, Chinese and Indian. His results support the suggestion that recalling positive episodic memories may contribute to people's attempts to develop a sense of purpose or meaning in life, both directly but also in conjunction with narrative awareness. His study suggests that positive autobiographical memories serve as building blocks for developing more extensive life narratives, but further experimental and longitudinal studies will be necessary in order to establish causality.

Part 3, Implications of Reminiscence, Life Review and Life Story Work for Health and Wellbeing, contains seven very different chapters that illustrate the rich variety of reminiscence methods employed with varied populations and their influence and outcomes on health and wellbeing. The latter term is used here to refer to a preponderance of general life-enhancing, positive experiences and positive emotional responses. Some of the chapters in this section are generic and apply to people of all ages while others are more specific, concentrating on defined characteristics such as age, contexts of living, or being beset by frailty, loneliness, depression and dementia. It is in this broad domain of health and wellbeing where most practical reminiscence projects are situated, and they are usually designed to contribute towards reducing the deleterious effects of ill-health, social isolation and ill-being.

Christine Bryden's chapter is unique because here is the authentic voice of an author reflecting on her own lived experience of dementia, having been so diagnosed in 1995. She writes from an 'insider's' viewpoint and as a practising Christian about her lived experience of dementia and as a person who is determined to challenge the dominant negative discourse of inevitable loss of narrative identity in dementia.

She persuasively describes the endurance of her narrative self, even though her language and recall are impaired. Despite her diminishing ability to express her unfolding story, she argues that her narrative nevertheless continues. We are entrusted with a moving account of one individual's life story, situated in time and place, and how it is possible to retain a continuing narrative of living despite the profound assault of having a prolonged progressive neurological condition.

Philippe Cappeliez and Gerben Westerhof, in separate chapters, write about their long-established interests in researching the links between reminiscence and depression in older people and in identifying the varied functions served by such recall and its relevance to mental health and quality of life. Their work demonstrates commonalities of functioning despite differences of language, nationality and ethnicity and highlights the different functions served by reminiscence. Like Peter Coleman, they stress that reminiscence is not necessarily appropriate for everyone.

Cappeliez focuses on the clinical implications of using reminiscence with clinically depressed older patients in his report of research concerned with a large number of community-dwelling depressed older people. He revisits his earlier tripartite model derived from Webster's eight reminiscence functions that consists of three second-order functions – self-positive, self-negative and prosocial. He stresses that in reminiscing with depressed older people it is critical to encourage specific, less generalised autobiographical self-positive memories and to discourage or curtail reminiscence used for bitterness revival and boredom reduction. He argues that such reminiscences may unhelpfully stimulate depressed older people to ruminate adversely on negative views of their past lives. Alternately, self-positive memories should be encouraged. For such work, careful selection of participants and skilled enablers are essential.

Kate de Medeiros and Sara Stemen, like several other authors, are interested in how life story narratives serve the purpose of assisting people who are actively engaging in searching for meaning in life. They suggest that it is the power of being heard as much as the content that is recalled that holds such potential for life enhancement and improved wellbeing. They present a detailed case study of 'Bill' and his changed interactions with other members of a writing group over the lifetime of the group. The social context of the group, they suggest, as well as its individual members, plays a significant part in the co-construction of the life story. The interactions between the teller and the listeners assist the individual to develop a story consistent with their lifetime values but also allow them a safe space for sharing frailties and doubts.

Marian Ferguson and Geraldine Gallagher report on an extensive project that sought to combat loneliness and social isolation in older people with substantial physical, emotional and social problems arising in later life by mobilising and actively promoting the sharing of memories of past competence. This was a large, five-year community-based Northern Ireland creative arts project called Sharing Memories Building Communities, where participants had already undertaken a 16-week re-ablement programme. The project used reminiscence as its starting point and as a bridge to assist socially isolated older people to develop impressive personalised art works depicting aspects of their lives, and in the process, to re-establish social links.

Pam Schweitzer's chapter presents her work when at Age Exchange in London, especially the reminiscence theatre activities that used professional actors and novice older actors to dramatise life experiences that were revisited by means of reminiscence and recall and then scripted and performed as theatre. The work of the European Reminiscence Network and, particularly, the long-established approach known as Remembering Yesterday, Caring Today (RYCT) as a means for supporting people with dementia and their family caregivers and its related apprenticeship training are also described. Pam invites her readers to join her on a journey that traces a number of projects and events in which intergenerational theatre and other creative formats such as a touring exhibition of memory boxes are harnessed in the service of older people, particularly those who have dementia.

Juliette Shellman takes as her starting point Barbara Haight's four characteristics of one form of life review, namely structured life review using Haight's life review form (LRF). This format guides individuals through a defined number of eight weekly one-on-one discussions, that chronologically cover the whole of the life course, closely following the developmental tasks proposed by Erikson. In a review of the 15 studies reported in the literature of the last ten years purporting to implement this approach and using the LRF where structure, duration, individuality and evaluation are considered essential, Shellman found that there was very little adherence to all four requirements but nevertheless a high degree of satisfaction with the reported outcomes. She identified a lack of consistency in the definitions used, a lack of rigour and variations in the methodology employed, including the length and number of sessions and differences in how structured life review, as defined by Haight, was employed. These findings led her to question whether the considerable satisfaction reported by the life review participants might possibly be due to the relationship developed between the interviewer and the life reviewer, regardless of the intervention of structured life review.

Gerben Westerhof contends that life review is not restricted to old age but is a process that occurs throughout the lifespan. It involves different aspects as people of varying ages seek to ascribe meaning to their lives through engagement in the processes of attributing evaluation, identification, reasoning and integration of personal memories. Life review is important for mental health, he contends, because it helps older people and those with depression and life-threatening illnesses to build psychological resources, which in turn contribute to promoting a sense of wellbeing.

In Part 4, Technology in Reminiscence Practice, Training and Development, Mary O'Brien Tyrrell, a nurse by original profession, shares her appreciation of cultural differences when she writes about founding and running a life story business, the inspiration for which arose from experiencing Native Americans' respect for their elders. She provides an abbreviated template to guide anyone wishing to emulate her successful personal history business that is devoted to interviewing and recording the life stories of older people. These stories, mostly commissioned by family members, she then crafts into limited editions of hardbacked published books, copies of which are distributed to family members at presentation parties. Many of the books have also been deposited in the Minnesota Historical Library, thus contributing to local historical knowledge and cultural preservation as well as being much prized by their title holders and appreciated by their families.

Assumpta Ryan, a nurse educator from Northern Ireland, reviews various approaches to utilising information and communication technology to stimulate the recall of memories. She describes the creation of an app named *Inspire*, which involved dyads consisting of people with early to moderate dementia and their family carers, in all stages of product development, including need identification and appraising interest, testing, training, specification refinement and improving functionality. Technology such as this is now readily available and is being increasingly used in reminiscence work.

It enables reminiscence triggers to be personalised by being matched to the interests, backgrounds and present circumstances of the users and their varying and fluctuating levels of interest and cognitive functioning.

Juliette Shellman, Loriena Yancura and Esther Gieschen pay tribute to John Kunz and his work in establishing the International Institute for Reminiscence and Life Review within the University of Wisconsin–Superior. They describe the work of the IIRLR, its networking and membership opportunities, biennial conferences, publications and its online journal and the online distance learning Reminiscence and Life Review Certificate course. This course is provided in conjunction with the Continuing Education Division of the University of Wisconsin–Superior. Its structure, content that includes a mentored practicum and its evaluation by students from different parts of the world are described.

Chapter 2

RECENT PROGRESS IN REMINISCENCE RESEARCH[1]

Thomas W. Pierce and Ann N. Elliott

From the very beginning of the field of reminiscence and life review, in Robert Butler's (1963a, 1963b) ground-breaking article asserting that reminiscence is a normal part of mental life, a wealth of questions regarding memory for personal history became apparent. Although Butler made a number of predictions and assertions as part of his discussion, many of them had not been empirically tested. For example, he speculated that as a result of life review 'it seems likely that in the majority of the elderly a substantial reorganization of the personality does occur' (p.69). Clearly, the presence of a 'likely' but as yet undemonstrated relationship is a powerful invitation to future researchers. Butler also calls for answers to important questions, such as when, how, and for whom reminiscence has beneficial effects. In these ways, the seeds of research were sown into the field at its start.

As reviews have carefully documented (e.g. Birren and Schroots 2006; de Medeiros 2014; Gibson 2011; Pinquart and Forstmeier 2012), hundreds of studies investigating memory for personal history have now been published. While many address basic research questions geared toward understanding memory processes, much of the reminiscence and life review literature is directed to questions of an applied nature. In keeping with the powerful human connections established through shared memories, practice-oriented research

---

[1] We consider the terms 'reminiscence,' 'life review' and 'life story work' to represent a set of closely related but conceptually distinct approaches to the study of memory for personal history and its many practical applications. Throughout the chapter, whenever we employ phrases such as 'reminiscence research' or 'the field of reminiscence and life review' our coverage of the topic under discussion has incorporated research conducted under any of these three umbrella terms.

assesses the degree to which reminiscence can improve the lives of people in a variety of settings. In fact, the field of reminiscence and life review is appealing to many precisely because it provides a synthesis of basic research and applied practice.

This dual nature of the field leads to the question of how best to characterize the role of research in reminiscence and life review. Specifically, is reminiscence and life review a field of basic research with strong practice applications? Is it a field of practice and application with a strong research component to support it? Or is it both? Certainly, within the wider reminiscence community there are members who fall close to both ends of a basic versus applied research continuum. Anchoring one end, researchers in autobiographical memory and cognitive neuroscience investigate a fascinating array of fundamental questions surrounding the ability to recall events from one's personal history. Their findings are generalizable across large groups of people and form the basis of many practice-oriented interventions. At the other end, the primary concern of practitioners is not with identifying basic principles of memory function that apply to virtually everyone but with using them to improve the lives of the people with whom they work.

Regarding the question of whether the field of reminiscence and life review should be considered a field that is basic or applied, we lean heavily toward the argument that it is both. We view each of these very different scholarly traditions as linked symbiotically within the gravitational pull of the other – making them more effective together than either could be alone. We argue that the force which allows the basic and applied aspects of reminiscence to complement each other so well – to bind them together – is research. In this chapter, we examine the role of research in the field of reminiscence and life review. In doing so, we highlight recent progress within particularly active fields of inquiry, identify research designs and data analytic techniques which have the greatest potential to move the edge of the field forward, and address the degree to which theoretical models of reminiscence guide the design of empirical studies. None of the sections describing research on a given topic provides a comprehensive review – the studies described serve only as interesting examples of recent research in each area. Taken as a whole, however, these studies convey the tremendous range of questions addressed by reminiscence research and the difficulty faced by theorists hoping to model relationships among the many variables considered relevant.

One particularly effective and influential attempt to model the structure of reminiscence research was made by Webster, Bohlmeijer and Westerhof (2010) in 'Mapping the future of reminiscence: A conceptual guide for research and practice'. Specifically, Webster *et al.* proposed a 'heuristic model of reminiscence' which lists and organizes the categories of variables most likely to appear in reminiscence research, ranging from initial memory cues or 'triggers' to ultimate outcomes (both positive and negative). As part of their model they include four additional categories of variables which could serve in either mediating or moderating roles:

1. Modes of reminiscence (memories are shared or unshared with others).

2. Contexts (settings for reminiscence are determined by cultural, institutional, and interpersonal factors that are capable of influencing memories).

3. Moderators (individual difference variables such as age, ethnicity, gender, and personality).

4. Reminiscence functions (motivations to engage in reminiscence, which are presumably determined by the context- and person-specific variables defined previously as modes, contexts and moderators).

Although Webster *et al.* list and organize these well-defined collections of variables, they explicitly do not arrange them in a fixed causal pathway. Rather, their model consists of a flexible framework that can be rearranged and updated as advances in theory predict and empirical observation suggests. As such, it provides the ideal conditions for research – a firm foundation from which to start and the opportunity for elaboration based on creative ideas and clever experimentation.

The clear appraisal of the state of reminiscence research by Webster *et al.* (2010) makes their recommendations regarding its future development well worth considering. They begin with an observation and an appeal:

> Whereas earlier research often, of necessity, was confined to making very general, relatively unsophisticated inquiries...contemporary researchers...need to ask and answer more conceptually rigorous questions. (p.548)

They then describe what these conceptually more rigorous studies might look like. To begin, they draw the distinction between studies focusing on depth versus those that emphasize breadth. In a *depth path*, 'questions are domain specific (e.g. they might focus exclusively on modes or on particular moderator variables such as ethnicity). Here, work will flesh out specific details resulting in specific micromodels' (p.548). Alternatively, a *breadth path* 'will examine the broader linkages among the model components, resulting in a macromodel perspective' (p.548). As a final component, they express the belief that studies in either category should be guided by theoretical predictions which may or may not be borne out in the data. If data does not support theory-derived predictions, then, according to Webster *et al.* 'we need to rethink the who, what, where, when, and why components of reminiscence processes' (p.549). Research thus completes a self-correcting loop in which increasingly comprehensive theories prompt empirical observation of novel combinations of variables, and these observations in turn determine the confidence researchers can place in these theoretical positions.

In the following two sections, we describe recent research in both basic and applied areas of reminiscence and life review. We draw special attention to studies which contribute to:

- a depth of understanding regarding a single category of reminiscence-relevant variables (e.g. triggers/cues)
- a breadth of knowledge regarding patterns of association among two or more categories (e.g. the degree to which engaging in particular types of reminiscence mediates the relationship between negative life events and depression).

We also highlight studies where basic research has led to practice applications and, conversely, where reminiscence interventions were guided by basic research. Overall, we hope these studies illustrate the degree to which the field is following Webster *et al.*'s (2010) recommendations for future research.

Recent advances in basic research

Basic research in reminiscence investigates foundational questions regarding when, how and why we remember events from our past. In this section, we describe work in three especially active areas of basic research: new technologies for triggering/cueing memory for personal history, reminiscence functions and cultural influences.

New technologies to elicit and preserve reminiscences

The first component of Webster *et al.*'s (2010) framework of reminiscence-related variables is that of memory cues or triggers. These events can be internal (with a particular thought cueing a memory into consciousness) or external (engaging any of the senses). In everyday life, autobiographical memories are evoked spontaneously and automatically, with specific cues determined by the situations in which we find or place ourselves. Researchers and practitioners in reminiscence, however, often intervene in these normal circumstances by eliciting specific personal memories through the introduction of prompts. Dozens of clever techniques for cueing personal memories have been introduced and the pace of innovation in this area continues to accelerate, particularly with regard to the use of digital technologies.

Family and historical photographs provide powerful reminders of the people, places and events that form the core of memory for personal history. Products for displaying digital photographs include digital picture frames (e.g. Williams *et al.* 2011), tablet devices (e.g. Hamel *et al.* 2016) and computers using presentation software, such as *PowerPoint* (e.g. Pierce 2013). The recent availability of high-quality software for video recording and editing makes it possible for people without special training, for example undergraduates (Yancura 2013), to record reminiscence interviews and produce engaging video materials that participants can share with family and friends or review themselves. Internet-based resources have also proven effective in stimulating reminiscence. We offer two brief examples. First, the Pensieve project[2] (Cosley *et al.* 2012) provides automated prompts to reminisce through emails containing personally significant materials acquired from social media accounts. Second, Thomas and Briggs (2016) compiled materials available from participants' Facebook accounts (e.g. photographs, posts, status updates) using the web service My Social Book[3] and then printed them in book form so they could be used later as reminiscence cues.

---

2   https://reimagine.hci.cornell.edu/projects.php
3   www.mysocialbook.com

One intriguing recent innovation is the introduction of technology to make continuous or near continuous recordings of events taking place throughout a person's life, a practice commonly referred to as 'lifelogging' (Bell and Gemmell 2009; Whittaker *et al.* 2012). As one example, SenseCam uses a small camera placed on the upper chest to record a digital image every 30 seconds. These sequential photographs can then be uploaded to a computing device for review at a later time. As a research tool, this technique provides the ability to compare the accuracy of memory for a specific event against information recorded at the time it occurred (e.g. Muhlert *et al.* 2010), enabling researchers to examine the degree to which review and discussion of recorded images results in more accurate recall of an event at a later time (e.g. Seamon *et al.* 2014). In an applied context, review of images for important events has the potential to promote reminiscence in those with impairments of memory function (e.g. Allé *et al.* 2017; Berry *et al.* 2007) or to provide cues for critical life events that can form the basis of discussions between mental health providers and clients.

Reminiscence functions

Perhaps the most basic of basic research questions regarding reminiscence asks why we engage in it at all. Early conceptualizations described reminiscence as behavior observed in older adults which serves the negative or, at best, the non-generative function of filling time in lives left empty of purpose. Butler's (1963a, 1963b) article rebutted this position and argued successfully that life review can cultivate a deeper appreciation of the meaning of one's past near the end of life. Since then, as researchers began to acknowledge reminiscence as behavior that takes place for many different reasons and under widely different circumstances (e.g. Wong 1989; Wong and Watt 1991), more comprehensive theories and descriptions of reminiscence functions have emerged.

A number of classification systems for reminiscence functions have been proposed. Webster (1993, 1997) identified eight functions using exploratory factor analysis of items from his Reminiscence Functions Scale (RFS): Death Preparation, Identity, Problem Solving, Teach/Inform, Conversation, Boredom Reduction, Bitterness Revival, and Intimacy Maintenance. Cappeliez and O'Rourke (2006) later showed that these eight functions could be organized into three larger groupings: 1) *Self-positive functions*, which represent attempts to enhance self-understanding (i.e. Death Preparation, Problem Solving and Identity), 2) *Self-negative functions* that prevent those engaging in them from achieving a coherent and positive self-narrative (i.e. Bitterness Revival, Boredom Reduction and Intimacy Maintenance); and 3) *Social functions* which allow us to enjoy the company of others by imparting either experiences (i.e. Conversation) or the benefits of experience (i.e. to Teach/Inform others). O'Rourke, King and Cappeliez (2017) recently demonstrated in a large longitudinal study that this three-facet grouping of functions remained stable over a 16-month period.

Adopting a cognitive approach, Bluck *et al.* (2005) described three theoretically derived functions of autobiographical memory. Using Bluck *et al.*'s (2005) terminology, a *directive function* uses memory for decisions made in the past to guide decisions we make in the present, a *self-function* uses memory for personal history to maintain continuity in one's sense of self or identity, and a *social function* allows individuals to use reminiscence to establish and nurture social relationships. Based on these categories, Bluck *et al.* developed the Talking About Life Experiences (TALE) measure of autobiographical memory functions.

In the context of employing reminiscence as part of mental health interventions, Westerhof and Bohlmeijer (2014) identified two reminiscence functions which appear conceptually similar to Bluck *et al.*'s directive and self functions. Specifically, Westerhof and Bohlmeijer refer to *instrumental reminiscence* as accessing memory for actions that were previously effective in coping with challenges, and they describe *integrative reminiscence* as a process through which negative memories are re-evaluated in ways that promote a more positive life story.

The RFS and TALE represent two well-respected but largely independent attempts to capture ways in which people use reminiscence. Harris, Rasmussen and Berntsen (2014) contributed a valuable link between these two approaches by examining the factor structure of the 11 subscale scores provided by Webster's eight RFS functions and the three subscales contained in a revised version of the TALE (Bluck and Alea 2011). Exploratory factor analysis revealed the presence of four factors, which they identified as generative, reflecting, social and ruminative functions.

In a recent example of research on simple, unstructured reminiscence, Henkel *et al.* (2017) observed that while considerable work has been done to identify the functions and effects of reminiscence in community-dwelling older adults, relatively little research has examined these questions in long-term care residents. To provide additional information regarding this important population, Henkel et al. (2017) administered measures of reminiscence use to residents in long-term care facilities. Consistent with results from a sample of community-dwelling older adults (Bluck and Alea 2009), residents in long-term care reported thinking about their past more often than they spoke about their past with others. Participants also rarely shared stories of past events with healthcare providers but, compared to community-dwelling adults, long-term care residents were more likely to engage in reminiscence for Intimacy Maintenance and Boredom Reduction and less likely to reminisce for Problem Solving or to promote a sense of Identity.

Cultural differences in reminiscence

Reminiscence may not be universal, in the sense that it is practiced and valued by every member of a given culture, but we are unaware of any society for whom it plays no part in the lived experience of individuals and the collective memory of the group as a whole. Even if not *universal*, in the sense proposed by Butler (1963a, 1963b), it is clearly *fundamental* to understanding the attitudes, aspirations and antipathies within a given culture. As such, reminiscence and life review is, at its core, an international and omnicultural field, with active research programs present in many countries.

One important factor in researchers' ability to examine cross-cultural similarities and differences is the extent to which standardized measures are available in multiple languages and have been modified to fit the specific requirements of target cultures. A number of recent studies have made significant contributions in this area. For example, Choy and Lou (2016) translated a 14-item short form of the RFS into Cantonese and administered the scale to a large sample of Hong Kong residents. Their measure included the Boredom Reduction, Bitterness Revival, Problem Solving, and Identity scales from the original RFS. Confirmatory factor analysis revealed that Problem Solving and Identity should be treated as separate reminiscence functions in this Chinese sample and that these four scales could be captured by two higher-order factors, reflecting self-positive and self-negative functions. In another example, Shellman and Zhang (2014) investigated the psychometric properties of a Modified Reminiscence Functions Scale (Washington 2009), designed for use with a Black population. Confirmatory factor analysis revealed that a model based on the eight RFS factors/functions identified by Webster (1997) did not fit well with data from this population. Good model fit, however, was obtained for an alternative seven-factor solution combining items from Webster's Problem Solving and Self-Identity subscales to create a single new factor which Shellman and Zhang referred to as Self-Regard. In contrast, in a Spanish sample, using a Spanish translation of the RFS, Ros *et al.* (2016) reported that better model fit was obtained by separating Problem Solving and Identity into different factors. Taken together, these studies demonstrate that translations of widely used measurement instruments now make it possible to compare patterns of reminiscence use across participants from different cultural and language groups.

Building on studies collecting data from participants within a single culture, cross-cultural studies provide direct comparisons of different cultures within the same study. For example, King *et al.* (2015) administered a short form of the RFS to samples of Israeli holocaust survivors, older Israelis and older Canadians to learn about the effects of early trauma on reminiscence use. The inclusion of comparison groups from both Israel and Canada allowed the researchers to determine if differences involving the survivor group were due to the effects of trauma (i.e. if the survivor group differed from non-trauma groups in both countries) or to nationality (i.e. if the Israeli survivor group differed only from the Canadian group). RFS functions were used to calculate scores for the three higher-level uses of reminiscence identified by Cappeliez and O'Rourke (2006) (self-positive, self-negative, and prosocial functions). King *et al.* (2015) found no group differences in the self-positive or prosocial functions but, as predicted, found that holocaust survivors engaged in more frequent use of self-negative forms of reminiscence than did either comparison group, indicating an overall effect of early trauma. Despite these observed group differences, King *et al.* interpreted their findings as largely reflecting greater similarities than differences in reminiscence use among the groups, suggesting that resilience on the part of holocaust survivors – and trauma survivors in general – is a variable worth pursuing in future research.

In additon to quantitative approaches using standardized rating scales, qualitative methods provide additional tools for data collection and analysis. Whether for extracting common themes from the recollected experiences of group members (Ando *et al.* 2012) or for using verbal feedback to evaluate reminiscence programs and interventions (Pierce 2005), qualitative methods bring the perspectives of participants to the foreground and have a vital role to play in documenting nuances of culture that cannot be captured by quantitative instruments. Sabir *et al.* (2017), for example, recorded recollections of older African Americans who participated in the Great Migration from the southern United States to the North during the 1920s and '30s. They identified three themes (*generative success*, attaining a role helping others; *generative desire*, prevention or delay in attaining a helping role; and *generativity unmentioned*, descriptions of helping roles were absent in recollections) which illustrate the opportunities and obstacles that shaped the lives of individuals occupying this historical and cultural space.

In another example, which emphasized gender identity rather than race, Johnson, Singh and Gonzalez (2014) employed the technique of Collective Memory Work (Haug 1999) to explore memories related to sexual or gender identity development in college students identifying as transgender, queer, or questioning (TQQ). Using written responses describing positive and negative memories related to identity development, as well as statements made in focus groups, the authors reported three themes:

- Gender identity and sexual orientation issues are complex and fluid.
- Persons identifying as TQQ faced concerns for their physical safety while in high school.
- Specific actions by educators could at least partially address safety concerns and create a more welcoming and accepting climate within school systems.

While not itself an intervention study, Johnson *et al.*'s analysis of the physical and psychosocial needs of this population represents an example of how reminiscence can be used to lay the groundwork for effective intervention within a larger cultural community. This path from basic research to intervention leads us into the large and growing area of practice applications for reminiscence and life review.

Recent advances in practice-oriented research

Although Butler's (1963a, 1963b) article drew needed attention to the benefits of spontaneous, unstructured reminiscence for the psychosocial health of individuals, we distinguish reminiscence practice from these informal settings and occurrences by the clear intent of an outside party to use reminiscence to intervene for the betterment of others. Westerhof, Bohlmeijer and Webster (2010) classified reminiscence interventions as falling into one of three general categories. Persons engaged in *simple reminiscence* are not participating specifically for the purpose of improving some aspect of their mental health, but benefits emerge naturally through promotion of positive feelings and interpersonal connection. *Life review* (e.g. guided autobiography – Birren and Cochran 2001; structured life review – Haight and Haight 2007) provides a highly organized set of reminiscence-based prompts and activities which have the potential to improve aspects of mental health by promoting integration of positive and negative memories across the lifespan. While life review is not intended to address serious mental illness, it helps people within the normal range of psychosocial functioning to achieve higher levels of self-acceptance and increased understanding of the meaning of their life. *Life review therapy* is a recognized treatment option for addressing serious mental health issues (e.g. depression, anxiety, post-traumatic stress disorder) under the care of highly trained and experienced mental health practitioners. Treatment strategies target specific sources of psychological distress using carefully guided recall of relevant life events. It also includes elicitation of positive memories for people who find it difficult to do so without guidance and the cueing of negative or traumatic events so they can become embedded within the context of a larger self-consistent and self-affirming life narrative.

In the sections that follow we describe the therapeutic application of reminiscence to three populations: persons with dementia and their caregivers; individuals struggling with mental illness, particularly depression; and persons who have experienced a traumatic life event. These applications represent active areas of research on reminiscence practice, but this list is by no means exhaustive.

Research on persons with dementia and their caregivers

There is growing evidence that structured reminiscence has significant benefits for persons with dementia (Woods *et al.* 2005). However, the question quickly arises of how to implement reminiscence programs on scales large enough to benefit significant numbers of people. The DARES program (Dementia Education Programme Incorporating Reminiscence for Staff) (O'Shea *et al.* 2011; 2014) addressed this issue by training staff members to engage residents in at least four episodes of reminiscence each week (one formal and three spontaneous). In a randomized controlled trial, residents received either the DARES program (n=153) or care-as-usual. Greater improvements in self-assessed quality of life were observed in the DARES group than in the care-as-usual group at an 18–22-week follow-up. No significant effects were observed for measures of agitation or care burden, and regrettably, participation in DARES was associated with slight increases in depression.

Cooney *et al.* (2014) supplemented quantitative assessment of the DARES program with a qualitative study of residents, care staff and family members participating in the program. Interviews with these groups yielded statements consistent with the program's theme of 'Seeing Me through My Memories,' which captured the ability of reminiscence to promote greater levels of understanding between staff members and the persons they care for. The presence of these enhanced personal connections identified through qualitative analysis in turn provides a plausible explanation for the positive effects of reminiscence on quality of life observed in quantitative analyses. This powerful combination of mixed quantitative and qualitative methods has much to recommend it, and we endorse and anticipate its application to many future research questions.

Reminiscence as cognitive training for memory for personal history

In addition to effects of reminiscence on measures of psychosocial function such as depression and anxiety, another potential benefit of reminiscence programs for dementia is improved memory function itself. In one study, Lopes, Afonso and Ribeiro (2016) tested the effects of a reminiscence program designed to improve memory function in persons with dementia residing in long-term care. Participants were randomly assigned to a reminiscence intervention group or to a usual-care control group. The intervention took place in five weekly individualized sessions under the guidance of a nurse facilitator. Sessions were largely unstructured, with a detailed timeline of each participant's life history serving as a prompt for further reminiscence. Participants and the facilitator also compiled memory prompts (e.g. photographs, newspaper clippings, etc.), and the facilitator encouraged detailed recall of positive events. The researchers administered a battery of cognitive and psychosocial measures both before and after the five-week intervention period. Participants in the reminiscence group displayed significant and sizeable improvements in measures of cognitive status, memory, anxiety and depression, while improvements were not observed in the control group. Effects obtained for the Autobiographical Memory Test (Williams and Broadbent 1986), which evaluates both the nature of memories generated in response to cue words and the time needed to retrieve these memories, were particularly noteworthy. The reminiscence group responded significantly more quickly to prompts for autobiographical memories after the intervention than before, and memories cued after the intervention period were more specific in nature.

Combined participation by caregivers and care recipients

Building on previous research (e.g. Haight *et al.* 2003), a number of researchers and practitioners have made significant recent contributions to the development and evaluation of reminiscence activities for the joint benefit of persons with dementia and their family caregivers. For example, the Couples Life Story Approach (Ingersoll-Dayton *et al.* 2016) supplements structured life review activities with the guidance of a practitioner who encourages care recipients and spousal caregivers to collaborate on the shared story of their life together. This study provided evidence that such interventions can improve communication between dyad members and enhance a sense of shared identity as a couple.

In another much larger series of studies, a multi-site research team in the UK evaluated the psychosocial benefits for both caregivers and care recipients derived from participating in the Remembering Yesterday, Caring Today (RYCT) reminiscence program (Schweitzer and Bruce 2008). RYCT adopts a joint reminiscence approach by including persons with dementia and their caregivers as dyads participating together in two-hour sessions incorporating a wide range of engaging reminiscence activities. In a full-scale test of the program, Woods *et al.* (2012) randomly assigned care recipient/caregiver dyads to one of two groups: a treatment-as-usual group (completed by 144 dyads) or a group taking part in the RYCT program once a week for 12 weeks and then once a month for the next seven months (completed by 206 dyads). Caregivers provided self-reports of quality of life, anxiety, depression, somatic symptoms, social dysfunction, caregiver stress, and the quality of the caregiver–patient relationship. These same measures were obtained three and ten months later. For persons with dementia, researchers obtained measures of quality of life, anxiety, depression, autobiographical memory and the quality of the caregiver–patient relationship. In contrast to positive results from an earlier pilot study of the program (Thorgrimsen, Schweitzer and Orrell 2002), the reminiscence group did not display more favourable outcomes than the control group at the three- and ten-month follow-ups. To the contrary, at the ten-month follow-up, caregivers in the reminiscence group displayed significantly higher anxiety scores than those at initial baseline, and their mean anxiety score was significantly higher than that observed for the control group.

In a follow-up study to determine if the RYCT program had a facilitating effect when combined with additional peer support from an experienced caregiver, Charlesworth *et al.* (2016) examined the separate and joint effects of peer caregiver support and the RYCT program on quality of life for both persons with dementia and their caregivers. Consistent with the pattern of results obtained by Woods *et al.* (2012), no significant changes in quality of life were observed for caregivers or persons with dementia in the RYCT condition at a 12-month follow-up. Unlike the Woods *et al.* (2012) study, however, no negative effects of the RYCT program were observed for either persons with dementia or their caregivers.

In a study following up the disappointing results of Woods *et al.* (2012) and Charlesworth *et al.* (2016), Melunsky *et al.* (2015) conducted semi-structured interviews with 18 caregivers who took part in the Charlesworth *et al.* (2016) study. The authors discovered that the experiences of caregivers in the program were complex and varied. Caregivers appreciated the fact that attending the reminiscence group with the person they cared for gave them more things to talk about at home and the opportunity to socialize with other people who shared the same challenges. Although caregivers were pleased to see care recipients 'come alive' when engaged in group activities, they were also disappointed when this active level of participation did not transfer to life at home. In addition, some caregivers noted frustration that memories triggered during group sessions were soon forgotten once the person with dementia returned home. Overall, the results of this study help to explain the higher levels of anxiety experienced by RYCT caregivers in the Woods *et al.* (2012) study, and they provide a more nuanced view of the effects of reminiscence groups for persons serving in caregiving roles.

While the results from this series of RYCT studies (i.e. Charlesworth *et al.* 2016; Melunsky *et al.* 2015; Woods *et al.* 2012) are disappointing to those who believe that reminiscence has beneficial effects for persons with dementia and their caregivers, they provide an excellent illustration of the ability of research to move the field forward. Both Woods *et al.* (2012) and Charlesworth *et al.* (2016) employ randomized controlled designs, standardized measures, and sample sizes large enough to detect small statistical effects. The presence of non-significant quantitative effects in these studies prompted the researchers to adopt a qualitative approach to gain a more fine-grained knowledge of the reminiscence group experience for caregivers. This combination of quantitative and qualitative designs thus contributes significantly to our knowledge of how best to provide reminiscence interventions for these groups in the future.

Reminiscence therapy for individuals struggling with mental illness

Reminiscence has been used in the context of psychotherapy for many decades (Westerhof and Bohlmeijer 2014), and the efficacy of reminiscence therapy for a variety of serious mental health issues has been well documented by recent review articles and meta-analyses (e.g. Istvandity 2017; Keal, Clayton and Butow 2015; Pinquart and Forstmeier 2012). In particular, recent research has contributed significantly to understanding when, how and why reminiscence therapy is effective. In light of basic research demonstrating that reminiscence serves a variety of positive and negative functions, cognitive-reminiscence therapy (e.g. Cappeliez 2002; Watt and Cappeliez 1995) applies these findings by promoting the use of two positive functions of reminiscence. First, clients engaging in *integrative reminiscence* are theorized to gain a greater degree of self-understanding, self-acceptance and meaning by re-appraising life events associated with feelings such as regret and failure. Second, clients engaging in *instrumental reminiscence* acquire higher levels of confidence and self-worth by noting episodes where their behavior was successful in meeting difficult life challenges. Therapists use both integrative and instrumental aspects of reminiscence to guide clients through an analysis of their past, with the goal of achieving a more fulfilling and meaningful future. While itself a theory of reminiscence-based change that has considerable explanatory power, cognitive-reminiscence therapy draws on strong theoretical and empirical roots found in earlier systems of cognitive-behavioral therapy (e.g. Beck et al. 1979).

In this section, we highlight the use of two designs to illustrate their potential to explain the relationship between engaging in reminiscence and effects on psychosocial outcomes. The first, a randomized controlled design, allows researchers to compare changes observed in one treatment condition to those observed in one or more others. The second design, a mediational model, provides information about the degree to which the effect of one variable on another is direct or whether its causal action flows first through a third (mediator) variable.

Randomized controlled trials

Korte et al. (2011a) replicated and extended previous studies examining the effectiveness of life review therapy using a randomized controlled design in 14 Dutch mental health service clinics. Participants had moderate levels of depression at initial baseline and ranged in age from 55–83 years. Sample sizes were large enough to test the potential moderating effects of age, gender, education level, personality, RFS reminiscence functions, as well as prior history of major depressive episodes, chronic medical conditions and critical life events. Participants in the treatment condition received a combination of life review and narrative therapy for eight weeks in two-hour group sessions with a trained clinical therapist and four to six participants. Individuals in the control condition received treatment as usual over the eight-week intervention period. The results showed that scores for depression, anxiety, and positive mental health improved significantly in the life review therapy group by the end of the eight-week intervention, while scores for the control group remained largely unchanged. Improved scores observed for the life review group were maintained at three-month and nine-month follow-ups. Moderation analyses revealed that life review therapy was associated with greater levels of improvement in extroverts and persons who engaged in less frequent reminiscence for the purpose of boredom reduction.

Using a Chinese sample, Choy and Lou (2016) compared the effects of instrumental reminiscence therapy and a no-treatment control condition on life satisfaction in participants 60 years of age and older who had mild to moderate levels of depression. Each of six weekly intervention sessions focused on a different theme or choice point in life and emphasized participants' past use of effective coping strategies. Significantly greater reductions in depression were observed in the instrumental reminiscence group than in the control group from baseline to post-intervention, and improvements observed in the reminiscence group were maintained at two- and six-week follow-ups. No significant effects of reminiscence therapy on life satisfaction were observed.

Tests of mediational models

The randomized controlled studies just described, as well as others (e.g. Chippendale and Bear-Lehman 2012; Hallford 2016; Latorre *et al.* 2015; Meléndez *et al.* 2015; Sabir *et al.* 2016), have moved the field forward by broadening our knowledge of:

- the outcomes most likely to be affected positively by reminiscence-based therapies
- the groups and cultures who derive benefit from it
- those individual difference variables most strongly linked with beneficial effects (ie. moderator variables).

However, mediational models have the potential to deepen our understanding of how and why these interventions work and they seek to identify causal pathways linking a root cause of psychosocial change (e.g. reminiscence) to a variety of ultimate outcomes (e.g. depression, anxiety and quality of life). They provide information about the sequence of changes that takes place when people recall and struggle with especially salient positive or negative memories under the guidance of a trained therapist. For example, does reminiscence cause lower levels of depression directly, or does it cause changes to other aspects of psychological function, such as psychological resources, which in turn act directly to reduce levels of depression?

The answers to these types of questions are essential for designing interventions that are more effective in terms of outcomes, efficient in terms of required resources, and tailored to meet the needs of specific types of individuals. In the context of psychotherapy itself, they are important for deepening our understanding of what it means to replace depressive thoughts with more positive and fulfilling frames of mind.

Korte *et al.* (2011b) tested a mediational model examining the extent to which two RFS self-positive functions (Identity and Problem Solving) and two self-negative functions (Bitterness Revival and Boredom Reduction) mediate relationships between critical life events and three psychosocial outcomes (depression, anxiety and life satisfaction). Although results indicated that all three relationships between the presence of critical life events and outcome measures were weak (depression, $r = .07$; anxiety, $r = -.16$; life satisfaction, $r = -.12$), the researchers found that one reminiscence function, Problem Solving, partially mediated the relationship between critical life events and anxiety. This mediational model is consistent with the assertion that at least part of the effect of critical life events on anxiety may be traced to a causal path in which a history of critical life events causes people to search their memories for effective instances of coping in the past, and that it is the access of memories of effective coping which acts directly on anxiety regarding effective coping in the future. Again, these effects, though suggestive, are small in size.

In a sample of participants exhibiting mild to moderate levels of depression, Korte *et al.* (2012a) used structural equation modelling to test a more complex mediational model. Specifically, they examined the extent to which a latent factor representing psychological resources (based on measures of meaning in life and sense of mastery) mediates the ability of self-positive and self-negative reminiscence to predict values for a latent variable of psychological distress (constructed from measures of depression and anxiety). Self-positive reminiscence was modelled as a latent factor based on scores for Identity and Problem Solving from the RFS, and self-negative reminiscence was a latent variable constructed from the RFS Bitterness Revival and Boredom Reduction scales. The authors found that self-positive reminiscence was unrelated to either psychological resources or psychological distress. However, they observed a significant relationship between self-negative reminiscence and psychological distress, and this relationship was mediated by psychological resources. This pattern is consistent with a causal pathway in which greater use of negative reminiscence functions causes lessened availability of the psychological resources of meaning in life and a sense of mastery. Then, in turn, decreased psychological resources are the direct cause of higher levels of depression and anxiety.

Adopting the theoretical perspective of cognitive-reminiscence therapy, Hallford, Mellor and Cummins (2013) conducted a cross-sectional study testing two mediational models. First, variables assessing psychological resources (meaning in life, optimism and self-esteem) were tested as potential mediators of the relationship between integrative reminiscence and depression. The second model tested the ability of primary control (belief in the ability to control events in one's life) and self-efficacy to mediate the relationship between instrumental reminiscence and depression. Hallford (2016) found significant relationships between positive reminiscence functions and depression, which were in turn mediated by measures of psychological resources. This pattern was later replicated in a more complex longitudinal study (Hallford and Mellor 2016b) demonstrating the ability of psychological resource variables to mediate the relationship between adaptive (instrumental) reminiscence measured at baseline and depression measured one week later.

Taken together, these investigations of mediating effects represent significant progress towards a more fully articulated causal model in which reminiscence results in improved psychological resources and then, in turn, higher levels of psychological wellbeing induce lower levels of depression. They therefore represent potent examples of how research can contribute to a greater depth of understanding regarding 'how' and 'why' reminiscence therapy works.

Reminiscence therapy for treatment of outcomes related to trauma

Another useful application of reminiscence therapy focuses on clinical populations reporting histories of significant trauma, including individuals with a history of childhood maltreatment and war veterans experiencing post-traumatic stress disorder (PTSD). Addressing child maltreatment first, theoretical and empirical work has emerged recently regarding the effects of parent–child reminiscence on reshaping memories of childhood maltreatment. In one recent example, Valentino *et al.*

(2013) provided a short-term, dyadic home-visiting program to enhance effective parent–child communication for maltreating parents and their 3- to 6-year-old maltreated child. Specifically, the researchers used Reminiscing and Emotion Training (RET), a parent–child reminiscing technique that trains and encourages parents to engage in frequent conversations with their children. When reminiscing about everyday past events with their children, parents are encouraged to ask frequent open-ended questions, utilize detailed descriptions and elaborations, build on the child's description of those events, draw causal connections between children's experiences and emotions, and discuss ways to resolve negative emotions. Results from this pilot study provided evidence that a short-term home visitation intervention is feasible and may lead to positive cognitive outcomes, such as richer memories for past events in preschool-age children. Additionally, maltreating parents improved their ability to understand their child's negative emotions, and maltreated children improved their ability to reflect on their own emotions when reminiscing about past events with a parent.

Empirical evidence also suggests that recall of traumatic war experiences under the guidance of skilled and experienced practitioners can promote the integration of these memories into psychologically healthy patterns of thought, emotion and behavior. One example of work in this area was reported by Westwood *et al.* (2010) in which 18 Canadian veterans participated in a group therapy program addressing combat-related trauma. Over the course of 80 hours, veterans in groups of six shared stories of traumatic events, first in written form and then through re-enactment of those events under the guidance of therapists. According to the authors, having veterans share their experiences and actively express their emotions with other veterans helped them to make sense of what occurred and make progress toward cognitive re-integration. Westwood *et al.* refer to this process of 'dropping the baggage' (2010, p.49) as one in which group members learn to anticipate triggers for unwanted memories and regulate their reactions to them.

Westwood *et al.* (2010) assessed the effectiveness of their program using both quantitative and qualitative methods. Participants provided scores for the Beck Depression Inventory and the Self Esteem Rating Scale prior to, immediately following, and three months after they completed the intervention. Data from the Trauma Symptom Inventory (TSI) were obtained at baseline and at the three-month follow-up.

TSI results showed reductions from baseline to the three-month follow-up in nine of ten subscale scores, with large reductions observed for the Tension Reduction Behavior, Anger/Irritability, Dissociation, and Impaired Self-Reference subscales. Improvements in scores for depression and self-esteem were observed from pre- to post-intervention and these improvements were maintained at the three-month follow-up. Qualitative analysis of interviews conducted following treatment indicated that veterans experienced a number of benefits, including improved relations at home, reduced feelings of shame and guilt, and increases in introspection, self-awareness, and the ability to trust others. In addition, veterans reported that they greatly appreciated the availability of ongoing support from group members after formal completion of the program. This latter finding may be especially important in light of the recent theoretical work by Davison *et al.* (2015) emphasizing that many aging veterans reengage with memories of war experiences in later life in an effort to find meaning, build coherence and experience post-traumatic growth (Neimeyer 2004).

The present and future of reminiscence research

Reminiscence and life review has developed into a thriving and diverse field which features an engaging synthesis of practice and research. In this chapter, we have focused on recent research and provided an overview of work in particularly active areas. Regretfully, we have been able to include descriptions of only a small sample of the many papers published in recent years. However, we hope our selections illustrate the tremendous variety of populations studied, variables assessed, research designs employed, and data analytic techniques brought to bear on questions regarding memory for personal history – questions which probe to the very heart of what it means to be a person with a past.

Our primary reference points in evaluating recent research have been the framework of reminiscence-relevant variables compiled by Webster *et al.* (2010) and the aspirational goals they proposed for future research. Our observation is that published research since the appearance of their article has yielded many examples of studies contributing to both a greater depth of knowledge within specific categories of variables and an expanding breadth of knowledge regarding associative and causal links among these categories of variables. We have every reason to believe the field will continue to move forward quickly along these lines.

When we examine the degree to which reminiscence research has become guided by theory, as Webster *et al.* (2010) recommended, the story is not as simple. Our examination of the role of theory in empirical studies of reminiscence and life review tells us that relatively few studies test predictions derived specifically from theories. The introductory sections of research articles often state the theoretical perspective from which the authors are working (e.g. Erikson's (1950) stage theory of psychosocial development, Baltes' (1987) theory of lifespan development, Watt and Cappeliez's (1995) Cognitive-Reminiscence Theory, Attachment Theory (Bowlby (1969) and others), but these studies appear more to be *affiliated with* or *embedded within* a particular theoretical perspective than designed as *tests of* these theories. To date, we see limited evidence that researchers have responded, or been able to respond, to Webster *et al.*'s (2010) appeal to falsification of existing theories as a route to better theories with better explanatory and predictive power. With that said, because theory development is a long and difficult process, we believe this present state of the field is normal and natural in areas of inquiry as young as ours. As significant as recent theoretical developments have been, we believe it is fair and accurate to describe reminiscence and life review as primarily a data-driven rather than a theory-driven discipline. At the present time, it may simply be the case that the field has not yet reached a critical mass of information necessary to formulate a comprehensive theory of reminiscence.

In summarizing our observations about the current position of research in reminiscence and life review, we see tremendous progress over recent years in the degree of methodological sophistication applied to research questions in the field. The presence of complex research designs and advanced statistical procedures provides compelling evidence of a maturing field with an evolving network of explanatory and outcome variables. In the future, we believe the increasing depth and breadth of empirical findings will yield a compelling theoretical structure that can fully incorporate the products of five decades of research on reminiscence and life review.

Chapter 3

REMINISCENCE WORK WITH PEOPLE WITH DEMENTIA

Making Sense of the Evidence Base

Bob Woods

I have been fascinated by the effects of reminiscence work on people with dementia for about 40 years. In the late 1970s, I was a relatively newly qualified clinical psychologist in Newcastle-upon-Tyne, and my work included frequent visits to the specialist dementia care homes run by the local authority. I had been approached by a community photographer, who was finding archive photographs of the city from the early years of the 20th century, and then taking an equivalent photograph, to compare 'then' and 'now'. He wanted to try these out with people with dementia, and I arranged for him to visit one of the homes with me. He had a pair of pictures of the quayside in Newcastle; 'then' it was teeming with life and industry, dock-workers unloading ships laden with all manner of goods; 'now' (40 years on), it was devoid of life, few ships on the River Tyne, derelict buildings, and only the famous Tyne bridges providing a focus of interest. A quiet gentleman, who rarely communicated and usually seemed withdrawn in a world of his own, picked up the 'then' photograph, pointed to one of the really quite indistinct figures of a dock-worker, and exclaimed, to everyone's surprise, 'that's me, there'. He became animated and began conversing with other residents, to the surprise of the care staff, who knew nothing about his background and life story. In an instant, his position changed from being just another elderly man with dementia to that of a person who had lived a life, who had once been young, who had worked and laboured, and so much more. It really was not important whether it was actually him in the picture – the story, the emotion, the coming to life was what mattered.

From that time on, I have sought to understand more about the ways in which reminiscence work might help people with dementia and those who support them. It has been a journey that has encompassed a wide range of reminiscence triggers and a variety of reminiscence approaches and functions. It has included: themed audio-visual presentations (slides plus music/archive sound recordings); groups in care homes and community settings; groups just for people with dementia, mixed groups of people with and without dementia and joint groups of people with dementia and their family carers; life review therapy; life story books; digital life story movies and life story apps; and much more besides. Clinical psychology is a discipline that embraces evidence-based practice, and so it has always been important to me to evaluate the effects of reminiscence work, in its many forms and in so doing to improve and develop practice further.

For the purposes of this chapter, a distinction will be drawn between two distinct types and functions of reminiscence work that may be carried out with people with dementia. Simple reminiscence involves people being 'given general cues about their past to stimulate associations with pleasant memories and to exchange these memories' (Bohlmeijer *et al.* 2007, p.292), with the aim of pleasure and interaction. In contrast, Wong and Watt (1991, p.272) describe integrative reminiscence, where the aim is to 'achieve a sense of self-worth, coherence, and reconciliation with regard to one's past'. Life review therapy, defined by Haight and Dias (1992, p.279) as 'a structured evaluative reminiscing process performed most effectively on a one-to-one basis', is an exemplar of integrative reminiscence.

This chapter aims to assist the reader in making sense of the evidence base that has developed over the years, in a context where no two applications of reminiscence work appear to be the same, where the quality of research available is highly variable and where it is often unclear what effects, on whom, we should be evaluating. It begins with a brief discussion of evidence-based practice, before reviewing the most recent and highest quality evidence available. It then focuses on the surprising results arising from the evaluation of joint reminiscence groups, and seeks to draw lessons for both research and practice from these, before looking briefly ahead to the rapidly growing field of digital reminiscence and identifying some of the challenges and opportunities this growth area provides.

Evidence-based practice

For many involved in reminiscence work, there are few doubts regarding its effectiveness with people with dementia. They see with their own eyes the response of people with dementia to memory triggers, or witness the social interaction in a reminiscence group. Why is it necessary to carry out research and, over time, build an evidence base? One important reason is that often public funding is required or utilised in care settings in order to provide reminiscence-based activities. With limited resources, many would consider that it is important to use these resources where they can have the most impact. Those who commission health and social care services, as well as care home and day-centre managers, may need to be convinced that investing staff time and resources, or establishing a new programme, will make a difference to people with dementia, and good quality evidence may be a factor that could influence their decision making. When guidelines are issued for health and social care regarding best practice, such as the National Institute for Health and Care Excellence (NICE) guidelines in the UK, they are typically based on the best available evidence, and services as well as individual professionals may well be obliged to follow any recommendations made. Research can also lead to improvements and refinements in treatment approaches, and assist in practice development.

There are challenges in evaluating reminiscence work, as there are with any psychosocial intervention. It is classified as a 'complex intervention'. It will typically involve person-to-person interactions and possibly group dynamics; even with the same theme and the same participants and facilitators the nature of the work may differ greatly on different occasions. A pill may be packaged, and its chemical constituents be analysed as identical from day to day, month to month, place to place, but a psychosocial intervention will vary naturally and unpredictably. Indeed, attempts to standardise its delivery run the risk of losing the essence of the approach, the unexpected memory, the free-flowing interchange between participants, sparked by a particular trigger but then taking off in a completely different direction. Beyond this inherent variation in psychosocial interventions, as has been referred to previously, there are a number of quite different approaches to reminiscence work, and even within one approach there is much variation in application. Also of course, people with dementia vary greatly in strengths, abilities, interests and preferences.

All this complexity means that we cannot simply apply the evaluation methods that would typically be used in relation to a new pharmacological treatment. A double-blind, placebo-controlled randomised controlled trial is usually neither feasible or desirable in this context. 'Double blind' implies that neither the person with dementia nor those evaluating the effects of the treatment is aware as to whether the person is receiving the active treatment or the placebo 'dummy' pill. By the nature of the intervention, the person with dementia will be aware they are attending, say, a reminiscence group, and so 'double' blind is not feasible; although it is possible to keep those making assessments 'blind', it is difficult at times to maintain this if the person with dementia begins to mention the groups they have been attending! Although it is possible to envisage and design placebo, inactive treatments, in practice it is difficult to ensure that there is no overlap with the active treatment, while retaining the interest and motivation of participants and facilitators.

What then is the way forward for evaluations of reminiscence work? Woods and Russell (2014) describe an approach based on the Medical Research Council (MRC) Framework for evaluation of complex interventions that can be applied to this context. Here, a randomised controlled trial is seen as just one aspect of the evaluation process. This should follow considerable development work, to address questions including the following:

- The intervention: has it been piloted and shown to be feasible? Can others be trained to deliver it? Does it have a clear basis in theory and practice? Is there a manual providing a detailed framework of guidance as to how it should be delivered, while retaining scope for individual choices and preferences? Can a process be established so that delivery can be monitored, to ensure fidelity to the treatment model? Will facilitators benefit from regular supervision from an experienced practitioner or from peer support? What 'dose' of the intervention is needed – in terms of duration of each session and number and frequency of sessions?

- Outcome measures: what are the domains where it is thought the intervention could feasibly contribute to change? What would be the mechanism of change in these domains? What are the best measures for these domains? Are these measures sensitive to change? Have they been validated with those who will be completing them (e.g. people with dementia)?

- Who is the target group for the intervention? If it is people with dementia, what profile of dementia severity, communication abilities, mood and distress and so on is being considered? For example, if the aim is to improve depressed mood, it would be most appropriate to include people with dementia who report low mood in the study, so that there is the potential for change. Are effects on others anticipated, such as family carers, care staff and so on? Have outcome measures for these other groups been considered? What will be the setting for the intervention? Different issues arise between care home and community settings, for example. In care homes, participants are 'on site' and readily accessed, but there may be other pressures related to staffing levels and staff turnover, and the support of management. In the community, identifying a suitable venue, arranging transport and finding convenient times for people to attend become important considerations to ensure attendance is maintained.

- Implementation: if the intervention appears effective in a research study, what would be needed for it to be implemented more widely? Could it be incorporated within existing service structures and professional roles, or would new programmes need to be established? Would it be possible to justify the costs of the intervention in relation to the likely benefits?

In this framework, a randomised controlled trial (RCT) is part of the overall evaluation programme. Typically, it will be single blind (with assessors unaware of whether the person is receiving the intervention), and will be pragmatic in that it will mirror the real-life context of the intervention as far as possible, with a view to a realistic appraisal of how implementation might proceed (Woods and Russell 2014). Often, there will be a parallel economic evaluation, so the cost effectiveness can be estimated. The trial will often evaluate what additional effect the intervention as a whole has, over and above usual care, so the control condition is likely to be 'treatment as usual', rather than a placebo condition. This means that non-specific effects of treatment, such as attendance at a group, are included in the active treatment, as of course they would be in the actual implementation of the intervention.

Other designs are needed if the aim is to identify the most important components of an intervention. Increasingly, process evaluations are embedded in the RCT, so that an understanding of the experience of the intervention from the perspective of the participants may be gained. Woods and Russell (2014) indicate the results of RCTs should be viewed alongside other sources of evidence, including case studies and qualitative research, echoing Moos and Bjorn (2006), who caution that qualitative evaluations are still required because much remains to be learned regarding the best ways of delivering life story interventions.

Cochrane reviews of reminiscence therapy for people with dementia

Background

Generally regarded as the most authoritative, reliable and relevant sources of evidence relating to interventions in healthcare, Cochrane reviews are produced under the auspices of the international Cochrane Collaboration, a global independent network of researchers, professionals, patients, carers, and interested lay people. Internationally, these reviews are recognised as providing high-quality, trusted information.

These reviews systematically identify and bring together the relevant original research regarding a particular intervention, apply rigorous quality standards and then synthesise the evidence to address the effectiveness of the intervention, making recommendations for practice and further research. These reviews make use of statistical techniques, described as 'meta-analysis', to combine data from multiple studies, to examine whether there are consistent effects across studies and to estimate the size of these effects. Cochrane reviews are peer reviewed to ensure the quality remains high, published online in the Cochrane Library, and plain language summaries aim to make the findings accessible to patients, carers and the general public, as well as to healthcare practitioners. Cochrane reviews are updated on a regular basis to incorporate new research, ensuring that decisions regarding the use of interventions can be made using the most up-to-date and reliable evidence.

Cochrane reviews of reminiscence therapy for dementia

The first review of reminiscence therapy for people with dementia was published in 1998 (Spector *et al.* 1998), and major updates have been published in 2005 and 2018 (Woods *et al.* 2005, 2018). The development of the field is evident over this period of almost 20 years, with barely a handful of studies being included in the earlier reviews, and these being considered to be of low quality. In the 2018 review, 22 studies have been included, involving a total of 1972 participants, with a number of these being of high quality, although only 16 (1749 participants) could be included in analyses combining data from different studies to evaluate cumulative effects.

In the 2005 review, my colleagues and I concluded that: 'The evidence-base for the effectiveness of reminiscence therapy continues to rest largely on descriptive and observational studies, with the few RCTs available being small, of relatively low quality and with some variation in outcome, perhaps related to the diverse forms of reminiscence therapy used' (p.8). We called for more RCTs following clear treatment protocols, to enable the more precise definition of the key elements of the different approaches to reminiscence work, and to evaluate their relative benefits. In particular, we called for evaluation of the effects of different modalities. These would include approaches using reminiscence groups versus individual reminiscence work versus joint groups with family caregivers. By 2018, more RCTs had certainly been reported, and a number of these had included fuller details of the treatment approach adopted. For joint reminiscence groups, for example, a full treatment manual concerned with reminiscence groups for people with dementia and their carers has been published (Schweitzer and Bruce 2008) and several of the individual reminiscence studies had taken as a basis Haight's life review experiences form (Haight 1992), but the review noted that for many studies sufficient descriptive details were still not available in treatment protocols.

Overall effects

The review first examined whether there were any effects of reminiscence therapy overall, irrespective of reminiscence type, modality or setting. We considered quality of life and wellbeing to be the most important of the numerous outcomes included across studies, and were able to conclude that overall there was probably no appreciable effect on quality of life, either immediately after the main treatment period or after a follow-up period. However, the analyses revealed considerable inconsistency between studies, indicating the need to explore the effects of other factors such as modality and setting.

In contrast, there was an effect of reminiscence overall related to performance on cognitive tests immediately after the treatment period. The benefit associated with reminiscence therapy was rather small, and it is not clear that it would be seen as clinically important in making a real difference to the lives of people living with dementia. Nine studies, with 437 participants, included the widely used (but much criticised) brief cognitive screening tool, the Mini-Mental State Examination (MMSE) (Folstein, Folstein and McHugh 1975) as an indicator of cognitive performance. On this scale, there was a clear improvement at the end of treatment of 1.87 points. It is estimated that the average person with dementia shows a decline of around 3 points per annum on the MMSE, so this benefit is equivalent to preventing just over six months of the expected disease progression. Thus, in studies using this specific scale we see a stronger effect than the overall picture, and there was an indication that this effect may be maintained at longer term follow-up, although the quality of the evidence for this was weaker.

A smaller number of studies (six studies, with 249 participants in total) included an assessment of communication and/or interaction as an outcome measure. Taking into account the quality of the available evidence, the review concluded that there may be an effect of reminiscence therapy overall in this domain, but noted there was inconsistency between studies, suggesting again the importance of examining sub-groups of studies. The benefit noted appeared to also be evident at longer term follow-up. Other outcome domains examined for the person with dementia included mood, functioning in daily activities, agitation/irritability and relationship quality. No clear effects were identified in these domains. We found no evidence of any harmful effects on people with dementia.

Outcomes for carers examined included stress, mood and quality of relationship with the person with dementia (from the carer's perspective). In general, we found no evidence for effects on carers apart from a potential adverse outcome related to joint reminiscence groups, discussed below.

Reminiscence modality

In homing in on differences in findings between studies, the review examined two aspects of potential significance. The first of these was whether the reminiscence work undertaken was on a one-to-one individual basis, as opposed to being conducted in a group context. Although individual work does not necessarily involve integrative reminiscence, following a life story perspective, it is more likely in this context, and the small number of studies available did not make possible a more fine-grained analysis.

All but one of the studies reporting a quality of life outcome involved reminiscence groups, and the combined results for these mirrored the overall finding, with no effect evident and considerable inconsistency between studies. The one individual study, which used a life review intervention to develop a life story book (Subramaniam, Woods and Whitaker 2014), may have shown some benefit, but on its own, with just 23 participants, does not provide strong evidence in this context. Combining data from five studies using individual reminiscence, with a total of 196 participants, showed a small improvement on performance on a variety of cognitive tests, but there was little or no difference for the nine group studies that included 1023 participants. For the six group studies using the MMSE, with a total of 281 participants, the result was similar to the overall finding, with a benefit of 1.81 points.

In the communication domain, reminiscence groups were associated with probable, though small, benefits both immediately after the treatment period (four studies, 153 participants) and at a later follow-up. Unfortunately, the evidence relating to communication outcomes for individual reminiscence work was of very low quality, and so the effects were uncertain.

Group reminiscence appeared to lead to little or no benefit in relation to depressed mood (six studies, 842 participants), whereas individual reminiscence was probably associated with a small benefit on depression scales (four studies, 131 participants) immediately after the treatment period. The one, very small, study with a longer term follow-up of individual reminiscence including a mood outcome also reported a probable benefit.

Setting: care home versus community

The results from the five community studies reporting a quality of life outcome, with 867 participants in total, were consistent with the overall findings, showing little or no effect on quality of life. In contrast, there did appear to be a positive effect on quality of life associated with reminiscence work in care homes. This conclusion was drawn from combining the results of three studies, with a total of 193 participants. The findings for performance on cognitive tests were similar, with little or no effect evident in community settings (eight studies, 989 participants), but a probable small improvement in care home studies (six studies, 230 participants).

It was only in the domain of communication and interaction that probable benefits associated with reminiscence work in community settings were evident, both at the end of the intervention period and at a longer term follow-up. However, this result was based on three small studies with a total of only 65 participants. For care home participants, the results were inconsistent between studies and while there may be an improvement at follow-up, at end of treatment the quality of evidence was very low and effects were uncertain (three studies, 184 participants).

Joint reminiscence groups

The results from community studies are strongly influenced by two large UK studies of joint reminiscence groups – REMCARE and Support at Home: Interventions to Enhance Life in Dementia (SHIELD) – with people with dementia and family carers participating together (Woods *et al.* 2012, 2016; Charlesworth *et al.* 2016). These studies contribute over 500 participants to many of the previously reported analyses of overall group and community effects. Both studies followed the Remembering Yesterday, Caring Today treatment manual (Schweitzer and Bruce 2008), and neither study showed indications of benefit to people with dementia or to the family carers involved from participation in any of the domains they examined. However, there was a suggestion that these groups might be associated with increased carer anxiety at longer term follow-up, although the size of the effect would be unlikely to be of clinical significance.

Cochrane review conclusions

The review concludes: 'Whilst this updated review has shown that reminiscence therapy (RT) can improve outcomes for people with dementia, its effects are inconsistent, often small in size and differ considerably across settings and modalities' (p.42). There does seem to be better evidence for effectiveness in care home contexts, where quality of life and cognition show improvements. Individual reminiscence is also associated with improved cognitive test performance and with improved mood, whereas group and community-based reminiscence may have some effects on communication and interaction. Joint reminiscence groups do not find any support for their effectiveness in this review.

It is perhaps no surprise that 'reminiscence' is not a 'magic bullet' for people with dementia – the term covers such a diverse range of activities and approaches, a point that has been made for many years (Haight and Burnside 1993). This meant that the review could not pin down important aspects such as the distinction between simple reminiscence and integrative reminiscence, for example. It was not possible to include some types of reminiscence work, such as where the intervention was simply to train staff (Gudex *et al.* 2010) or to facilitate the use of life story in care planning (Eritz *et al.* 2016).

The strength of the Cochrane approach is its rigour and the emphasis on the quality of the evidence reviewed. Other reviews with less stringent inclusion criteria have resulted in slightly more positive conclusions. For example, Subramaniam and Woods (2012) reviewed studies of individual reminiscence work. From the five RCTs they identified, only three of which were included in the Cochrane review, they considered that a consistent pattern emerged. Positive outcomes appeared to be associated with 'individual reminiscence work that includes a life review process, uses specific memory triggers and results in the production of a life story book' (p.8), i.e. integrative reminiscence work. In contrast, more general, simple, reminiscence work did not appear to have such effects. Testad *et al.* (2014) reviewed psychosocial interventions in care homes, including six studies of reminiscence therapy, most of which did not meet the inclusion criteria for the Cochrane review (e.g. three were not RCTs). Reminiscence was associated with improved mood, but the evidence for other outcomes was inconsistent. A third, more comprehensive, review is reported by Huang *et al.* (2015) and included 12 studies, with 1325 participants.

The review focused on two main outcomes – cognition and depressed mood – with nine studies contributing to meta-analyses in each case. As with the Cochrane review, they identified a small benefit for cognitive test performance, but they also reported an effect on depressed mood, although this was greater in care home studies than in the community.

Taking the evidence from reviews together, we can conclude that reminiscence work has the potential to be of benefit to people living with dementia, but that these benefits cannot be assumed for every implementation of reminiscence work in every context. More work is needed on who will benefit from which type of approach, and on understanding why implementation in care homes appears to have a wider range of effects. One factor may be that, in general, care home settings offer less stimulation to people with dementia, so that any intervention will have larger effects than in the community. Another factor, more directly related to the nature of reminiscence, is that in the care home setting inevitably the person with dementia will experience a less familiar environment, with less of their own personal possessions and memory triggers such as photographs and souvenirs. Reminiscence may be especially helpful in this context in contributing to a sense of identity. Of all the reminiscence modalities, the evidence appears least positive for joint reminiscence groups, which have been the focus of two large-scale rigorous RCTs. The next section will consider some of the factors contributing to this situation.

Joint reminiscence groups – why no positive findings?

To date, the predominant implementation of reminiscence groups involving people with dementia and family caregivers together has been the Remembering Yesterday, Caring Today (RYCT) approach, the development of which has been documented elsewhere (Gibson and Bruce 1998). In essence, this approach grew out of a project aiming to train family caregivers to use reminiscence techniques with their relatives. The family caregivers took part in a reminiscence group, and their relatives were invited along to some sessions so the facilitators could model the techniques with them. These sessions went so well that the whole programme became a joint one, albeit with some time set aside in some sessions for carers and people with dementia to work with facilitators and volunteers separately from each other.

A small-scale evaluation of the approach was reported by Thorgrimsen *et al.* (2002), involving 11 people with dementia and their family carers. This showed some promising trends in terms of improved quality of life for people with dementia and reduced stress for carers, and encouraged Martin Orrell, Errollyn Bruce and myself to seek funding for a larger evaluation study, working closely with Pam Schweitzer, the originator of the approach. We were initially successful in 2004 in receiving funding from the UK Medical Research Council for a 'trial platform' (see Woods *et al.* 2012, appendix 10, pp.95–96). This funding allowed us to explore a number of areas regarding the evaluation about which we were uncertain, as well as providing an opportunity for the intervention to be written up in the form of a treatment manual, so that new facilitators could be trained to deliver the approach in a consistent manner across centres (Schweitzer and Bruce 2008).

We had been struck by descriptive reports that the approach could improve the quality of the relationship between the person with dementia and the carer, benefiting both. Accordingly, during the trial platform we tested out different measures of relationship quality, to see which could be completed reliably by both people with dementia and carers. We also considered a number of other outcome measures, including cognitive tests. We decided against using the MMSE, as it did not appear directly relevant to the aims of the intervention. We preferred instead a measure of autobiographical memory – the person's memory for events relating to their life over the years – which we considered directly relevant to the content of the reminiscence groups.

In the trial platform, we conducted a small pilot study and included two comparison conditions. Those people with dementia randomised to one condition attended a series of reminiscence groups without their family carer present; the other condition comprised 'treatment as usual', i.e. there was no additional intervention.

Fifty people with dementia and their carers completed assessments immediately after the intervention period, with 45 followed up three months later. Recruitment to the study went well, across three centres, and participants were prepared to be randomised (and so potentially not receive the intervention) and to complete the range of assessments used. Participants enjoyed the groups so much that they asked for additional reunion sessions following the 12 weekly sessions – and these monthly maintenance sessions were later incorporated in the subsequent full-scale RCT.

The results of the pilot were very promising for what was a relatively small-scale study. The results for the primary outcome measures – quality of life for the person with dementia and stress for the family carer – were not statistically significant, but showed a reasonable effect size. People with dementia showed a significant benefit on autobiographical memory, compared with the treatment as usual group, immediately after the intervention period, and carers showed less depressed mood and distress immediately and at follow-up (see Figures 3.1 and 3.2). Benefits appeared to accrue from both joint groups and groups for people with dementia alone. Where the person attended a group without the family carer, the carer seemed to benefit from the break this provided.

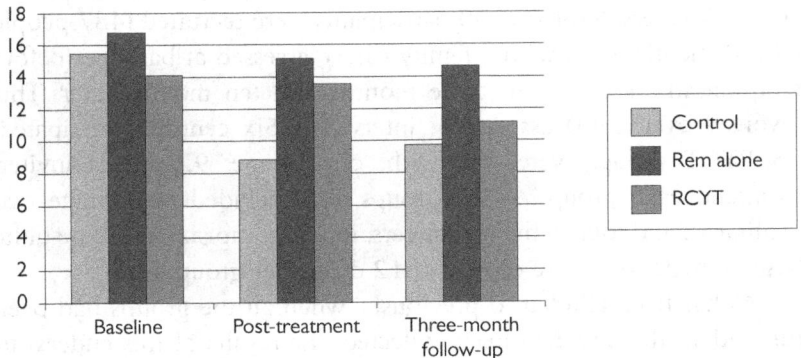

Figure 3.1: Trial platform – Autobiographical Memory Interview (Autobiographical Incident Scale) (Post-treatment, p = 0.007; Follow-up, p = 0.26)

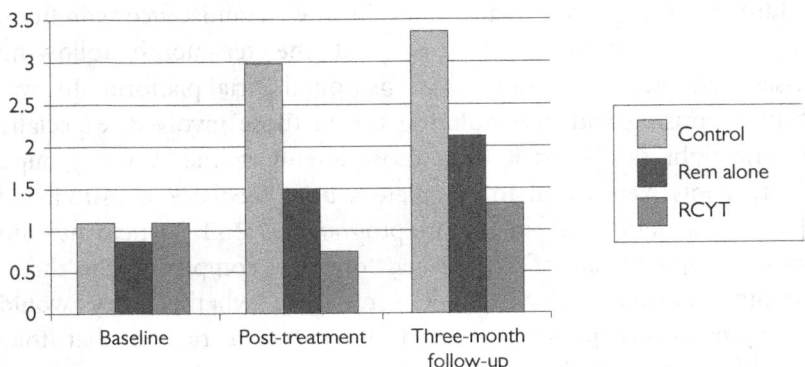

Figure 3.2: Trial platform – Carer depression (GHQ28-D) (Post-treatment, p = 0.013; Follow-up, p = 0.024)

These results, showing benefit for both the person with dementia and the family carer, formed the basis for a successful application to the UK National Institute for Health Research Health Technology Assessment programme for a full-scale RCT of the RYCT approach, the REMCARE study. Full details of the study procedures are available in the trial protocol (Woods *et al.* 2009). Although identifying any differences between the outcomes from joint reminiscence groups and groups for people with dementia alone would have been of interest, the results from the trial platform suggested that the differences, if any, were relatively small and would require an unfeasibly large trial to identify. Accordingly, 'treatment as usual' was the only comparison group utilised.

REMCARE was at the time probably the largest study ever undertaken of a psychosocial intervention for people with dementia and their carers. Nearly 1000 participants were recruited (487 people with dementia, each with a family carer), assessed at baseline (before randomisation), and then three months and ten months later. This involved over 2500 assessment interviews. Six centres participated; 28 RYCT groups were run, with, on average, 9.6 dyads invited to attend each group. As the groups also included on average two facilitators and four to five volunteers, initial group size could be quite large – invitations were capped at 12 dyads per group.

As has been alluded to previously, when all the groups had been run and all the data had been collected, the results of this endeavour were disappointing. There was no evidence of any benefit for people with dementia and their carers allocated to the joint reminiscence condition, compared with those receiving treatment as usual. In addition, it appeared that carers in the reminiscence condition reported higher levels of anxiety at the ten-month follow-up assessment. After the positive findings from the trial platform, this was both surprising and disappointing for all those involved, especially in the light of feedback from those attending the RYCT groups. Participants were asked to complete a brief feedback questionnaire at the conclusion of the group programme; 263 participants did so – a response rate of 58 per cent of those completing the three-month assessment. Participants were asked whether they would recommend the programme, and 86 per cent replied that they would do so. Only 1 per cent said that they would not recommend the programme, with 13 per cent not responding to this question.

Many respondents elaborated on the reasons for recommending the programme:

> I am not the only one with a bad memory. I have enjoyed it very much. I would definitely recommend this project to a friend. I have had fun. (*Person with dementia, Bangor*)

> Got very friendly with everyone. We were all in the same boat and how much fun I have had. (*Person with dementia, Bangor*)

> A very nice two hours every meeting and the time passed quickly and was very relaxing and really enjoyed it and it was very beneficial. (*Person with dementia, Bangor*)

> Because it helps you to remember things of the past, make new friends. (*Person with dementia, Bangor*)

> It wasn't just a Tuesday session. We were both stimulated – looking forward to the sessions and discussing these afterwards. (*Carer, Bangor*)

> At first, I was sceptical about this work, thinking it would not do much, but I was amazed when, after and in-between group sessions my mum was remembering the past and trying hard to remember more…these sessions make them feel worthwhile and special again. They come away with more confidence I think. (*Carer, Bangor*)

Such reports from participants raise the question as to whether any alternative explanations for the lack of benefit should be considered. These might include the following suggestions.

The trial platform results were misleading

Inspection of Figures 3.1 and 3.2 suggests that the reminiscence interventions were in general not actually associated with any improvement for people with dementia – rather the people with dementia and carers allocated to those conditions deteriorated less rapidly than those in the treatment as usual control group. This is a perfectly acceptable outcome in the context of a progressive condition, of course, but in the REMCARE study, the control group did not appear to show such a rapid decline. Although this was not documented, the greater availability of community groups, including choirs and Alzheimer cafes, for example, may have contributed to a more stimulating environment for 'treatment as usual'. Such activities were, of course, equally available to those randomised to the reminiscence condition, but timetable clashes led to some participants not attending reminiscence groups in view of a long-standing commitment to another activity.

The outcome measures used were not sensitive enough to capture the changes taking place

The primary outcome measure for people with dementia was a widely-used quality of life scale, the QoL-AD (Thorgrimsen *et al.* 2003), which can be completed in an interview with the person with dementia or by the carer, acting as proxy. Both forms were used in REMCARE. The scale asks for a rating of quality of life in 13 standard domains, such as friends, energy, food and so on, on a four-point scale. There are clear limitations to the scale, as each person's quality of life may be influenced by other, personally relevant factors; it relies on a complex judgement, and memory to appraise the current situation; it does not allow for qualified responses, if some aspects of a domain are good but others less so; scores are heavily influenced by the person's mood and self-concept (Woods *et al.* 2014). However, it has proved sensitive to change in studies of other psychosocial interventions, such as cognitive stimulation (Spector *et al.* 2003). The quality of relationship scale used (the Quality of Carer Patient Relationship (QCPR); Spruytte *et al.* 2002) has also proved sensitive to change in cognitive stimulation studies (Orrell *et al.* 2017a). Thus, while the outcome measures were far from perfect, they might have been expected to show benefit if it had occurred.

The measures were not taken at the right time

There are two aspects to this issue. First, it has been suggested that measuring quality of life after the conclusion of the 12 weekly reminiscence sessions (at the three-month follow-up) or the seven monthly maintenance sessions (at the ten-month follow-up) might have meant that participants felt the loss of something they had enjoyed. This is especially pertinent as sometimes due to logistics of researchers being able to arrange to see participants, up to two months might elapse between the final session and the assessment taking place. This might then have diluted any effects which did occur.

Second, wellbeing was not measured during the reminiscence sessions. Observations and reports of much laughter and fun suggest that many participants experienced considerable wellbeing during sessions. Should this have been one of the outcome measures? This is a valid point but changes the nature of the evaluation. It is perfectly reasonable to develop interventions where people with dementia have positive, uplifting experiences, and these will be worthwhile in their own right. However, we cannot claim any enduring effect unless this is evaluated after the sessions in some way. There would also need to be some activity for the treatment as usual control group, if this were part of an RCT. Brooker and Duce (2000) showed higher levels of wellbeing for people with dementia in reminiscence groups compared with control activities, but in this study, people acted as their own controls rather than having a separate control group.

The participants did not receive the intervention as planned

Typically, in studies of psychosocial interventions there are concerns that the treatment has not been delivered appropriately to a sufficient quality. In the REMCARE study, there was a clear and detailed manual, and group facilitators and volunteers were trained by Pam Schweitzer, the originator of the approach, meeting regularly for supervision. In addition, a simple checklist was used, completed by a volunteer at the group, encouraging self-monitoring of adherence to the manual. The much greater concern in REMCARE was that a significant number of those allocated to receive the reminiscence intervention did not do so, because they did not attend many of the group sessions. In analysing the data for the study, best practice is to use the 'intention to treat' approach, so that the results for a participant attending one session (or indeed no sessions) are given equal weight to those attending all 12 weekly and seven monthly sessions. If there is an effect of the intervention, having significant numbers of non-attenders could dilute the results obtained, of course.

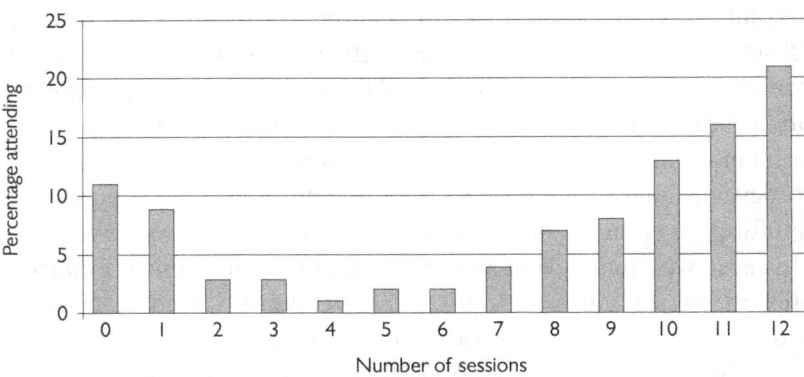

Figure 3.3: Total number of weekly sessions attended by REMCARE participants (Woods et al. 2012)

Figure 3.3 indicates the scale of this problem, with 26 per cent attending three or fewer sessions, and 11 per cent attending no sessions at all. It is important to note that these participants had all agreed to take part, were aware of the nature of the intervention, and remained in the research despite not attending the majority of sessions. The reasons for non-attendance included illness or declining health, the group clashing with attendance at a day centre, or the carer's other commitments, and either the carer or person with dementia being reluctant to continue attending. In some cases, this reflected a discomfort with groups and there were certainly examples of people with dementia who had shown some enjoyment of the groups being withdrawn by their relative who was less enthusiastic about attending.

It is possible to re-examine the REMCARE results according to the level of attendance. In doing so, it is important to consider that those who continue to attend may differ in important ways from those who do not, as attendance is no longer randomly determined. The findings should then be treated more cautiously than the main trial results, but are of some interest, nonetheless. For most outcome measures, including quality of life for the person with dementia, level of attendance did not influence the outcome. However, for autobiographical memory, attendance at weekly sessions was related to outcome at the end of the weekly sessions (three-month time-point), although, as with the trial platform, this effect was not maintained at follow-up, at ten months in this instance (see Figure 3.4 and Woods *et al.* 2012, pp.36–37).

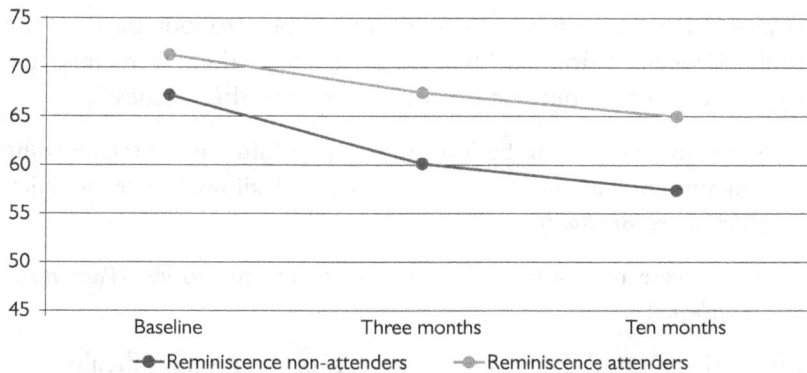

Figure 3.4: REMCARE study – Autobiographical Memory Interview total scores
Autobiographical Memory Interview total scores; attenders at three months had attended at least 6–12 weekly sessions; attenders at ten months had also attended at least 3–7 monthly sessions. Difference from baseline to three months was statistically significant ($F = 4.64$, $p = 0.03$); difference from baseline to ten months not significant ($F = 1.48$, $p = 0.224$).

Those people with dementia who attended more weekly and monthly sessions also scored more highly on a generic quality of life measure (the EQ-5D) and on the quality of relationship scale, the QCPR, at the ten-month follow-up. However, the negative effect on carers' stress levels also appeared to be related to level of attendance, with those carers continuing to attend scoring significantly higher on the Relatives Stress Scale at the ten-month follow-up. Thus, while factoring in attendance levels does suggest that the reminiscence groups may be benefiting people with dementia in the domains of autobiographical memory, quality of life and quality of relationship, there remains a concern that this may be at the cost of greater stress for the carer.

It's not for everyone

The REMCARE study attendance rates (Figure 3.3) certainly support the proposition that – for whatever reason – many people with dementia and carers choose not to attend reminiscence groups when these are made available to them. In the research context, it appeared that a number of people signed up to the project to assist with research, rather than to gain an opportunity to attend a group. As well as some finding groups difficult, we have known for many years that not all older people wish to reminisce (Coleman 1986b). For some, this is because memories are painful; for others, memories of better times make the present time seem disappointing; and for others it is because the present time is too fulfilling and busy to look back. In the feedback received from REMCARE participants, there were very few negative comments, but one or two did relate to these issues:

> Some memories can be exceptionally painful and perhaps time and support has not been satisfactory and allowed time of quiet. (*Participant, Bradford*)

> These were not particularly good times and memories. (*Participant, Manchester*)

A few others found the enactment aspects of the group difficult:

> I feel the group was not for me. I felt degraded by the childish enactment. I don't think I am in my second childhood just yet. (*Participant, Manchester*)

> I'm not cut out for these sorts of sessions. The 'play acting' bits I found excruciatingly embarrassing. (*Participant, London*)

These were, of course, isolated comments and for many other participants acting out a wedding or bathing a baby and so on were cited among the highlights of the group experience. Outside the research setting, the person's choices and preferences may be recognised more readily. Having people with dementia and carers attend together does add the complication of one party enjoying the group and the other not, and as mentioned previously we were aware of people with dementia who were not able to continue attending because of their carer's reluctance, despite their evident enjoyment. Again, outside the research context, opening up groups to people with dementia (and carers) without involvement of care-partners becomes more feasible.

An evidence-base cannot rely on one study alone

Despite the size of the REMCARE study and its adherence to the highest standards for conducting a trial of a psychosocial intervention, as with any study, conclusions can be more powerful when results are replicated. This has in fact already been accomplished, through a study carried out under the auspices of the SHIELD programme, funded in the UK by the National Institute for Health Research (Orrell *et al.* 2017b). This particular study included two distinct interventions: RYCT and a carer support programme (CSP) offering one-to-one peer support (by volunteers) to participating carers (Charlesworth *et al.* 2016). The study used a more complex factorial design, with participants allocated randomly to receive either RYCT or CSP or RYCT and CSP together, or treatment as usual. In total, 291 dyads of carers and people with dementia took part in the study. A total of 194 dyads were offered a place in a RYCT group (half of these also being offered a CSP), with 112 attending at least one session (58%). Reasons for non-attendance were as for the REMCARE study, together with the severity of the cognitive or physical impairment of the person with dementia (as the inclusion criteria allowed a greater range of impairment in this study). The results were similar to the REMCARE results, with no benefit evident for the person with dementia, from either the RYCT intervention or the combined RYCT/CSP intervention, in terms of quality of life and other outcomes. However, there was no evidence of a negative effect on family carers, and indeed it appeared that those carers receiving the combined intervention were reporting an improvement in their relationship with the person with dementia at the end of the study. It is possible that the greater focus on carers in the RYCT/CSP study was able to ameliorate the negative effects found previously. For example, where the carer was also receiving the CSP intervention, their peer-volunteer supporter was able to attend RYCT groups with them, and all carers may have benefited from the extra emphasis given to addressing carer needs in the sessions.

It is natural for carers to have mixed feelings

Although some feedback was obtained from participants in the REMCARE study, as discussed previously, this was not sufficiently in depth to understand factors that might have led to increased anxiety and stress for participating carers. As the SHIELD study was still continuing when these results emerged, some additional qualitative work was commissioned, interviewing individually 18 carers who had participated in the RYCT groups in that study, including a few who had attended less than half the sessions (Melunsky *et al.* 2015).

Although some carers had experienced the intervention as entirely positive, some mixed feelings were elicited. Positive feelings included the social aspects, sharing with other carers and with the person with dementia, and seeing how others coped with and managed their situation. More negative feelings included a lack of emphasis on the carers needs in the groups and a lack of respite through attending the group along with the person with dementia. Particularly poignant were comments made regarding the person 'coming alive' in the group session, but this not being maintained afterwards, adding to the carer's sense of loss. The range of severity of dementia of people in the group was difficult for some carers, who did not wish to think about what the future might hold, in terms of the further deterioration in the condition of their relative. Unmet expectations of improvement were also difficult. Feelings of guilt and stress at not being able to put into practice skills and coping strategies acquired in the group were expressed in these interviews, and were also evident in some of the REMCARE qualitative feedback:

> It has been very helpful seeing how each of them cope but they all do seem to be much better than me. (*Carer, Manchester*)

There are clearly a number of factors that can contribute to carers' negative feelings from involvement in RYCT groups; most might well arise in any group bringing carers and people with dementia together and are not specific to reminiscence work. Mixed feelings are perhaps inevitable, but the importance of directly addressing carer needs in this context is clear. This is especially the case in a large group where it may be difficult for facilitators to be aware of the range of experiences and reactions in the group, and where the participants with dementia are being given particular attention to support their full involvement.

Conclusions

This chapter has attempted to set out the current state of the evidence base for the use of reminiscence work in dementia care. Despite, or perhaps because of, a growing number of research studies of greater quality, the picture presented is not clear cut. There are many inconsistencies and unanswered questions. Small changes, more often in care homes, and the potential benefits of individual reminiscence work emerge. The perplexing lack of changes associated with joint reminiscence groups in the community has been explored in greater depth and detail than has been possible in other publications, and the complexity of evaluating dyadic interventions in dementia care illustrated.

Looking forward to future development of the evidence base, there is a rapidly growing interest in digital life story work, with many systems and apps now being available to assist the person making a digital life story book. See, for example Chapter 2 by Pierce and Elliott and Chapter 19 by Ryan. However, the Cochrane review did not include any studies of this approach, as, to date, RCTs have not been reported. One challenge that may need to be overcome in order for these approaches to take their place in the evidence base is the rapid rate of change associated with any information technology application. Typically, RCTs may take three or more years, from funding to reporting, by the time approvals have been obtained, participants recruited and evaluated, and a reasonable follow-up period included. By this time, the application being evaluated will probably have changed dramatically, or no longer be compatible with current devices. More timely, flexible and agile evaluation approaches will be required.

The fundamental issue of reminiscence type will continue to arise with digital media, just as it has in the past. The Cochrane review was not able to clearly distinguish simple and integrative reminiscence approaches (in view of insufficient studies of the latter). Will digital apps effectively be a store of photographs, music and video clips from the person's life, offering personal, specific memory triggers, accessed almost at random? Or can they be organised in a personal narrative, to tell the person's story in the way in which he or she wishes to do so, perhaps based on a life review process? (See Chapter 14 by Ferguson and Gallagher for one such example.) The sheer volume of potential triggers may make this a more daunting task than the old-fashioned approach of sorting through a drawer full of fading photographs and a rack of CDs. One approach to digital reminiscence involved the construction of life story movies, so that there was a clear narrative and sequence (Subramaniam and Woods 2016). Although simple reminiscence (responding to a photograph pulled at random from the digital 'drawer') may well be enjoyable, and support communication and enjoyment, are there additional benefits to being able to share a coherent life story, reinforcing identity and continuity and potentially providing a pathway to person-centred care?

This chapter has documented where I have arrived on my 40-year journey to define and understand the effects of reminiscence work for people with dementia. I remain convinced that it can be a powerful intervention for some people with dementia, but recognise we need to become better able to identify for whom it is useful, and under what conditions. There remain many questions for future reminiscence researchers in dementia care to answer.

Acknowledgements

I am grateful to my co-authors of the Cochrane review, especially Laura O'Philbin and Emma Farrell, for their painstaking work in updating it. I am also grateful to colleagues from the REMCARE study and especially John Keady and Ruth Elvish, who compiled the qualitative feedback from participants.

Part 2

AGE AND CULTURAL VARIATIONS AND APPLICATIONS

Chapter 4

REMINISCENCE AND LIFE REVIEW IN LATER LIFE

The Southampton Longitudinal Study

Peter G. Coleman, Christine Ivani-Chalian and Maureen Robinson

The study of older people's memories and their contribution to quality of life has become a significant field of research on ageing and it seems strange to recall that there was a time, less than 50 years ago, when the importance of past memories for older people was neglected. Even in care settings, reminiscence tended to be seen as a symptom of mental decline rather than of wellbeing and was often actively discouraged. Only in the 1970s and 1980s as observations and research on the social and developmental aspects of reminiscence began to be recorded was recognition given to the life-enhancing character of recall of past memories in later life.

Two of the major contributors to the changed attitudes were the psychotherapists Erik Erikson and Robert Butler, the former in his emphasis on the acceptance of and appreciation of the life that one has lived as a crucial developmental task of later life, the latter in his concept of 'life review' as an inevitable aspect of growing old, sometimes experienced in the return of important but neglected troubling memories needing resolution. One or the other and sometimes both men's writings were usually credited with stimulating researchers' and therapists' interests in the role that reminiscence both played and could be encouraged to play in later life.

As a result of the growing interest in reminiscence, research on older people's wellbeing began to include questions on reminiscence. An early example was the Southampton Ageing Study (1977–2002), a joint project of the Faculties of Medicine and Social Sciences at the University of Southampton, in which a limited number of questions on attitudes to the past and to memories of the past were included as part of an initial survey of health, activities, social relations and subjective wellbeing at the first observation point 1977–78. Recruitment of 340 participants was conducted from the lists of general medical practices in Southampton, a medium-large city with a population fairly representative of the central south of England. These people were re-interviewed in both of the next two years, with a ten-year follow-up in 1988.

The Economic and Social Research Council (UK) funded further qualitative study of the remaining sample, and up to six subsequent in-depth interviews were conducted with these people between 1990 and 2002, focused on sources of identity and wellbeing in later life. The interview schedule included assessments of self-esteem and its sources (Coleman 1984) as well as depression (Montgomery and Asberg 1979). The participants also completed written accounts of themselves, responding to sentence-completion statements on self-perception (Dittmann-Kohli 1990) and life attitudes (Kivnick 1991), which they posted back to the researchers. A total of 40 persons (23 women and 17 men) subsequently gave permission for accounts of their lives to be written (drafts of which we encouraged them to read and comment on), using pseudonyms. These case studies were eventually published 13 years after the last interviews were conducted (Coleman, Ivani-Chalian and Robinson 2015).

Although reminiscence was not the focus of these studies most of the participants took the opportunity during the interviews to talk in some detail about their past lives. In this chapter, we provide a description of how life review, accounts of life stories, and more general reminiscence featured in these case studies. It has often been assumed that engagement in life review can be understood as a mode of reaching final acceptance of one's life story. But in fact, neither Butler nor Erikson ever acknowledged the relevance of the other's thinking to their own vision of development in later life. This is despite the fact both of them cited Ingmar Bergman's film *Wild Strawberries*, with its depiction of the impact of the return of unbidden memories, as examples of 'life review' and 'integrity' respectively (Butler 1963a, 1963b; Erikson 1978). Jeff Garland and Christina Garland (2001, p.33) have commented insightfully on the difference between the two accounts from their own experience of using reminiscence in therapy:

> Comparing Erikson and Butler, the authors' experience suggests that each is right. We find that some narrators in later life are trying to make sense of their life as a whole, as Erikson proposes, while others, as Butler reports, are more concerned to limit their efforts to dealing with certain issues from the past which have re-emerged with ageing.

We draw on a similar distinction in dividing up our study material, between close involvement in dealing with disturbing past memories, which one might call active life reviewing, and the telling of an integrated life story, which might or might not be the result of close attention to particular difficult periods of life. We analyse first the interviews from five of our women participants who wanted to engage us in their own examination of disturbing and painful memories. In the following section, we describe material from 12 other members of our sample who provided us with integrated stories of their lives. Inevitably in a very partially completed longitudinal study, a researcher can only perceive fragments of a person's long trajectory of reminiscence activity. Furthermore, since we only began interviewing our participants in depth much later on in the study, when the youngest was already 78 years old and the average age of the participants was in the mid 80s, we would have missed earlier periods of active life reviewing.

In the last section, we consider the character of reminiscence observed in the remaining 23 members of our final sample. Although the majority of our participants did reminisce with us in the course of their interviews, as many as 13 (thus almost one third of the total sample) spoke relatively little about their past lives. Of course, this is not to say that they did not reminisce in other social circumstances or in private, but it is significant that they did not do so in interviews that were focused on sources of self-esteem and identity in later life. Analysis of these cases is therefore of particular interest. Why were past memories apparently of little relevance to the accounts of their past lives? In conclusion, we draw some comparisons with the results of another partial longitudinal study of naturally occurring reminiscence and life review conducted in London 20 years earlier. We also comment on noticeable differences observed in the Southampton study between the lives told to us by older men and older women.

Wrestling with difficult memories

The data from interviews over the first three years of our study showed that a significant minority had negative attitudes to their past lives and memories of them. As many as 34 per cent admitted that they had 'not got most of the important things which they had wanted in life', 12 per cent expressed themselves 'dissatisfied as they looked back on their lives' and 18 per cent said that they did not enjoy thinking about the past (1977–78 data). The response to the 10-year and 20-year follow-up questionnaires showed similar proportions. As other researchers in this field (e.g. Wink and Schiff 2002) have emphasised, life review tends to be the product of life's difficulties rather than successes. The five members of our sample, all women, who engaged in intensive life reviewing during the course of our interviews had all expressed elements of disquiet with their past lives earlier in the study, but at the 20-year follow-up all but one expressed themselves 'satisfied'.

ELSIE DARBY

Elsie Darby was one of the oldest members of the whole sample. We had interviewed her first at the age of 75 years. At the age of 86 years she entered a residential care home to escape a stressful relationship with her third husband which had led her to have a heart attack. Five years later, with the help of her children's families, she returned to sheltered housing where she lived for another six years. We interviewed Elsie only a few months after she had moved back to sheltered housing, and it was then that she began spontaneously reviewing her life with us and making connections between the difficulties of her early life and her subsequent experiences.

Elsie's mother had died when she was very young, after which she and her sister had spent unhappy years being passed around from one 'mother' to another while their father was often absent.

> My past life wasn't very happy... We didn't have a mother, a proper mother and a proper father when he was away... The children used to gang up on us, my sister and I... There was so much up and down and upheaval... We never knew what it was to have a cooked meal... I took a handful of dog biscuits to eat and fill us up because we were really hungry.

An important factor contributing to her bewilderment as a child was her inability to understand and cope with the death of her mother.

> I was so small to say goodbye to my mother, to say goodnight to her. I didn't know that she was dying then. That's remained in my memory... If I'd have been older when my mother died, I could have understood, I should have known how to cope... I didn't know how to... I had to just let other people do what they had to do.

Elsie made an explicit comparison with her recovery of her own home. 'Now that I am older I know what to look for and know what to expect.' Independence and control had become central values to her, which she expressed through her ability not only to carry out various activities but also contribute to children's welfare through her making of soft toys.

At subsequent interviews, Elsie continued to elaborate on her life story. Especially striking were her memories of her mother's early death and the lasting visual images that accompanied them. She spoke emotionally of having been placed in a house across the road from where she lived, and 'peeping through the curtains' seeing a coffin being brought into her parents' house. 'Why was a big box being brought into her mother's house?' Her older brother had noticed blood dripping on to the pavement, and had later told her that their father had been 'bad'. He had been with another woman she knew as 'Auntie Min' before their mother had died. From then on Elsie's life had been rootless, moved around from one foster family to another. She and her siblings would ask each other, 'Who is going to be our next mother?' Elsie said that she was telling us these things because it helped explain why she chose to marry first a widowed man already with children of his own. She had felt sorry for them. The marriage had not been perfect but still he had given her three children of her own in addition to two stepsons.

NELLIE MORETON

Nellie Moreton's life review also provided an example of how continuing progress can be made in coming to terms with earlier wrongs. She had been faced with demanding responsibilities at a very early age. After her mother became seriously ill, Nellie had to leave school at 12 years of age to help look after her six younger brothers and sisters. She remained their principal carer when her mother died two years later until it was considered that the task had become too much for her and they were put into homes. But Nellie continued to play a significant role in their upbringing by visiting them regularly, and by trying to secure them employment.

Her responsibilities meant that she did not get married until she was 29 years old. But her husband, a merchant seaman, left her with two children before the end of the Second World War after only a few years of marriage. As a result, Nellie was again faced with the task of bringing up young children alone and on a very low income. Eventually, she obtained training in catering and for most of her working career was employed as a cook in a school for 'handicapped children'. She retired at age 62 as a result of increasing back pain due to cervical spondylosis and eventually moved to a British Legion sheltered housing scheme.

Nellie was first interviewed in depth about her life in her early 80s. Her self-esteem remained strong, supported by references to her active involvement in the life of the housing scheme and close contacts with her large extended family. She also expressed pride in her past achievements, what she referred to as her 'survival against great odds'. She did not see her life in story terms but more as consisting of 'things which had happened' to her which were out of her control. Yet she had derived personal satisfaction from the task of bringing up her siblings and own children alone and in subsequently focusing attention on others less fortunate than herself.

It was in these terms that we wrote about Nellie's evident achievement by the age of 82 years in accomplishing Erikson's developmental tasks of generativity and integrity. It might have been thought that there would be no further development of life review. But just two years later she had begun reconsidering her husband's role in her life. For example, she had come to acknowledge that it was thanks to his work in the merchant navy that she had been eligible for British Legion sheltered housing. She said that she may at times have done him an injustice because he had been so entirely dominated by his mother. She had found out later that her mother-in-law had kept the money her husband had put by regularly for the upkeep of their two children. She had forgiven her although she could not forget how much harder her life had been as a result, having to take her very young son and daughter with her to work, whether cleaning or embroidering. In subsequent interviews, Nellie continued to reflect more on her early experience of her mother's illness and death, and how at the age of only 12 she had had to take care of the family. It had been especially hard because her father drank (as did her husband).

Her children as well as her surviving siblings were in regular contact with her. There were many photographs of them around the room and most telling of the family's centrality to her own identity was that Nellie wore a small photograph of her first great-grandson in a chain around her neck. She said she was very sad for older people when they told her how they did not see their families for weeks. She seemed also to imply that she who had been so unfortunate in her family early in life was so extremely fortunate now.

EVA CHESTER

Eva Chester also referred to missing important elements in her early life, but especially a mother's love. Her life review was provoked by her husband's death when she was aged 76 years. She and her husband had had a comfortable life together but without children. His death was preceded two months earlier by a serious accident in which she fractured a hip and thigh bone which kept her in hospital for three weeks. At the time of the interview a year later she was 'trying to carry on' with her household tasks but was experiencing a high degree of depression.

When we next interviewed her two years later Eva had recovered her zest for life. She had been travelling, meeting people and reflecting on her experiences. These thoughts had led her to make connections with her earlier life experiences. Her theme was her lifelong search for a full-hearted relationship. This had its roots in her early childhood in Hungary where she did not experience 'much of a family life'. She had begun to search for new companions to compensate for the loss of her husband and other close friends. This led her on one cruise into a romantic relationship with an older man from which she had some difficulty extricating herself.

When we interviewed Eva again at the age of 83 she continued her life review. She spoke a lot about her husband, how they had met in Paris, and how she had been lucky to have such an 'understanding' and 'considerate' husband. She had come from Hungary to Paris just before the war in order to learn French, but then could not travel back. She went to Lourdes where she prayed for a husband. She had met him soon afterwards and felt therefore that she could not turn him down. It seemed that Eva needed to get the love she missed in childhood, where she said she 'did not know the love of a true mother'. She had not wanted children – perhaps because of this need of hers to be at the centre of attention.

For many years, she said, she had been keeping a diary, which she found not only helped her to reconsider the past but also to express herself. As she wrote to us, she valued it greatly:

> To write down my feelings which are my very own. It's nice to look back on happy days and not so happy days – which don't seem so important after a few years. I couldn't do without that diary.

A further source of inner strength was derived from reviewing how she coped with past problems, which seemed to help her to look at the present in a positive light.

> Definitely. It gives me satisfaction that I was on my own and had to make my own decisions, guide my own destiny… I look through and am surprised at what I've accomplished. I come to terms with past events

She had loving memories of her husband but had surprised herself by how easily she had adjusted to her loss of him.

> Lots of things remind me of him. It was the first time in my life I had somebody whom I had loved and lost, and I was surprised I quickly adjusted… He had a quick passing…a happy long life…but my loss it wasn't so big…'

At the time of these interviews, a Hungarian friend had become 'very much a part of my life'.

> He is so alone, and men can't take it. I know I give more than I get but I am interested in his life. We are important for each other.

There was still a void to be filled but she was at peace. 'All my life I look for love. I don't find it…but I'm contented.'

VERA WRIGHT

Vera Wright, in contrast to Eva, had a happy early life to remember. Her father had promoted her education from school days onwards. She had obtained a degree in chemistry and had worked as a pharmacist both before and after her marriage. But she suffered a massive blow at the age of 34 when her husband left her for another woman whom he had met during the war, leaving Vera to bring up two sons alone. She had retired a year before our first interview with her when she was 65 years old. However, because she missed work she had already taken up a new position as a part-time secretary at the local general hospital, which she converted to full-time in the following year. Through her 70s, Vera continued to enjoy an active lifestyle, also taking on voluntary work as a member of the governing body at two schools.

At the age of 80 she had a serious fall which necessitated two operations for hip replacement. When we interviewed her at the age of 83 years, worsening arthritis in her knee was severely limiting her mobility. She engaged enthusiastically with our analysis of her sense of self, agreeing that a key part of her identity was her sense of inner strength and determination which helped her to surmount difficulties. 'My father brought me up to be independent... I learned a lot at university – they were honest and straightforward. I came back with that attitude...' She also agreed that she adopted a stance of living day to day rather than looking to the past or the future. In particular, she did not dwell on the past. 'It is no good looking back on things; never look back – it's defeating.'

It was surprising for us therefore that at a further interview some months later Vera clearly did wish to reminisce, and in considerable detail. She reflected on the formative experiences that had led her to her present-day attitudes, particularly the end of her marriage and its aftermath, as well as the death in early adulthood of her younger son. She attributed the failure of her marriage to the Second World War. When her husband returned after war service he seemed 'morose' and looking through his papers she found out about an affair he had been having with a woman living in the north of England. After some time, Vera agreed to her husband's wish to visit his lover and he never returned. A difficult time followed as her husband tried to gain custody of their children, whom he wanted to send to his mother. The bitterness lasted many years, as he never made Vera any payments. It was only when, many years later, she sued for divorce that the court obliged him to make regular payments. Only recently he had asked whether he could make a final lump sum payment, but she had refused, making it clear to him that he had been the one 'to walk out' on the marriage.

Vera had clearly not yet resolved the strong feelings she still felt about the end of her marriage. As a result of it she said her subsequent life had had many hard moments. She expressed considerable anger towards her husband and also to others who had treated her less than generously as she had struggled to make a living for her children and retain a home of her own. However, she had been successful in finding jobs and places to live when needed. She stressed a belief in making the best of life.

In our last interview with her at the age of 86, she appreciated again the opportunity to analyse her life with us. Her mobility was further reduced, and her social world diminished. Nevertheless, she remained resilient and was not going 'to give up'.

RITA FLETCHER

Rita Fletcher provided the most difficult case of late life review in our sample, probably because it was forced on her by a sudden and unexpected trigger for recall of disturbing past memories in an already vulnerable person. In the first years of our study, Rita had consistently shown raised depression scores which she associated with the difficulties arising from caring for both her husband and her mother. By the ten-year follow-up, both had died and Rita had been admitted to hospital with severe depression.

On her return home, she was contacted in regard to tracing the natural mother of a 54-year-old woman who had been adopted as a baby. Rita was that mother and shortly afterwards met and began establishing a relationship with her daughter. When we interviewed her three years later, aged almost 80, she was eager to speak with us about the mixture of emotions that had marked the intervening time. Initially she had been concerned that she would lose her son's respect when he found out that his mother had had an illegitimate child. This fear had turned out to be unfounded.

More disturbing, however, were the unhappy memories that had been brought to the surface associated with the period when the baby was conceived. She had already spoken about the death during the war of her fiancé as one of the 'tragedies' of her life. But the baby who had been born shortly afterwards had not been his child. 'Now with this coming up, it's all raked it all up again, you know what I mean. Some of it, murky past, I'd rather it be buried and finished...' Her dead fiancé was uppermost in her mind. 'I've got his last letter. You wouldn't think that was possible, would you? Well, I have. It's there. I want it in my coffin too when I'm gone. I've asked that they put it in. I hope they will.' Although her depression score was raised she showed markedly higher self-esteem than before, feeling more important to her family, expressing confidence in speaking with people and being in their company. Her daughter's re-appearance had provided the link to enable Rita to articulate her full life story. She appeared to have settled down into a pleasant relationship with her daughter and it was a source of particular pleasure for her that she and her son got on so well. 'And now what I think is, he's got someone when I'm gone, hasn't he?'

However, Rita was to remain prone to depressive feelings and at the interview two years later her self-esteem had also diminished. She said that she had 'lost confidence' since a fall down an escalator in a shopping centre, and the discontentment that she felt about her past life remained.

> I've never had a good life; what I mean I've never had a life when it's been cheery. My brother brought me up, life was dull then, there was only Grandma and I, so I never had a really what-do-you-call-it life.

At the time of our last interview with her, she expressed herself still very dissatisfied with her past life and was becoming even more worried about the future. Sadly, she no longer had contact with her daughter after a row on the telephone a year before.

Life stories: review and acceptance

There were other participants who told us of difficulties in their lives but they were expressed already with a strong element of acceptance. A striking example of a life both endured and accepted was that of Mavis Dawes.

MAVIS DAWES

Mavis Dawes had moved from Lancashire to communal housing in Southampton in the year prior to her first interview at the age of 72 years. She consistently described her past life as 'hard', and in her interviews in her early 80s gave a detailed account of the various losses and disappointments she had suffered. Mavis had possessed academic abilities, winning a scholarship, but as a result of ill health had been unable to progress her education. She would have liked to have become a school teacher.

> I started with a rheumatic disease, then I was off school for four months, but I didn't get a chance. I was going in for the Oxford exams at the higher grade school and I had instead to go out to work at 14.

As with Nellie Moreton, her mother had died young and she had had to take over family responsibilities.

> I've had a sad life, you see my mother died when I was 19. She died when she had a baby in her charge. She was 44. I had to give up work then… I was left at 19 with a family and a young baby to look after.

Some years later she also lost her younger sister to whom she was very close. She described the loss as even worse than losing her mother.

Mavis's marriage had been troubled as her husband had developed psychological problems. Mavis said that she had had to bring up her children – two sons – almost singlehandedly. From the age of 50 she ran a successful corner shop for 13 years until she had to give it up because of lung problems. She allowed her younger son and his wife to take it over but it failed within a year. When her husband died, her other son encouraged her to come down to the Southampton area where both sons were now living. She lived with them for a while before finding her present accommodation. Subsequently her son tried to start his own business, which Mavis invested her money in, but that was all lost when the business failed.

However, Mavis settled well into her new life in Southampton, attending church and older people's clubs as well as visiting family. But difficulties continued. Her younger son was sentenced to prison for some months, and continued to have a lot of problems, primarily as a result of alcohol abuse. This was a major concern for Mavis. As she entered her 80s, her physical health began to decline noticeably. When she was interviewed at the age of 83 her older son, who had moved to work in Scotland again, was asking her to come back there to be there with his family. But Mavis was reluctant to agree, also because her younger son in Southampton had become very dependent on her financially and she worried about his failure to care for himself properly.

In her written comments to sentence prompts at this time she gave a positive view of her life despite the difficulties:

> When I think about myself…I've had a fair amount of courage to stand my life. I like to dream about…the happiness I had before my husband took ill and when my sister was alive.

Her religious faith was also a strong part of her self-image: 'When I feel unhappy…I believe in prayer. Maybe I can…thank the Lord for the good things.'

By our last interview with her at the age of 86 years Mavis had become almost housebound. Yet despite her awareness that her health had continued to deteriorate and that she had become much less active than she used to be, she expressed a more positive set of attitudes towards her present life, agreeing that she 'found it nice to grow old' and that 'old age is a happy time for me'. She referred to her importance to her son and her usefulness in helping friends at the day centre. Underpinning meaning in her life was provided by her religious faith. The state of inner peace she had now reached and her positive attitude to growing old were in striking contrast to the negative descriptions of the hardships of her past life.

TED JACKSON

Ted Jackson presented a life story with a most dramatic positive transformation in midlife. His early experiences both of family responsibilities and family breakdown seemed to lie behind the very strong value he placed on creating a happy family. Born into poor circumstances in the north of England, he had entered the army as a young man. At that stage of life, he already appreciated the importance of family solidarity.

> I joined the army because I was hungry. It was a relief for the family to get a little donation of your pay each week to help them because we were a big family.

Ted's first marriage collapsed while he was in India during the Second World War. His wife left him for another man and with four children to care for. His superiors 'shipped' him and his children back to England, where the children were cared for by his mother, while Ted continued his war service on the home front, including the D-Day preparations. At the end of the war he met his current wife, who was also obtaining a divorce and already had two children of her own. They married in Gibraltar and joined their families together before his posting to Egypt. When his wife became ill there with tuberculosis he decided to retire and joined the Post Office where he worked until his retirement at 65 years old.

When we interviewed him soon after his 80th birthday, Ted's inner satisfaction came out most clearly in his subsequently written answers to sentence prompts:

> When I compare myself to others...they with their cars, yachts, mansions and so on. I wonder are they as happy as I am? My life up to now...maybe with a bit of thought I could have bettered my position in life, but I could not have been happier.

Ted's health continued to decline and in his last years his family developed a rota of care for him and his wife. At our interview with him a few months before his death he wanted to reminisce again. He spoke about his childhood in Lincolnshire, his army career, the shock of his first wife leaving him, but that it had been for the good in the end, and his involvement in preparations for D-Day. He had enjoyed his army career, the parades and conviviality (which he had missed in his later work in the Post Office). The letter we received on his death showed how much he had been loved and respected by his children.

EMILY SHIELDS

Emily Shields by contrast had nostalgic memories of her childhood and early adult life in Scotland. She had been sad to leave when her father decided to move south for the benefit of her mother's health. By then Emily was already established at work in the Scottish Civil Service, and she described how much she missed the rich social and cultural life of Aberdeen on coming to Southampton. Her life improved after she met her husband, a policeman, who had also been transplanted from his native Northern Irish culture.

Emily was one of the few married women in our sample to comment in detail on her relationship with her husband. Whereas Emily was quiet her husband was 'exuberant'.

> ...it didn't matter what Brendan did, it was noisy. He had an aura of noise around him, if you know what I mean. You always knew he was about when he came in and everything was so quiet afterwards you know, it wasn't that he shouted about or anything, it was just he had this noisiness about him.

Nevertheless, Emily felt that she and her husband complemented each other very well and their marriage endured despite his very busy working life in the Criminal Investigation Department, which meant that she 'never knew where he was, where he was going, when he was coming back, or when he was going out...'

Memories of Scotland came back to her more strongly after her husband died when she was 80 years old. Two years later she and her daughter took a two-week motoring holiday visiting Aberdeen and the surrounding area. In particular, she was delighted to find her grandfather's grave. She liked reminiscing about her earlier life in Scotland. She spoke of the 'beautiful white sands' on the coast north from Aberdeen, how she used to swim from 'Dee to Don' with her friends on Saturday mornings and go dancing in the evening. She expressed regrets about how she had been unable to pursue medical studies due to poor health when she was young. Her parents had been advised to concentrate on her brothers' education. Clearly for her, as for Mavis Dawes, this had been a great disappointment and it was reflected in the answers she gave to the self and life attitude questionnaires she completed for us. 'In achieving life's goals', she wrote that she had not 'felt completely fulfilled'.

DENNIS WILCOX

Dennis Wilcox also expressed regret about lack of education. He had experienced a tough life as a young boy and man, having to work hard for everything.

> Sometimes I used to take two goats on the way to school, tether them and pick them up after school and take them back and put them in their hut. I got a shilling a week for that. I worked for a chemist, taking films to be developed... I used to take the films about twice a week to be developed, take some down and bring some back, and they used to give me the tram fare... I didn't go on the tram, I went on an old ladies' bike to save the tram fare... But that's how my life was, nobody ever gave me anything. I had to earn it...and I think if you've been like that...it makes you be careful.

After leaving school he tried several jobs, working first as a van boy on a horse-drawn bread round for a local baker before being transferred to the post of uniformed porter at a city centre cafe. He then became a trainee butcher, and for about six-and-a-half years he worked as a van driver. When he needed more pay in order to be able to get married he dared not ask for more money from that employer who had already given him two raises, so he was advised to try the Automobile Association (AA). War provided him with new opportunities. As the AA had an arrangement with the War Office that enabled its riders to join the supplementary reserve of the Military Police, Dennis could be employed as an outrider on security duties, providing escort and protection to such key figures as King George, Churchill and Montgomery. The war, he believed, had an important effect on his personal development, making him more broad-minded and tolerant.

Despite these notable experiences, Dennis expressed a rather low sense of self-esteem. This contrasted with his pride in his childrer's success. By comparison he felt himself to have been disadvantaged.

> I am very proud of our children, their academic achievements... [listed]. When I think about myself... I am sure that had I had the same educational opportunities as our children I would have had a better life.

As he passed into his 80s, Dennis's life story remained fundamentally the same. He continued to reiterate his pride in his children's achievements while retaining a low sense of self-esteem. He subsequently wrote to us that the most meaningful aspect of his life had been his children's education and academic achievements and his contribution to them. He continued to underplay his own career, despite being invited at 83 years by the AA to appear on its anniversary video as one of the oldest surviving AA patrolmen.

Another eight persons – six men but only two women – also gave us detailed and coherent accounts of their lives of which they were evidently proud. Difficulties they had encountered, even in the later stages of life, had all been successfully resolved.

RALPH HODGKIN

Ralph Hodgkin told a story of striking out on his own to build a successful career. He and his older brother had begun working for their father, a painter and decorator. However, when Ralph wanted to marry after the age of 30 he confronted his father with the fact that his pay was insufficient – his father would only work in good weather – and he left to work for a house builder in a town elsewhere in Hampshire. Soon Ralph was able to set up his own business. He also developed the clever idea of buying up old houses at auction which gave his men work to do indoors when the weather was bad. His father was amazed at his success, initially having questioned whether his son 'knew what he was doing' and could afford this way of doing business. Ralph retired early at 58 years, moved back to Southampton in order to be near his wife's family, bought a new house and made sure all the fittings were 'first class' and able to 'last a lifetime'.

HAROLD RANK

Harold Rank told a story of overcoming successive setbacks, beginning with the hardships of life as a child during the First World War, his love for both his wives, his distress when his first wife died of meningitis during the Second World War, leaving him alone with two children, and his subsequent marriage to a younger widow with two children of her own. During our study, his second wife developed a severe form of early dementia and Harold suffered from both physical ill health and depression. But he was able over time to recover a robust sense of self again, based on his memories of his former resilience.

GEORGE ROWAN

George Rowan had never expected his younger wife to predecease him and when she became ill and died in her early 80s he was devastated. As he was already 93 years old, we did not expect him to recover from the severe grief reaction he displayed. But he recovered well and lived another seven active years. He seemed to benefit greatly from being able to reminisce freely about his life with his wife. He described how he had first met her: 'how lovely' he thought she looked when he first saw her standing in the bank where he worked, 'within a shaft of dusty sunlight'; how they had met again playing tennis; the war years and a train accident of 1945, resulting serious injuries to her and how this led to the three-year delay in their marriage. Their marriage had been one of 'tremendous companionship'. They used to sit in the evening, holding hands, watching the sun go down across their back garden. He never wanted to be away from her. They had benefited, he said, from being 'fully formed' characters when they married. He 'thanked God' for their happy married life.

STUART MURRAY

Stuart Murray told a story of his transition from a life of restless conflict to one of calm order. The son of travelling theatrical artists, he walked out on his parents at the age of 17 and, declaring himself a year older than he was, signed on for the army. He served in the notorious 'Black and Tans' regiment sent to counter the Irish rebellion after the First World War, was then posted to Asia Minor during the Greek-Turkish conflict and finally to India where he lived for 35 years, transferring at some point from the army to the Indian Civil Service and staying on after Indian Independence. At the age of 92 years, he spoke with us in detail about what he described as the major transition of his life in his early 20s when he was converted to Christianity by an American missionary in India. He showed us the well-used books he had used throughout his life to meditate on the Bible.

ALFRED PARKER

Alfred Parker had also come to a different more spiritual perspective on life. In his early adulthood, he had been very active in politics, but had become disillusioned, and after his son's hearing became impaired as a result of meningitis, he took up voluntary work in helping disabled people. He also became a more committed church member. At the time of our first interview he had recently been appointed a 'special Eucharistic minister' in his local Roman Catholic parish church, taking communion to sick and disabled parishioners. His strong belief in an afterlife and continued active participation in prayer and church services sustained him in his later years as his wife became ill and died. Shortly afterwards he married a mutual friend of theirs who subsequently developed dementia. He endured these experiences too with a serene faith that all that happened to us was 'pre-ordained' but that we could count on God's support to 'bolster us up'.

BILL BLACKBURN

Bill Blackburn gave an account of a financially insecure but happy life based on the relationships he had had from childhood onwards and especially with his late wife. The focus of all his conversations was on the overriding importance to him of social contacts. Over time he gradually told us more, and in his 99th year, now living in a residential care home, was more expressive than ever, speaking of his mother who had been 'so kind' to her children, and his wife – 'a beautiful Scottish girl', only four feet, ten inches high. Her womb had been too small to bear children. Their GP had told him to 'forget it'. They had had cats and chickens, a two-week holiday every year, and a very happy marriage. He spoke of his old neighbourhood in Southampton and the friends whom he missed. He continued to express his need for social contact and he stressed how much he 'loved people'. He described how he was compensating for his loss of vision and hearing by visualising his life in the past: 'I think a lot. I don't think of the present or the future. My mind goes back to me sisters and me brothers.'

Only two women provided such comprehensive life stories. Both had lived busy lives outside as well as inside the home.

ETHEL WILLIS

Ethel Willis began reminiscing with us after she encountered a series of major health problems in her later 80s. In an interview at the age of 92, she provided vivid descriptions of every period of her life: her childhood in the countryside outside Southampton; her early years working as a tailoress in the centre of town before the Armistice of 1918; subsequent marriage and births of her children, including an ectopic pregnancy which was still difficult for her to speak about. Her husband had earned three pounds a week as a ship's carpenter. In the early years of their marriage he had been away on ships around the world for much of the time, but a trade union official had helped him obtain a job in the docks after their son was born in 1935.

Perhaps as a consequence of her husband's frequent absence Ethel became active outside as well inside the home. She had always done a lot of sewing. But thinking back on the situation she was surprised how her husband tolerated her outdoors work. She had become secretary of her local ward's Conservative Party Association and was also active in a number of other organisations, so that she was out many evenings a week. In her last years, she had many questions about how British life had changed in her lifetime. She was puzzled by many of these changes and sought to understand them in her conversations with others.

IRENE MONROE

Irene Monroe had worked when young as a nurse and had also qualified as a chiropodist. But her identity had long been rooted in her religious faith. From their early married life, she and her husband had determined to live their Christian vocation, making the choice to live on a council estate in order to help others. After her husband's death and suffering from severe arthritis as well as angina, she moved into a residential care home in her later 80s. She found the loss of an active life hard but gradually began to draw on past experiences as a source of satisfaction. We interviewed Irene on various occasions up to the year before she died at 95 years. She reflected on her early achievements as a nurse and spoke about her career as a Christian missionary in Asia (she showed a painting she had made of mountains in Sri Lanka) and her association with the evangelical ministry of Holy Trinity Brompton. Memories of her husband seemed to have an increased presence in her life. She was proud of the MBE he had been awarded, which she had recently given to her granddaughter.

> I've still got his letters and I sometimes read them. I read them the other day. There was a wonderful letter written about him by the Church… I want to be buried with him and have the service in the same church.

Reminiscence in older people's lives: evidence from a longitudinal study

We have already given account of the character of the reminiscences of 17 members of our study. All of them – with perhaps the exception of Rita Fletcher who was suddenly confronted with very difficult memories she previously had kept at bay – clearly benefited from their recall. Their past stories, whether of achievement or of survival against the odds, strengthened them in the difficulties they encountered as they aged.

But what about the other 23 members of the sample? We have records of at least another ten participants sharing memories of episodes or aspects of their lives with us even though they did not express a rounded account of their life as a whole. Common subjects for the men were stories of the Second World War. Thomas Johnson, for example, liked to reminisce about serving in the navy throughout the Second World War – he had been at the Battle of Cape Matapan, the relief of Tobruk and the Normandy invasion – and spoke with great pride and affection of the comradeship he had experienced. He lent books on the war at sea to one of the authors. But at the end of his life his greatest interest was in showing us photographs of his eight great-grandchildren. Similarly, other men spoke about their service in the Second World War but it did not dominate their conversations, which were more focused on their present life and activities.

Women by contrast tended to refer more to memories of family and also church life. They commonly referred to how they were 'sustained' or 'comforted' by their memories of happy family life, although involvement with their present family predominated. For example, Hilda Smith retained for many years active responsibilities within her very large family – 25 great-grandchildren – and as she grew old in her 80s she expressed sadness that she couldn't 'go and mind the babies any more'. The past then became more prominent in her written answers to sentence promts 'When I feel lonely...I just go back over the years and remember many things that happened.'

In her 90s, she reminisced more about her earlier married days and how she had earned extra money for the family by detailing how she had taken in washing – 'two pence a sheet, a penny a pillowcase, washed, boiled and ironed'– and cleaned houses.

A further six of our participants did not seem to feel the need to reminisce with us. In all cases this appeared to be because they remained completely involved with their current hobbies and activities or with their families. Their identity was sufficiently expressed in these. Descriptions of earlier working days were brief and to the point. Their engagement in the present day seemed almost total. Of course, our perspective remained limited to the few occasions when we visited them.

More striking, however, were the remaining seven participants in our sample who conveyed a distinct preference for avoiding speaking about their memories. The reasons were diverse. Some found it difficult to speak about past happiness because of the depression they were encountering following bereavement or sudden disability, for example following a stroke. Doris Iveson found the loss of her husband to be irreparable, and repeatedly referred to the meaning of her life being 'buried in the past'. There were no children or grandchildren who could provide a greater relevance for her current life. She had been fulfilled in the past but was now left without any significant role or purpose. 'It's a really nice life I've had. That's why I notice it now... It's totally different to what it was before... Since my husband died, I've had nothing.' She lived through her 80s until her death at 87 unable to change this basic attitude to her present life.

Perhaps the most intriguing case in our sample was Margaret Baker. She consistently expressed a very low self-esteem over the 20 years that we interviewed her. This appeared to have its roots in childhood but also in her perceived lack of control over her earlier adult life which she had spent caring for her invalid mother. She had been obliged to delay marriage until middle age, and her husband had died after only seven years. However, she eschewed any signs of self-pity and remained resolute in her focus on the problems of the outside world rather than her own. 'We should not be kind of self-centred...we often get trapped in our little worlds and that in a way is wrong.'

We considered similarities and differences with a longitudinal study of conversational reminiscence conducted in the 1970s and early 1980s on an earlier generation of older people living in London (Coleman 1986a, 1986b). This produced a similar typology of life review and life storytelling, as well as avoidance of reminiscence either because of pain of what had been lost or because of the greater attraction of present interests. But the previous study also contained more emotionally charged reminiscences, more accounts of painful life regrets and difficulties in resolving them, as well as of pleasure in the recall of joyful childhood and other early memories, and pride, wonder and amazement at what they had experienced including the events of both world wars.

Participants in that study also tended to draw a stronger contrast between the present and past and generally gave a much higher evaluation of the past. Adjustment to the post-war social changes from the 1960s onwards appears to have been harder for that earlier generation.

What emerged most clearly from the present study is the very large difference between men and women's reminiscences. Noticeably more men told integrated stories of their lives whereas it was only women who appeared to need to review the difficult episodes of their lives. The evident reason for this difference is that the women had encountered more setbacks, for example in education, even as opportunities for women generally were improving after the First World War, and as a result experienced lower control over their lives. Now that women's sense of external control has increased in Western societies it is good to be reminded of how a previous generation of women had often to cope with disappointments in realising their potential.

Acknowledgements

We acknowledge the assistance of the Economic and Social Research Council in funding our follow-up studies of the participants in the Southampton Ageing Project with four grants from 1990 to 1999

(R000232182, R000234404, R000221633, R000222535), and thank the University of Southampton and particularly the Department of Academic Geriatric Medicine for its continuing and steadfast support of our work. Above all, of course, we thank our participants for entrusting us with information about their lives over so many years.

Chapter 5

DEVELOPMENTAL FOUNDATIONS OF LIFELONG REMINISCING

Robyn Fivush and Jordan A. Booker

Since Robert Butler first introduced the practice of life review as a way of creating a coherent integrative narrative at the end of one's life in order to provide a sense of positive closure (Lewis and Butler 1974), the practice of engaging in life writing has blossomed (Birren and Svensson 2013). Indeed, life writing has emerged as a critical part of clinical care across the lifespan, to help individuals cope with ongoing physical ailments, psychological distress, and, even more broadly, simply as a way to gain more reflective self-understanding (see Pennebaker and Chung 2006 for a review). The ability to narrate the self in coherent, elaborate and emotionally regulated ways is linked to positive wellbeing across a wide age span and across a wide diversity of contexts (Adler *et al.* 2016). Yet, there are also wide individual differences in the ability to create self-narratives in beneficial ways.

In this chapter, we argue that self-narration is a skill that is begun to be fostered early in development, as children are just starting to verbally recall their personal experiences. Across childhood and adolescence, children are learning the forms and functions of self-narrative through socioculturally situated stories that are both told to them, and with them, especially within the family. These parentally guided narrative interactions set the stage for a lifetime of reminiscence. Moreover, narrative interactions within the family are situated within larger narrative ecologies (Fivush and Merrill 2016; McLean 2015). Stories of self are embedded within more encompassing family stories and intergenerational narratives that pass on family history and family values, and these family stories are embedded in larger culturally mediated narrative structures that provide shared understandings of the form and function of self-narratives.

We first provide a framework for understanding narratives within these larger sociocultural frames. We then turn to how children are socialized into these narrative frames early in development, focusing on parent–child co-narration of children's personal experiences. We then expand the discussion to include family narratives and, more specifically, parental intergenerational narratives – stories parents tell about their own childhood experiences. Here, we focus on adolescence and emerging adulthood, a developmental period when narrative identity becomes a central task (McAdams and McLean 2013). We discuss how intergenerational narratives provide models for developing self-narratives, as well as directly influencing adolescents' sense of self and wellbeing. Our goal is to delineate how both engaging in telling stories about one's own life and listening to stories of other lives helps facilitate a more coherent, elaborated and emotionally regulated self-narrative across childhood and adolescence. We end with a discussion of how parents and grandparents – the bearers of family insights and life lessons – may benefit from engaging in narrative interactions with younger generations. Thus, we argue that storytelling benefits both tellers and listeners, and that in the process of telling stories to, with and about self and others, children and parents build coherent shared narratives that maintain emotional bonds and family identity across the generations.

Stories of self are socioculturally situated

Stories are fundamentally how human beings make sense of experience (Bruner 1990; Gottschall 2012). Whereas experience unfolds in undifferentiated time, stories carve experience into meaningful units, beginnings, middles and ends (Ricœur 1991), creating a temporal landscape of meaningful events. Even more, stories move beyond chronological accounts of what happened to include thoughts and emotions, human intentions and motivations, in ways that link actions in the world into meaningful endeavors, triumphs and failures, stories that make sense of human lives (Fivush and Graci 2017). Sharing personal stories is one of the most frequent forms of social interaction (Merrill, Gallo and Fivush 2014). Personal stories emerge about every five minutes in conversations among family and friends

(Bohanek *et al.* 2009; Pasupathi, McLean and Weeks 2009). When we talk, we talk about the past. As stories are told and retold, tellers and listeners create evolving interpretative understandings of their own and others' experiences, developing shared understandings of what happened and what it means (McLean, Pasupathi and Pals 2007). And these evolving meanings are created in both local interactions and within socioculturally mediated ways of understanding stories and understanding lives.

Although storytelling is universal, the narrative forms of storytelling are culturally variable; cultures define the shape of a life and the evaluative interpretive frames for telling life stories (Breen *et al.* 2016; Wang 2013), or what have been called master narratives (McLean and Syed 2015). For example, in Western industrialized cultures, autonomy and independence are prized, and narrative frames in these cultures highlight the benefits of individual achievement. More specifically, perhaps especially in US culture, redemption is a classic master narrative (McAdams 2004). In this narrative, the protagonist begins with little but due to individual hard work and perseverance achieves success. This is the classic American rags to riches narrative that ends with material redemption, but it also echoes in narratives of recovering addicts hitting rock bottom, but through individual abstinence and perseverance, achieving sobriety and psychological redemption (Dunlop and Tracy 2013). Culturally defined master narratives provide the frameworks for culturally appropriate ways of telling stories about individual experience, and individuals who conform their own life story to these cultural frames show higher levels of wellbeing. For example, middle-aged and older US adults who tell redemptive life stories show higher levels of life satisfaction and higher levels of generativity, the personal sense that one has provided something of importance to the next generation (Lilgendahl and McAdams 2011). Thus, the way in which individuals tell their own story is influenced by cultural norms and, in turn, influences individual wellbeing.

This process begins early in development. From the moment of birth, parents and grandparents engage infants in storytelling, including stories of family adventures and exploits, bringing the infant into the family fold by placing them within the family narrative (Andrews *et al.* 2015; Fiese *et al.* 1995). Throughout childhood and adolescence, children continue to hear these stories, most especially family stories, intergenerational narratives of their parents' lives growing up, their grandparents and family history (Fivush, Bohanek and Duke 2008). It is within this context that children begin to tell their own stories. As soon as children begin talking, at about 18 months of age, they begin to reference the past (Uehara 2015) and, across the preschool years, children begin to participate more fully in co-constructing narratives of their personal experiences with the adults around them (Fivush 2007). In these early narrative interactions, children are learning the forms and functions of self-narratives in ways that set the stage for a lifetime of narrative understanding of the self.

In the remainder of this chapter, we delineate these processes in more detail. We first discuss the extensive literature on how children learn to tell their own stories in parentally guided reminiscing interactions. We then turn to the burgeoning literature on family stories more broadly, how listening to the stories of parents and grandparents facilitates children's and adolescents' understanding of their own stories, and of themselves. We then broaden our discussion by showing how it is not only children who benefit from co-constructing self-narratives with their parents, but that adults also benefit from sharing their stories with others, especially their children. We end with broader implications from our review of family narrative interactions for life reminiscence.

Parent–child reminiscing and the emergence of a narrative self

As argued by Nelson and Fivush (2004), the ability to construct a coherent, detailed narrative of personal experience is a valued cultural skill, perhaps especially so in modern industrialized societies where individuals are called on to present themselves to new people in new contexts on a regular basis. Following Vygotsky's (1978) sociocultural model of development, Nelson and Fivush argue that narrative interactions are structured in such a way as to pull children into learning narrative skills. Two-year-olds are asked to tell Mommy what happened at daycare; preschoolers are asked to tell what they did over the weekend during story circle; school age children write essays about their summer vacation; and by late elementary school, children are asked to write their autobiography. Whether one is applying to college, in a job interview, or meeting a possible romantic partner, one is expected to have a coherent story of self.

Learning the forms and functions of these self-narratives begins early in development, as parents help their young children construct coherent narratives of their personal experiences and establish links among children's relevant life events. For example, an 18-month-old child may look up from play and say 'Berries' and the mother responds, 'Yes, we had strawberries for breakfast this morning. Weren't they delicious? You really love strawberries!' In these small, everyday interactions, parents are already socializing young children into the culturally appropriate forms for expressing their thoughts and evaluations of personal experiences, as well as relating these experiences to a developing sense of self. Early in development, when toddlers can participate in these conversations by offering just a word or two, parents provide most of the narrative, interpreting relevant goals and emotions and elaborating on the few pieces of information offered by their child, thus providing models of narrative understanding of experience. Children quickly begin to participate in these co-constructed narratives to a greater extent, and by the end of the preschool years, most children are able to provide a reasonably coherent account of specific personal experiences (see Fivush, Haden and Reese 2006 for a review).

Importantly, whereas narrative socialization appears to be universal (Tõugu et al. 2011), there are also substantial and enduring individual differences in how parents co-construct narratives with their preschoolers, and these individual differences have profound effects on children's developing narrative skills and their emerging sense of self. Some of these differences are related to cultural values and master narratives (McLean and Syed 2015; Wang 2013), and some of these differences are related to gender, both of the child and of the parent (see Fivush and Zaman 2013 for a review). Although a detailed review of cultural and gender differences in parent–child reminiscing is beyond the scope of this chapter, these patterns underscore that, even within a universal phenomenon, sociocultural processes canalize development along certain lines (Nelson and Fivush 2004). Thus, whereas telling our story is universal, how we tell our story is shaped by sociocultural and individual differences. Here, we focus on individual differences within broadly middle-class Western families in how children come to tell their own life stories.

Elaborative reminiscing style

Some parents, like the example that follows, are highly elaborative in structuring narrative reminiscing with their children. More elaborative parents reminisce more frequently with their children and, more importantly, provide more elaborative detail about the facts and emotions of an experience (see Fivush *et al.* 2006 for a review). Especially when their young children are not recalling very much, more elaborative parents continue to scaffold the conversation, providing additional details, and weaving them into a narrative that connects to the child's experience, as this example between a mother and her four-year-old child, who we will call April, illustrates. In this study (Zaman and Fivush 2013), the parent was specifically asked to talk about a time the child felt sad.

Table 5.1: Mother–child reminiscing

Mother: So, what's something that would make you sad? Can you think of something that maybe happened before that made you sad? Child: I can't remember. Mother: What happened today that made you sad? Remember something that happened after school? Child: I lost my Tinker Bell book. Mother: You lost your Tinker Bell book? Child: Mm-hmm. Mother: And why did that make you sad? Child: Because I didn't know if we were going to find it or not. Mother: Yeah. And what did Mommy say when you were saying you were sad? Child: We would get it back tomorrow – I mean, on Monday. Mother: On Monday, yeah. So, are you still sad about it? Or you feel a little bit better about [inaudible]? Child: Well, I feel better because I just like staying with you now.	The mother defines the type of event they will be discussing but leaves it open to the child to select. When the child explicitly does not contribute a possible event, the mother asks another, more directed question, that focuses the child on a specific recent experience, still keeping it open enough for the child to provide her own response. When the child does provide a response, the mother validates it through repeating, and then elaborates on the emotional reaction, asking the child to reflect a bit more about why this event made her sad. Again, the child provides an explanation for sadness which the mother validates, and the mother moves on to scaffolding the child's memory of how they resolved this emotional reaction. The mother validates the ability to solve the problem and resolve the emotion, but she still returns to validating the emotional feeling itself – it is still sad, but because there is a resolution at hand, it is maybe a little bit better, so emotions are complex and enduring.

Mother: You like staying with me now? Do you think that Mom ever gets sad? Child: Uh-huh. Mother: You do? Child: Uh-huh. When you were a little girl. Mother: You think I [was] sad when I was a little girl sometimes? Child: Uh-huh. Mother: Do you think I ever lost things? Child: Yes. Mother: Like sometimes you lose things? Yeah? So, what's the – Child: Did you? Mother: I did. You know, one time I lost my purse when I was about six years old and I left it at a restaurant and it had my favourite lip gloss in it and it made me really sad. But you know what? You know Grandpapa is my parent? Child: Uh-huh. Mother: He found it for me. Child: Where? Mother: Back at the restaurant. We remembered where I left it. So, I think we'll get your Tinker Bell book back on Monday. So, do you know what the opposite of sad is? Child: Happy.	The child responds with what seems to be a non-sequitur, and her mother re-focuses the conversation to ask the child if she thinks the mother is ever sad, thus helping the child understand that everyone feels sad sometimes. The child now explicitly connects to her mothers' childhood experiences – perhaps the mother was also sad when she was a little girl. The mother immediately picks up on this, and even links her own sad experience to a similar childhood event to what the child is experiencing now. These kinds of intergenerational links help children and adolescents model their own emotional lives on those of their parents, as we will discuss later. The mother makes an explicit connection between herself and her daughter; they are the same, they both lose things. The mother resolves her own childhood sad experience, also through parental intervention, to find and return the lost object. In doing so, she makes another explicit connection about family relationships, from grandparent to parent to child. Finally, the mother brings the conversation back to resolving the child's current situation and ends the conversation with a more abstract lesson about emotions more broadly.

In contrast to this example, some parents are less elaborative, providing little new information, and often simply repeating the same questions again when the child does not recall information. Even when the child does participate by recalling some details, less elaborative parents do not follow up and extend on the child's response, but simply ask another repetitive question, often leading more to a list-like recall, such as a listing of who was present at a family picnic, or which animals were seen at the zoo, rather than a narrative account that weaves together what happened into an evaluative story.

Many studies have confirmed that parental reminiscing style is both consistent across time and siblings, and distinct from other conversational contexts, although it should be noted that most of this research is with mothers and not fathers (Fivush and Zaman 2013). Parents who are highly elaborative when their children are toddlers, remain more highly elaborative than their less elaborative counterparts as children develop through the preschool years, and mothers who are highly elaborative with one child are also highly elaborative with their other children. Finally, elaborative reminiscing is not simply talkativeness. Mothers who are highly elaborative during reminiscing are not necessarily more talkative in other contexts such as book reading, free play or caregiving routines (see Fivush *et al.* 2006 for a review). These patterns suggest that mothers are displaying a consistent reminiscing style, and that they may have specific implicit or explicit goals in co-constructing narratives with their children that are unique to this conversational context. Indeed, mothers self-report engaging in reminiscing with their preschoolers in order to create emotional bonds through a shared history, and to help their children better understand themselves and their emotions (Kulkofsky, Wang and Koh 2009).

Emotion reminiscing style

Most of the stories we share are at least nominally emotional; obviously emotional experiences are ubiquitous, with individuals experiencing, identifying, regulating and sharing emotional messages throughout daily life (Halberstadt, Denham and Dunsmore 2001), both as emotions occur and in narrative retrospect. Along with elaboration of factual details, parents also provide scaffolding for understanding and expressing emotional content in daily reminiscing about even mildly emotional experiences (Denham, Bassett and Wyatt 2007; Eisenberg, Cumberland and Spinrad 1998), as seen in the narrative between April and her mother. Parental scaffolding supports and coincides with children's developing emotional competence (Saarni 1999).

As with elaboration, some parents show greater awareness and acceptance of children's experiences and expressions of emotions, and strive actively to guide their children's emotional experiences, as in the example above (Katz, Maliken and Stettler 2012). These parents make more efforts to direct and validate children's emotional experiences during reminiscing, as well as coach children through recollections of their emotion experiences, such as accurately labelling the emotion, identifying the causes of the emotional experience, discussing the consequences of the emotion, and identifying ways to better regulate emotional responses going forward, including discussions of coping strategies (Fivush *et al.* 2003). Through scaffolding of emotion experiences in reminiscing, parents instil sociocultural values of appropriate experiences and displays of emotion and improve children's ability to regulate their emotions independently (Grusec 2002).

Parents' accepting values (Dunsmore and Karn 2001) and supportive behaviors (Eisenberg, Fabes and Murphy 1996) toward children's emotions promote socio-emotional competence among children, and children's competence coincides with personal adjustment and interpersonal skill (Eisenberg *et al.* 1996; Garner, Dunsmore and Southam-Gerrow 2008; McElwain, Halberstadt and Volling 2007). We can see this clearly in the example above. April's mother begins the conversation asking April to make attempts at spontaneously identifying the cause of her sad experience, and then goes on to validate both the type of emotion and the appropriateness of experiencing such an emotion given the event. April's mother also redirects the conversation to maintain a coherent focus on sad feelings, before advancing the discussion by normalizing experiences of sadness (given the context) and providing a possible resolution to sad experiences, and, interestingly, also by providing a similar personal experience. After walking with the child through the experience, the mother provides a brief, abstract lesson on an alternate, and here opposing, emotional experience and definition – finding ways to enhance understanding of emotions through contrasts.

Elaborative and emotional reminiscing style and narrative development

Children of more highly elaborative parents come to tell more coherent and detailed narratives of their own personal experience across development (see Fivush *et al.* 2006 for a review). More specifically, longitudinal research indicates that children of more highly elaborative parents provide more information when reminiscing with their parent, and these relations emerge across the preschool years, suggesting that children are learning specific styles of how to participate in co-constructing narratives. Moreover, children of more highly elaborative parents provide more information, more specific details, and a more coherently organized narrative when asked to tell an independent narrative to an unfamiliar adult interviewer (Fivush, Haden and Adam 1995), suggesting that these children have internalized a more coherent elaborative frame for narrating their experiences. Finally, experimental intervention studies indicate that training mothers to be more elaborative with their preschoolers during reminiscing results in children showing improved coherence and details in their independent narratives up to a year later (see Salmon and Reese 2016 for a review). Clearly, more highly elaborative parents are fostering a more elaborative coherent narrative style in their children.

In learning to tell more coherent and detailed narratives about their personal experience, children are also learning how better to understand themselves and others. Children's skills in socio-emotional competence, including anticipating, understanding and managing their emotions and the emotional experiences of their interaction partners are directly influenced by parents' emotion socialization (Denham et al. 2007; Katz et al. 2012). In the above example, the mother directs April's attention to reflecting on her subjective emotional experience, including the underlying cause of her sadness (recognizing what about losing the book was upsetting) as well as a possible resolution (getting the book back) before discussing ways that possible resolution is likely – and, hence, worth anticipating – given past experience. As can be seen from this example, these emotion-focused conversations provide opportunities for parents to address both coping skills and children's sense of self (Fivush 2007). This kind of elaborative, emotionally focused parental narrative socialization promotes children's ability to relate to themselves and those around them, and children's emotional competence is reciprocally informed by and informs children's sense of self (Halberstadt et al. 2001). For example, when parents make more effort to explain and validate children's emotional experiences, children have higher self-esteem (Reese, Bird and Tripp 2007) and fewer internalizing and externalizing problem behaviors (Fivush and Sales 2006).

Emotion socialization also promotes children's development of positive social roles and self-understanding of social status with others (i.e. acceptance versus rejection). They learn how to fit in in social scenarios, and are better equipped to manage emotional experiences across pleasant (i.e. making friends, building close relations) and unpleasant (i.e. social conflict and rejection) scenarios, as well as perceptions of their standing with others. Thus, through elaborated, emotionally focused reminiscing across the preschool years, children are learning both how to reflect on and how to narrate their personal experiences in ways that facilitate more coherent and more emotionally regulated ways of understanding self and relationships.

Reminiscing and socialization through adolescence

As children progress into adolescence, capacities for forming more abstract narratives and life scripts coincide with increased skills and situational demands for socio-emotional competence (Booker and Dunsmore 2017; McAdams 2013a). As young people are transitioning from childhood to adulthood, they face the major developmental challenge of creating a healthy adult identity (Erikson 1968). It is during this key developmental period that individuals develop the sophisticated cognitive and socio-emotional skills to begin to think about the self and individuality in more nuanced ways and face the socioculturally mediated challenges of making decisions about who they want to be and what they want to stand for (Habermas and Bluck 2000; Habermas and Reese 2015). Part of the creation of an adult identity involves creating an overarching coherent life story. Whereas we see great developmental strides in telling coherent, expressive narratives of specific experiences throughout childhood, it is only in adolescence that individuals begin to link these disparate experiences together into an overarching life story that provides causal and thematic cohesion across experiences (Habermas and Reese 2015; McAdams and McLean 2013).

With these developmental changes come shifts in the ways adolescents reminisce with parents; notably, adolescents' abilities autonomously to narrate life events with coherence and deeper meaning become more advanced (e.g. Chen *et al.* 2012; Reese, Jack and White 2010), and forms of parental scaffolding change accordingly (McLean and Mansfield 2011). Although youth are now less reliant on parental scaffolding for expanding factual story details or defining the implications of emotions in the context of specific experiences, parents continue to play an important role in helping children frame a more overarching life story, connecting specific experiences together into a larger framework of self over time.

Initially, parents help young adolescents with the temporal structure of a life, and with increasing skills, parents help older adolescents to create personal evaluative frameworks (Habermas and Reese 2015). As with children, more sensitive socialization from parents (and particularly among mothers in past studies) predicts ongoing personal and social adjustment for youth, including higher self-esteem and fewer behavior problems (Bohanek *et al.* 2009). The ongoing support of experienced and supportive parents may become especially important during challenging life events that disrupt adolescents' sense of self and the framing of the life story that has been established to date (e.g. a jarring shift in the social network; challenges to sexual or religious identity; a change in plans for the future), as youth are better equipped to re-establish coherence and meaning in the life story relative to children, but are not as skilled or as efficient in reframing elaborative meaning and emotional clarity from lived experiences as adults are (Fivush, Booker and Graci 2017).

Stories of family

Perhaps most important, adolescents' worlds are expanding. Thus far, we have focused on how children and adolescents are learning the forms and functions of narrating their own personal experience through participating in parentally structured narrative interactions. But as we argued earlier, we tell our own stories in story-rich environments in which we hear, listen and participate in telling stories of others as well. Again, this begins within the family, with stories of both shared experiences and family history (Fivush and Merrill 2016). One critical type of family stories is intergenerational narratives – stories told by the older generation to the younger generation – and within these types of stories, the stories parents tell their children about their own childhood experiences may be particularly formative. Parents are obviously important identification figures for their children, and hearing these stories may aid children and adolescents in formulating models of how to cope with challenging and difficult experiences as well as how to tell a coherent integrated life story (Fivush *et al.* 2008).

These kinds of parental intergenerational narratives are, perhaps not surprisingly, reasonably frequent in everyday family conversation, such as around the dinner table, where most families tell at least one intergenerational narrative during a 30-minute conversation (Bohanek et al. 2009). More interesting, when these stories are initiated, the children often participate in the retelling, asking questions but also adding details, indicating that these stories are told and retold and that the children are both familiar and interested in these stories. Indeed, children initiate these stories (e.g. 'Mom, tell us about that vegetable garden you and Grandpa planted') as often as parents do, perhaps even in very early childhood, as April did with her mother. Thus, these kinds of intergenerational narratives are clearly part of family storytelling; children hear these stories and even participate in telling some of them. How might intergenerational stories provide scaffolds and models, especially for adolescents as they begin to construct their own life story?

Across several studies, we have found that adolescents and emerging adults know and easily tell stories about their mothers and fathers when their parents were growing up (Merrill, Booker and Fivush 2018). Moreover, they can tell multiple kinds of stories – stories that are simply entertaining, as well as stories that are more deeply self-defining or that represent serious challenges the parents faced when they were younger, including transgression experiences, regrets and failures (Merrill et al. 2018). Interestingly, parents tend to tell their child stories that are developmentally matched; that is, parents tell stories to their young adolescents about when they themselves were adolescents, and they tell stories to their emerging adult children about when they themselves were that age.

This suggests that intergenerational narratives may focus on experiences that may be most relevant for what the child is currently experiencing in terms of identity challenges. This is further evidenced by the reasonable frequency with which adolescents and emerging adults make an explicit connection between the parents' experiences and their own experience as they narrate, although this varies greatly by type of event being narrated. About a third of narratives will include a specific connection between self and parent, but this drops to less than 5 per cent when the narrative is about a parent's transgression experience. The overall patterns indicate that parents tell these stories, even of difficult and challenging experiences, perhaps especially developmentally relevant stories, and that children are actively hearing these stories, and are often making specific connections to themselves.

And these stories matter. Adolescents and emerging adults who tell more coherent, elaborated and emotionally expressive intergenerational narratives show higher levels of psychological wellbeing and a greater sense of personal identity (Fivush, Bohanek and Zaman 2010; Merrill, Srivanas and Fivush 2017; Zaman and Fivush 2011).

The benefits of telling family stories

Our focus to this point has been the benefits of elaborative reminiscing for children and adolescents, but engaging in more highly elaborated, emotionally focused reminiscing may also benefit the adults who scaffold these interactions with the younger generation. Here, we briefly review the benefits of life reminiscing more broadly, and then turn to a more focused discussion of the specific benefits parents and grandparents may derive from sharing intergenerational stories with the younger generation.

Reminiscing in later adulthood

Reminiscing throughout adulthood continues to involve coherent reflections of one's experiences and accomplishments as defining of the life story and life review to date (see Caldwell 2005) and provides opportunities for meaning-making from reflections on the past to additional impacts and accomplishments one still plans to obtain (e.g. Lewis and Butler 1974; Rappaport 1995). As individuals mature into later stages of adulthood, broad life review and introspection become more commonplace and salient (Lewis and Butler 1974), and events across the lifespan are connected for the purpose of constructing extended narratives of the relevant themes of one's life (see Sommer and Baumeister 1998).

For middle-aged and older adults, opportunities to constructively express themselves through reminiscing and life review can provide meaning and reaffirm identity from extended and causally connected events accumulated over the years. Opportunities to share life stories with others – to have an audience receptive to one's lived experiences and life lessons – is gratifying for storytellers (Chonody and Wang 2013). Further, opportunities to engage in life review and identify positive meaning and resolution from life's events are linked to fewer depressive symptoms for older adults (e.g. Serrano *et al.* 2004).

This process of finding one's life to have been meaningful and impactful, to feel appreciated and valued, continues to be important for individuals moving into later stages of the lifespan. Reminiscing can also promote social bonds with others, fulfilling needs for belonging and intimacy that remain salient across adulthood. In fact, older adults recognize opportunities to connect and build intimacy with others as a major reason for reminiscing, in contrast to the identity development goals of adolescents and young adults (Webster 1995).

Intergenerational storytelling

Bridging our discussion of the benefits of scaffolded storytelling for children and adolescents, and the benefits of life reminiscence for older individuals, it becomes clear that the older generation telling stories to the younger generation has specific benefits for both tellers and listeners. As reviewed by Merrill and Fivush (2016), sharing the past with the younger generation may have positive benefits and functions for storytellers, including promoting wellbeing, building and maintaining intimate bonds, and building one's contributions and lasting legacy for future generations. Shared family stories can help scaffold events for inexperienced storytellers, provide context and life lessons for children and adolescents struggling with personal challenges and identity development, and provide support for adult children managing additional life pressures. Further, life reflections that find positive meaning, and do not neglect past pitfalls and current challenges (i.e. diminished agency, exposure to disease, etc.), but incorporate positive growth and resolution from these challenges (e.g. Eschenbruch 2007), provide valuable insights about both the storytellers – windows into their history and identity – and critical life lessons passed on to younger individuals (Merrill *et al.* 2018).

Reminiscing from more experienced storytellers can also enrich the lives of family members in need, passing along valuable lessons of perseverance and wisdom for children experiencing distress, adolescents and young adults unsure of the next steps for their independence and autonomy, and middle-aged adults coping with pressures of parenthood and midlife challenges in the family and community (e.g. Merrill *et al.* 2018; Myers 1989). Hence, reminiscing can uplift and promote upcoming generations. Intergenerational family stories, couched within sociocultural norms and framings, reaffirm and transmit family and cultural lessons and expectations from one generation to the next, serving as a means of maintaining valuable heritage and organizing for others the events that are important for achieving a meaningful and positive life.

Implications

Early family narrative interactions set the stage for a lifetime of reminiscing. Parental sharing and scaffolding of stories helps children and adolescents construct more coherent and emotionally regulated stories of self across development, and children and adolescents who are scaffolded in more elaborated ways show higher levels of narrative coherence, emotional regulation and psychological wellbeing. In turn, adults who sensitively scaffold these narrative interactions with the younger generation show beneficial effects, including higher levels of generativity and positive emotional bonding. Thus, reminiscence has a long developmental history, and the benefits of coherent, elaborated and emotionally expressive storytelling show continuity across the lifespan. Moreover, the critical and central role of family storytelling in this process highlights the deep socio-emotional components of this process for building family history and values across the generations.

Our review leads to two interconnected implications. First, children and adolescents who are the recipients of coherent, elaborated and emotionally expressive stories from the older generation – stories that model challenges and difficulties as well as achievements and redemption – learn to tell their own personal stories in beneficial ways. Second, the very act of sharing these stories benefits the tellers; those who pass down the family stories, who engage the younger generation in the co-construction of meaningful family histories, are themselves beneficiaries of these tellings. Life reminiscence is a skill and an art that develops early and provides a lifetime of benefits for both the tellers and the listeners.

Chapter 6

REMINISCENCE AND LIFE REVIEW WORK IN TAIWAN

TsuAnn Kuo

Nobody knows where the cycle of storytelling begins. However, someone once said:

Everyone has a story to tell,

if only someone will ask,

if only someone will listen.

In the olden days, in Taiwan, it was common for older men to gather under a big big tree. Here, they chatted among themselves about their work lives, politics and current events, and how they viewed the world around them. These scenes, which happened day after day, were also where some people talked about their life stories with the old men around the big tree as well as with anyone else who happily stopped to listen. This naturally occurring practice usually happened around certain times of the day, with multi-coloured tea cups and a seasoned clay teapot often present. Some men drank tea and talked, other men played chess on the side while passers-by, young and old, happily stopped to listen to the life stories.

Fast forward to today's modern and urbanized Taiwan where four major ethnic groups live under diverse influences inherited from the Dutch, the Portuguese, the Japanese and the Chinese, and society changed from a predominantly Japanese culture between 1895 and 1946 to Chinese after the Second World War (Su 2017). The country moved from an agricultural to an industrial society from the 1950s to the 1980s, where young people left rural areas for better jobs, people went abroad to study and nuclear families with high mobility became the majority. The elderly population percentage is rapidly increasing as the fertility rate falls, making Taiwan one of the fastest ageing countries in the world (Taiwan National Development Council 2016). More elderly or older couples now live on their own, and the practice of gathering together to chat about life stories has become a 'task' and is no longer a frequent everyday practice. Instead of seeing people gathering under the big tree, special arrangements have to be made for professionals or community volunteers to facilitate life storytelling with older adults. The feeling is that the world has begun to move too quickly for those deemed too slow to keep up and too fast for the young to slow down and listen. These changes further highlight the need for reminiscence and life review interventions in Taiwan to reinstate old practices in modern settings.

After 25 years of living and studying in the United States, I returned to Taiwan to initiate life review and reminiscence practices with Taiwan's expanding older adult population. While I was studying at the then Andrus School of Gerontology at the University of Southern California, my colleagues and I worked with many older adult volunteers, who eventually became our mentors. Under the supervision of Dr James Birren, we learned about older adults' life stories through a series of practices involving interviews and conversations. I was fascinated by how happy those older volunteers looked when talking about their lives, and how proud they were about the different roles they had played during their lives. I was also reminded of my own childhood when I would pull up a stool to sit next to my grandfather and listen to him share stories with his friends. The combination of these experiences – studying gerontology, valuable childhood memories with my grandfather, and modern Taiwan's rapid progression towards becoming a super aged country – prompted me to become a promoter of life review and reminiscence in Taiwan.

In 2018, Taiwan will be classified as an aged country (i.e. more than 14% of the total population is aged 65 years and older), and it is projected to become a super aged country within the next eight years. At the same time, the life expectancy of Taiwan's older adults aged 65 and older continues to grow slowly and currently they are expected to achieve an average age of 85 (Taiwan National Development Council 2016). This means that on average a 65-year-old person may have 20 more years of life to live, which may possibly include close to 12 years of being active, followed by 8 years of being frail or inactive (Lin and Liu 2013).

With this increased life expectancy and increasingly more socio-economic advancement among the current older generations, the Taiwan government initiated the Aged Friendly City program by following the Active Ageing guidelines announced by the World Health Organization, designed to keep most older adults healthy and active (World Health Organization 2008). Many cities in Taiwan started to engage older adults in various types of programs, including health promotion activities, communal exercises, lifelong learning, leisure events and volunteering (Hsu 2015). Of all the programs, many community-based organizations and educational institutions focused on starting reminiscence and life review programs for older adults. These programs can be divided into four categories: art-based, community-based, computer-assisted, and guided autobiography (GAB).

> *Art-based reminiscence programs* allowed older adults to use different expressions of art work to tell their own life stories or engage with others to exchange shared life experiences. An example of this approach is Legacy Art Work, a program that originated in New York and was implemented in Taiwan in 2003 that enabled older adults to use various forms of art as a medium to tell stories (Legacy Art Work 2018).

> *Community-based story book projects* made it possible for older adults to create their own book, scrapbook, photo album or sketchbook from scratch and recount different stages of their lives by including complementary photos that had been collected throughout their lifetime. A Memory Box program is another example where older adults were encouraged to use a big shoebox as a container for personal memorabilia – a sort of window through which their life stories were illustrated (Liu-Huang *et al.* 2010; Lu 2012).

> *Computer-assisted programs* focused on using computer technology to generate a simple story book for the older adults' families. This computer program first asked the older adult to answer a series of pre-arranged life course questions, then it allowed users to pre-select art designs for backgrounds and frames, and it concluded by merging the answered questions and selected art design to form a quick electronic life story book for the older adult to share.

Guided autobiography (GAB) programs first developed by James Birren (Birren and Cochran 2001) were adapted by Dr Kuo in 2009 and later implemented in Taiwan. GAB was developed to improve the psychological wellbeing of older adults in various states of health and at different life stages. This program required a group of older adults led by trained life review leaders (LRLs) to follow a structured program. Within the program, the older adults and LRLs worked together to examine how the older people's lives had passed through different stages and how they viewed their achievements and interpreted the meaning of the challenges they had faced. Group members were encouraged to comment or respond to each person in the group when they shared their stories. The group dynamics also allowed members to bond and form close relationships through which they could be empowered, encouraged and inspired.

Development of a life review program in Taiwan

Over the years, many scholars have developed their own versions of reminiscence and life review programs (Birren and Svensson 2013; Cappeliez and Robitaille 2010; Chiang *et al.* 2010; Haber 2006). Alwin (2012) also suggested that there were five ways of looking at the life course and undertaking a life review, which could be structured by:

- time or chronological age
- life stages
- events, transitions and trajectories
- lifespan of human development
- early life influences on later adult outcomes.

As mentioned previously, not only did reminiscence and life review programs in Taiwan come in four different types, programs such as History Alive and Real-Person Library Book were being developed (History Alive 2018). These two programs asked older adults to serve as storytellers, describing history or interesting life experiences to families or audiences in community settings or libraries. The stories that these older adults told were often so lively and vivid that they were described as a 'real book' themselves.

In order to develop evidence-based life review programs that could be shown to have positive psychosocial effects when undertaken by older adults, I decided to adopt Birren's guided autobiography tool for use as a life review program in Taiwan (Birren and Cochran 2001). In addition, a literature review was undertaken to identify relevant studies concerned with cultural or intellectual factors that differed from the American culture in which Birren had primarily worked. For further discussion of guided autobiography see Chapter 9 by Svensson and de Vries. The original nine topics suggested by Birren and Cochran (2001) were:

- the major branching points in your life
- your family
- the role of money in your life
- major life work or career
- your health and body
- your sexual identity
- your experiences with and ideas about death
- your spiritual life and values
- your goals and aspirations.

A panel of Taiwan experts was convened to evaluate the appropriateness of these topics as well as to suggest how each topic should be translated or interpreted for use in Taiwan. The expert panel also focused on the cultural sensitivity of each topic and analyzed any potential negative psychosocial impact this may have for older adults when discussing each topic.

In the end, the panel of experts decided to keep six of Birren and Cochran's (2001) original nine topics. The three excluded topics pertained to discussions of money, sexual identity and ideas about death. While these three topics are important with regard to the life review process, they were found to be potentially too sensitive for most Taiwanese older adults or their families at this stage of family, national and cultural development. For instance, in Taiwan, it is rare for families to discuss economic or monetary issues with strangers, and dialogues about death and dying between a younger person and an aged adult are not considered culturally appropriate. This decision was further supported by Cappeliez and Robitaille (2010), who wrote about cultural considerations in life review and suggested that death preparation may be considered negative while reminiscing for maintaining intimacy may be regarded as positive in most Western societies. While European Americans usually reminisce for functional reasons (i.e. to educate, to write a history or to pass down family traditions), the Chinese may lean towards more non-functional reasons to think and tell their stories for socialization purposes (Cappeliez and Robitaille 2010). Cappeliez and Webster (2017) also mentioned that regardless of culture, people across continents or ethnic groups seemed to agree on the 'what' to reminiscence about but the 'why, when, where and who' components can vary greatly between different cultures.

Therefore, in the interests of goodness of fit for use with current elderly population groups in Taiwan, the three topics were changed and replaced by topics focusing more on:

- identifying the inner self and life values
- recording achievements
- relieving or ameliorating regrets in life.

The expert panel believed that the current generation of older Taiwanese people was relatively conservative, receiving fewer years of education than younger generations and believing more in collectivism (i.e. being family oriented), thus the replacement themes focused more on guiding the older adults to look inside of themselves, reflect on their values and hopefully develop more self-esteem and confidence. These tasks were considered to be more important at their stage of development. A ten-session life review program was developed, with emphasis on reviewing one's life history, considering one's own identity and developing self-esteem, as well as reflecting on one's own dreams for the future. In addition, to evaluate the effectiveness of the program, two scales were used as pre- and post-test measures of psychological wellbeing and personal fulfilment. The two scales were

Geriatric Depression Scale by Sheikh and Yesavage (1986) and the Satisfaction with Life Scale by Diener *et al.* (1985) (see Table 6.1).

Table 6.1: Program for older adults' life review groups developed by Dr Kuo

Unit	Event title	Session goals for group leaders	Session content for older participants
1	A happy beginning	Introduce self and participants	Make introductions and get acquainted
		Introduce and outline the program	Explain the nature and importance of life review and life review groups
		Explain purpose and nature of pre-testing	Cover basic group rules and discuss ethical issues such as respect, confidentiality, regular attendance and making positive contributions to the group
			Complete pre-testing
2	My lifeline	Explain the idea of major milestones throughout life	Use a soft wire as a symbol of life and fold it to resemble the course of one's own life
		Encourage participants to identify and reflect on personal milestones in discussion with other participants	Identify major life events and describe these life events in group discussion
			Reflect on the significance of these positive and negative milestones and how they were managed
3	My family	Participants identify and describe close family members	Identify, describe and discuss significant family members
		Identify one's family values	Reflect on how a person could be shaped by family values, culture and traditions
4	The circle of my friends	Participants identify significant friends in their lives, their importance and how they behave in relation to these friends	Make a list of friends who were significant in one's life
			Discuss and reflect on how one's social behaviour or relationships could be shaped by friends and/or experiences with friends
		Encourage participants to make a pictorial representation of the significance of these friends	Complete the 'Circle of Friends' exercise

cont.

Unit	Event title	Session goals for group leaders	Session content for older participants
5	Who am 'I'?	Assist participants to create a self-portrait by recognising and appreciating the importance of different roles that one plays in life and how a comfortable self-identity is created	Create a self-portrait and interpret the different sides of self (outside, inside, and real me) Identify a role that each participant is deeply associated with and reflect how this role is playing out in the current stage of their life and what satisfactions are associated with the role
6	Happy moments in my life	Encourage participants to appreciate the highlights of their lives and to reflect on their self-identity and personal confidence	Using various prompts and questions participants are encouraged to 'walk through their lives', identify happy events and how these contributed to the development of personal life values, successes and satisfactions
7	Old picture shows a 'golden self'	Encourage discussion about the proudest moments and personal characteristics and values participants identify about themselves so as to assist them to appreciate themselves	Choose a photo that can best identify one's achievements, personality or character Look deeper and appreciate what made this identified character great
8	Regrets in my life	Discuss the likelihood of everyone having some regrets in life Encourage participants to identify personal regrets and consider what action(s) could be taken to relieve such regrets	Identify or re-evaluate how regrets play a part in daily life Take action on relieving the regrets in order to move on with life
9	Dreams of my life	Help participants to think about re-organising their life by identifying unfinished dreams in life Encourage participants to create a to-do list for the foreseeable future	Reflect on dreams or unfinished business that one would like to take some action on Think deeply about how these 'dreams' can help one move on and create a better life
10	Story of my life	Individuals create a life story book and share the book with the group Conduct the post-test	Take the opportunity to assemble or put the final touches to a book about one's life which will likely have been begun in earlier sessions Share stories and talk about how the 'story-making' process has affected each person

Adapted from Birren and Cochran (2001) and Svensson (2018)

Implementation of training program for leaders of older adults' life review groups

In 2013, a Train the Leaders program for leading older adults in life review groups was developed after three years of testing, and was directed by Dr Kuo for the Hsiang Shang Culture and Education Foundation (2018). The aim of the training was to equip group leaders to conduct and lead life review groups for older adults living in the community or in institutions. Participants who joined the training were mostly social workers, nurses, senior volunteers or organizational leaders who were responsible for developing programs in community care sites, assisted living facilities, nursing homes and adult continuing learning centers. The 40 hours of training consisted of three parts (see Table 6.2). The trainee leaders were asked to conduct an actual full life review program with older adults and to make detailed observation and reflection notes in order to receive a basic certificate of competence for leading a life review group. The training included:

- basic knowledge of and skills in working with older adults
- principles and skills needed to conduct life review groups
- practice, performance, coaching and evaluation.

Part 1: this concerned basic knowledge and skills in working with older adults and included:

- basic competencies and ethics
- lifespan and public history, including major public events and pop culture in different historical periods
- art therapy and applications
- basic group work skills of listening, leading, reflecting, accompanying and empowerment.

Although some of these topics were fundamental in working with members of any age, this training content placed more emphasis on the importance of seeing an older adult's life through their own eyes. Hence, learning about the history and significant events that the older adults might have lived through was important for group leaders who would be leading life review groups. This was especially important in cases where the group leaders were relatively young and may have had difficulty developing empathy due to lack of understanding about the older adults' historical contexts. Moreover, the addition of art therapy encouraged more creativity and comfortable, enjoyable opportunities for older adults to express the events of their lives in non-verbal ways. Part 1 consisted of topics 1–5; Part 2 of topics 6–10; and Part 3 comprised the practicum.

Table 6.2: Content of training program for leaders of older life review groups for older adults, developed by Dr Kuo

	Topics
1	Introduction to gerontology and reminiscence, life review and undertaking life story work in groups
2	Working with older adults: ethics and basic competencies
3	Major historical events and pop culture within a lifespan: historical perspective of older participants
4	Narrative therapy theory and applications
5	Art therapy and applications
6	Basic group work skills: attending, listening, leading, reflecting, accompanying and empowering
7	The process and power of storytelling: sharing stories within life review groups
8	The design of a life review group and its content
9	Observing, recording and evaluating a life review group
10	Preparation for practicum: arrangements for leading two to three sessions and their assessment

Part 2: this was about training in the principles and skills needed to conduct life review groups, which included:

- introduction to life review groups: basic theories and applications
- the power of storytelling: sharing a story with the group
- the design of a life review group and its content
- narrative therapy and applications.

The importance of life review as a therapeutic method requires leaders with a strong theoretical foundation and life-course perspective to lead throughout the process. Depending on the physical condition of the older adults and the organizational setting in which the groups met, group leaders needed to use different applications and alter or adapt the life review process. For example, if an older adult was depressed and isolated in a community setting, or if older adults had impaired cognitive or physical functioning in a mixed group, the group leaders needed to have sufficient judgement and skill to change the way they conducted the life review group.

Part 3: this was about real practice and performance, which included:

- coaching
- skills of observation and record keeping
- conducting evaluations
- doing a practicum where leaders were asked to lead two or three sessions.

Group leaders were asked to practise by conducting the actual life review groups in front of the class and received constructive feedback from the instructors and the audience. Group leaders were advised to follow the same structure and choose two or three topics to conduct the life review group (see Table 6.1). Moreover, the observation notes were especially emphasized to remind group leaders to pay attention to verbal and non-verbal messages that older adults might have expressed when talking about their life stories as well as changes occurring in individuals throughout the life review process.

In addition, depending on the literacy level or the physical functioning of the older adults, which may limit their capacity to write or tell their story, the group leader had to use different art therapy techniques as ways to facilitate the storytelling process more easily. For example, for people who were older, more isolated or with mild depression, it was difficult for them to come up with a list of friends. Thus, the activity of drawing a full hand (palms down) reminded participants of the activities they used to do as a child. With a list of guiding questions and prompts (such as 'Think about who you used to play with when you were a child', 'Who do you remember the most when you were a student in grade school?' or 'Can you think of any childhood sweetheart?'), the participants were asked to identify at least five friends who were significant in their lives. The friends could be from any stage of their lives and could be remembered as having been either a positive or negative influence. Friends' names were identified, and the participants were asked to recall and record their best memory of some shared event or activity. At the end, the older adults were asked to write a short conclusion about what 'friends' meant to them in their lives.

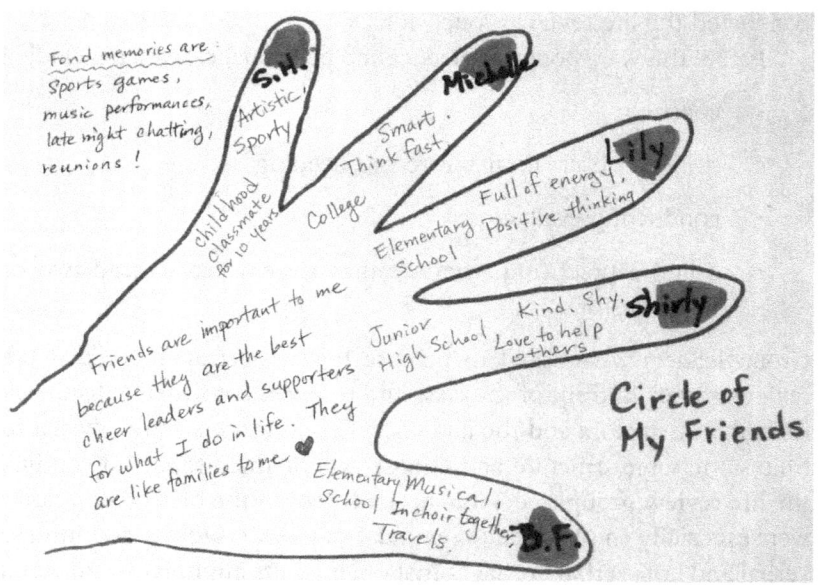

Figure 6.1: The circle of my friends – a sample page from a life review group (photograph by Kuo 2018)

Other art therapy techniques were also used, including scrapbooking, drawing (with different mediums such as crayon, watercolor, colored pencil, etc.), sculpting, collaging, origami, cropping photos or magazine pictures and die cutting. For example, sculpting was used when talking about regrets in life; collaging was used to express happy moments in life. Since there were ten sessions in the life review program, the combination of art techniques used relating to thematic topics not only allowed trained leaders to elicit stories from the older adults but also helped facilitate learning and creativity within the older group members (Madori 2007). For other examples of art linked to reminiscence programs, see Chapters 14 by Ferguson and Gallagher and 15 by Schweitzer.

Once the leaders were trained, they were required to lead a life review group completing the entire ten sessions (see Table 6.2) and complete full observation notes as well as pre- and post-test assessments of participants. The ten sessions were developed based on the modification of Birren and Cochran (2001) and the Taiwan expert panel review discussed previously. The topics and the sequence of the ten sessions were tested three times before they were finalized. The three tested sites were a) an urban setting, with a mixed membership of both genders and educational levels; b) a rural setting, predominately of women with only a few years of formal education; c) an urban setting, predominately of men retired from different types of work. All the ten topics were well received by the group participants at the three test sites, but the depths of the stories elicited and leaders' choice of facilitating mediums varied, depending on each group's dynamics and changes over time. After testing the ten-session program three times, the group leaders, program organizers and the older adults all agreed that the life review program should be further promoted and widely implemented. Some of the comments the participants gave on the outcomes of the life review program were: 'the best gift in life', 'something to give to their grandchildren', 'a chance to organize my life', 'something stimulating, and it will help maintain good cognitive functions', 'opened dialogue between parents and children', and 'every older person should do it'.

Evaluation and results of the life review program

Between 2010 and 2014, 32 life review groups were conducted in various parts of Taiwan (north, central and south), with more than 400 older adults from different educational backgrounds and geographic settings. Participants' average age was 77.3 years, with the majority being women (71.6%), married (47.8%) or widowed (41.2%), more than half having elementary school education (57.2%) and being Buddhists (53.7%) (Kuo 2015). These participants were invited to attend the life review groups pre-arranged by non-profit organizations or adult day services where a trained life review group leader was used to conduct the ten-session program.

Although these life review groups took place in different settings with older adults with a variety of physical and cognitive conditions, the pre- and post-tests using the Geriatric Depression Scale (Sheikh and Yesavage 1986) revealed that the depressive symptoms of the participants reduced by 6 per cent and the Satisfaction with Life Scale scores (Diener et al.1985) increased by 5 per cent (Kuo 2015).

Some of the groups also conducted post-group interviews with the participating older adults, and some also included their family members in the evaluation. Results were compiled from a qualitative analysis of the information contained in the group leaders' observation notes, their records of verbal and non-verbal expressions as well as inspirational phrases used by the older adults in the life review sessions. Since the design of the life review program was about personal life history, self-identity and dreams for the future, the qualitative analysis also reflected how participants changed during the course of a life review group and what they discovered about themselves. The results from the qualitative analysis indicated that four main themes emerged in the life review groups in Taiwan during the five-year period (2010–14):

1. Pride in the life stories and inspiration gained by reviewing them.
2. Recognition of self-achievements and contributions made.
3. Resolution of uncomfortable feelings and relationships.
4. Hope that the future can be as colorful and hopeful as the past.

Pride in the life stories and inspirations

The participants found that they had lives full of interesting stories and inspiration. Many older adults said that they rarely had a chance to sit down quietly and feel 'safe' to talk about their lives. The life review group gave them an opportunity to think through every period of their lives, systematically. The older adults mentioned that they enjoyed doing the reminiscence about childhood, adulthood and even retirement. Since most of the elderly participants had been through the Second World War, many said that they could not imagine thinking about that part of life because it was full of hardship and unpleasant memories. However, when they revisited those life events during the group sessions, the thoughts about them being unpleasant were replaced by feelings of being released from sad memories and gratitude that they had survived. It was as if they had a new appreciation of themselves for having lived through the hardship of the war, so they were afterwards able to face different challenges. Some even said that they now appreciated the hardships they had endured because these difficult times or challenges had made them tough and resilient.

> I never thought I would think about the past because it was full of sad and hard memories. In fact, I was resentful and felt that my life as a whole was full of bad luck. However, I never realized how much I can appreciate life now because the past taught me so many life lessons, so I can survive until now. (*86-year-old woman with three years of education*)

In addition, the chance to talk about the past and re-examine the different kinds of social roles that older adults played in life brought back pride and self-esteem and gave meaning to life. As many older adults mentioned, they did not realize that they had done so many things in life. Some established a family because their neighbors or elders arranged 'match-making events', which was quite common in the agricultural society existing before the 1950s. Others mentioned reasons for their success in life, both at work and through other times, that were as diverse as 'receiving help from others', 'self-determination', 'family working together', 'not wanting to fail' and 'endurance'.

> I was told to marry my husband when I turned 18. I only saw him once before we got married. When I got married, my husband's family had 14 members but soon grew up to 20 in three years. Each day, being the 'eldest daughter-in-law', I had to coordinate and arrange for meals to be cooked enough for the entire 20 family members. I was so busy that I never sat down to eat at the dinner table with the other family members. And then, I had ten children in 14 years, but my husband passed away when I was 38. The youngest son was only 4 years old. It was so hard to raise my children and I told myself never to look back… I cannot die because my children need me. So, a day passed, a year passed, a decade passed… I am happy, I am still alive. And the children and grandchildren are so good to me. (*93-year-old woman without a formal education, widowed for 55 years*)

Recognition of self-achievements and contributions made

Many of the older adults mentioned that they felt uncomfortable at the start because it was not easy to talk about themselves. Most of the women were housewives who had been devoted to their families for a long time, so they had tended to lose their own self-identity as time passed (Hu and Chou 1996). Historically, the older adults grew up in an environment where the society was rather conservative, and Taiwan was under martial law for a long time. So, talking about what happened in the family to non-family members was often not trusted and forbidden by 'elders' in the family. The traditional culture influenced by Confucianism taught people to be humble, which also limited older adults' willingness to think and talk about themselves, especially when it was time to describe their lifetime achievements.

However, the life review process gave them a chance to talk about their past life experiences from another perspective. Those experiences that seemed to bring hardships turned into proud moments or were recognized as achievements, when the group leader would guide people slowly to pay attention to their inner self and appreciate their own resilience. Gibson (2011) mentioned this as 'giving a sense of self-worth' and 'countering social isolation' in reference to reminiscence with minority ethnic groups. In the many life review groups conducted in Taiwan, women talked about how helping their family members had been their first priority throughout their lives. It seemed that they were more likely to suffer identity loss and not to see themselves as the one who contributed to the success of their family members. Many started by feeling lost, hopeless, useless and frail until they were encouraged in the groups to remember past achievements and realize that they were once strong 'super women'.

> I don't think I have anything proud to share. I only had a couple of years of education and only know about how to raise six children, which was considered as normal among my peers. My husband came from a well-off family, so my mother thought it was good for me to marry into that family. But ten years into marriage, I realized that he took for granted all of what he had and never seriously worked for. He started making bad friends who asked him to drink and spend money on other women, and then he became so bad tempered that my kids and I were afraid of him. So, I decided one day to take all my kids away and we lived as far away as possible from him. I had to work four jobs: one where I helped cook breakfast for construction workers very early in the morning before the kids woke up, one during the day to do household cleaning for rich people, one at home to do simple assembly work or sewing shoe parts or making small tools, and one on weekends to work at the market selling things I made. So, I learned to make everything, canned vegetables, food such as rice balls or dumplings, and beautiful dresses; and I knew how

to fix everything. I made anything that could turn into money. And my children helped me do the small assembly jobs and sell things at the weekend market. That's all I did – raise kids and try to survive. (*83-year-old women living alone who had mild depression*)

Resolution of uncomfortable feelings and relationships

The issue of death and dying was still quite sensitive to many older adults who tended to suppress or ignore their feelings about resolving any uncomfortable or residual issues connected with their loved ones. In one of the life review sessions when talking about 'regrets in life', one elderly man talked about his regret about his 'adopted' father.

> I was sent to my uncle's family when I was five. The adults did not tell me why, but my birth mother told me to start calling my uncle 'father' from then on. My birth family was relatively well off but my uncle's family was poor. Every day, I had to help with family chores and work very hard on the farm. I dreamed about going back to my birth family all the time because my uncle (oh, I should have said my father) never gave me enough to eat. Deep inside I was very resentful of my birth parents, and I told myself not to grow close to my 'adopted' family. I was very lonely as a child. I carried this 'hate' for 70 years when my mother told me that before my adopted father passed away he actually kneeled down in front of my birth father, thanking him for giving him a son to carry the family name and to save him from being 'looked down on' by neighbors for not having a son. I never thought how significant that me being 'transferred' from one brother to another brother was so important. And of course, I did not have a chance to grow close to my adopted father (i.e. my uncle). In fact, if I had another chance to talk to my adopted father, I would forgive him and really thank him for using his whole life to love me, and to help me grow up. (*73-year-old man talking about being a rebellious son*)

Hope that the future can be colorful and hopeful as the past

Many older adults changed their life perspectives after finishing the ten-week sessions, as many started to say that they would want to go back to do what they used to like doing, or to plan for the future. Family members of the older adults also saw differences, as some mentioned that they started to see the more cheerful and positive part of the older adults. A few family members, who read the story books that their older adults produced, mentioned that they would now appreciate and know how to interact better with their elderly loved ones. The phrase 'start thinking about the future' seemed to mean different things to different people. Many thought of it is a rebirth, others thought of it as an adventure.

> Life review sessions were the first activities after my husband passed away suddenly. Yes, I had been a widow for five years and it was too difficult for me to go out to socialize with others. I thank my friend for pulling me out of my house to attend the life review group. It was really hard at the beginning because all I could think of on the earlier topics were to do with my husband. So, I did not share much. However, when we were at about the second half of the process, when the group leader asked me about what I was most proud of in my life, I really puzzled and did not have an answer…
>
> That night, I went home and asked myself, what do I want to do with my life? Before my husband died, I told myself to enroll in a cooking class, because I never knew how to cook. I consider not being able to cook shameful, especially for a woman. Now I go to the lifelong learning center to learn how to cook, and I also want to learn English, so I can travel. Learning is important because we never had a chance when we were children. Those were all day dreams for me because I was too dependent on my husband. So, I thank the life review group for giving me a chance to think what I want to do with my life. I don't think I could even imagine, had I not been pulled out of my house and met the people, listening to their stories and doing imaginations after going home each time, I would not have come up with now 12 'to do' items on my 'dream list'. (*68-year-old woman with a new approach to life*)

Besides the qualitative results, the impact of life review groups in Taiwan made the society as a whole focus more on the psychosocial wellbeing of older adults. Since Taiwan was implementing its national long-term care and community-based care programs, the creation of life review groups provided a movement for older adults to fulfill their dreams as well as helping to engage more older adults in civic affairs or productive efforts. 'Self-actualization' placed at the top of Maslow's hierarchy of needs (see Burton 2012) was observed in members of the groups, both in terms of personal growth and for altruistic contributions to others. One of the examples of this was the 'Grand Riders', where a group of older adults rode motorcycles around the island as an unfulfilled dream in life.[1] This group experience was made into a documentary film, which made the whole of Taiwan society focus more on developing different programs promoting active ageing.

Another impact of the life review groups has led older adults to be more productive and active. One example was the 'Silver Legends', where older adults with special talents or resilience were found after reviewing their life stories. These Silver Legends were then trained to tour various sites in communities, including schools, senior centers, libraries, adult day care centers, nursing homes and cultural centers. There they shared their life stories, demonstrated how they survived hardship, were living with positive minds and passing down their special skills or talents to other people. Many Silver Legends mentioned that the practice of sharing their life stories and in the process recognizing their own skills reminded them how meaningful their lives were. The ability to be productive and helping others allowed them to stay positive and hopeful in life (Hsiang Shang Culture and Education Foundation 2018).

Conclusion

In reviewing the benefits of reminiscence and life review conducted in Taiwan for the past 12 years, many scholars indicated positive results on increasing life satisfaction, reducing depressive symptoms, increasing social interactions and preventing social isolation (Chao *et al.* 2006). The Taiwan government is actively promoting various versions of reminiscence and life review programs in community-based settings as part of its Ten-Year Long-Term Care Plan 2.0 (Taiwan Ministry of Health and Welfare 2017). The life review leaders training program and the life review groups for older people that I developed and implemented over the past seven years in Taiwan began to make an impact on older adults' social engagement and psychological wellbeing. Both qualitative and quantitative data indicated that not

---

1 See www.gograndriders.com

only life satisfaction and depression were improved but also many dreams were identified and fulfilled, and regrets were relieved. Moreover, the feedback from the administrators and family members indicated that many older adults developed a stronger sense of self and greater confidence and optimism about future directions. It was due to the ten-session process that older adults started to appreciate what they had done in life and found meaning in life both past and present.

Based on the success of the life review program, a follow-up project was developed to empower older adults to become 'Silver Legends' or 'Living Libraries' where they would share lifetime skills and experiences, or help other people realize their life potential, especially assisting frail elderly people and encouraging younger generations. As Taiwan becomes the fastest ageing country in the next eight years, this will dramatically change the demographics, with up to a quarter of the population aged 65 years and older. Therefore, preserving the valuable life lessons of the current elderly generations and preparing them to face a hopeful future can be achieved through training more leaders and implementing more reminiscence and life review work.

Chapter 7

SPIRITUAL REMINISCENCE IN LATER LIFE

Elizabeth MacKinlay

There is something deeply intriguing about human story. It is closely associated with identity and can come to engage the person's whole sense of being, meaning and purpose in life. When I first felt drawn to listen to the stories of older people in the 1990s, seeking to find what life and meaning looked like for these older people, I had a sense that it would somehow be connected with the depths of being or the spiritual dimension. I was also conscious of the fact that, in the 1990s, the word 'spiritual' might not be the best word from which to begin to explore older people's stories. It was a word ill-defined and according to some could be termed a 'weazle'[1] word. But I felt uncertain about any other more appropriate word at the time. What I hoped to do in my studies was to map the spiritual dimension of older independent living people to learn if the spiritual dimension was important to them, and whether this might be so for those who had a religious faith and also those who did not. In other words, was the spiritual dimension a factor in the lives of older people, and if so, how important was it? This chapter focuses on the process of searching for and finding meaning as the basis of spiritual reminiscence. Spiritual reminiscence has been defined as 'a particular way of communication that acknowledges the person as a spiritual being and seeks to engage the person in a more meaningful and personal way' (MacKinlay and Trevitt 2015b, p.9).

---

[1] Attributed to former Bishop of Durham Rt Rev David Jenkins (2004)

Background

My interest in this field began with my desire to discover how older people found meaning in their lives, taking a particular perspective of spirituality. My work at that time was as an 'outsider' with little personal experience of being older myself. However, two decades on, I feel that I am now becoming an 'insider' in the experience of ageing, and am able to write about what I have heard and learned from others, tempered with my own life experience.

My background came from working with older people as a nurse and then, later, from my experience of pastoral ministry, and from there on, combining the two strands of knowledge and experience. The major factor that had intrigued me for a long time was how different older people with seemingly the same medical diagnosis and treatments might come to have quite different health and wellbeing outcomes. It seemed that outlook and attitudes were vitally important, but where did these attitudes come from, what made the difference for those who did well compared with those who did not do well? It was obvious that it was more than the physical condition with which the people had been diagnosed, but what was it?

My sense was that if we could more adequately identify the factors that made or influenced the difference, perhaps we could help those who were not 'doing' well to achieve more fulfilling outcomes. It seemed that this knowledge must lie in the psychosocial and/or spiritual dimensions of life and that new lenses were needed to explore the factors responsible for wellbeing in older people. Within the context of many more people living into their later years, I believed it was important to find how we may assist these people to come to new ways of being and to be able to flourish in later life, rather than simply survive.

An important starting point was to map the spiritual dimension as experienced by independently living older people. The means chosen to achieve this was through narrative.

Narrative in later life and finding meaning

Story is largely about reminiscence and Butler found reminiscence to be important among older people in psychiatric care in his work in the 1960s (Butler 1963a, 1963b, 1995). It seems there is now wide agreement that most people do engage in reminiscence – even younger people do so at times, but it certainly becomes more frequent and more intentional for many older people. (See Chapter 5 by Fivush and Booker for a discussion of this topic.) However, there are different functions of reminiscence. Is it to remember and share the facts of particular events from one's past? Or is it even to remember just a particular event and be able to re-engage in that event, perhaps as an enjoyable activity for older people? It has been my experience that when people have the opportunity to share their story, it often has deeper meanings and is closely associated with the search for meaning and identity.

At the core of our being we seek meaning and purpose in our lives, sometimes consciously, or perhaps in some ways not even realising we are doing so. Life can have purpose and meaning even in the face of great difficulties and challenges (Frankl 1984). Yet, for some people, life seems to hold no meaning, and despair may ensue, as described by Erikson, Erikson and Kivnick (1986). It is through finding meaning that we are able to transcend the difficulties and losses of life. Vitally important in finding meaning for most people are their deepest relationships and this has been evident in my studies of older people and their search for meaning (MacKinlay 1998, 2006, 2017) (see also Webster's discussion on reminiscence and meaning-making in Chapter 10). Ultimately, finding meaning brings the ability to transcend and find transformation in life, moving from self-centredness to other centredness. It is through working with reminiscence that story can be articulated, refined and re-storied, particularly when facing the challenges of later life. This process enables the person to actually transcend and find hope and joy at the depths of their being, even when all outward signs seem to point otherwise.

This is not a new revelation of the 21st century; it has been so for millennia. Taking a Christian perspective, Paul wrote of this mystery in his second letter to the Corinthians where he encouraged them, 'So we do not lose heart. Even though our outer nature is wasting away, our inner nature is being renewed day by day' (Bible, New Revised Standard Version 2, Corinthians 4:16). It would seem that these changes Paul was writing of relate especially to older people, where bodily decrements become more common, but at the same time, our 'inner nature' or the spiritual dimension may continue to grow and develop. It is through growing self-awareness that we may become more sensitised to our inner nature. Then, as we come to terms with living with more chronic diseases and disabilities, as well as the major losses of loved ones and threats to autonomy, we have the opportunity to focus more on the questions of our individual human identity; this occurs in the context of our relationship to family, to community and to the wider society. It is then that self-transcendence and, for some, transformation can more fully develop. The process of spiritual reminiscence supports and facilitates the finding of life meaning, and hence, transformation that explores matters of relationship and the discovery of hope.

Using narrative to map the spiritual dimension among older people – the original study

In my study (MacKinlay 1998), I used exploration of narrative to gain a greater understanding of the life experiences of independently living older people that in turn informed their spiritual wellbeing. I invited reflection from each of the participants in extensive interviews by having them take a broad perspective of their understanding of where they found meaning in life, their relationship with God and/or others, their hopes, joys and fears, and I invited them to explore their experiences of growing older. From the analysis of the stories recounted in these interviews I developed a model of spiritual themes that led on to a model of subsequent spiritual tasks of ageing (MacKinlay 2001, 2017). The model has since been tested with older people who are well, those who are frail and those who have a diagnosis of dementia. In each case, the model has proved valid (MacKinlay 2006, 2017; MacKinlay and Trevitt 2012, 2015a).

This year, I have again listened to stories of older people, this time, of the same age cohort (although not the same people) as my original studies, but 20 years on. My target audience this time was frail older people in residential care.

Responding to narrative

One of the very positive experiences for me as a researcher, and as nurse and pastoral practitioner, was the informal feedback from participants in that first study; many told me how good it felt to be able to tell their story. Further, some of those participants stayed in contact with me for the rest of their lives. It was as I sat listening that I discovered how privileged this role of speaking and listening to story was – for the speaker, to call forth their story and to be listened to, and for the listener, to be able to be part of the speaker's life, to be invited into the journey at this point in the person's life.

Listening to story

How we listen can make a difference as to what we hear and to how free the storyteller feels able to share. As I listened to the words of those who agreed to participate in my initial study, I became fascinated with how their stories unfolded. I found it a privilege to be the listener, and I realised that my listening was often being worked out in what could be best described as sacred space. These older people were telling their stories and coming to new senses of meaning that were being processed as they spoke, in light of their whole life journeys and experiences. There were instances of listening as the person suddenly had an 'Aha' moment, realising that they understood something about their story and therefore their life for the first time. Some of these people were coming to understand who they were, refining their sense of identity and their purpose in life; this included coming to a new sense of meaning that had not been apparent to them previously. For further exploration of the experience of finding meaning through the process of storytelling and being entrusted as a listener with hearing another's story, either within a group or individually, see Chapter 13 by Kate de Medeiros and Sara Stemen and Chapter 18 by Mary O'Brien Tyrrell.

I have become aware over the years since I did my first in-depth interviews that these older people were sharing important insights into their lives, and were processing meaning, sometimes even reframing the meaning of something from perhaps years back (MacKinlay 2017). I realised that those I listened to were at different places in their understanding of their lives and ranged from those who had a greater depth and sense of the spiritual in their lives, to those who had never thought about such matters at all. I began to understand the importance of being able to tell one's story to another human being, one on one, and of knowing that you were really being listened to and accepted with the unfolding of the story. I also became aware that some people seemed to have blockages that prevented them from examining their life story and its meaning, and in some instances, it seemed fear was holding the person back from exploring this potential journey of discovery and healing. At the same time, I realised how liberating it was for those who did share and who engaged in processing their life story. It seemed that the individual's story illuminated life's meaning and held an important key to both the identity of the person and their individual spiritual journey of searching for personal meaning and purpose in life.

It was certainly my experience that comparing the people I interviewed in 1988 who were living independently with people no longer able to live independently in 2006, and more recently, with frail older people in residential care interviewed in 2017, that the search for meaning seemed to become more central and more focused in later life, and with this came an increasing sense of the deeper things of life.

Developing a method for spiritual reminiscence

Taking the perspective of Erikson *et al.* (1986), it seemed that a developmental approach to ageing had merit for the work I intended to do. Erikson's eighth stage – integrity versus despair – with an outcome of wisdom, had the potential to situate my work in a fruitful place. (See also Chapter 16 by Shellman and McNeil for further discussion of Erikson's life stages.) It was important to identify the main differences between reminiscence and spiritual reminiscence. Reminiscence is usually remembering the events of the past; it may or may not have a deeper purpose. However, I use the term spiritual reminiscence in this chapter to mean an intentional process of finding meaning through the process of reminiscence. Spiritual reminiscence does not focus on a chronological history, rather it seeks to find answers to questions such as: Why did that happen? Why did I respond that way? How important was it? Can I bring closure to that happening? What did it (any event in my life) mean then and what does it mean now? For people of faith, spiritual reminiscence includes their story (including identity) and their story of faith. For people who do not hold a religious faith, the search for meaning is as important as it is for all human beings, and entering into the process of spiritual reminiscence may be of value for them too. These questions and reflections are often best addressed when the person is older and becoming more aware of the fabric of their life, as it lies behind them. Nevertheless, it does not focus on a dwelling in the past, rather the process aims to set the past in context and to bring peace now, in the present.

Taking a deliberate focus on meaning from my model of spiritual tasks and the process of ageing informed the way that narratives were explored and shared by the study participants when we began working with story and people who have dementia (MacKinlay and Trevitt 2012). In this work, we did not seek a chronological account of the person's life, unlike Haight's work on a structured life review approach as discussed by Shellman and McNeil in Chapter 16. Rather, we concentrated on the important and meaningful episodes and events of an individual's life that the person wished to share. It became apparent that this learning could be beneficial for people who were cognitively intact, when engaging in spiritual reminiscence. It may be that we tend to concentrate too much on facts and dates, rather than the meaning of our life experiences. The matters shared were both positive and negative memories and stories. The relationship between storyteller and story listener was an important one, with willingness to listen being a vital prerequisite for the story to unfold. Kenyon's words of the 'desire of the story listener calls forth the words of the storyteller' (Kenyon 2003, p.31) are apt.

Ways of engaging with narrative in a spiritual dimension

Spiritual reminiscence has at its heart story or narrative. Some older people have examined their lives and have a clear sense of self-identity and meaning, while others seem not to have really thought about it at all. For many older people, while the task becomes more focused and perhaps more urgent as a sense of time limits draws in, there remain many twists and turns still to be negotiated and resolved. It is here that the person is able to reflect on their life, connecting life experiences as reviewed and evolving into final meanings and discarding other memories perceived as not key to personal identity. It may not be until the very last that they will come to see the final meaning and purpose of their lives, if they come to realise final meaning at all in this life (Frankl 1984). For some people, this process has a long history, perhaps of years, often commencing in midlife and growing in importance as they perceive increasing frailty or perhaps loss through the death of or separation from loved ones.

What is important about story and growing older?

For those who follow the Abrahamic faiths, story lies at the core of faith. It connects with identity as individuals and as communities of faith, it informs daily lives and values and therefore can be said to shape the lives of believers. This remains, even in the face of societal changes in Western cultures of the 21st century, when so often the news and fake news seem instantly to shape worldviews that are constantly changing. But, perhaps, in the midst of rapid societal change, story remains as an anchor point to sustain and support us on our life journeys.

The fact that spiritual reminiscence may occur naturally, especially in people who are spiritually aware, is acknowledged and affirmed. However, in a secular world, many people have focused on the material and physical perspectives of life and have not lived lives of reflection and introspection. This may leave the person without the intellectual, emotional and spiritual resources needed to engage in this final life career, of discovering final or ultimate meaning. Simply telling a historical account of one's life does not necessarily reach into the deeper aspects of meaning and purpose, making it difficult for the person to come to a sense of their meaning in life.

The spiritual themes and tasks of ageing as a basis for a process of spiritual reminiscence

The model of spiritual tasks and process of ageing (MacKinlay 2001, 2017) outlines six spiritual tasks. The first four tasks are:

- self-transcendence or, according to Frankl (1984), self-forgetting
- the process of searching for meaning
- finding intimacy with God and/or others
- finding hope.

The remaining two spiritual tasks both influence and are influenced by these four tasks. Thus, at the core of our being are found the outcomes of our searches for meaning:

- the task (outcome) of finding ultimate or final meaning
- response to meaning and the outcome results in how we respond to all of life.

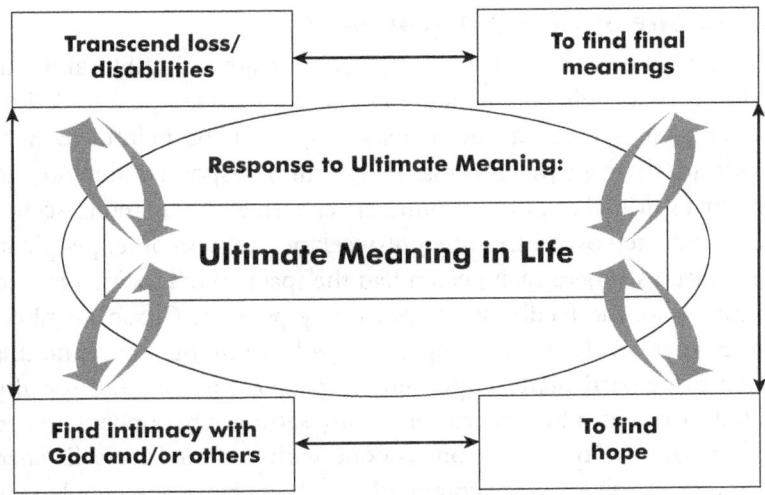

Figure 7.1: Spiritual tasks and process of ageing – a continuing process
The arrows in the model indicate the interactions between the tasks.
Reprinted from MacKinlay, E. (2017) Figure 5.3, p.116

Essential in this process is the search for final meanings. It has sometimes been said that human beings are meaning-makers, and in some respects, this is so, but rather I prefer the point made by Frankl (1984) that meaning is found, not manufactured. There is something deeply authentic in finding answers to the fundamental question of 'who am I?' and coming to see our purpose in life. It is not to be given to us by any other person but revealed in the process of our searching. Thus, in the model in Figure 7.1, which is reproduced with permission from MacKinlay (2017, p.116), based on my studies, there is a search for provisional meanings – the way we understand events in our lives at the time the event was experienced, and the subsequent processing of these provisional meanings to come to final meanings as we approach our own mortality, if indeed, we are able to reach this stage of understanding. This process is closely associated with our identity as a human being. It is indeed through coming to know who we are at the very depth of our being that we can at last come to fully self-transcend losses and disabilities, come to final intimacy with others and/or God and find hope. This process of finding final or ultimate meaning is processed through our own narrative; spiritual reminiscence is a valuable means of working through the process.

The process of spiritual reminiscence one on one or in small groups

There are numerous ways to reminisce that are enjoyable and can provide for satisfying activities, especially for older people. While spiritual reminiscence can occur naturally, it can be helpful to have a guide to share in the process. People may respond differently to individual spiritual or group reminiscence. In small group reminiscence work, conducted over a six- or eight-week period with older people in parish settings, where each person had the space to tell their story and be listened to, the feedback has been very positive. Group members reported that bonds of friendship developed within the group, and this seemed to be particularly important for people who had felt socially isolated. It can also be undertaken in any setting where people meet, in other community groups, one on one with a trusted story listener, and in residential aged care communities. Of course, some people may not be comfortable sharing in a group, no matter how supportive the group may be; these people may be much more secure sharing one on one with a trusted companion.

We have found that small groups work particularly well for people who have dementia. The process is the same; it's about finding meaning within one's life story. In our research with people who have dementia, we examined the use of art, music, language and pastoral care as means of supporting these people in finding meaning, with positive outcomes (MacKinlay 2011; MacKinlay and Trevitt 2015a; Byrne and MacKinlay 2012). (See Chapter 3 by Woods for a review of the literature about reminiscing with people with dementia both individually and in small groups, in community and residential contexts.)

The difficulties of another person telling the story

Each story is unique for that person. Their life experience, including social, education, cultural and religious faith, influences the composition of the story and the way in which the particular person sees life. Sometimes it may seem that the person is no longer able to tell their story, perhaps following a stroke, where speech becomes difficult, or in cases of advanced dementia. In these circumstances, a close family member may be called on to tell the story, but we must be very aware of the potential dangers of this. Telling the story for another person without their input produces a second-hand account of a life. Each one of us has a unique story that only we can tell if it is to have authenticity. Each person sees the story from their own perspective – even my sister and I recount the same event differently in some situations. This makes it important for people to come to understand their own story and the shape of their life while they are still able to articulate the story. In our work (MacKinlay and Trevitt 2012, 2015a) with people who have dementia, we have shown that it is still possible for these people to be able to tell their story at least into moderate dementia. However, loss of language makes this increasingly challenging as dementia progresses into the late stage. Some sense of the person always remains, but a supportive environment is vitally important to call forth the words of these people. The role of the story listener becomes even more crucial; it is a privilege and should not be undertaken lightly.

The process of finding meaning in later life

Essentially, the spiritual task of moving from understanding provisional meanings to finding final meanings (and an outcome of wisdom) is a process, while ultimate meanings is the outcome of this search, and the final meaning will be held at the core of one's being. It is the goal that one aims for (although often not consciously). It is what lies at the centre and is modified and informed by the other four tasks of relationship, finding meaning, transcendence and hope. Ultimate meaning is also what drives the response to meaning. The goal of coming to ultimate meaning is to arrive at a sense of peace and joy and acceptance, but not resignation. Resignation infers a giving up on life, but I see this process as an active, dynamic and continuing process until death.

As people age they are likely to become more introspective and more intentional in examining their lives but are also unlikely to have come to final meanings – there is still work to be done. It is in the fourth age of life that this task becomes more urgent and the process of searching for and finding meaning and the purpose of one's life takes on greater urgency for many. The finding of final meaning is the process that will, all being well, lead to finding ultimate life meaning. The answers to questions such as 'Why was I here?' may be asked with more urgency. Questions of forgiveness and reconciliation, of closure and coming to peace may be important at this stage. But this stage may not be completed by everyone.

Examples of spiritual reminiscence from narratives of older people and from small group work

While older people are more likely to engage in spiritual reminiscence than younger people, those in the third age of life are still often in the midst of 'doing' and the business of living, and may subsequently have less time for the processing of life's meaning. As well, during the third age, it seems that there is often a sense of having plenty of time for reflection in the future, but not today. In the first study I completed (MacKinlay 1998), the participants were certainly all still in the third age and vitally engaged in life. Finding final meaning in life remained a work in progress, with all of them focusing on remaining independent and autonomous human beings. As these older people reflected and shared their life story, all of them expressed fears and apprehensions about their future; largely these were fears of facing suffering or feeling they could no longer retain control of their lives. I have chosen the following example of spiritual reminiscence from a woman who had developed a deep spirituality but had no church affiliation throughout her life. Her changes in the spiritual dimension can be seen in her reflections on her earlier life and compared with her increasing introspection in recent years.

A journey of discovery in the third age

Mary,[2] divorced and a single parent, lived in a small rural community. When I met her, she was very socially engaged in the community, enjoying painting (I saw a number of lovely paintings she had done) and she also had recently learned to play the violin – a skill she was very willing to share with a local community group.

Mary remarked, 'There's more to life than this' [bringing up children] (MacKinlay 2017, p.328) as she reflected on how her life

---

2   Pseudonyms are used throughout. The story is drawn from the data published in MacKinlay (2001, 2017)

was opening up and the joy she found in life now. She had brought up five children largely by herself. Tragically, two of her adult sons had been killed in separate situations in recent years. She found meaning in life now with her family and in the wider community.

Mary had never had any contact with a church, yet she remembered her birth family living very 'religiously'. She remembered not being allowed to go to the pictures or do things other children did. She remembered her father reading the Bible to them at home. She had developed a deep spirituality in later life, tied mainly to her love of nature, expressions of creativity in her art and music and concern for other people.

Mary saw religion as the cause of wars, a view based on her childhood teaching but, at the same time, Mary also spoke of God as creator, 'Well there must have been a creator, I just know, now well, he'd have to take me and surprise me…the world really is a beautiful place' (MacKinlay 2017, p160).

She believed the religious teaching of her childhood kept her shy and reserved. Now, later in life, Mary seemed to have found a place of acceptance and peace. Mary said that a new beginning started for her, 'About 45 or so, I got back into things after being married and divorced' (MacKinlay 2017, p.218). In her experience, she did not connect spiritual things with church. She went on to say of the spiritual, 'I think that's in yourself, it's something that's in yourself'. She spoke of life as a journey, 'I've always felt that life is quite a trip you know, it's an experience and shouldn't just be wasted' (p.219).

Mary said behind her love of painting lay a love of nature. She liked to be with people, and, 'I like to think that even my painting gives people encouragement' (MacKinlay 2017, p.202). For this woman, there had been a midlife blossoming, a realisation of talents she did not know she had, and a new freedom to use them. These she had developed and used wisely, often for the benefit of others. This fits with Neugarten's (1968) and Jung's observations of changes in midlife (Sawin, Corbett and Carbine 2014).

Mary particularly feared dementia and physical disabilities: she felt that she 'wouldn't like to be off my legs or lose my mind' (MacKinlay 2017, p.243). This woman voiced her fears of possible happenings in the future. Her main regret was that she was always shy and didn't have confidence in herself until midlife. Now she liked to be with people. She saw things differently now. Asked what she thought had made a difference to her self-confidence, she replied that she thought it was when she had had a few paintings accepted. As for emotional and spiritual supports, she spoke of how she liked to help others. She was involved in community activities. It is also worth noting that she had breast cancer about eight years before the interview, and she reflected on how, since then, she had found herself reaching out more to others. Mary said:

> I'm just hoping to keep well and be able to keep on doing what I'm doing…and whatever comes afterwards well, I have to just, you know, because, I s'pose I'm as religious as most people are, in my way. (MacKinlay 2017, p.280)

This woman had never been part of a church-going family. She was involved in a wide range of community interests. As an older woman, she had developed a deep spirituality through life experience and reading. Mary's story shows the changes that may occur in mid to later life, and in her case, through tragic events in her earlier life. There is some evidence of self-transcendence and wisdom in her story at this stage. It would be expected that she may continue to re-process these provisional meanings in the light of her further life experiences as she grows still older.

Still journeying in the stage of frailty

However, on becoming older and frail, life becomes more precarious. Often things can no longer be planned with any degree of certainty, and the sense of autonomy that a person once had is seen for what it is – fleeting and lost. As a staff member speaking of the frail residents in an aged age care facility said:

> But what happens here is, you're old and you're in a nursing home, and if it gets tough, the best you can do is get back to where you were, or somewhere near it, but then the next thing is, you die. So, it's a different kind of experience…it can't be handled like past crises in life can, because they always come with a kind of an optimism, yeah, it's tough now but it'll get better, we can make it better, things always get better. (MacKinlay 2017, p.94)

The importance of finding meaning when it is no longer possible to live independently

In some respects, the real search for meaning does not become urgent until the fourth age of life. It is then that physical disabilities accumulate and reality about the ageing body must be acknowledged. The struggle to find meaning and transcendence was evident in the words of Judith, a participant in a study by MacKinlay (2017). She reflected on her ageing body and the multiple problems she was experiencing with increasing disability. She turned to her knowledge of scripture and in particular, the story of Job in the midst of his afflictions and Job's relationship with the Lord. It was from this that she drew strength in her current journey. In the excerpt below, she seems to have achieved a degree of transcendence evidenced by being able to move beyond what is happening in her body and, in the process, find humour as she speaks of the uncertainty of what will happen next:

> I never know what part of my body is going to go next, you know, and I think the Lord is sometimes testing me to see what [laughs] he can do to aggravate me. But anyway, I was only reading Job the other day [laughter], and I thought it didn't matter what the Lord did to Job, he accepted it, and all the people saying, 'denounce the Lord' and I think 'oh, Job knew better'. I know the Lord always comes to my side when I need it. But yeah, that's about all. A bit of tummy trouble and that, just generally old – the memory's getting a bit faint at times.

In each in-depth interview that I conduct, I always invite the person to talk about what is hardest for them now. The following elderly frail woman, Yvonne, seemed to have difficulty in self-transcendence:

> Interviewer: [what is] The hardest thing for you?

> Yvonne: The hardest thing for me now is being in the position I'm in with the sickness, I know that it's not going to get any better, which I accept, but to be honest I wish to goodness that I could just go like that, go to sleep and finish it because I'm fed up of being the way I am. I've never been, I've always been a hard worker and full of life but now, life it means nothing to me now, I've got nothing really. I mean I'll be in a nursing home for the rest of my life so that's not living, you know what I mean, with this breathing it means now that I can't go out because I've got to have oxygen all the time.

This participant was struggling with her physical condition and seemed not able to move beyond her immediate (and real) physical problems to be able to transcend them and find meaning. In such instances, it is apparent that a blockage to finding meaning and to being able to touch the deeper aspects of life prevents the person coming to a sense of final meaning, peace and joy. She was still very focused on 'doing' rather than 'being'; doing had been a way of life for her, and now she could not see past that. It is, as Erikson and colleagues (1986) wrote, that the eighth stage of psychosocial development was a stage of finding integrity rather than despair. The associated struggle may move either way. In the fourth age, of frailty, where this woman was, Erikson and Erikson (1997) identified a ninth stage of psychosocial development, somewhat aligned to Tornstam's (2005) gerotranscendence, where being rather than doing came to dominate the daily life, even if the individual was unprepared for this change.

The interactions between the spiritual tasks of ageing – the decrements of the ageing body versus being able to move beyond these towards self-transcendence, the continuing search for meaning, for finding relationship and finally hope – may become the focus for struggle (and achievement) in these final years. Spiritual reminiscence through applying the spiritual tasks of ageing can assist the person to come to a state of peace, joy and hope at the end of life (MacKinlay and Burns 2017).

In our work with people who had dementia, we found that small group participation worked more effectively when continued weekly for 18 or 24 weeks. It took much longer for these people to interact in the group and to develop relationships, but they achieved both when given time (MacKinlay and Trevitt 2012). This contrasted with the much shorter time required for cognitively intact people doing spiritual reminiscence.

Conclusion

Spiritual reminiscence can be a powerful process, undertaken either informally or with a spiritual guide, or as part of a group process, in assisting older people to come to an understanding of their life's meaning. In one sense, we live our lives seeking meaning at each and every part of our life journey, but much of this processing is done at an unconscious level, and we are often not aware of it happening at the time of the event. At other times, events move too quickly for us to be able fully to process their meaning. But it is not until we become cognisant of our own mortality that we may become really aware of the meaning of our lives. This may be devastating for some who see only loss, defeat and despair. For others, this may become a time of peace and joy even in the face of seeming disasters, as they are able to self-forget and see the deeper meaning of their life.

The process of spiritual reminiscence assists older people to find final or ultimate life meaning. The process is valuable for people with religious faith and for those who have no religious faith. The case examples in this chapter have been drawn from the research projects undertaken with cognitively intact older people, with in-depth interviews using spiritual reminiscence. But in other settings, small group work over a period of six to eight weeks has led to participants gaining a deeper understanding of their life journeys and life meaning. These groups have also supported continuing deeper friendships among some otherwise isolated older people. Our small group work with older people with dementia over a longer period has also been fruitful. Of course, some people are able to engage in their own spiritual reminiscence unassisted and to come to the knowledge and understanding of what their life finally means. There are many differences between human beings, and never more so than in later life. It has been a joy to work with these older people and to accompany them for a time on their spiritual journeys.

Chapter 8

THE LOSS OF A LOVED ONE
Remembering the Life and the Dying Days

Emily L. Mroz and Susan Bluck

The American sitcom *How I Met Your Mother* follows five friends living in New York City. The show explores their triumphs and failures, new experiences and old challenges, the beginnings and endings of lives. In one salient episode, one of the friends, Marshall, loses his father and becomes fixated on his dad's final words. He is distressed that his father's last words involved trivial advice about a silly movie he should see whereas his family members recall last moments involving professions of love or pride. Marshall's wife attempts to sooth him, saying, 'You have so many great memories of your dad. Who cares about the last one?' Marshall, however, is not consoled. Having a good ending to remember, he believes, would bring comfort as he goes on in life without his dad. This example demonstrates a sentiment found in literary and popular culture: memories from the dying days of a loved one, including final memories, are often given extra significance by those who remain.

Though individuals cherish a variety of memories from across the lives of their lost loved one, why might memories of the dying days hold special significance? In this chapter, we argue that such memories serve psychosocial functions for the bereaved (Bluck and Alea 2002). We begin by reviewing the role of reminiscence in processes that occur in the early period of bereavement (e.g. meaning reconstruction, personal growth). Long after this initial period of mourning is over, however, it is normative for memories of the lost loved one to drift to mind or be brought to mind intentionally (e.g. de Vries and Rutherford 2004; Marwit and Klass 1995). We address how memories of the loved one's life, including explicit memorializing (e.g. Schwab 2004), can help the bereaved maintain a healthy connection to the lost one over time. Finally, we speculate on the functions served particularly by recalling and sharing memories from a certain life period, the dying days. We argue that such memories may be unusually valued because they serve both self-continuity and social bonding functions (Bluck 2003). The chapter concludes by examining the implications of seeing memories of the dying days as serving important functions. That is, the environment (i.e. death in hospital, hospice, at home) may play a key role in what is remembered about those days. As such, the setting in which individuals die may be critical not only to a good death for the patient (e.g. Wright *et al.* 2010) but also for the wellbeing of their loved ones as they remember the deceased over time.

Scope

Three issues are clarified here before beginning. First, reminiscence can be public (i.e. sharing stories with others) or private (i.e. recalling events in one's own mind). Both occur regularly in daily life (e.g. Bluck and Levine 1998). This is also true following a loss: bereaved individuals commonly recall their loved one to themselves, and also reminisce with others (Neimeyer, Klass and Dennis 2014; Robinaugh and McNally 2013). As such, reference to memory or reminiscence in this chapter refers to both public and private forms. Second, the review is limited to situations that involve a lingering death trajectory as opposed to sudden, unexpected deaths that do not afford the opportunity for final moments or conversations. As such, use of the term dying days refers to the time before the death (i.e. months, weeks, days) when it is known that the loved one is terminally ill or dying. Finally, we use the term, the bereaved, to refer to any person who has lost a loved one (Genevro *et al.* 2004). The loss may have occurred recently or at any point in the individual's life. As such, he or she may not consider that they are actively grieving but are simply remembering a loved one who was once part of their life, and is no longer.

The role of memory in meaning reconstruction and personal growth

We all face the deaths of loved ones in our lives. We all carry loved ones with us in memory. Immediately following a loss, one needs to both emotionally comprehend the death and navigate the changes it brings to daily life (i.e. *dual model of coping with bereavement*, Stroebe and Schut 1999). Loss has historically been characterized as a negative life experience, for example melancholia (Freud 1917), and much of the current work on grief and loss also details how remembering the loved one can lead to maladaptive post-loss attachment (Neimeyer, Baldwin and Gillies 2006) or an inability to function due to depression or anxiety (Prigerson and Jacobs 2001). Though it is important to recognize that some individuals will face *complicated grief* (Prigerson *et al.* 1995) which may require clinical attention (Granek 2010), the loss of a loved one is best characterized not only as negative but also as a dynamic, multi-dimensional life event. This includes variation in the severity and length of grief responses (Wortman and Boerner 2011).

Though the loss of a loved one commonly comes with suffering, theoretical thinking about grief has expanded – it is no longer considered as something that people should 'recover from' (Tedeschi and Calhoun 2008). Instead, grieving is now considered an emotionally challenging activity (Baddeley 1988; Stroebe and Schut 2010) that can include learning from reviewing memories of the lost loved one. That is, remembering a lost loved one is sometimes painful but can also lead to beneficial outcomes over the initial grief period. Particularly we argue that memory, remembering the loved one, is central to both *meaning reconstruction* (Neimeyer 2001) and *post-traumatic growth* (Calhoun and Tedeschi 1998; Tedeschi and Calhoun 2004).

Meaning reconstruction

When a loved one dies, the overwhelming finality of their death can challenge one's internalized representation of the deceased (Shear and Shair 2005) and one's worldview more generally (Moules 1998). This may require reconstruction of basic psychological meaning structures. The majority of individuals appear to navigate loss well over time (Bonanno 2004), using memories of lived experiences with the deceased not only as painful reminders, but also to provide solace. When bereaved individuals first face the reality of a loss, they often recall, review and reconstruct personally significant memories of experiences with their lost loved one. *Integrative reminiscence* (Wong and Watt 1991) following a loss can include re-telling of stories and memories to make new meanings of past experience. Recalling and sharing memories can help individuals process and, in some ways benefit from the loss experience (Baddeley and Singer 2009). As such, meaning reconstruction involves the use of memory to come to terms with how the loss unfolded and the larger implications that the loss holds for the one who carries on (Janoff-Bulman and McPherson 1997).

Humans are keen to tell the stories of their lives, creating narratives of life's events that can be shared and compared – in part to forge meaning (Reker, Birren and Svensson 2012). Individuals do this throughout life including to forge meaningful narratives in the face of loss (e.g. Dennis 2008). Ultimately, the use of memory, the retelling of stories, and reminiscing with others can result in reconstruction of meaning that allows the bereaved some comfort (Gillies and Neimeyer 2006). This can occur in at least two specific ways, namely *sensemaking* and *benefit-finding* (Davis, Nolen-Hoeksema and Larson 1998). Sense-making involves recalling information about the deceased's life in a way that helps explain why the loss had to happen and why it unfolded as it did. This may include, for example, spiritual validation (e.g. recalling the deceased's devotion to religion across their life and thereby feeling that they were ready to transition to an afterlife) or assignment of responsibility for the death (e.g. recalling the rich, full life that the lost loved one lived, with old age as an explanation for their death). In contrast to sense-making, benefit-finding includes reviewing of the lost one's life and death that results in positive insight for the one who remains, for example understanding that the loved one is no longer suffering. Such benefit-finding is common when loss occurs, and even more so when facing other difficult life events (Mackay and Bluck 2010). In sum, individuals use memory to reconstruct meaning after loss, attempting to create stories about their experience to fit with the worldview they held before the loss, or to re-forge a positive worldview (Balk 1997).

Personal growth

Adverse life events such as the loss of a loved one can also lead to personal growth. We suggest that memory plays a central role in this process. Growth refers to positive self-development, including the ability to identify lessons or perceive life progress. This can occur, partially, through recalling and reviewing even the distressing loss of a loved one (Tedeschi and Calhoun 1996; Tedeschi and Calhoun 2004).

As such, bereavement is one example of an opportunity for *post-traumatic growth* (Gillies and Neimeyer 2006). Note that while this term includes the word trauma, the construct refers to growth occurring in the wake of any significant, difficult life event and not only a traumatic or violent death. This construct includes coming to terms with a loss by focusing on how one has grown through sharing life with the lost one, or through experiencing their death. As such, the occurrence of post-traumatic growth following the loss of a loved one fits closely with Tedeschi and Calhoun's (2008) delineation of bereavement as a period of resolution that includes holding the deceased in memory as opposed to 'recovery from grief', which implies an illness and a cure.

Personal growth is typically experienced within the first few months after loss, as a person reflects on their relationship with the deceased (Caserta *et al.* 2009). Individuals may experience growth in the form of feelings of increased strength and competency or improvements in social relationships. Growth outcomes related to loss (Calhoun and Tedeschi 1998) have been categorized as changes in perception of:

- the self, including becoming a better version of oneself
- social relationships, including feeling closeness with living family and friends, or with the lost loved one (Affleck *et al.* 1985)
- philosophy going forward, including increased appreciation for life.

In sum, the use of memory to reflect on the life or death of a lost loved one can provide a unique opportunity for personal growth.

Meaning-reconstruction and personal growth largely occur in the early period following the death of a loved one, often as part of accepting the loss (Gillies and Neimeyer 2006). We have argued that autobiographical memory and reminiscence play a role in these processes. The important role of memory, however, also extends well past the initial period of grief. As time goes on, individuals strive to maintain an ongoing connection with their loved one (Klass, Silverman and Nickman 1996) or to integrate the loved one's death into their own life story (Bluck and Mroz 2018). We suggest that they do that, in part, by remembering the life of the lost loved one over time, sometimes over a lifetime.

Remembering the lost loved one's life

Maintaining an enduring relationship with a lost loved one has been formally considered through the concept of *continuing bonds* (Klass et al. 1996). One aspect of continuing bonds is feeling a sense of calm through recalling memories of the deceased, as suggested, for example, by Currier *et al.* (2015). Exploration of how individuals maintain some kind of relationship with the deceased through memory, however, dates back more than a century (Shand 1920; Stroebe and Schut 2005). It has been studied across disciplines, indicating wide interest in the idea that the deceased can play ongoing social roles in individuals' lives (Sweeting and Gilhooly 1992).

In contrast to early theory suggesting that individuals should disengage from the deceased (for a review, see Wortman and Boerner 2011), research now suggests that it can be beneficial to maintain certain types of connection with a lost loved one, even long after they are gone. Such a connection is maintained most directly through remembering and reflecting on experiences shared (Boerner and Heckhausen 2003; Hagman 1995). As Buchsbaum (1996) writes, memories of the deceased are 'an essential bridge between the world with and the world without the loved person' (p.113). Indeed, verse or poetry at funerals and memorials – readings meant to comfort individuals and set them on a path to continue life without their loved one – include themes of how the lost one remains in memory. For example, one poem suggests: *Keep my memory with you, for memories never die. I will be there with you, when you look across the sky* (Allison Chambers Coxsey 1996, p.1). Christina Rossetti (1992) writes: *Remember me when I am gone away, Gone far away into the silent land.* These examples represent how, in society, the idea is widespread that memory is important in the face of loss: it can help us maintain a connection with those who have died, to not forget them, though we continue with our life.

Individuals' feelings regarding their ongoing connection with the deceased indicate the benefits of remembering the life shared with the loved one. Following a loss, individuals are sometimes fearful that they may forget the deceased (Kastenbaum 2015), again pointing to the importance individuals place on remembering those they have lost. Spontaneous reminiscence or *involuntary memory* (Berntsen 2008) about a lost loved one may occur in the day-to-day lives of the bereaved. When asked to identify the role, if any, the lost loved one played in their ongoing life (Marwit and Klass 1995), college students endorsed several positive ones. Remembering the deceased was seen to provide *a role model, situation-specific guidance,* or *values clarification.* Reminiscence about the lost one was also seen as generally useful for *remembrance formation* (i.e. retaining strong memories that elicit positive emotions). Thus, reminiscing about the times one shared with a lost loved one continues to occur and holds value for individuals long after the initial period of grief. Indeed, recalling the life shared with the deceased and incorporating them into our lives appears to be a healthy approach to facing the unavoidable reality of death (Bluck and Mroz 2018).

Though spontaneous or involuntary recall of cherished memories of the loved one does occur, so does directed, intentional remembering (Field *et al.* 1999). This includes engaging, over the long-term, in memorializing behaviors (Leming and Dickinson 2007). Memorializing can be seen as a type of strategic, voluntary remembering to honor the loved one but also to ensure a continuing connection with them (e.g. eating something that person loved on their birthday each year). Saving intimate objects such as jewellery, clothing or books is a common practice used to help the bereaved bring the loved one back to mind in day-to-day life. Technology now makes it easy to store digital 'heirlooms': artefacts of a lost loved one's life that can be accessed virtually to help individuals connect with memories of their loved one (van den Hoven, Sas and Whittaker 2012). The internet also allows for direct association with the deceased, through maintaining online social networking profiles of lost loved ones, or viewing specific memorial pages to review their life, maintaining a connection through text, pictures and stories (Degroot 2012; De Vries and Rutherford 2004).

Clinical psychologists have noted the possible benefits of exploring the life of the lost loved one through remembering them, using reflection on the shared past to create new feelings of connection after the loved one is gone. For example, sharing memories with others who knew the deceased may provide a chance to relive one's own memories but also to enhance one's sense of relationship with the deceased through hearing others' stories of them (Neimeyer 2001). Reviewing photographs that the deceased left behind may also bolster the sense of relationship (Attig 2000) by providing cues that provoke reflection on the lost loved one's life, beliefs and feelings. Indeed, contemporary sympathy cards reflect the societal view that we are comforted best by remembering our loved one, and by cherishing those memories. Sympathy cards often include reference to remembering the lost loved one's life. For example: *Always in our hearts, forever in our memory;*[1] *Death leaves a heartache no one can heal, love leaves a memory no one can steal;*[2] *Those we love can never be more than a thought away...for as long as there's a memory they live in our hearts to stay.*[3]

This individual and sociocultural propensity for remembering the life of lost loved ones have also been formalized in therapeutic techniques that involve the production of legacy documents that individuals can leave for their remaining loved ones to review. These records left by the deceased have the explicit goal of helping others to remember them once they are gone.

Records left by the deceased

The practice of leaving a written record such as a life review, legacy document or memoir has grown in the last few decades (Gulotta *et al.* 2013; Hunter and Rowles 2005). This again suggests the importance placed on remembering and reminiscing about the life shared with the deceased. Reminiscence, particularly integrative reminiscence (Wong and Watt 1991) that includes re-evaluating past experiences, can promote mental health (Westerhof *et al.* 2010). This occurs partly through reflection leading to a greater understanding of life's purpose (Reker *et al.* 2012). Based on these findings, individuals working in the field of palliative care have created a therapeutic technique known as dignity therapy whereby dying individuals create legacy documents (Chochinov *et al.* 2002; Chochinov *et al.* 2005). The dying person speaks about the things in life that matter most, sharing events and experiences that they want remembered by the people closest to them, after they are gone. Recorded interview sessions are transcribed and streamlined, and edited for clarity and to bring out important life themes. After being reviewed by the dying person, these records are passed down to their close family or friends.

---

1   www.askideas.com
2   www.funeralresources.com
3   www.quoteambition.com

While dignity therapy was established relatively recently, other reminiscence techniques have long been used to create records that individuals can eventually pass on to loved ones (e.g. Allen *et al.* 2008; Birren and Deutchman 1991). For example, guided autobiography (Birren and Deutchman 1991) was crafted with one of its goals being to create an autobiographical record that could be utilized by family or friends to remember the life of their lost loved one. (See Chapter 6 by Kuo and Chapter 9 by Svensson and de Vries.) Other reminiscence activities were not necessarily created with this goal in mind, for example digital life story books (Westerhof 2017b), but could easily be used in the same manner. All of these reminiscence techniques result in records left by the deceased that can serve an explicit role in helping the bereaved remember the life of the lost loved one.

The use of memory to maintain some type of connection to the lost loved one has been demonstrated here through reference to empirical work as well as common societal practices such as sympathy cards and memorial readings and therapeutic techniques like dignity therapy or guided autobiography. All of that work is based on explicit or implicit assumptions that a person will find comfort, and potentially even growth, through remembering the life shared. When individuals die, however, remembering the shared life also includes remembering the final stage, the dying days. Research on memory of the dying days is sparse. We therefore speculate in the next section on how memories of the dying days may be particularly important and argue that they can serve adaptive psychosocial functions (Bluck and Alea 2009).

Remembering the dying days

Individuals recall emotional memories about the life shared with their loved one long after the initial grief period (Rubin 1984). This includes stories of the dying days. What function might these memories serve? We argue that positive memories of the dying days are recalled because they serve psychosocial functions in the current life of the bereaved. In particular, we discuss how memories of the dying days may help individuals maintain self-continuity and strengthen social bonds. This discussion of memory of the dying days includes remembering final visits, or conversations, with the deceased. If dying days do serve important psychosocial functions, we discuss how this has implications for the environments in which people die.

Cherished stories of the dying days

Remembering and sharing memories of the end of a loved one's life is considered helpful in American culture (Baddeley and Singer 2008), especially when memories from this time period encapsulate positive or significant themes. Indeed, an individual's story of how their loved one died is often used in grief therapy (Sedney, Baker and Gross 1994). Recall, however, continues well beyond the initial grief period. Widowed older women, for example, often recount stories about their husbands' dying, long after they have adjusted to the reality of the loss (van den Hoonaard 1999).

Memory researchers have focused little on this issue. Mackay and Bluck (2010), however, asked middle-aged and older adults (not currently grieving) to recall 'a specific memory about any death or dying-related experience' from any time in their life. Though they could talk about any aspect of the experience, individuals often shared a memory about a loved one's dying days. Though not specifically asked to talk about this period, 65 per cent of participants shared a memory that took place in the dying days, and 83 per cent of participants mentioned the dying days as a part of their memory narrative (Bluck 2017, personal communication). The narratives included themes of positive emotional connection with the lost loved one and other family and friends. Memories were recalled with detail, even years following the loss. One participant offered this memory:

> Many things in that last two weeks in the hospital have stuck with me…what also sticks in my memory is the help and support of my family… From my 13-year-old daughter who took my wife's part in a church play, to the friends she stayed with and my cousin who sat with me using his vacation time to do so.

When considering memories of the dying days, it needs to be acknowledged that there are different endings for each person: not everyone has a *good death* (Flaskerud 2017). Some endings may not be as easy as others. Beyond the nature of the death itself, the way that those who live on and remember it may also vary based on their own personality, relationship history and other factors. While the dying days may include tranquillity, peace and tender moments, this period of a lost loved one's life may also include turmoil, confusion and pain for both the dying individual and their loved ones.

For memories to serve adaptive functions over time, they must be either of positive moments or of difficult moments that were made positive through their meaning or poignancy (e.g. cherished memories). As such, in discussing the functions served by recalling the dying days, we refer to these sort of positive memories (Bennett and Vidal-Hall 2000). Constant recall of distressing or discomfiting memories of the dying days is likely to be maladaptive. As such, the environment in which individuals die may have critical implications for the ways in which the memories of the dying days may serve adaptive functions following a loss.

The functional perspective on autobiographical memory

The functional perspective on autobiographical memory suggests that recall of one's personal past is adaptive (Bruce 1989) and that memory (Bluck 2003) and reminiscence (Webster 1993) serve psychosocial functions in everyday life.[4] The flexible, constructive nature of autobiographical memory helps individuals to constantly update their knowledge in order to navigate daily life in an ever-changing world (Newman and Lindsay 2009). That is, memory provides a record of lived experience but also involves reconstruction, including personal interpretation (Ruth, Birren and Polkinghorne 1996) and meaning-making (Sedney *et al.* 1994). The nature of the memory system thus aids in the storage and recall of memories that can serve specific functions (Bluck, Alea and Demiray 2010).

Researchers denote several broad functions that autobiographical remembering serves (Bluck 2009; Bluck and Alea 2011). The self-function involves the use of memory to understand one's own identity

---

4   The functional perspective on autobiographical memory suggests that this memory system is adaptive; however, not all stored or recalled memories serve adaptive functions. Reminiscence for bitterness revival (Webster 1993), for example, is considered a maladaptive use of memory (Harris *et al.* 2014). Although the bereaved may sometimes engage in rumination or bitterness revival, the focus of the current chapter is on adaptive, functional use of memories of the lost loved one.

(Neisser 1988), including maintaining self-continuity over time (Bluck and Liao 2013) or enhancing one's view of self (Wilson and Ross 2000). The social function involves using memory to develop, maintain and deepen personal relationships (Alea and Bluck 2007; Neisser 1988). This perspective on memory is useful in understanding the importance of remembering the final days of life. Individuals recognize the importance of time spent with a dying loved one, even if those days are not necessarily happy, and cherish some memories long after the loved one has passed. For example, Freeman (2016) writes about his final days with his mother: 'I wouldn't call these times "good". But nor were they bad. They were just…times. All I could do, all any of us could do, was just take them in, be there with her, be present.'

Theoretical functions of remembering can be applied to how individuals recall and reflect on the dying days of a lost loved one. For example, Baddeley and Singer (2009) propose that memories of the lost loved one particularly serve self and social functions. We argue, this is likely to be true also of memories of the dying days; remembering this period may help maintain self-continuity and foster relationships with others as well as feelings of closeness to the lost loved one.

Self-continuity

In Western culture, identity formation and maintenance occur through creation of a *life story* (McAdams 2001). Significant life events, both positive and challenging, are coherently incorporated into a story of one's life. For some time, psychologists have agreed that memory plays a role in both identity formation (Erikson 1959) and growth (Jung 1933). Reminiscing about life can help build and maintain identity (Cappeliez, O'Rourke and Chaudhury 2005; Webster 1993). When a loved one dies, the bereaved may feel discontinuity in their life, a disruption to their own identity. They have lost a person who was a large part of their life story. As such, memories of the lost loved one may be recalled to re-forge a sense of continuity, to strengthen a sense of personal identity. Memories from the dying days may be crucial in making sense of the death in relation to the individual's own sense of self, following the loss (Davis *et al.* 1998). People sometimes share salient recollections about their loved one's death because such memories are closely connected to, and help to reify, their sense of self (Baddeley and Singer 2009; Neimeyer 2001; Walter 1996).

Discussing loss experiences in a supportive social environment allows not only for emotional recovery but also helps in reconstructing a stable sense of personal identity (Kübler-Ross and Kessler 2005). Individuals selectively share memories of their lost loved one. These memories are often generated in order to present a stable narrative that reinforces a sense of self (Walter 1996). The bereaved may try to validate their experience of the end of their lived relationship with a loved one by sharing memories that have unique or special emotional significance, particularly cherished and intimate memories from the dying days. Indeed, it may be beneficial to select these particular memories *because* they are connected to key values of the narrator (e.g. being loved by the lost loved one during provision of care, being able to please the loved one when visiting).

One bereaved individual from Mackay and Bluck's (2010) study reflected on their caregiving responsibilities during the terminal illness of their loved one: 'It was quickly established that I would be the caregiver 24/7... It was an honour and a gift. I kept her clean, comfortable and laughing at all times.' Memories from the end of a lost loved one's life thus allow the bereaved to connect back to their loved one, maintaining a sense of self by reliving the connection with a significant figure in their life story. Privately reminiscing or publicly sharing vivid, intimate memories of tender moments with a dying loved one may provide needed stability, serving a self-continuity function (Bluck and Liao 2013).

Social bonding

Recalling memories of the dying days may also serve a social-bonding function. Losing a loved one is a social experience (Walter 1996). Rarely do individuals navigate loss alone – they engage in social rituals and memorializing (Leming and Dickinson 2007), look to friends and family for emotional support, and rely on their connection with the lost loved one for comfort (Schwab 2004). Recalling the final days spent with a loved one may serve a social-bonding function in two ways. Autobiographical remembering has been shown to: a) enhance closeness with others (Alea and Bluck 2007) and b) help maintain intimacy with the lost loved one (Bennett and Vidal-Hall 2000; Webster 1993).[5]

Sharing significant personal memories from the dying days should enhance closeness between the listener and the teller. When difficult events occur as part of loss this can lead to increased self-disclosure, sharing intimate aspects of important memories with others. Such sharing provides an opportunity to further develop and enhance interpersonal relationships (Alea and Bluck 2007; Calhoun and Tedeschi 1998). For example, one study participant (Mackay and Bluck 2010) shared a symbolic experience from the dying days of her husband:

> He (the doctor) explained they needed to cut the ring off his swollen finger. I held the two pieces to the light and saw that it had been cut off exactly between our two names. To me it was a sign and I whispered to my husband 'It's okay, honey, you can let go now.'

Clearly, this memory would be a powerful one for this woman to share with her family and friends. Baddeley and Singer (2008) argue that closeness between the narrator and the listener (e.g. more acceptance, less social awkwardness, greater social support) occurs when individuals tell memories that include redemptive aspects, that is, when difficult situations are described as having led to an improved outcome or insight. As such, sharing memories of the dying days may lead to greater intimacy with others, particularly when the memory is constructed as a redemption story. While memories from other life periods are often shared widely with friends, family and even acquaintances, memories of the dying days may feel precious, even sacred. Such memories can be infused with deep meaning and may thus be shared more sparingly, though able to deepen intimacy with those who are already trusted, close others.

---

5 Immediately following the loss, individuals may share such memories to elicit empathy from others, another functional use of autobiographical memory (e.g. Bluck *et al.* 2013; Pillemer 1992). However, when considering the use of such memories over the life course of the bereaved, it is likely to be uncommon that eliciting empathy will be a primary goal of memory sharing once the immediate grieving period has passed. As such, we focus on the functions these memories may serve following the grieving period, when an individual has navigated the majority of their distress in response to the death of their loved one.

We have suggested that recalling and sharing memories of the dying days may bring us closer to others in our lives. Recall may also help to maintain the narrator's sense of closeness to the lost loved one. Retaining some sense of connection to a lost loved one over the course of one's life is considered normative (Klass *et al.* 1996). Memories from the time preceding the loss are particularly important for maintaining this valuable connection (Tedeschi and Calhoun 2008). Remembering positive, unique or meaningful experiences from the end of a loved one's life may help individuals grapple with sometimes shifting emotions and attitudes towards the deceased (Baddeley and Singer 2010). Taking time to remember and reminisce about specific memories of the lost loved one leads to greater mental health than enacting behaviors such as simply holding on to their possessions (Field *et al.* 1999). Final experiences with a lost loved one, often including themes of love or strength, may be particularly beneficial for maintaining continuing bonds. Memories from this time period that may hold particular emotional weight include final conversations one had with the loved one.

The dying days: remembering final conversations

Individuals recall stories of a loved one's death, including the time leading up to the death, the experience of the death itself, or the aftermath (Sedney *et al.* 1994). Final conversations may be salient from this period. Although end of life is a difficult time, both for the lost loved one and for the family, memories of final conversations are often treasured (Bennett and Vidal-Hall 2000). Such moments are thought about privately and sometimes shared, usually with close others.

As a culture, we tend to give final conversations and last words special importance, collecting them on websites[6] and even recording the last words of specific groups of people, such as inmates on death row.[7] Aside from these examples of 'famous last words,' the Marie Curie Foundation has collected memories of final conversations as part of its work with terminally ill patients and families in the UK. Its recent poll found that 83 per cent of adults who had lost a loved

---

6 For example, https://en.wikiquote.org/wiki/Last_words
7 www.goodbyewarden.com

one remembered their final conversation.[8] Such recollections were specific, even when they involved stories of deaths that had occurred many years before. Some individuals recounted final conversations of reconciliation while others recalled expressions of love. These two examples provide a sense of the importance of final conversations from their poll. The first tells of a lasting love:

> My fiancé Ian passed away almost 19 years ago…10 weeks before our son was born. He was in hospital at the end. His last words to me were 'I love you'. He didn't say those words to me very often, but I knew he loved me. I'll never get over losing him, but those last words have bought me so much comfort over the years.

The second example concerns an important chance for forgiveness and gratitude:

> Two days before she passed away I held her hands and had a lovely conversation with her during which I told her how sorry I was for all the wrong things I did. She looked in my eyes and said, 'You have nothing to apologize for. You have been a wonderful daughter. Leaving you behind is like leaving myself.' She said, 'Always look for something good in every situation, doesn't matter how bad – and it will help you to cope with whatever life throws at you.' The best thing she's ever told me as it really helps.

Overall, many of those who chose to share their memories told heart-warming stories with personal significance. Final words or conversations with lost loved ones often result in profound memories. Such memories may allow us to meaningfully mark an end to our lost loved one's life as part of our own life story (Bluck and Mroz 2018).

Implications: where we die

Every story unfolds in a given setting. 'All the world's a stage, and all the men and women merely players. They have their exits and their entrances' (Shakespeare 1623). We have argued that memories of an individual's exit from the stage, the dying days of a lost loved one, serve important psychosocial functions. Reflecting that, part of the construction of dignity therapy transcripts with a patient at the end

---

8 www.mariecurie.org.uk/blog/last-words/49569

of life involves making sure the legacy document is structured so as to include a meaningful ending to the story. Memories of the dying days are important to bereaved individuals as they incorporate the death into their own life story. We suggest that the end of a loved one's story – the memories the bereaved carry with them – depends in part on the 'setting of the stage' in which the loved one dies.

As an example of the importance of the setting of death, Bennett and Vidal-Hall (2000) found that wives whose husbands died at home remember their experiences during this time much more vividly than wives whose husbands died in hospital. This reflects current research citing dying at home as more favourable than dying in a hospital setting (Kinoshita *et al.* 2014). Indeed, terminally ill individuals rate dying at home as superior to dying in hospital both for maintaining their own happiness, and also for maintaining good relationships with their close loved ones. Though many people would prefer to die at home, however, the actual end-of-life environment for over half of terminally ill Americans is a hospital ward, or an intensive care unit (Gomes and Higginson 2008). Though modern medicine has made amazing strides and some hospitals provide exceptional care, the modern medicalized approach to end of life, traditional in the American healthcare system, places relatively low value on creating an environment that fosters positive memories for families and loved ones.

Those working in hospice and palliative care offer a fresh perspective. They are concerned with creating environments that facilitate positive social interaction and meaningful family involvement during the dying days (Parker-Oliver 2000). Such services also make it more feasible for individuals to die at home, respecting important patient wishes about how they wish to die (Steinhauser 2000). One participant from MacKay and Bluck's (2010) study notes the setting distinctly, when telling the story of the dying days of a loved one:

> I went to the house, held her hand, cried and talked to her. Knowing she was where she wanted to be to die, I can live with her memory and feel that we did something she wanted. If possible, people's wishes should be a reality.

Compared to one's familiar home, impersonal, unfamiliar hospital environments may not necessarily foster the formation of adaptive memories of a dying loved one. The disturbing reality of losing a loved one in a sterile, busy hospital setting is aggravated by the unfortunate reality that often doctors and hospital staff provide underwhelming psychosocial support for those who have just lost their loved one (Prigerson and Jacobs 2001). Earlier referral to hospice care, on understanding that a patient is dying, can result in a positive hospice transfer, with fewer markers of aggressive care and a more comfortable setting in which to die (Amano *et al.* 2015). If we take an ecological approach to the understanding of end of life, place of death may thus have strong implications for the likelihood that dying individuals have a good death (Kinoshita *et al.* 2014). We argue in addition that, due to the important functions that such memories continue to play after the death, the wellbeing of their loved ones is also affected by the memories that family and friends carry with them of the dying days.

Conclusion

Everyone eventually loses someone they love. While these losses can be painful, the trajectory that individuals take following a loss is not typically exclusively negative. Remembering the lost loved one is an essential aspect of meaning reconstruction and growth, particularly in the initial period following a loss. Across a lifetime, memories of the deceased can serve adaptive psychosocial functions. This includes recalling the life shared with the deceased, but also remembering the end of their story, the dying days. Reminiscing specifically about the dying days may help maintain and re-forge self-continuity for the one left behind. It may also help to create stronger social bonds with loved ones and maintain a sense of closeness with the one who has gone. As such, fostering peaceful, humane environments for the dying and their loved ones is an essential goal. Providing settings such as home, hospice or hospital palliative care units where meaningful, poignant, tender memories can be made will allow individuals to end their life story in a way that also brings comfort to those who live on.

Chapter 9

GUIDED AUTOBIOGRAPHY

Scope, Implementation and International Applications

Cheryl Svensson and Brian de Vries

Guided autobiography (GAB) is a method that helps people write their life stories – two pages at a time. In the 1970s, James E. Birren, a pioneer researcher and educator in the field of aging, created the guided autobiographical writing process. In his long and highly acclaimed career (J.E. Birren, 1918–2016), he changed from studying memory and age-related cognitive processes to developing and expanding the GAB method to reach thousands of people. He recognized the great potential in this method. Among his hundreds of publications and scientific contributions, Birren wrote three books on guided autobiography (Birren and Deutchman 1991; Birren *et al.* 1996; Birren and Cochran 2001) and numerous articles and book chapters, and conducted many research projects exploring the processes and effects of GAB (Birren and Svensson 2009; de Vries and Thornton 2018).

Introduction

Jim Birren literally stumbled on the power of writing and life stories in the early 1970s. He was teaching a class on the psychology of aging at the University of Hawaii while on a summer sabbatical from his post as founding dean of the University of Southern California (USC) Andrus Gerontology Center. While teaching the class, which included students of all ages and backgrounds, he became frustrated with the lack of enthusiasm and engagement of the students and with having to compete with sunny skies and the calling surf. In an attempt to encourage class interaction and involvement, he told the entire class to, 'Go home and write two pages on a branching point in your life;

a road taken versus the many alternatives open to you. Bring this with you tomorrow and be prepared to read it to the class.' The following day, the class gathered and began to share their two-page stories. Birren was amazed at the immediate change in the class. The students were enthusiastic and interacted and connected with each other across generations. Being the ever-questioning and empirical researcher that he was, Birren took this experience to heart, returned to USC and gathered graduate students to help him understand this experience and the basics of personal writing, autobiographies, small group processes and journal writing. At the same time, he engaged other graduate students and together they reviewed the primary themes of life as reflected in the life course and developmental literature. This became the framework for guided autobiography. He sought to recreate the ultimate success of that summer experience and he developed a syllabus and tested out this new life story writing process at the USC summer institute in the mid-1970s. Thus, a powerful new method for writing meaningful life stories was created, based on life themes and built on small group processes, and a new path and legacy for Jim Birren was initiated.

Below, we describe the scope of GAB – its content, process and outcomes – exploring its operation and reviewing what we, and others, have learned through its implementation and delivery and the research that has emerged in its support. We conclude with examples from our international colleagues of their experience using GAB in other countries, languages and settings. GAB is a legacy of Jim Birren that offers insights and provides opportunities for personal growth and a deeper awareness of the human life course, with its perils and potential.

Guided autobiography: content, process and outcome

Guided autobiography is a method of reminiscence and life review that teaches people how to write their own personal life stories, two pages at a time (on selected themes). It is conducted in a group setting wherein these brief stories are shared, using prescribed themes and processes. GAB has yielded very positive outcomes for individuals and groups (such as families) – and beyond – as reviewed below, organized by the content of the writings, the method of its implementation, and anticipated and experienced outcomes.

Content

GAB is built on what are believed to be core life themes that form the threads of life. Beginning with the major branching points in life as the first theme, the nine weekly life themes increase in depth or sensitivity. The themes in sequential order are: your family, the role of money in your life, your major life work or career, your health and body, your sexual identity, your experiences with and ideas about death and dying, your spiritual life and values, and the last theme, goals and aspirations.

Along with each theme there is a short introduction to the topic and a list of sensitizing questions. These questions are meant to prime or stimulate the memories of the GAB participant; the questions also serve to uncover any triggering events that may help participants decide what to write. As such, the review of life is not always done in a chronological fashion; rather it often happens that formerly unconscious events surface and become the focus of the two pages written on the theme. Subsequent themes may stimulate recall of previous events and experiences. Participants are encouraged to write as much as they wish but when it is time to read their story, only two pages will be shared in the class. This helps achieve a focus on salient issues and experiences; it also helps to manage time. All writing is done at home and the emphasis is always on 'capturing the story' rather than on grammar and critical writing skills.

Process

The GAB process is what makes this life review method so unique and powerful. A typical GAB workshop may consist of 20 participants meeting weekly; however, the large group is broken up into smaller groups of six to eight participants. It is within these small groups, which remain together for all the GAB sessions, where the life stories are read and shared. For the first hour of every GAB workshop, the large group meets together.

Each week, the facilitator introduces a new topic that sets the stage for the writing theme to be introduced that week (i.e. the writing assignment to be shared the following week). The facilitator leads a mini-lecture that lays the groundwork for the theme. At this time, there are often large group discussions and experiential exercises to engage all the participants and to prepare them for the theme. Towards the end of this period, the facilitator introduces the new theme and a more thematic-focused discussion ensues as the participants read over the sensitizing questions. Typically, one or more of the questions will resonate with the participants and 'prime' memories for them to jumpstart their writing. After the first hour, the larger group breaks up into the small groups where they read the stories they have written with only their small group members. It is in the small group where personal growth, interpersonal connection, and new perspectives typically occur.

Outcomes

There are five key components to GAB that make this a powerful and empowering writing method: life themes, priming questions, expressive writing, the small group process and confidentiality.

- *Life themes:* The themes Birren has chosen reflect universal guideposts that illuminate the journey through life. For example, everyone has 'branching points' that reflect opportunities and challenges that arise or have arisen and change the direction of one's life. Everyone has a family, whether the traditional nuclear family consisting of parents and child(ren), an adopted or foster family, or a chosen family – but every child was nurtured and supported (to varying degrees) through infancy to maturity. In a similar manner, every person has (or had) a life's work or career, whether raising a family or climbing the corporate ladder, that is a reflection of how they have spent their time and energy throughout life. Money is similarly a universal theme. People in all cultures use money in some form of exchange, whether currency or barter. In the American culture, the so-called hard-earned dollar is a basic value that often defines who and what we are. In contrast, shells are the money used for exchange in some parts of the Papua New Guinea culture. And so it is with all nine themes Birren has selected for GAB; they are universal and applicable to all people. It is believed, and it is our experience, that focusing on one theme at a time seems to make writing about one's entire life much easier. It's like completing a jigsaw puzzle one piece at a time.

- *Sensitizing questions:* A list of questions accompanies each theme and is meant to stimulate memories and to provide participants with a focus as they write their two-page story. The questions range from the general to the specific – from more superficial to more sensitive, deeper issues. Participants choose which question(s) they might respond to, or come up with their own if none seems applicable to their life situation. The decision concerning what to write is based on how deeply they may choose to explore their past and/or how comfortable they feel in sharing the story with the small group. Participants may ask themselves, 'Who am I writing this for?' We have found that many older adults have joined the GAB workshop on the urging of an adult child or grandchild to 'get your story written down before it is too late'. But as often happens, and typically by the second or third session, they decide and proclaim, 'I'm writing this for myself. It can be edited for the family later.'

- *Expressive writing:* Expressive writing happens when the participant allows the story to write itself. That is, when they are able to write what they believe needs to be written rather than what they think they should write. It is writing that is personal and emotional and both uncovers and reflects the meaning of the experience. James Pennebaker, of the University of Texas at Austin, first studied expressive writing and wellness in the 1980s with college students (Pennebaker and Beall 1986). The students were divided into two groups. The experimental group was asked to write for 20 minutes a day for four days on a traumatic event in their life, expressing their deepest emotions and feelings, while the control group was told to write unemotionally about a neutral topic for 20 minutes. Both groups were told to write with no regard for grammar or spelling. The results showed that the experimental group who had written about a traumatic event, even though it had been more difficult for them to write at the time, made fewer visits to the health center in the ensuing months compared with the control group. Subsequent studies have replicated this seminal work and have shown that writing about one's personal experiences has a number of beneficial effects, including enhanced immune function (Petrie *et al.* 1995) and even reduced health issues (Greenberg and Stone 1992). In GAB groups, the stories that emerge are from the heart, they are deeply felt and reflect significant events from the participants' past. Given this, participants may risk stepping in a pothole, as Birren described the situation when painful memories were uncovered and expressed. However, with the support and understanding of the group, the feedback and reinforcement gleaned from insights and new perspectives, the participant may emerge stronger and perhaps better able to cope with life. The writing expressed their deepest feelings and they could move forward.

- *Small group process:* Each week the participants join their small group of six to eight people to read the story they have each written. This process is a critical component of the GAB process; it deepens and intensifies the writing experience, as each person feels truly 'heard' by the group members. The group helps realize the full potential of expression. Camaraderie and connectedness grow as the stories are shared each week. Birren called this the 'developmental exchange' and it is this mutual sharing of significant, personal life events that reveals the important emotional depths of the life stories (Birren and Deutchman 1991; Thornton *et al.* 2011). It is not unusual in a GAB group to hear someone say, 'I've never told this to anyone before.' After each story is read, group members are free to share constructive comments with one another. Strengths may be pointed out that were not previously considered, and personal insights into ways of being in the world may be more deeply understood and help participants to grow in a truly transformational manner.

- *Confidentiality:* Trust and confidentiality are critical components to the success of any GAB workshop. Confidentiality is built into the process from the very first meeting when participants learn that for the duration of the GAB sessions, whatever is shared in the small group remains in the small group. The stories are not to be shared with anyone outside the small group without express permission from the storyteller. This sets the stage for trust and allows free expression to occur.

When GAB participants know their privacy is held in a safe place, confidence builds and deeper and deeper self-exploration – and personal growth – may occur.

Benefits

Personal

Through the weekly GAB meetings and writings, participants learn about themselves and others in deep and profound ways. To begin, reading through the sensitizing questions often uncovers memories long forgotten – or on which individuals have stumbled and struggled. The stories that emerge are not the stories readily told of the successes and accomplishments of life – in fact, these may be the stories that have never been told before. The stories often reflect personal discovery and understanding that may lead to personal growth. Jim Birren repeatedly said that GAB was not therapy but was very therapeutic. Participants don't come into a GAB workshop with a problem they need fixed. Rather it is through the process that they uncover insights into themselves, much like peeling the layers of an onion. For example, one participant wrote about the betrayal of her husband, whom she had worked to put through college, and their subsequent divorce. She was left alone to raise their two young sons. Each theme she wrote contained a reference to this event and she seemed unable to 'let go' even though it had occurred more than 30 years earlier. Then, after writing on spiritual life and values, she reported a breakthrough insight. She exclaimed, 'I just realized. There was nothing wrong with Bill. We never should have been married. We never shared the same values.' This participant, in her late 70s, was free to let go of the past and move on, and she began to travel alone, became a hospice volunteer, and developed a new relationship. The GAB group and the personal weekly writing had helped to set her free to move forward.

Similarly, the stories shared comprise the threads that create the tapestry of each person's full and colourful life. The life themes of GAB are not a chronological listing of life events; rather, they may document the emotions, issues and lessons that occurred with the life event. For instance, one participant related the story of growing up, the oldest of three, with a frail and sickly, single mother. They lived with her maternal grandparents. Her grandmother died when she was 15 and her mother died five days later, leaving her with a bereaved elderly grandfather and two younger siblings to support. The participant reflected on how these losses impacted her life. She wrote, and spoke, about where one turns when there is no one left to turn to. These are the typical stories that are written and shared in GAB groups. Writing the text for one's self is only half of the experience. The story, shared within the deep embrace of a small group of attentive listeners, completes the experience. Comments are exchanged after each story that reflect back to the writer, 'You've been heard, understood and valued.' Participants may grow into their true and full selves. One participant described this experience succinctly in comments to her GAB companions after sharing the stories on death, 'Just the sharing of these very personal experiences with death reflects for me a collective experience that transcends any physical differences that we may have, whether age, time, distance, ethnicity, faith, etc. Know that I feel a bond with each of you.'

Communities

We often live our lives in a hurry, rarely taking the time (or perhaps more accurately, making the time) to reflect on our lives and share them with others in our closest spheres, such as family members. However, it is through the stories of our lives that friend and family alike truly know us. Our stories connect people and generations. Whether it is an adult child, grandchild, other family member or friend, we may learn, understand and grow in affection for one another through our stories. A deeper understanding and appreciation for others happens when we know and understand the stories of their life. Generations may begin to understand one another. For example, an older grandparent becomes accessible to a grandchild when the child hears the stories of how they too struggled with school, were bullied, or rebelled against their parents. This understanding may deepen the affection between generations. This also happens in GAB groups that frequently have a wide range of ages. For example, in a USC college GAB class, the ages ranged from 20 to more than 80 years when for-credit students joined retired faculty and staff for a class. The older students became mentors who could relate their life stories of the Great Depression or the early, more sexist academic environment of their careers and what they did to survive and excel. They personalized these experiences in a way that made the historical event come alive. The understanding was reciprocal. The older adults began to see and understand today's youth in a very real and profound manner. They were no longer perceived as privileged and entitled children attending an expensive university, for example; rather, they became full and multi-dimensional as they learned that many of the students were carrying enormous student debt into a very uncertain future. Where would the students find a job when they graduated and how could they pay back their student loan? It is not difficult to imagine that the intergenerational understanding helped each of them understand and cope in their own family and other multi-generational situations in a much fuller and compassionate way.

Duke, Lazarus and Fivush (2008) have completed ground-breaking research into the importance of knowing one's family history and the wellbeing of children. They studied the correlation between what children know about their own personal family history and their coping and behavioral skills. They developed a 20-question measure titled, Do You Know? for the research project. The questions reflect family events and history that the children could only know from another source, such as a story told to them or a written record of the event. They were simple questions: Do you know how your parents met? Do you know where your father grew up? Do you know the names of the schools your mother went to? This is information the child could only have learned from another family member. The findings were remarkable.

Children who knew more about their family history had higher self-esteem, internal locus of control, less anxiety, better family functioning and fewer behavioral problems. It is not just the knowing of the family history or the content, but the process and how the children acquired the information that is important. They learned that mothers and grandmothers were usually the ones to pass on family information and typically during meals and vacations and at other times the family gathered together. In our highly technological society, with even young children computer savvy and with smartphones and similar devices, it is easy to see how a grandparent's story could be read and shared with young family members. What better motivation for grandparents to write their life story than to know that they are helping their grandchildren, and even great-great-grandchildren they will never meet, to become better adjusted and resilient and more able to cope with the slings and arrows of life?

Society

An African proverb tells us that when an old person dies, a library burns to the ground (Amadou Hampaté Ba 2017) – such is the depth and prominence of life stories. Jim Birren called GAB stories, 'bottoms-up' history. The stories written and shared in GAB workshops are the personal experiences of ordinary people. They express the insights and emotions of having been there and having participated in the event. This contrasts with stories written by a third party or authority figure, or 'top-down' history. In this case, the information is uncovered and often pieced together from historical records of the event, but the writer was not there. An example would be authors who write about the Second World War but were not involved in it in any direct way. The bottoms-up stories are rich in emotion, recollections and the abundant nuances available only to those who have been a participant. These are the first-person stories that need to be written or told and archived so that future generations will understand what it was like, in the 1900s, to write and receive a letter and mail it with a postage stamp; or the soon forgotten stories of ice men delivering the block of ice for the icebox and milkmen delivering bottles of milk to the doorstep. Participants in GAB workshops, as well as other life story-writing classes, write these personal, informative stories. The importance of this writing goes far beyond just the family and extends to all biographers and historians who require these written records for their work. Personal stories show how life was lived in a different era.

Research

Research into GAB is still in its infancy, although growing significantly given the interest in this method. In the section below, empirical research is reviewed and organized around the dimensions introduced above: content of GAB stories, the GAB process and its effects (i.e. outcomes). de Vries and Thornton (2018) reviewed empirical research, organizing their appraisal in terms of these same dimensions. What appears below summarizes much of the same literature but also draws on a broader research base, including conference presentations and student theses.

Content

The nine themes typically addressed by GAB have been described above. It is worthy of note that these themes were established through an intensive review of the literature (on the primary themes of life as reflected in, largely, the empirical literature of developmental psychology and gerontology); they were adapted through repeated administrations of GAB leading to the creation of the sensitizing questions. Ruth *et al.* (1996) took a macro perspective on the themes to uncover the overarching constructs governing what participants wrote in their sample of ten female and ten male participants. Describing these constructs in the terms of life projects, they found five overarching dimensions: achieving (and accomplishments); being social (e.g. engagement in life with others); loving (and being loved); family life (and intergenerational connections); and struggling (and often overcoming). These findings add support for the themes adopted in GAB through highlighting the underlying constructs or dimensions (defined as projects in this case) by which they are governed.

Alternatively, de Vries, Bluck and Birren (1993) adopted a more micro perspective, examining the specific ways in which participants addressed a single theme – in this case, the theme of death and dying – in the writings of 54 women and men. Using content analytic measures, reliably applied, they found that GAB participants wrote on this theme in ways that reflected high personal involvement and impact and with moderate complexity. These results suggest that participants are significantly engaged in the activity. Interestingly, 'death' was more frequently referenced than 'dying' – with implications for both GAB and life course literature more generally. This data suggests that, to varying degrees, the existential and philosophical issues of life's end dominate our thoughts and concerns across the life course. These are the 'Who am I' questions so well addressed by GAB.

Process

Birren and Svensson (2009) have been among the few to directly examine the GAB process. Using a pre-test-post-test design, they asked participants to evaluate the usefulness of particular dimensions of the GAB process. Significant increases were found on active participation in the group discussions (both in the large and small groups), the writing and reading of the weekly stories, the facilitation of the small group, and the focus on one topic per meeting. In addition, the value of listening to the stories of others was significant. That is, participants experienced these dimensions as more useful to their GAB experience than they had anticipated.

Vota and de Vries (2001) also examined the GAB process but with a virtual, online implementation. Following some initial disagreement with the structure and between a couple of participants, the small group of all female participants ultimately expressed great satisfaction with the process and in the cohesive group that was established. They enjoyed (as did the participants in the Birren and Svensson in-person study above) their online version of small group discussions (posting comments, in this version). However, the participants felt constrained by the one theme per week assignment (in contrast to the in-person group participants above). Perhaps this difference was wrought by the uniqueness of this online process and those drawn to this virtual version.

Thornton (2008) and Thornton and Collins (2010) have conducted probably the most extensive exploration into the educational process of GAB. With a sample of 88 women and 26 men with an average age of 62 (a typical average for GAB groups), they examined learning scripts ('What am I learning in the guided autobiography workshop?'). Neither age nor gender contributed any significant effects – an interesting and typical pattern with findings related to GAB. Participants frequently mentioned their experiences of learning throughout GAB – learning about the process and about others. To an even greater degree, however, participants spoke about learning about themselves – as is often heard from participants (and as is noted above). They spoke of new interpretations, understandings and frameworks for considering the self and recognition of both the many and varied aspects that comprise the self and efforts to integrate these aspects and establish a coherent life story.

This integration is a common theme of several smaller studies into the GAB experience – bridging process and outcome. Reedy and Birren (1980) were the first to describe this. They asked participants to complete standardized instruments three times, each with a different referent: their real selves, their ideal selves, and their social selves. The results showed that over the course of the GAB sessions, participants' views of these different selves moved closer together – a type of integration, as suggested above. A related finding was that participants' view of others moved closer to these integrated selves; that is, there was less distance between the participants' self-ratings and their ratings of others. They began to see other people as more like themselves. Similar findings have been reported by Schroots and van Dongen (1995) and Reker, Birren and Svensson (2014).

Reker *et al.* (2014) also reported evocative age differences, mostly as interactions with time of testing and measurement. In particular, they found greater change from pre-test to post-test among older adults (those over 50), relative to younger adults (i.e. ages 19 to 50), on actual/ideal self and actual/social self-image. They interpreted these effects as evidence of the appropriateness of GAB, or perhaps life review in general, in the later years.

In summary, GAB is an integrative process, coalescing self-perceptions and bringing the view of others closer to the view of the self. Participants recognize these processes and their utility, although there may be individual, age or implementation differences in such appraisals. Participants often recognize the ways in which they have changed over the course of their participation in the GAB, as reviewed below.

Outcomes

Jim Birren and many others have long recognized the power of GAB to promote positive individual change and wellbeing. Birren and Svensson (2009) have identified many of the changes informally observed through numerous GAB courses. As described above, these benefits range from the tangible (such as a written legacy of their lives, as told in the pages of text prepared for each of the themes) to many intangible psychological and social benefits. These include a renewed or expanded self-understanding, a sense of resilience, courage and personal confidence (in having overcome the stressors and hardships described in their thematic essays), and connection to others at a profound level having shared personal stories, secrets, hopes and fears. Individuals have reported feeling less alone; the skeletons in their closets are not as scary or unique as they initially felt, with a greater acceptance of both self and others. The documentation of these outcomes has been somewhat more complex.

Fagerstrom (2002) studied the effects of participation in two settings (a GAB group versus a walking group) on older adults' psychological wellbeing, using a pre-test-post-test design. Setting 1 consisted of a ten-week GAB group held in a university extension class. Setting 2 consisted of a five-week GAB group and a control walking group. Using Ryff's Personal Well Being scale (1989), significant increases occurred pre-test and post-test scores in Setting 1 in personal growth. In Setting 2, participation in GAB resulted in significant increases in personal growth and positive relations with others relative to the walking group. These findings support previous research that indicates the benefits of GAB with older adults.

In Reedy and Birren's (1980) study comparing participants before and after GAB engagement, significant differences were found, echoing the outcomes informally observed by others. In particular, participants reported increased self-acceptance and energy or vigor for life, more positive views of others and greater connectedness, as well as decreased anxiety and tension. Using a format structurally analogous to GAB, Bohlmeijer *et al.* (2005) found significant decreases in depression and increases in mastery. Malde (1988) compared different GAB groups (traditional GAB, modified GAB, waitlist control) and found no group differences on the three dependent measures of self-concept, time competence and purpose in life. Several methodological interpretations were offered for the lack of difference, including sample size and measure sensitivity. Malde (1988) reported a follow-up with a subset of these participants and reported that changes in the sense of self may be more apparent over time as participants integrate the knowledge and experiences taken from participation in GAB.

Further challenges in charting and understanding the effects of GAB participation have been identified by Westwood and colleagues (Brown-Shaw, Westwood and de Vries 1999; Kuhl and Westwood 2001). Brown-Shaw *et al.* (1999) have commented that GAB has significant therapeutic potential, but also suggest some limitations in this context. They suggest, for example, that in GAB, and more generally the review of one's life, critical life events may be identified and possibly resolved (e.g. over time or in the retelling, as in the previous account of the participant's betrayal and subsequent divorce) but may also remain open – along with their potency and impact. For Westwood and others, in such instances GAB may serve a diagnostic function, setting the stage, in some ways, for further intervention and reparation. They describe one such intervention, group-based enactment, wherein GAB participants (or others) re-enact the distressing event, under the skilled direction of a therapist. The story is enacted along the lines of the original script, interrupted for discussion and clarification; the story or event is ultimately resolved, often through acting out what might have been, in an extension of the original script. New interpretations and integration may emerge – for both the storyteller and those in supporting roles; as de Vries and Thornton (2018) have described, 'this approach moves the natural and therapeutic aspects of GAB into an active therapy intervention' (p.14). Notwithstanding its emergent nature, research on GAB content, process and outcome reinforces and provides direction for both the practice of GAB as well as future research. Such research could include optimal circumstances for the administration of GAB and further inquiry into its effectiveness with regard to some of the myriad other approaches to life review.

Guided autobiography: multi-cultural and multi-dimensional

Gender, sexual orientation, race, ethnicity, culture, income, education, language or any of the number of ways we identify and define ourselves do not preclude participation in GAB. Jim Birren evaluated and chose the nine life themes based on their universality and applicability to all people; for example, he offered GAB workshops in Singapore, Brazil and Japan. The process can be adapted to fit specific populations and venues. Since 2009, GAB instructor training classes have been offered in eight, weekly, live, interactive online classes by the Birren Center for Autobiographical Studies (2017). Thus far, more than 350 GAB facilitators have been trained worldwide, including facilitators from Greece, France, Germany, Taiwan, Korea, Australia, New Zealand as well as across the US and Canada. Each GAB facilitator is encouraged to adapt GAB to fit their participants' needs, culture and language. For instance, the questions and exercises have been translated into other languages, the exercises and writing have been adjusted to fit participants with little literacy, and questions and themes have been changed for specific purposes, such as a spiritual GAB class. The following are examples of how GAB has been adapted around the world.

In Taiwan, Professor TsuAnn Kuo (see Chapter 6 in this book) has offered a number of GAB classes with a variety of participants. She not only translated the questions and exercises into Mandarin but also adapted the process to work with older Taiwanese adults who could not read or write proficiently. Exercises were devised involving collage, sculpture and drawing that enabled the participants to create their life story in a novel and creative format. In addition, GAB classes were offered that combined older Taiwanese adults and younger students. Deep and emotional bonding occurred when the participants were able to better understand their own families based on the stories the older adults shared in the GAB class.

In Freiburg, Germany, Orth, a historian, and Wetzstein (2016) translated and adapted GAB to fit the needs of older people who were children during the Second World War. When the group first started, they were hesitant to write and only wanted to talk about their childhood during the war. As the group continued to meet they became more open, trusting and willing to participate and write about their experiences. The participants all shared a common understanding, background and bond with each other through their Second World War experiences. Their stories were subsequently published in a book called, *Kinder im Zweiten Weltkrieg–Spuren ins Heute* or *Children During World War II: Traces from the Past in the Present*.

Leoni Thanasoula has translated the GAB material into Greek and offered workshops at the Katakouzenos Museum in Athens. This particular museum was chosen because it had been the residence of Angelos and Leto Katakouzenos, a well-known Greek couple and patrons of the arts. It is now a salon for artists and intellectuals, narrating a part of the history of modern Greece. The GAB material was enriched with references to Greek authors and the history of autobiography from antiquity to the present. After the workshop, one participant mentioned that they were now connected – part of a team.

Jinsoo Jason Kim has incorporated guided autobiography into his doctoral dissertation with elderly Korean immigrants: 'Spiritual Development Through a Guided Autobiography Group Among Elderly Korean American Immigrants' (2008). In the course of his research, he studied the theories underlying guided autobiography and then designed a method to use GAB with elderly Korean American immigrants to understand the spiritualty of their immigration through writing on GAB themes. He concluded that the Korean immigrants grew spiritually through the GAB process.

Katie Tran, a young Vietnamese GAB instructor, has brought the workshops to the Vietnamese community in southern California and in doing so, changed GAB to fit the special needs of this population. It was determined, for example, that many of the questions and exercises were not culturally appropriate and needed to be changed; Vietnamese heroes replaced American historical figures. Also, it became clear that many Vietnamese are reticent to talk openly on all matters of life, particularly men, who often seemed to stop themselves before they became too emotional. Therefore, some themes were changed, as was the order of presentation. For instance, the end of the Vietnam War in 1975 was a turning point for all of them (the biggest turning point for many) and something they all shared in common – and something they seemed to yearn to discuss. This became the final writing theme in the workshop. Writing and sharing their experiences with the group helped them to feel proud of their resilience and survival. Facilitators in GAB groups often learn as much as the participants; Tran reported coming to understand the sadness that resides in the older Vietnamese community in the US in ways that she had not previously understood.

In addition to using GAB material translated into other languages, GAB workshops have also been offered in a variety of venues. Ana Rita Melo, in Portugal, has translated the material into Portuguese and offered the workshop in a yoga studio; the participants were all women in their early 40s. GAB has been helpful in working with female inmates incarcerated in a local county jail in Indiana. Women found writing in response to the weekly themes to be cathartic, and it enabled them to reflect on where they had been and where they wanted to go. At the end of the eight-week workshop, each participant received a published booklet of the writings submitted by the writers. Their sense of pride and accomplishment was very rewarding for the GAB facilitator. The possibilities for venues and participants for GAB workshops are endless.

Conclusion

We live our lives through our stories; our lives are as much biographical as they are biological (Birren *et al.* 1996). Perhaps that is part of what makes it so devastating when dementia and memory loss occur: we've lost our stories, and hence our lives. There are many ways to record life stories: memoir writing classes, personal historians, videographers, how-to-write-your-life-story books and more. Of all these methods, it is GAB alone that takes the participant on a guided and thematic journey of their life, accompanied by the support of other, like-minded writing partners. Whatever method a person chooses, life stories have something to offer individuals, their communities (in multiple forms) and society more generally.

Personal stories

Write your story for yourself. Every life has value. Everyone deserves to have their life remembered as more than an old, faded photograph with a name scrawled on the back, or a digital photo with only a date and place stamped on it. Writing your life story provides both a better understanding and acceptance of the past and a sense of direction for the future. In her book, *The Power of Meaning* (2017), Emily Esfahani Smith states 'happiness' is not the goal that satisfies and fulfills our lives, rather it is 'meaning in life'. According to Smith, the three components for a meaningful life are: belief that your life matters, a sense of purpose to move forward, and that your life is coherent and makes sense. Writing your life story gives meaning, it provides the understanding and clarity to see your life as lived, the opportunity to retell your story and perhaps move forward with a new (or revised) story.

Community stories

Write your story for your community – your family, those who are present in your life now and for the generations yet to come. This is not a self-centred, egotistical undertaking to show the world how great you were (as so many people fear and state when first hearing about life review and GAB). Rather, it is a way to leave your legacy for future generations, to help them learn and grow by understanding their family history. We live in an ever-changing, highly technical and seemingly disposable society. Your story can provide a solid base for your great-great-great grandchildren to know that the 'Smiths' stand for strength, integrity and determination. They will know that their great-great grandfather emigrated from Germany to America (for example), attended seminary in Minnesota, became a pastor and travelled by horseback on a preaching circuit in rural outposts to deliver the word of God. Your story will connect you with your current family in profound and meaningful ways. You will become more than the role of father, grandfather, uncle. Similarly, your story could be read by younger gay men or lesbians (for example) who can learn of the struggles you have experienced and survived, leading to their current acceptance and freedoms, or less positive circumstances – the spirit of the 'It Gets Better' campaign.[1] Through your stories, others may understand you more fully – your weaknesses, strengths, hopes, and fears – and you will connect with them. Write your story for your community.

Societal stories

Write your story for your society. Leave a written record of, 'I was here, and my life counted.' Historians and archaeologists search ancient tombs and hieroglyphic writings to understand the times of the Pharaohs. They uncovered the Dead Sea Scrolls and learned the lessons and history of the past. As distant as it may seem, the stories you write today about your life as a war veteran or a single-working mother or as someone who is marginalized in some way will provide a fuller picture and better understanding of life and times in the 20th and 21st centuries. Some struggles are time specific; some seem eternal. Write truthfully and honestly with a recorder's eye to include the details that make your story come alive in time and place. Ursula Le Guin said: 'There have been great societies that did not use the wheel, but there have been no societies that did not tell stories' (Le Guin 2017).

The value of GAB

Guided autobiography rests on a solid foundation of research and testimonials to secure a place of honour and respect among life story writing methods. For more than 40 years it has proven time and again to provide the space and support for people to write their own

---

1   https://itgetsbetter.org

story, to learn about themselves and teach others. Jean Stumpf, a GAB facilitator, wrote:

> The value GAB offers is amazing. It has been magical for me to reframe some of my own 'broken records'. For me, it has been a therapeutic and emotional experience. This transformation or reframing of the story-that-kept-me-stuck had to be experienced. I could not 'think' myself there. I allowed my writing to go places I did not know. Words to describe this seem inadequate. I hope I can create a space for others to tell, and retell, their stories.

There are myriad reasons for reviewing our lives and writing our stories. GAB is a process amenable and responsive to these many reasons: it has a logical and rational history, with organic origins stemming from interpersonal interactions; it has a well-considered, practical and emerging empirical foundation on which to base decisions for use; it is adaptable to other cultures, languages and settings. Guided autobiography has depth, breadth and reach that are integral to its appeal and success.

Chapter 10

REMINISCENCE, NARRATIVE AND THE PRESENCE OF MEANING IN LIFE

Jeffrey Dean Webster

Remembering our personal past, or reminiscence, is a fundamental process which affects many psychosocial outcomes. Autobiographical retrieval serves many functions (Webster *et al.* 2010) and enables us to consolidate our sense of self, interact with others with respect to shared prior experiences, and learn from earlier life mistakes and accomplishments. Moreover, organizing discrete reminiscences within personal narratives in particular ways may allow us to discover a sense of purpose and meaning in the myriad twists and turns of our life story. This suggests that reminiscence, narrative structure and meaning-making are interrelated processes, the investigation of which constitutes the major rationale for the current study.

Readers of this volume will be aware of the myriad ways in which reminiscence has been linked with psychological wellbeing (for reviews see Webster *et al.* 2010), including decreased anxiety and depression levels, and increased levels of adaptive coping, happiness and physical health. Both reviews and recent empirical investigations have shown, however, that it is particular uses of reminiscence which are associated with positive results. For instance, several important collaborative papers by Cappeliez and O'Rourke (e.g. Cappeliez and O'Rourke 2006; O'Rourke *et al.* 2011; O'Rourke *et al.* 2017) have shown that specific reminiscence functions (i.e. *identity, problem solving* and *death preparation* – collectively called *'self-positive' functions*) as measured by the Reminiscence Functions Scale (RFS: Webster 1993) consistently predict positive outcomes.

Recall of individual autobiographical memories, therefore, may enhance immediate wellbeing by improving mood or suggesting coping strategies for current problems. In isolation, however, such discrete reminiscences may not achieve their maximum potential to produce more enduring forms of wellbeing. In contrast, examining personal life events over a more extended period, such as in a life review (Butler 1963a, 1963b), may facilitate outcomes such as Erikson's (1963) construct of ego-integrity. Indeed, the examination of life stories, or personal narratives, is currently a robust and productive research area encompassing many aspects of the social sciences (e.g. de Medeiros 2014).

Within psychology, for instance, narrative approaches are making major contributions in several subdomains such as personality (e.g. McAdams 1993), clinical (e.g. Adler 2012; Bohlmeijer, Westerhof and Emmerik-de Jong 2008), developmental (e.g. Habermas and Bluck 2000; McAdams and McLean 2013) and gerontology (e.g. de Medeiros 2014; Demiray, Mischler and Martin 2017; Kenyon, Bohlmeijer and Randall 2011; Randall and McKim 2008). Narratives include not only the content (i.e. specific autobiographical memories) but several other fundamental components, such as plots, actions, actors, obstacles, logical sequencing, foreshadowing and temporal organization, to name a few. These elements provide a structure within which important reminiscences are rendered comprehensible. Weaving memories into a broader and more extensive autobiography, for instance, may facilitate recognition of life themes, goals and a sense of coherence (Waters and Fivush 2015). McAdams (2013b) identifies powerful themes such as agency, contamination and redemption. Persons become aware of values, emotions and psychological attributes which have jointly contributed to their lived lives to date, as well as to the refinement and maintenance of an integrated sense of identity.

Recently, Hallford and Mellor (2017) introduced the intriguing notion of narrative awareness, which they conceptualize as a metacognitive recognition concerning the importance of personal narratives in identity formation. They argued 'that the basic awareness of having life stories that bring cohesion and meaning to events from a person's life, irrespective of the content of those stories, may itself be adaptive' (p.400). They found that their newly developed scale (the Awareness of Narrative Identity Questionnaire; ANIQ) correlated in predicted ways with components of 'turning point' narratives, specific reminiscence functions (e.g. identity consolidation) and measures of wellbeing such as self-esteem and the presence of life meaning.

The pursuit and discovery of a sense of meaning in life has been described as a fundamental motivator of human growth (e.g. Frankl 1984) and a salient developmental task (Mayseless and Keren 2014). At different moments throughout life, persons may question their values, goals and behaviors in an effort to understand whether their life is worthwhile or has some underlying purpose. Such self-evaluation can be existentially troubling to some. For others, or the same persons at different times, identifying attitudes and actions which make life valuable contributes to a sense of meaning.

Empirical research in meaning-making is extensive (see Heintzelman and King 2014; Park 2010 for reviews) and shows that the presence of meaning in life is associated with a host of positive psychosocial outcomes. For instance, persons experiencing higher levels of meaning in their lives show higher levels of wisdom (Webster *et al.* 2017), identity commitments (Negru-Subtirica *et al.* 2016), adaptive personality traits (Steger *et al.* 2008a), health-related behaviors (Brassai, Piko and Steger 2015) and psychological wellbeing (e.g. Krok 2017). Such findings illustrate important outcomes but leave open the question as to what sources provide the raw materials for acquiring meaning in the first place. Bringing us full circle, I suggest that reminiscence is an important source of meaning-making (e.g. Reker *et al.* 2012), and one which has been relatively under-examined to date. Indeed, Bohlmeijer *et al.* (2008) state that 'the effects of reminiscence on meaning in life…have hardly been studied' (p.644).

Finally, it is important to examine possible cross-cultural variability in positive reminiscence, narrative awareness and meaning in life. With respect to reminiscence and narrative awareness, for instance, it may be that cultural 'macro-narratives' influence and shape the content, frequency and uses to which autobiographical memories are directed (Kober and Habermas 2017). In some cases, particular negative functions might occur more frequently in certain populations such as older Jews incarcerated in concentration camps during the Second World War (O'Rourke *et al.* 2013). In other cases, however, results from empirical studies show many cross-cultural similarities. For instance, Ros *et al.* (2016) found that self-positive functions predicted less mental health problems in a Spanish sample, as did Lou and Choy (2014) using a brief Chinese version of the RFS.

In terms of meaning in life, there has been little research to date focused on cross-cultural differences. One of the few studies to examine this issue (Steger et al. 2008b) investigated different levels of the presence of meaning in life in young American and Japanese adults. Results indicated that Americans had higher levels of meaning in their lives whereas the Japanese participants rated higher on searching for meaning in life. Ostensible differences in cognitive style and individualistic versus collectivist attitudes towards self and life were offered as possible explanations.

Summary and hypotheses

Reminiscence, narratives and meaning in life have all, individually, been associated with positive psychosocial outcomes. However, direct empirical tests of the relationship between reminiscence and meaning are relatively few. Moreover, some of these studies (e.g. Bohlmeijer et al. 2008; Westerhof, Bohlmeijer and Valenkamp 2004) have been pilot projects with low sample sizes and restricted to older adults with particular mental health issues (e.g. depression levels) and so additional research is warranted.

Narratives include multiple reminiscences and so measures assessing these two variables should be related. Further, meaning in life is determined, at least in part, by reflecting on our past experiences as organized within narrative frameworks (which provide structure and coherence). Therefore, I hypothesize that: 1) reminiscence, narrative and meaning will all positively correlate with each other at the bivariate level, and 2) since reminiscence can be considered a building block or foundation of larger narratives, reminiscence will explain additional variance (i.e. show incremental validity) in meaning-making beyond demographic and narrative variables in a regression analysis. Finally, given the possible influence of culture on reminiscence, narrative awareness and meaning, I first evaluate whether there are cultural differences on mean levels of these three variables before conducting further analyses.

Methods

Participants

Participants in the current study were part of a larger project examining time perspective and mental health. Only those individuals who self-classified into one of three specific ethnic groups (Caucasian, 21.1%;

Chinese, 34.2%; and Indian, 44.7%) were considered in the current study. One hundred and fifty-two participants (45 men and 107 women) ranging in age from 17 to 57 (M = 22.27, SD = 6.53) completed all measures. Participants were first and second year community college students in Vancouver, Canada. Participants received nominal course credit for participation and the study was approved by the Research Ethics Board (REB) of the institution.

Measures
Reminiscence
Reminiscence was measured with the 'Past' subscale of the modified Balanced Time Perspective Scale (mBTPS; Webster 2011; Vowinckel et al. 2015). The mBTPS is a 38-item scale containing two 14-item subscales, one reflecting a positive past orientation and one reflecting a positive future orientation, and one ten-item subscale reflecting a positive present orientation. Participants respond to each item on a six-point Likert-type scale where 1 = strongly disagree and 6 = strongly agree. Sample items from the past subscale include: 'Tapping into my past is a source of comfort to me', 'Recalling previous successes helps motivate me now' and 'The pattern of my life makes more sense to me when I reflect on my past.' Cronbach's alphas for the past, present and future subscales were .90, .89 and .94 respectively.

Narrative awareness
Narrative awareness was measured with the Awareness of Narrative Identity Questionnaire (ANIQ; Hallford and Mellor 2017). The ANIQ is a 20-item measure assessing four aspects of narrative identity (five items each using an 11-point Likert-type scale ranging from 0 = completely disagree to 10 = completely agree). Sample items include: 'I use my stories about my life to work out the kind of person I am' (awareness); 'I can put the events of my life in order of when they occurred' (temporal coherence); 'Things that have happened over the course of my life are meaningfully tied together' (causal coherence); and 'I can perceive common themes about who I am across memories of my life' (thematic coherence). Cronbach's alphas for the four subscales in the current study were .87, .74, .87 and .89 respectively. Cronbach's alpha for the total ANIQ was .90.

Meaning in life

The presence of meaning in life was assessed with the five-item 'presence of meaning' subscale of the Meaning in Life Questionnaire (MLQ; Steger et al. 2006). Responses are made on a seven-point scale where 1 = absolutely untrue and 7 = absolutely true, to sample items such as, 'I understand my life's meaning.' Cronbach's alpha was .87.

Results

As noted in the introduction, culture may play a role in all three of the main variables examined in this study (i.e. positive reminiscence, narrative awareness and meaning in life). I therefore conducted an initial series of one-way analyses of variance (ANOVAs) in which the three cultural/ethnic groups (i.e. Caucasian, Chinese and Indian) served as the independent variable. Results indicated that none of the three analyses produced a statistically significant result, meaning that there was no mean difference among the ethnic/cultural groups on any of the three dependent variables tested. All three ethnic/cultural groups were therefore combined in subsequent analyses.

The descriptive statistics and bivariate correlations among all main study variables are presented in Table 10.1.

Table 10.1: Descriptive statistics and bivariate correlations among main study variables

	Variable Mean	SD	Age	ANIQ	Past	MLQ
Age	22.27	6.53	--	.07	.13	.14*
ANIQ	135.64	28.63		--	.42***	.20**
Past	3.96	0.84			--	.36***
MLQ	22.74	6.73				--

Note: ANIQ = Awareness of Narrative Identity Questionnaire; Past = the past subscale of the modified Balanced Time Perspective Scale; MLQ = Meaning in Life Questionnaire presence of meaning subscale; *p < .05; **p < .01; ***p < .001

Age is weakly and positively correlated with the presence of meaning, but not with either narrative awareness or reminiscence. Supporting my first hypothesis, reminiscence, narrative awareness and presence of meaning in life were all positively intercorrelated. The strongest association was between positive reminiscence and narrative awareness.

Given this pattern of bivariate results, I conducted a hierarchic multiple regression analysis to determine which of the variables explained unique variance in meaning in life after all other variables were accounted for (see Table 10.2).

Table 10.2: Hierarchic regression on presence of meaning in life

Variable	Model 1			Model 2			Model 3		
	Beta	t	p	Beta	t	p	Beta	t	p
Gender	.009	.108	.914	-.011	-.134	.894	.018	.237	.813
Age	.14	1.726	.086	.130	1.612	.109	.093	1.201	.232
ANIQ				.196	2.442	.016	.059	.692	.490
Past							.324	3.799	.000
R	.143			.241			.377		
R2	.020			.058			.142		
ΔR^2	.020			.038			.084		
F change	1.54			5.96*			14.43**		

Note: * p < .05; ** p < .001

In step 1, the demographic variables of gender and age were entered as a block. Overall, the model accounted for only 2 per cent of the variance in meaning and this was not statistically significant, $F (2, 149) = 1.54$, $p = .217$. In step 2, narrative awareness was entered as a block and this explained an additional 3.8 per cent of the variance in meaning which was statistically significant, $F (1, 148) = 5.97$, $p = .016$. Finally, in step 3, reminiscence was entered as a block. Supporting my second hypothesis, positive reminiscence explained an additional 8.4 per cent of the variance in meaning which was statistically significant, $F (1, 147) = 14.43$, $p = .000$. Combined, the three variables accounted for 14.2 per cent of the variance in meaning. Finally, only reminiscence remained as a significant predictor in the final model. This means that reminiscence is a significant mediator of the narrative awareness to presence of meaning link.

Discussion

This study investigated in a preliminary way the relationships between reminiscence, narrative awareness and the presence of meaning in life in a cross-cultural sample. As predicted at the bivariate level, reminiscence, narrative awareness and meaning were positively associated with each other. Positive autobiographical memories serve as building blocks for more extensive life narratives. Recalling successes, directive behaviors and the pursuit of purposeful goals provides the basis for a sense of meaning in life. Similarly, structural elements of personal stories (e.g. temporal sequencing, theme identification and identity clarification) also contribute to meaning. Results are generally consistent with Hallford and Mellor (2016b), who found that both groups of participants assigned to either an identity or problem-solving reminiscence functions group improved post-test on a meaning in life measure. Moreover, persons in the problem-solving functions group showed a weak, but significant, increase in narrative awareness post-test.

In the current study, positive reminiscence was more strongly related to meaning than narrative awareness was to meaning. Indeed, the regression analysis showed that narrative awareness no longer explained unique variance in meaning after positive reminiscence was added in the last step of the analysis. Perhaps specific and salient personal memories have a more direct connection to meaning compared to the more abstract and conceptual awareness of narrative identity. Narrative awareness may provide the structural scaffold, or template, which helps us organize our memories, but the memories themselves are more vivid and powerful. For instance, one of the subscales of the ANIQ is temporal coherence, which concerns knowing the chronological sequence of events in one's life, such as that dealing with a child's serious illness occurred before one was promoted at work. Although such temporal knowledge is helpful, the images, thoughts and emotions surrounding a particular event (e.g. child's illness) may provide a more visceral connection to a person's sense of meaning.

The strongest bivariate correlation in the current project was that between positive reminiscence and narrative awareness (r = .43). Again, these results are consistent with Hallford and Mellor (2017), who found that, across two studies, the identify function of the RFS was positively correlated with all four subscales of the ANIQ (average r = .45). These findings support the supposition that having a reservoir of positive autobiographical memories which one can draw on serves as a building block for life stories. This claim cannot be equivocally supported by the current correlational data (see the next section on limitations and future directions), but Hallford and Mellor's (2016b) study, in which they experimentally manipulated reminiscence prior to testing for narrative awareness, provides more compelling evidence for the claim.

Finally, the lack of any significant ethnic/cultural differences on any of the main study variables warrants attention. With respect to positive reminiscence, it may be the case that, at least for younger adults, recalling the types of general past experiences which contribute to positive mood states (e.g. pride, happiness) and elevated personal evaluations (e.g. self-esteem) represents basic and universal needs (Cappeliez and Webster 2017). In contrast, more specific reminiscence functions (e.g. teach/inform) have shown some cultural differences (e.g. between indigenous and non-indigenous Australians; Nile and Van Bergen 2015). Regarding meaning in life, as noted previously, little research has been conducted explicitly examining a culture-meaning link. The current results showed that, although the difference was not statistically significant, the Chinese and Indian participants scored lower in absolute value on meaning relative to the Caucasian participants. So, these results show a comparable trend of Asians scoring lower on meaning than Caucasians (Steger *et al.* 2006). Finally, in terms of the ANIQ, there are no cross-cultural comparisons available to my knowledge. Hallford and Mellor (2016b) did have a large Indian sample (55%) but no analyses were done examining possible cultural differences. In the current study, there was again a trend for Caucasians ($M = 142.32$, $SD = 28.97$) to be higher in narrative awareness relative to both Chinese ($M = 138.15$, $SD = 24.72$) and Indian ($M = 130.56$, $SD = 30.69$) participants, but as previously noted, this did not attain statistical significance, $F(2, 149) = 2.18$, $p = .116$.

Limitations and future directions

The current findings are generally consistent with, and build on, prior research. Several possible caveats, however, need to be addressed. First, the results are correlational, which precludes any causal statements. It is certainly possible that increases in positive reminiscence enable individuals to identify personal strengths and accomplishments which subsequently bolster that person's sense of meaning in life. However, it may also be that persons who have achieved a relatively high level of meaning in life through other means gravitate towards recalling positive personal memories. Supporting the first interpretation, however, Hallford and Mellor (2016b) experimentally demonstrated that persons randomly assigned to positive reminiscence conditions subsequently scored higher on measures of self-esteem, self-efficacy, affect and meaning in life relative to a control condition, although the measure of meaning was only a single item from the MLQ. Additional experimental and longitudinal studies are required to investigate the order in which these two interrelated processes occur.

Second, the measurement of narrative awareness, while novel and potentially informative, is not the same as an actual life story or autobiographical narrative. It would be instructive to thematically code actual life narratives in conjunction with positive reminiscence and meaning in life variables. Such a direct measure of narrative might produce stronger associations with personal recall and meaning-making outcomes. On a related note, although Hallford and Mellor (2017) found positive correlations among their four narrative awareness subscales, they did not actually combine them into a single scale, as was done in the current study. The psychometric consequences of combining the subscales needs further validation.

Third, given that meaning-making is often triggered by stressful life events, future studies may profit by including negative reminiscence functions as well (e.g. bitterness revival) in order to investigate possible similarities and differences in outcomes associated with both positive and negative autobiographical reflection, as well as potential mediators such as mastery (e.g. Korte *et al.* 2012a). It is conceivable, for instance, that painful personal memories are more powerful predictors of meaning in life, but only after they have been assimilated into a life narrative. As a corollary, including measures of searching for meaning (in addition to actually obtaining meaning) may shed additional light on the use of reminiscence and narrative awareness in achieving meaning. For instance, measures of searching for and finding meaning are often negatively correlated (at least in North American samples). However, searching for and obtaining meaning are not necessarily mutually exclusive. For instance, wise persons have achieved a sense of meaning in their lives, but they also continue to search for new meanings and life purpose (Webster *et al.* 2017). Finally, all measures used in the current project were questionnaires and so the results may be unduly influenced by shared method variance. For instance, it is likely that item similarity among the three main measures inflated the bivariate correlations.

Despite these limitations, and the preliminary nature of the current project, results reinforce the notion that retrieval of positive episodic memories can play an important role in developing a sense of meaning in life, both directly and in conjunction with narrative awareness. Additional work, particularly experimental and longitudinal approaches, will help address the issue of causality and identify important new questions about how reminiscence contributes to mental health and wellbeing.

Acknowledgements

The author gratefully acknowledges the data entry and manuscript preparation assistance from Ivona Kutle, Sanya Oh, Michael Bamford, Athina Leung, Yuki Okemoto and Jacqueline Uppal.

Part 3

IMPLICATIONS OF REMINISCENCE, LIFE REVIEW AND LIFE STORY WORK FOR HEALTH AND WELLBEING

Chapter 11

THE NARRATIVE SELF IN THE LIVED EXPERIENCE OF DEMENTIA

Christine Bryden

A diagnosis of dementia often leads to significant fears of loss of narrative: with questions such as who am I and who will I become? I faced these questions after my diagnosis of dementia in 1995, and since that time have published a number of works (Bryden 2002, 2005, 2012, 2015a, 2015b, 2016; Bryden and MacKinlay 2002). These accounts reflected on key relationships and particular experiences in such a way that my narrative could be opened up for a new future (Ford 1985). Examining this evolving narrative was essential to discover meaning, as well as to repair my identity to incorporate living with dementia and to retain a sense of hope. In this journey of reflection, I have come to the view that people with dementia retain a continuing narrative throughout their lived experience.

My aim in this chapter is to give an insider's perspective, challenging the dominant discourse of narrative loss in dementia. People with dementia have a continuing ability to find meaning in life in the present moment, despite being unable to catalogue a series of life events. Therefore, like all people, we are a living narrative whose unity 'links birth to life to death as narrative beginning to middle to end' (MacIntyre 1981, p.91). With or without dementia, we are all developing biographically, as a work of art created over time.

Society's fear of dementia appears to focus on a loss of *episodic* memory, or an ability to recall past events, and an outsider's perception is that this means loss of the narrative self. Increasing recall dysfunction has certainly been my experience, but to suggest therefore I have lost my narrative assumes that this is dependent on recalling what *I did*, rather than on knowing who *I am*. More important than recall of factual events is to know my identity in terms of my commitments and underlying values (Taylor 1989). As a Christian, I have examined how the living story of God has shaped my narrative (Bryan 2016), which I consider will remain despite dementia. Although I am unable to recall accurately events throughout my life, I can be encouraged or assisted to search for meaning in my life. Outsiders assume that recall dysfunction leads to an incoherent narrative (Kevern 2012), implying that an accurately remembered factual chronology is vital to having a narrative. However, although I lack an accurate chronology of my life's events, with help, I can recall certain past events and discover meaning in my life's narrative. We may not be able to place events on our chronological timeline, but more importantly we can perceive *meaning* in our lives. I am not a robot dispassionately recalling and communicating a series of events over my lifetime, as my life is full of events of meaning to me. A robot can tell of its life in terms of an accurate chronology of factual events, but it cannot tell of experiences in terms of images, feelings and meanings, which is the essence of a narrative.

Narrative in the lived experience of dementia

The lived story of any of our lives is to some extent fictional and ever changing, according to our experiences, values, audience, and time and place. We are continually editing events into a plot, forming impressions, and assigning roles, to give a resultant blend of fact and fiction, which has been called 'faction' (Randall 2011, p.23). This editing process continues into the lived experience of dementia, when we are still trying to make sense of our experiences through the lens of our story, and how it is affected by, and affects, the stories of those around us (Clandinin 2006).

Since my diagnosis, I have been searching for meaning in my story in order to find ways to transform my experiences (Clandinin and Roziek 2006). Although I do not have the same cognitive capacity as I once had, I still have a sense of narrative as an 'I' *in relation* to the world. I am not merely an ageing bag of biology, but a story: 'More than bodies or brains, we are biographies' (Randall 2001, p.35). I am far more than an increasingly damaged brain, as I search for meaning from within my lived experience of dementia, in order to challenge the common discourse of loss of narrative.

The concept that loss of recall ability means loss of mind, or knowledge of our story, can be traced back to Plato and Aristotle, who viewed recall being similar to modern data storage and retrieval (Keck 1996). Such views still persist in our society; for example, a psychological view is that people with dementia lose their narrative due to their inability to recall events accurately (Bryan 2016). However, very few people have total accurate recall of the past, and indeed the Eastern Orthodox view is that recall is not essential to having a narrative (Zizioulas 1975). Despite my failing recall ability, my experience of each moment is a continuous narrative (Moen 2006), which has not altered after my diagnosis.

From my insider's viewpoint, I consider that narrative is retained throughout the lived experience of dementia, where our present-day existence is informed by glimpses of the future, as well as by a distorted recall of the past. I live within my narrative, where life is like a literary process, and we all have a unique story to tell (Randall 2001). We *have* and *are* stories, and we think, perceive, feel, decide and act on the basis of our life story, where 'to be a person is to be a story' (Randall 2001, p.57). Even when we are living with dementia, we still see life through the lens of our own unique story, searching for meaning. However, after the traumatic and disruptive experience of diagnosis, we do need to re-integrate a sense of identity, based on our new and altered future.

My story still reveals an indivisible unity of body and mind (Crites 1971), and the use of narrative counters the concept of the possibility of becoming a mindless body as the brain deteriorates (Crites 1971), or indeed of ever becoming a 'mindless empty shell' (Alzheimer's Disease International 2000, p.1). Focusing on retaining a continuing narrative throughout dementia provides an important counter to Cartesian dualism, which holds that the physical brain is the mind. The mind is thought to be the place in which our continuing narrative somehow resides, so that therefore there will be a loss of life story due to brain atrophy. However, despite loss of brain tissue, people with dementia still retain a narrative of meaning, which exposes this fallacy of Cartesian dualism. People with dementia continue to have and be a story, seeking meaning in the present moment, even if we may need some help to recall and reflect on past events.

My identity is not about me as an object in the present moment, but as a person who is growing (Taylor 1989), and this does not cease when living with dementia. I am still the same person at different times and places; even if I cannot recall this continuity, I retain a unity of narrative. I am the subject of my own unique story, shaped by narratives of others around me, just as much as I shape theirs (MacIntyre 1981). I am both what others think me to be, as well as 'the *subject* of a history that is my own and no one else's, that has its own peculiar meaning' (MacIntyre 1981, pp.102–103). However, my story is embedded within a sociocultural context of living with dementia, so is impacted by the discourses around me of expected narrative loss. I have roles crafted for me within these stories around me (Clandinin 2006), which assume that I am unable to sustain a narrative of meaning. Yet even when we are living with dementia, we can search for meaning in our life's story, which is entangled within the web of others' stories and the dominant culture (Bryan 2016).

We all face significant events, such as a diagnosis of dementia, which are not of our making, yet we need to find a way through these unpredictable dramatic turns in our individual lives. Place can play an important part in our narrative, so that often we can recall where significant events occurred. For me, a spotlight is shone on the doctor's office in which I received my diagnosis, where my narrative became sharply different from that which I had expected. Yet reflections on place can also lead us to visions of future possibilities; our story of place, of past highlights as well as of future hope, can enrich our stories.

For some of us, the dramatic event leads to us becoming subject to overshadowing influences, such as the dominant story of dementia. In this larger master narrative, our story is a subplot and we can be 'de-storied' by stigmatised assumptions about dementia and its consequences. Diagnosis becomes a significant intrusion into our story (Randall 2001), resulting in narrative foreclosure, where we believe that our story is now finished (Freeman 2011). The future often looks bleak, tainted with decline and despair, as well as with a seemingly inevitable loss of narrative when we may find memories increasingly difficult to recall. Nevertheless, we still have an evolving story, and our narrative is being formed and reformed within a larger set of narratives, which are like the threads of a tapestry being interwoven to create a picture within our sociocultural milieu.

Time and finding meaning in the present moment

Time can be meaningfully measured by important events where 'we are not in this time, but it is in us' (Niebuhr 1941, p.34). However, scientifically time is measured with the atomic caesium clock and is devoid of meaning (Baars 2011). Time for most of us falls somewhere in-between, having meaning as part of our inner history, but ticking away on the scientific clock as we age. We all experience story-time as well as clock time; yet events can warp our perception of time in our narratives (de Vries *et al.* 2001).

Clock time is linear, but story-time, depending on circumstances, is altered according to the way we see meaning and significance in the themes of our lives. For example, we do not always perceive the passing of time accurately, so that we may feel younger or older than our biological selves. My grandmother was 107 and when staying in respite care for a short while, she said she did not like to be there with all those old people! This highlights the way our lived time is not related to actual biological time. We live our life story, looking from the inside out, not looking from the outside in, and from that perspective we look at the world much as we have done for many years. Reflecting on our narrative in a process of making meaning involves feelings and emotions, as well as our sense of the past and future co-existing somehow in the present (Bryan 2016). Narrative provides insight into our experience of time (Kenyon 2011), where we all make sense of the past through rereading our story through the lens of the present (Schiff and Cohler 2001), weaving the past into a story that gives us meaning. The meaning that we attach to recalled events alters the way we perceive them: indeed, none of us tell the same story, even about the same event. The Gospel narratives are an example of how the writers gave differing perspectives of the meaning of the same events in a period of time. We all experience this incomplete nature of recall, where 'remembering is not yet knowing' (Crites 1971, p.75).

I have an altered perception of time, so that I feel more firmly situated in the present and less able to recall the past. My present moment is more vivid than the past, yet I will always be a historical being, who lives in time and continues to be a story in her world (Baars 2012). This experience of a disturbed sense of time, not an exact awareness of chronological time, means that my perception is of both living in the world, as well as living in time; my narrative gives meaning to this experience (Baars 2012).

Importantly, for those of us living with dementia, *the present moment is a pivotal point* in our story, as we glimpse threads of the past and attempt to imagine a future. This intensely present moment (Crites 1971), where past and future are co-joined, is like psychologist Stephen Sabat's 'personal present' (2001, p.232), within which my fear of future possibilities, as well as an awareness of my past, re-shaped my narrative shortly after diagnosis, and continues to influence my search for meaning. Although I have a disrupted timeline, I have a greater awareness of the present moment in which to find meaning.

Although my recall ability has been disrupted, my life story and bodily identity continue into an evolving future that is aptly described as the 'intriguing temporal dynamics of memories' (Baars 2012, p.151). For example, my memoir (Bryden 2015a) told my story in terms of past events that were important to me at the time of writing (with the assistance of others for recall); perhaps today it might be a very different story. This is true for all of us: we have differing perspectives on meaning at various times in our lives, arising from our ongoing experiences. There is more to me in the present moment than there is in my inadequately remembered timeline; therefore, my view is that being able to sequence events accurately over time is not essential to creating meaning (disputing Baldwin and Estey 2015).

For me, time is often warped and misshaped, and my recall of events is dysfunctional; yet what is of importance is the meaning that I attach to those events, even if I might need some help to recall them. Therefore, I disagree that my story is an essential part of my *'cognitive architecture'* (Bryan 2016, p.29; my emphasis). Instead, my narrative is set within the experience of the present moment, within which I can still explore meaning, beyond a limited cognitive timeline of events, towards a full and rich expression of all that I am. I can still search for ultimate meaning, where this is finding who I am in God's eyes, by reviewing meaning and reframing my narrative (MacKinlay 2016). My life still has meaning, even with dementia (Swinton 2012), and my present-moment reality is an important part of this narrative truth. Narrative for me is a *search for meaning in the present moment.* (See Chapter 7 by MacKinlay.)

Challenging the dominant story of dementia

Common views of a loss of narrative with dementia have led to an overwhelming *fear* of the condition, which permeates society. People may even be deterred from seeking a diagnosis, and when diagnosed, often experience a loss of hope. This fear profoundly impacts our stories, as we endeavour to live as best we can with the condition. We may also become isolated, as not only do we believe this story of loss, but those around us alter their behaviour towards us accordingly, assigning us limited roles, called malignant positioning (Sabat 2001). Diagnosis had a profound impact on my sense of personal identity, and was a negative and isolating event, disrupting my imagined future narrative. There was now a schism between growth and development, of a career trajectory before me, and the doctor's prognosis of future decline and loss, with a few years of diminishing capacity before death in care. At diagnosis, within the dominant discourse of dementia, we believe that only decline lies ahead of us, and that we will become unable to know or tell our story (Freeman 2011).

However, people with dementia can still ascribe feelings of meaning and value to our experiences, even if we cannot recall their factual details (Freeman 2011). These emotions provide substance for our narrative, far more than a list of facts devoid of feeling. I seek to challenge the dominant discourse of loss of narrative in dementia with an insider's view: we retain an ability to find meaning, within a narrative in the present moment. I still have a meaningful narrative, even though my language and recall are impaired, so that I have a diminishing ability to *express* this unfolding narrative of meaning.

I describe my lack of recall of past events and a disrupted awareness of the future as 'my life is like a carpet unrolling before and behind me' (Bryden 2015b, p.130). In this metaphor, life before and behind me is unseen, yet the pattern of meaning on the carpet beneath my feet is nonetheless vivid, although I might need more help and time to describe it. Despite my functioning on neuropsychological tests becoming increasingly defective, I can still explore my fear of loss, and develop the concept of having a narrative in relationships with God and with others.

Our narrative may become non-verbal, yet it is still rich with imagery and imbued with meaning, giving a thick, rich description of a life lived. My own experiences and observations of people in the later stages of dementia support this concept of a *non-verbal narrative*, which is proposed to emerge as a series of images from birth (Damasio 2010). Despite difficulties in finding the right descriptors, or being able to sort these images into an accurate order over time, I can still find meaning in life, and develop a narrative. Language is not critical for me to *be* a story, although to *share* my narrative I will need to be helped to convey this to others. Outsider views are that I need language as the basis for narrative (Baars 2012), yet I can retain my narrative despite my increasing linguistic problems.

Narrative care for people with dementia

Spiritual reminiscence work with people with dementia demonstrates that meaning can be found in the moment, and narrative is still possible (MacKinlay and Trevitt 2012). Similarly, people with dementia have been found to be semiotic, able to make and derive meaning (Sabat 2001). Dementia is just one part of the tapestry of life, which can be incorporated into a new and continuing narrative. Despite our diagnosis, we still have an interest in the future (Shadden *et al.* 2008), even if this involves *continually* combatting the fear arising from the master narratives of dementia surrounding us. We retain the ability to be biographically active, capable of some degree of narrative development (Randall 2011), sometimes with support, and importantly, we retain an *interest* in our life story, despite a loss of cognitive function (Blustein 1999).

Narrative relationships are a fundamental part of all of our lives, as each one of us is intricately embedded in the lives of others. We have an identity framed by our roles in the lives of others, just as they play a role in our life. However, this becomes increasingly important for those of us living with dementia (Shadden *et al.* 2008). At first, we may need some support from others for recall of the recent past, but then perhaps increasingly also for events in the distant past. Given that events seen from the outside by a non-participating observer only form an *outer* history of things, it is vital that people with dementia are supported to communicate events understood from within, as part of their *inner* history of self (Niebuhr 1941).

We all exist in a web of interconnecting life stories, and this interweaving of our story with those of others is more important for people with dementia, whose recall is dysfunctional. Our narrative care-partners need to have the *time* to attend to our stories. We might have lost the communicative tools to sustain and share the details of our life story, but we do not stop having a narrative, nor relationships with others. We can be supported in a narrative care-partnership to find meaning (Shadden *et al.* 2008). In these relationships of listening and telling, care-partners are like weavers who help us to reweave 'a poorly woven portion of the tapestry into the new weaving' (Coyle 2014, p.41).

The negative narrative of the biomedical view of dementia can have a profound impact on our stories, so we need our care-partners to focus on listening, or, as I write, to 'listen with your eyes' (Bryden 2015b, p.132). We need listeners who act as witnesses or conversation partners (Abraham 2016), even sitting with us in silence in what has been described as the 'sacrament of the present moment' (Swinton 2012, p.254). We need help in identifying the deeper *meaning* beyond the facts, looking at this from our perspective, and being assisted particularly when we feel overcome by the narrative of loss (Shadden *et al.* 2008). We should be encouraged to explore our narrative, despite perhaps having increasingly limited communication skills. Our narrative care-partners are to hear, reflect and record episodes of meaning, helping us to put together events in our life story (Abraham 2016), as our recall may become increasingly impaired. By attempting 'to interpret the worlds behind the text, of the text, and *in front of* the text' (Abraham 2016, p.732), narrative care-partners can support us to see our lives as a whole.

Assisting us to find meaning, despite our cognitive disability, can be regarded as being *disruptive*, like Jesus who disturbed established practices to refocus on the truth, such as in regard to children and Samaritans (e.g. Matthew 19:13–15, Luke 10:29–37; Metzger and Murphy 1991). Narrative care-partnerships can be regarded as disruptive approaches that help us to find meaning within a life lived with dementia and to identify a different lens through which to view our story. Despite the overshadowing narrative of loss, care-partners can help us to find new meaning in the present moment, moving towards horizons of future hope. We want to be able to live positively with dementia: *in*, *through* and *beyond* the diagnosis. We are not merely a medical diagnosis or prognosis, but a living story: *we are letters from Christ* (2 Cor. 3:2), written by the Spirit of the Living God.

Our narrative is sensitive to sharing, given the fragility of our recall ability, and can become changed in the telling and retelling (Bryan 2016), when others might influence our storytelling. Therefore, narrative care-partners need to avoid the risk of co-authoring, where they impute their own meaning to our behaviour. We may become increasingly dependent on care-partners to understand and respect our inner story, relying on them to do this without any distortion of our narrative. Their role is to assist in recall, identifying meaning and repairing the fabric of our narrative, which has been threatened by dementia (Randall 2011). In particular, narrative care-partners should avoid malignant social psychology (Kitwood 1997), whereby all our actions are interpreted solely through the lens of dementia.

Dementia has disrupted our story, which is socially situated and constructed; yet with some support, we can sustain our narrative, despite a decreasing ability to express ourselves. Despite a diagnosis of dementia, we still can explore our narrative, in a changing balance between our own agency and communion with others. Agency might have become diminished, due to our decreasing communication and recall skills, but communion with others then becomes even more important (Shadden *et al.* 2008).

The narrative quest

As we age, our narrative becomes a portrait through which to reflect and find sources of meaning in our lifelong experiences. We all want our lives to have meaningful unity and look to our narrative to uncover this (Taylor 1989). At diagnosis, I needed to look to my narrative in order to create a new portrait that would give me a sense of unity, as I faced a terminal illness that evokes fear and horror in our society. My quest was to work through the oppressive narrative of being a dementia victim, towards a positive portrait of becoming a survivor. By finding a narrative within, and despite dementia, I sought to prompt the church to see people with dementia with Godly eyes (Coyle 2014).

My narrative quest can be regarded as a *parable*, providing a different lens with which to view a story and discover new insights. Parables have a context, plot, beginning, middle and end, but the end is unexpected and redirects us to reflect further to discover a sense of meaning beyond what would be found in the straightforward narrative of experience. Similarly, narratives need not be linear, consistent, coherent and realistic, and can be more like a patchwork allowing for 'transcendence, mystery, and surprise' (Baldwin and Estey 2015, p.214).

After diagnosis, I wrote an embodied story of my illness, in a fragile chaos story in which my diagnosis was like a 'shipwreck' (Frank 2013, p.54) that would lead to inevitable cognitive decline. I reintegrated the story of dementia within my narrative, towards a sense of individual wholeness and survival. However, even now there is still a seesaw between my being able to tell the story of a non-linear chaotic lived life and yet also a coherent story of survival (Frank 2013). This tension is common to all of us in retelling the story of our lives (Clandinin 2006), yet is even more so the case for those of us trying to challenge a dominant narrative in society, which can overwhelm our struggles to narrate a new identity for ourselves.

I found identity as a dementia advocate, weaving events into my story to give a thick, positive perspective (Coyle 2014) and rejecting the thin descriptor of dementia that led to despair and fear. I sought to find unity in my life, despite the chasm that opened up after diagnosis, when I faced an unknown and unwanted future. This search for unity was my narrative quest (MacIntyre 1981) to uncover meaning in my life with dementia. Through advocacy, I sought to find a story larger than just my own concerns, and found meaning in this experience 'through acceptance or surrender' (Kenyon 2011, p.240). By sharing my reshaped narrative, I accepted the diagnosis, rather than surrender to the master narrative of decline. I became open to my changed story, and accepted my life as it had now become, not as I had previously thought it would become (Kenyon 2011).

By constructing a new narrative, I faced a radically new path of life (Kenyon 2011) and sought an understanding of future possibilities (MacIntyre 1977). By seeing life as a narrative, I could accept dementia as just one aspect of my story and remain open on the journey of life: 'Wisdom significantly involves the acceptance of our life story; as it is, as it has been, and also as it has not been – "the road not chosen"' (Kenyon and Randall 2001, p.10).

Summary

The master narrative about people with dementia is a biomedical prognosis that reduces us to deficits, yet the traumatic loss of an expected future is not a medical symptom (Frank 2013). An alternative narrative of dementia focuses on how our personhood can be sustained by others (Kitwood 1997). Yet I have my own desire to find meaning in *surviving and thriving despite dementia*, which presents a far more important *personal* narrative about who I am. This is not just about my body's medical defects or my dependency on others, but about my experiences and sense of meaning in the present moment.

The master narrative of dementia of future loss and decline has to be challenged, in order to give an improved understanding of the continuity of narrative in people living with dementia. At some time after our diagnosis, we may need to be assisted by sensitive narrative care-partners, in order to counter the tendency towards foreclosure and to encourage us to have hope for the future. We can be helped to revisit the past, looking at meaningful events, and to edit our story to find new meaning. We can identify our signature stories, and how these were of value in our storyline in giving us personal meaning and providing our lives with a sense of unity and purpose. With such help, we can rewrite our life stories, linking the past to the present and to the very different future. Crucial to this is the weaving into our story of the diagnostic crisis, modifying our narrative and giving new perspectives on meaning. In particular, we seek to challenge the interpretation of our story given to us by the dominant discourses of dementia.

I am in the midst of my narrative, and do not know how it will end, but seek a guiding metaphor. My aims are to live *well, beyond and through* dementia, and to be able to answer the questions now facing me: who am I now; am I only a life in retrospect; can I create a good enough narrative (perhaps with narrative support) to help me to live in the present moment with dementia? As agency fades and communion becomes more important, I can be assisted by narrative care-partners to recognise a new part of my living narrative (Bryan 2016), in which I am reflecting on meaning within the lived experience of dementia. My storyline has been and continues to be disrupted by a fading recall for events, and a warped sense of time, yet I can still search for a unifying narrative, based on my values and spirituality.

As I incorporate dementia into my narrative quest of searching for meaning in the Christian context, I plumb the depths of my emotional and spiritual being. I find meaning in a narrative that is a redemptive story, of finding meaning after trauma, and striving for a legacy that I might pass onto future generations: a sense of hope set within the traumatic text of dementia, founded on my Christian faith. My story is not just about living with dementia but is told *through* my life with dementia. Diagnosis disrupted my old story and has now become incorporated into my new narrative, so that dementia is part of who I am. I tell my embodied story of living with this condition, despite my body lacking language (Frank 2013). In sharing my narrative, I have sought to reach out to others who are learning to live with dementia (Frank 2013), and my story is retold each time it is read as 'the social rhetoric of illness' (Frank 2013, p.21).

Through looking to God, I find meaning, where God 'is not far from each one of us' (Acts 17:27). From my Christian worldview, I know that I can still relate to God and others, even without accurate recall (Poll and Smith 2003). I am so much more than my recall dysfunction, disrupted sense of time and communication problems – even if I can no longer speak, and my thoughts become more muddled, I know I will remain secure in God who created me. I have a continuing sense of being upheld by God in the fullness of my identity. Ultimately, it is God whom I trust to hold to all who I am, have ever been and will ever be.

My narrative is like shifting sand; as I age, develop and grow, I accrue the wisdom to reflect on my experiences in new ways. I see life as an hourglass, where the sands of time appear to be speeding up as they pass through to the bottom. There is only a limited amount of time left to narrate my story, despite, with and beyond dementia. I am a survivor of dementia, with a somewhat unclear past, intensively lived present moment, and uncertain and indistinct future. I am who I am, and I am not my dementia. This condition is only one small part of my life's experiences: I am far more than a person living with dementia, as I am Christine, a unique individual who is living her own story in the midst of the stories of others.

Notes

I use the term recall *dysfunction*, rather than memory loss as this is closer to my experience of being unable to store memories accurately and therefore needing help to access them. The memories are not lost, but rather access to them has become dysfunctional. Psychologist Stephen Sabat refers to implicit memory and observes that even if there are difficulties in recall, it is not the case that a person has no memory of the event (2001, 2016). This issue is discussed in more detail in Sabat (2018, p.31–32).

I use the term 'care-partner' (Bryden 2005, p.130), rather than caregiver, as it better reflects the journey of accepting and adapting to new roles within the shared journey of dementia. The person with dementia plays an active part in this circle of care.

Chapter 12

SELF REMINISCENCES OF CLINICALLY DEPRESSED OLDER ADULTS AND THE TRIPARTITE FUNCTIONAL MODEL REVISITED

Philippe Cappeliez

The objective of this chapter is to deepen our understanding of how reminiscences contribute to wellbeing in later life. It is divided into three sections. The first section reviews the empirical support for a tripartite functional model of reminiscence that pertains to the relationships between the reminiscence functions and physical and mental health. The second section presents a study on the uses of reminiscence that distinguish clinically depressed older adults. The third section incorporates these findings in a theoretical review of the tripartite model. It also draws out the clinical implications for reminiscence interventions with depressed older patients.

The literature on reminiscence interventions with depressed older adults is indubitably relevant to many points addressed in this chapter. However, this chapter chooses to focus on reports by older adults living independently in the community about occurrences of reminiscences in their daily life, and not on reminiscences prompted and coached in the context of interventions with a therapeutic intent for depression and anxiety, for example. Reminiscence is the recall of personal experiences from one's past. The role played by reminiscence has been a topic of sustained interest in gerontological theory and research for more than 50 years (Westerhof and Bohlmeijer 2014). After Erikson (1959) and Butler (1963a, 1963b) had established reminiscence as a constructive cognitive process in later life's psychological development, it did not take long for research to emphasize that reminiscence was a complex process, with various modes of reminiscence serving different psychological functions, and therefore having different effects on psychological functioning (Coleman 1986a, 1986b). In this literature, functions of reminiscence are defined as 'reasons for remembering personal experiences' or 'uses of personal memories'. These early insights led to the elaboration of several typologies of reminiscence functions (for reviews of early works, see Staudinger 2001; Webster and Haight 1995). One of these taxonomies proposed by Webster (1993) eventually gained pre-eminence in research, largely because it offered an empirically validated scale for measuring these functions: the Reminiscence Functions Scale (RFS). This taxonomy comprises eight functions: identity (activating personal memories to discover or clarify who I am as a person), problem solving (recalling experiences of coping and past problem-solving strategies), death preparation (using memories to face my own mortality with equanimity), bitterness revival (recalling repeatedly difficult life events, crises and conflicts), boredom reduction (using memories to fill a current void of stimulation or interest), intimacy maintenance[1] (recalling memories of those who are absent or deceased), conversation (narrating personal memories with simple communicative intent) and teach/inform (sharing memories to convey experiences and life lessons).

Initial work with the RFS focused 'internally', i.e. on the relations among the eight different functions. Our understanding of the role of these reminiscences in psychological functioning entered a new stage when the focus shifted from use of reminiscence to adaptivity of reminiscence, with the examination of the links between the distinct functions of reminiscence on one hand and psychological wellbeing and distress, and also physical health, on the other hand. This approach led to the discovery that, for the purpose of understanding the potential contribution of reminiscence to the physical and mental health of older adults, the best conceptualization of the eight functions was a model with three second-order factors (Cappeliez and O'Rourke 2006; O'Rourke et al. 2011), which were called: self-positive functions (identity, problem solving, death preparation); self-negative functions (bitterness revival, boredom reduction, intimacy

---

1   It should be noted that a similar terminology is used in the autobiographical memory literature referring to a completely different function of personal memories (Alea and Bluck 2007). These authors mean intimacy in romantic relationships, an aspect of the social bonding function or, more generally, prosocial functions of personal memories.

maintenance); and prosocial functions (conversation, teach/inform). In this context, the self is defined as the personal mental representation of one's own identity, formed on the basis of past experiences, images and thoughts encoded in memories.

Over time, this model with three principal reminiscence functions has gathered support from studies conducted with English and French speaking Canadians (O'Rourke *et al.* 2017), older Spaniards (Ros *et al.* 2016) and Israeli Holocaust survivors (King *et al.* 2015). Of note, the field of autobiographical memory research has also emphasized a model with three main functions for autobiographical memories: self, directive and social functions (e.g. Bluck *et al.* 2005). Discussion of the significant overlaps and the nuances of the two tri-dimensional models can be found elsewhere (Bluck and Alea 2002; Harris *et al.* 2014; O'Rourke *et al.* 2017). Harris and colleagues (2014) have argued for a model with four classes of autobiographical memory functions: reflective (comprising identity and problem solving from the RFS), ruminative (comprising boredom, reduction, bitterness revival, and intimacy maintenance from the RFS), social (comprising conversation from RFS), and generative (comprising teach/inform and death preparation from RFS). Except for the generative function, this model and the tripartite model are very similar in their ways of clustering the individual reminiscence (or autobiographical memory) functions.

Empirical support for the tripartite functional model of reminiscence

Self-positive reminiscence functions

Self-positive functions of reminiscence (identity, problem solving, death preparation) have been associated with better mental health and wellbeing in a number of studies (Alea and Bluck 2013; Cappeliez and O'Rourke 2006; Hallford and Mellor 2015; Hallford *et al.* 2013; King *et al.* 2017; O'Rourke *et al.* 2011; Ros *et al.* 2016; Waters 2014). Indeed, in these cross-sectional and longitudinal analyses, both direct and indirect associations have been observed between, on one hand, self-positive functions and on the other hand, greater life satisfaction and lower psychological distress manifested by reduced depressive symptoms, hopelessness, and anxiety level.

Concerning self-positive reminiscences, their particularly beneficial role in reducing psychological distress is further underlined by the finding that this latter effect mediates their long-term influence on physical and mental health (King et al. 2017). In other words, the enduring effect of self-positive reminiscences in reducing psychological distress may well be the process which leads to the improvement of physical health.

Self-negative reminiscence functions

Self-negative functions (bitterness revival, boredom reduction, intimacy maintenance) have been associated with lower wellbeing in later life. Direct relationships have been observed between the self-negative functions and indicators of poor mental health, including increased depressive and anxious symptoms, hopelessness, reduced life satisfaction, poorer perceived health and compromised physical health in cross sectional research (Cappeliez and O'Rourke 2006; Hofer et al. 2017; Korte et al. 2011b; Ros et al. 2016), as well as in longitudinal research (King et al. 2017; O'Rourke et al. 2011).

Although both self-positive and self-negative reminiscences are linked with physical health, the link is stronger for self-negative reminiscences, as indicated by standardized path coefficients, a finding already highlighted (Cappeliez and O'Rourke 2006). In other words, as it pertains to physical health of older adults, the harmful effects of the self-negative reminiscences appear more powerful than the constructive effects of the self-positive reminiscences.

Regarding self-negative reminiscences, the relative association appears stronger with physical health than with psychological distress (King et al. 2017). In other words, the ongoing negative effect of self-negative reminiscences on physical health may determine their influence on both physical and mental health in the long term.

Prosocial reminiscence functions

Research suggests that, in contrast to self-functions, the link between prosocial functions (conversation, teach/inform others) and health and wellbeing is indirect (Cappeliez and O'Rourke 2006; Ros et al. 2016). More precisely, it appears that the prosocial functions are associated with physical health and psychological wellbeing via the self-positive and self-negative functions (Cappeliez and O'Rourke 2006; O'Rourke et al. 2011). In other words, it is only in their subsequent impact on the self-functions that any predictive association with health and wellbeing may occur.

In this line of research on the tripartite model, data has been analyzed and discussed systematically at the construct level of psychological wellbeing, anchored on such indicators as depressive symptoms, level of anxiety and life satisfaction. It made sense for these studies to examine reminiscence at the higher level of construct since the primary focus was on the validity and features of the tripartite functional model. A finer-grained analysis of the associations between the individual reminiscence functions and depressive symptoms may elucidate further the tripartite model. A few studies have already pursued that track. In a study carried out with the eight individual reminiscence functions and a sample of older adults recruited from the general population, Cully and his colleagues found that the functions of bitterness revival, boredom reduction and death preparation were linked with both depression and anxiety symptoms (Cully, LaVoie and Gfeller 2001). This finding for bitterness revival and boredom reduction was replicated with a sample of depressed older adults (Korte et al. 2011b). Taken together these results demonstrate consistent connections between the self-negative functions of bitterness revival and boredom reduction on the one hand, and depression on the other. Further considering that these findings were obtained with both general and clinical populations, they underline once more the pernicious influence of these self-negative functions on mental health.

A complementary investigation of the relations between the functions of reminiscence and depression could consist of specifically targeting older adults with clinically significant depression. Clearly, identification of the patterns of reminiscence associated with these conditions is the most important for healthcare professionals who use reminiscence in their interventions with depressed older adults. The next section presents such a study.

Functions of reminiscence in clinically depressed older adults

Participants and recruitment
The initial pool of participants consisted of 1106 older adults initially recruited in the context of a larger longitudinal study on reminiscence

and wellbeing in later life (O'Rourke *et al.* 2011). The sociodemographic characteristics of that sample can be found in that article, which also contains more details on the procedure of participant recruitment and data collection.

Instruments

Reminiscence Functions Scale

The RFS (Webster 1993) is a well-known 43-item scale measuring the frequency of use of the eight types of reminiscence presented earlier. Respondents indicate how often they reminisce for each reason, endorsing from never (1) to very frequently (6) on a six-point Likert-type scale. The RFS has good psychometric properties. The internal consistency for each subscale, as measured by Cronbach's alpha, ranges between $.82 < \alpha < .88$ (King *et al.* 2017). Test-retest reliability was assessed using Pearson product-moment correlations between baseline and follow-up data collected 8 and 16 months later. As expected, they were in the medium range, between 0.48 and 0.63, most being above 0.60. Westerhof and his colleagues (2010) have declared that the RFS is the most empirically supported and useful measure of reminiscence functions, and it is widely used in different languages and cultures (e.g. Lou and Choy 2014; Mezred *et al.* 2006; Ros *et al.* 2016; Shellman, Ennis and Bailey-Addison 2011).

Centre for Epidemiological Studies – Depression Scale

The Centre for Epidemiological Studies – Depression Scale (CES-D) (Radloff 1977) is a 20-item self-report instrument that assesses symptoms of depression over the past week. Respondents rate the frequency of depressive symptoms on a four-point Likert-type scale, from rarely or none of the time (0) to most or all of the time (3). Some examples are: 'I felt lonely', 'I felt hopeful about the future.' The CES-D has been used in many community-based studies of the elderly, with generally favourable psychometric properties (Beekman *et al.* 1997; Radloff and Teri 1986). We used 16 as a cut-off for identification of those participants as depressed at a clinical level. Using this cut-off with community-based older adults provides a sensitivity for major depression of 100 per cent and a specificity of 88 per cent (Beekman *et al.* 1997). Two hundred participants in the total sample of 1106 had a score within the seriously depressed range (M = 24.30; SD = 8.23). This represents 18 per cent of the total sample, comparable to 15 per cent reported by Beekman and collaborators (1997) with an elderly community-based sample.

To eliminate mildly or transiently depressed individuals from the analysis, we determined as 'non-depressed' only those participants with the bottom scores of either 0, 1 or 2. It turned out that an equivalent number of participants, precisely 218 (i.e. 20% of the complete sample), had a score in that non-depressed range.

Analytic procedure

To determine whether clinically depressed older adults differed from non-depressed individuals in their frequency of reminiscing for the eight functions and the total frequency of reminiscences, we conducted a series of t-tests. Considering that we were running nine tests, we used a Bonferroni correction to set the level of significance at a more stringent alpha level of .001 (.01/9).

Results

Table 12.1: Means (and standard deviations), t-test and Cohen's d results for the comparisons between depressed and non-depressed older adults on eight functions of reminiscence (N for depressed = 200, N for non-depressed = 218)

Functions	mean (SD)	mean (SD)	t	Cohen's d
Identity	21.1 (6.3)	18.1 (6.7)	− 4.75*	0.46*
Death preparation	17.5 (6.4)	14.1 (6.1)	− 5.48*	0.53*
Problem solving	19.8 (6.0)	17.1 (5.9)	− 4.66*	0.45*
Boredom reduction	15.7 (6.4)	10.0 (4.5)	−10.48*	1.03**
Bitterness revival	12.4 (5.1)	7.9 (3.1)	−11.00*	1.08**
Intimacy maintenance	15.2 (5.1)	12.7 (4.6)	− 5.41*	0.52*
Conversation	15.5 (5.5)	14.5 (4.9)	− 1.94	0.19
Teach/inform	17.5 (5.2)	17.1 (5.0)	− 0.71	0.08
Total frequency	134.7 (45.8)	111.5 (40.6)	− 5.49*	0.54*

t test: * p < .001; Cohen's d: * medium effect size 0.5; ** large effect size 0.8

Table 12.1 shows the summary of results for the t-tests and Cohen's d statistics comparing depressed older adults with non-depressed. Compared with non-depressed individuals, depressed older adults reported significantly higher frequencies of reminiscences in general (21% more than non-depressed) and in particular for the three self-negative functions (boredom reduction, bitterness revival and intimacy maintenance; 34% more) and for the three self-positive functions (identity, death preparation and problem solving; 19% more). According to Cohen's d statistics, the effect size is deemed to be large (i.e. $d > 0.8$) for boredom reduction and bitterness revival functions. No differences were found between depressed and non-depressed participants for the frequencies of prosocial reminiscences.

In summary, compared with their non-depressed counterparts, depressed older adults reported higher use of all private self-reminiscences, cumulating in a higher frequency of reminiscence activity overall. In contrast, they did not differ in their reliance on reminiscences shared with others, i.e. prosocial reminiscences. These findings help to refine the tripartite functional model of reminiscence.

The tripartite functional model revisited
Total frequency of reminiscence

These findings clearly underline that depressed individuals think more often about their past than their non-depressed counterparts. Other studies have reported this association between propensity to psychological distress or actual depressive symptoms and increased reminiscing in samples of adults of different ages (e.g. Cappeliez and O'Rourke 2002; Cully *et al.* 2001; Grace, Dewhurst and Anderson 2016). Furthermore, it has been shown that interaction between a ruminative style of thinking and reminiscing predicts future depressed mood in older adults (Brinker 2013). As will be detailed later, it is clear from the results that higher frequencies of self-reminiscences, both positive and negative, are responsible for this overall increase in reminiscence activity. This demonstrates again that depressed older adults are caught in ruminations, frequently reflecting on causes and consequences of past events (Nolen-Hoeksema, Wisco and Lyubomirsky 2008). Ruminative reminiscing keeps exposing individuals to negative personal memories, reinforcing the associated negative feelings. Research on the interactions between cognitions and emotions has demonstrated that dysphoria is associated with enhanced maladaptive self-referential thinking (i.e. ruminations and self-blame) (Rochat, Billieux and Van der Linden 2012; Salovey 1992). Self-centered repetitive thought such as rumination both contemporaneously and prospectively increases depression in older adults (Segerstrom *et al.* 2010).

Self-negative functions of reminiscence

All three self-negative functions of reminiscence were enhanced in depressed individuals in the present study. These results again reaffirm the harmful nature of these reminiscences. Korte *et al.* (2011b) also found that the links between reminiscences and depressive and anxious symptoms were almost entirely attributable to reminiscences for bitterness revival and boredom reduction. A study conducted with long-term care residents also reported that more frequent reminiscences for boredom reduction and bitterness revival were related to higher intensity of depressive symptomatology (Henkel *et al.* 2017).

A few studies have uncovered analogous processes presumably mediating this negative impact on mental health. Generally speaking, self-negative reminiscences impair both assimilative coping (i.e. mobilizing personal resources to pursue goals) and accommodative coping (i.e. flexibly adjusting goals to constraints and limitations), in turn leading to increased depression (Cappeliez and Robitaille 2010). Even when older adults are only mildly to moderately depressed, self-negative functions undermine meaning in life and mastery (Korte *et al.* 2012a) and the satisfaction of basic needs for relatedness, competence and autonomy (Hofer *et al.* 2017). These findings are in agreement since the concept of mastery overlaps with facets of needs for autonomy and competence.

Boredom reduction

Boredom reduction has repeatedly been found as the reminiscence function that contributes most to the construct of self-negative functions of reminiscence (Cappeliez and O'Rourke 2006; King *et al.* 2017; Ros *et al.* 2016). This suggests that this function of reminiscence is especially harmful to wellbeing. Reminiscence for boredom reduction may connote a feeling that current life is boring and dull and that it pales in comparison with the past (for a discussion of the concept of boredom, see Rengade 2016). A significant body of literature underlines that such a negative subjective time perception is linked to lower levels of health and wellbeing (for a review see Gabrian, Dutt and Wahl 2017). Viewing the past as better than whatever can be experienced in the present and expected from the future fosters a scenario of deterioration over time. In earlier writing (Cappeliez and O'Rourke 2002), we had shown that reminiscence for boredom reduction is associated with a lack of goal seeking. This return to the past for lack of present or future personal goals may explain the particularly damaging contribution of these reminiscences because it deeply cuts into the sense of direction, coherence and purpose of life. In this respect, processes at work in boredom reduction reminiscence are the direct opposite of those involved in problem-solving reminiscence.

Interestingly, a positive use of nostalgia has been proposed as an antidote to the loss of meaning engendered by boredom (van Tilburg, Igou and Sedikides 2013). Nostalgic memories are typically associated with episodes of life during which challenges have been overcome (problem-solving reminiscence). They produce a feeling of self-continuity and wellbeing (identity reminiscence) by reducing the perception of distance between the past and the present (Hepper *et al.* 2014).

Bitterness revival

Bitterness revival represents the quintessential self-negative function of reminiscence. It implies going over and over again past mistakes, failures and losses. This bias toward self-negative information is a well-known characteristic of depressive cognitive patterns. The facilitated retrieval of these negative memories is promoted by a perceived discrepancy between actual self and ideal self, a core feature of depression. In turn, these self-discrepant memories aggravate and maintain depression. This increased frequency of bitterness revival reminiscences in depressed older adults can be understood with the help of cognitive psychology research showing that high levels of psychopathology are associated with increased retrieval of highly self-referential content, especially when negative emotional material is involved (Watson and Dritschel 2015).

This increased frequency of bitterness revival connotes the ruminative brooding that has been repeatedly shown to play a key role in the onset, maintenance and recurrence of depression (for a review, see Watkins 2015). Rumination involves dwelling on self-related material such as causes and consequences of upsetting events, personal difficulties and on depressed symptoms themselves. Rumination has far-reaching consequences, not only increasing negative mood and negative autobiographical memories but also negative thinking about the future (Nolen-Hoeksema *et al.* 2008). Rumination and over-general autobiographical memory reinforce each other (Watkins 2015). Over-general autobiographical memory, the recall of categorical summaries rather than specific events, is a marker or a vulnerability factor for depression.

Intimacy maintenance
The understanding of this function, and in particular of its consistently negative association with wellbeing, has been a source of controversy, in large part because of confusion about its nature. In Webster's taxonomy, this function refers narrowly to using memories in order to maintain some form of connection with those who have departed. It does not correspond to memories of close and romantic relationships. Such conceptualization allows us to interpret the substantial link with depression as evidence that this function encompasses reminiscences accompanying and/or aggravating extended grief (Cappeliez and O'Rourke 2006). Indeed, complicated grief is accompanied by pervasive memories of the deceased. This repetitive confrontation with losses conspires with the ruminations associated with bitterness revival to further lock the person into depression.

It is interesting to note that all three self-negative functions are aspects of *regret*. Although uncertainty remains about the origin of the word 'regret' in English, it could well originate from 're-grâta', a Scandinavian term which means 'to cry, to moan'. Thus, historically, 'regret' first refers to the longing for someone or something lost or absent, a feeling that is painful. It can be argued that this is akin to the reminiscence function of intimacy maintenance.

The term 'regret' has two other derived usages that interface with the other self-negative functions. It may carry a notion of personal discontent, and even guilt about having behaved in an indequate or reprehensible manner. In contrast to the first meaning, this one implies self-agency, and consequently an increase in the negativity of the feeling. Viewing one's past in this manner is central to the reminiscence function of bitterness revival.

Lastly, 'regret' may mean the discontent felt when events have not unfolded as one would have hoped or liked. It implies a negative comparison between what should have been and what actually happened. As in the first definition of regret, it involves some kind of longing for the past. This is akin to the process underlying reminiscence for boredom reduction. As we argued above, reminiscences for boredom reduction reflect the belief that good things are irremediably locked in the past (the 'good old' past) and that, in comparison, little positive is to be expected from what lies ahead in life.

Self-positive functions of reminiscence

The outstanding finding of the present study was the comparatively high reliance by the clinically depressed individuals on the self-positive functions of reminiscence. All the studies reviewed in the introduction above consistently point out a negative link between self-positive reminiscences and psychological distress. In other words, more reminiscing for these functions is typically associated with less psychological distress. Importantly, in that line of research, psychological distress is conceptualized on a continuum of levels of depressive symptoms, anxiety and life satisfaction and examined in the general population of community living older adults. As shown above, when the focus is made singularly on depression as a clinical entity, a different pattern emerges, one of activated self-positive reminiscences, one that seems exclusive to depression and not anxiety.[2]

The present study helps us understand the dynamic interplay between self-positive functions and depression. It appears that depression triggers a process of 'life reflection', a term proposed by Staudinger (2001) that corresponds to self-positive reminiscences, as an attempt to cope. This 'life reflection' involves reviewing negative and positive events, interpreting them in terms of a coherent life narrative, and comparing the past with present condition. In depression, these

---

2 Highly anxious participants (with a score > 43 on the state version of the State Trait Anxiety Inventory, STAI; Spielberger *et al.* 1983; n = 130) differed significantly from the 'not-at-all anxious' ones (bottom score of 20 on the STAI; n = 118) only in their increased uses of reminiscences for boredom reduction and bitterness revival (Cappeliez 2013)

processes, plagued by negative comparisons and images of failures, only meet sporadic success, and are thus repeatedly activated.

Identity

Findings from different studies suggest that the emotional turmoil of depression activates a search for purpose and meaning. A higher level of neuroticism predicts more reminiscence for identity (Cappeliez and O'Rourke 2002), a result that was interpreted as evidence that this disposition toward emotional vulnerability and negative affect fuels a drive for finding a sense of life coherence and meaning through recollection and review of the personal past. In support of this view, for older adults, more frequent confrontation with critical life events is associated with higher frequency of reminiscence for identity and problem solving (Korte *et al*. 2011b). Also, congruent with this line of thought is the finding (Grace *et al*. 2016) that higher levels of depressive symptoms are associated with increased recall of personal memories for self-continuity purpose, as measured with the Thinking about Life Experiences Scale (TALE) (Bluck and Alea 2011). Of note, this study was conducted with a sample of young adults, namely undergraduate students.

In contrast to our finding, Korte and her colleagues (2011b) found no significant relation between the function of identity and depressive symptoms (nor with anxious symptoms for that matter). The reason for the discrepancy may lie in the characteristics of the sample. These authors selected only mildly distressed older adults, excluding from their sample individuals with serious depression, i.e. those with scores of 24 and above on the CES-D with an accompanying diagnosis of major depressive disorder. In our study, individuals with scores of 24 or higher on the CES-D represented a sizeable 35 per cent of our depressed group. Considering the two studies together, it may mean that the higher use of reminiscence for self-positive functions is a feature of the most severe cases of depression.

The higher use of reminiscence for identity of depressed older adults reflects their attempts at maintaining a sense of self-continuity that constitutes a primary function of autobiographical memory. When facing crises, there is a drive to use reminiscence in order to re-forge 'retrospective self-continuity', a term coined by Bluck and Liao (2013) that refers to recognizing and reflecting on the self as continuous within one's continually evolving life story.

Problem solving

Reminiscences for problem solving represent recalling episodes of life in which one has tried to overcome challenges and crises. They entail accessing memories of previously used coping strategies to face problems. In other words, they involve making use of the past to direct one's present and future behavior. Because they proceed from linkages between past, present and future, they also contribute to meaning-making in one's life journey or, as pointed out by Bluck and her colleagues (2005), to updating current views of one's biographical self.

Additionally, insights gained from the practice of reminiscence interventions with depressed older adults suggest that these memories have the potential of repairing the sense of worth that is so undermined in depression. The reason is that problem-solving memories are potentially associated with images of oneself as capable of handling the difficulties or, at least, of confronting the problem instead of avoiding it. These representations of the self as competent contribute in their own way to fighting depression. The higher frequency of reminiscences for problem solving reflect the efforts the depressed person invests in accessing memories of formerly successful coping strategies for the purpose of re-establishing some sense of competence, personal worth and meaning.

Death preparation

The prospect of death often means reviewing one's life to feel at peace in the face of the inevitability of death. This raises questions about the nature and meaning of life. On one hand, this allows for better self-understanding and feelings of growth. But, on the other hand, confronting one's death may affect mood, and lead to depression and despair.

In earlier research, we had found that older adults who are more open to experience, as a personality trait, reported more frequent use of reminiscence for death preparation (and also for identity) (Cappeliez and O'Rourke 2002). Rasmussen and Berntsen (2010) replicated this and found that openness to experience correlated with RFS scales of problem solving, death preparation and identity – in other words with all three self-positive reminiscence functions. So, it seems that reminiscences constitute a privileged means for the intellectually curious, emotionally and cognitively receptive person to address existential issues of life purpose and meaning. Depressed older adults appear to be caught in repetitive thinking about these issues. In that vein, reminiscence for death preparation was reported as significantly correlated with depressive symptoms in samples of older adults, both cognitively functional and impaired (Alzheimer's disease) (El Haj and Antoine 2016), a finding the authors interpret as a manifestation of psychological distress towards approaching death.

Prosocial functions of reminiscences

Depressed and non-depressed participants did not differ significantly in their reliance on prosocial functions of reminiscence, a finding also reported by Grace and colleagues (2016). Community-dwelling older adults in general report using their memories for social bonding (and for directing behavior) significantly more often than for self-continuity (Bluck and Alea 2009). This pattern does not seem to apply to clinically depressed individuals. Social withdrawal, a common symptom of depression, and the dominantly self-referential thinking discussed earlier may be factors that seriously interfere with the engagement of depressed older adults in social interactions.

These findings invite a re-examination of the role played by prosocial reminiscences in the psychological functioning of older adults. As reviewed in the first section, research shows that prosocial reminiscences are not directly related to health and wellbeing, but rather indirectly through their own associations with self-reminiscences. One mediator of the contribution of prosocial reminiscences to health and wellbeing may be their influence on emotional regulation. We take our clues for this line of argument from several sources. For one, reminiscences for conversation appear to modulate positive affect in older adults, specifically generating and amplifying positive emotions (Cappeliez, Guindon and Robitaille 2008). The finding that extraversion, a trait that predisposes to experiencing positive affect, is positively linked with reminiscence for conversation and to teach/inform (Cappeliez and O'Rourke 2002; Cully *et al.* 2001) or generally reminiscence for serving social functions (Alea, Bluck and Ali 2015), is also consistent with a role played by prosocial reminiscences in positive emotional regulation. Also, it is known that positive memories are generally the ones that are recruited to serve social functions (McLean and Lilgendahl 2008).

Using an incident memory paradigm, a recent study reported that, consistent with their putative role of prosocial reminiscences in emotional regulation, participants remembered better the emotional contents of prosocial reminiscences (conversation and teach/inform) than those of integrative (i.e. identity) reminiscences (Cappeliez, in press). An integrative interpretation of these various findings obtained with very different methodologies is to assume that the primary role of prosocial reminiscences is to regulate emotion, more specifically to create and nurture context and contents for social interactions providing pleasure and self-enhancement (Cappeliez and O'Rourke 2006; O'Rourke *et al.* 2011). The positive affect promoted by prosocial reminiscences would in turn influence positively meaning in life, in unison with self-positive reminiscences. Indeed, correlational as well as experimental evidence support a causal link between positive affect and meaning in life (King, Heintzelman and Ward 2016).

Additionally, prosocial functions can be viewed as having in common a role of fostering relationships, which also contributes positively to wellbeing. Sharing personal experiences has been recognized as a means to facilitate and build social relationships, including setting up a context of intimacy (Alea and Bluck 2003, 2007). The globally positive effect of social reminiscences on mood has been underlined (Pasupathi and Carstensen 2003). Telling positive memories may increase self-esteem, and in turn improve wellbeing and health (Mather and Carstensen 2005). Actually, for older adults, using positive memories for conversation is related to the personal growth component of wellbeing (McLean and Lilgendahl 2008).

Clinical implications

These findings have important implications for reminiscence interventions with depressed older adults. They clearly underline that in order to optimize the effects of these interventions it is critical to curtail reminiscences for bitterness revival and especially boredom reduction, given their strong harmful effects. As indicated by Korte *et al.* (2012b), the beneficial effects of life review therapy on depression (and anxiety for that matter) are obtained largely through reductions of these two types of reminiscence.

Recent developments in memory-based interventions for depression have sprung from the hypothesis that, because of the link between over-general autobiographical memory retrieval and depression, training depressed patients in generating specific autobiographical memories will counter ruminations and thus be therapeutic (e.g. Serrano et al. 2004). However, there is a very different way of combating ruminations that is relevant to reminiscence interventions with depressed older adults. It can be found in mindfulness-based therapy (Segal, Williams and Teasdale 2002). This therapy approach fosters the ability to disengage from mind states characterized by patterns of ruminative, negative thinking. In this way, the person engages in a mode of reflection on the event that is self-distancing rather than self-immersing, with a resultant decrease in negative emotion associated with the event memory (Kross, Ayduk and Mischel 2005; van der Velden et al. 2015). It has been argued that a selfless psychological functioning (i.e. altruistic, kind, empathic, compassionate), which is fostered by meditation based on mindfulness, is a source of authentic and durable happiness and wellbeing (Dambrun and Ricard 2011).

These findings also point to risks of negative outcomes in reminiscence interventions, a subject rarely approached in the literature. Indeed, simply encouraging older depressed individuals to recollect personal memories may have the very adverse effect of activating a downward spiral, unless they are provided with a guiding context to review these memories, in a form of life review therapy as Westerhof and his co-authors defined it (2010). Engaging in problem-solving and identity reminiscences, even if only brief and limited in scope, enhances self-efficacy and meaning in life, as a unique experimental study with young adults recently demonstrated (Hallford and Mellor 2016b). However, it is clear that, in the case of intervention in depression, self-positive reminiscences need to be carefully guided for fear that the search for meaning will shift toward repetitive negative thought patterns. To further this aim, the adoption of a structured form of life review therapy is warranted. Additionally, the integration of life review and narrative therapy, as proposed by Bohlmeijer and Westerhof (2013), provides further means for the restoration of meaning.

Comments and conclusion

Some limitations of this line of research on the adaptivity of reminiscences must be noted. All these studies rely on data from questionnaires in which participants provide a retrospective account of their uses of the various reminiscence functions. As stressed by several authors in the field (e.g. Bluck et al. 2005; Cappeliez and O'Rourke 2006), there are inherent limitations to measuring reminiscence functions with self-report questionnaires due to the fact that individuals vary in their definitions of reminiscence and of their purposes. Responses may then be skewed toward reminiscence functions involving conscious awareness, possibly missing more spontaneous reminiscences. Basically, such self-reports are a hybrid measure of actual frequency of reminiscence uses compounded by perceptions and beliefs of the person regarding the relative importance and usefulness of the various forms of reminiscence. These perceptions and beliefs have a major influence on how an individual in fact uses reminiscence.

While self-defining memories sustaining a sense of identity are particularly resistant to the effects of age, the weakening of executive functioning with advancing age could in itself facilitate cognitive processes such as ruminations. Future research on ruminative thinking style could attempt to tease apart the interaction between healthy aging and depression.

Other reminiscence functions are likely to play a role in emotion regulation besides prosocial reminiscences. Other authors have suggested that emotion regulation may be served by self-functions generally (e.g. Harris et al. 2014). Further research is needed to determine if emotion regulation can be incorporated in existing conceptualizations such as the tripartite model or needs to be considered as another separate class. Research in that area has been impeded by the fact that the existing measures of reminiscence or autobiographical functions, the RFS and the TALE, do not address emotional regulation.

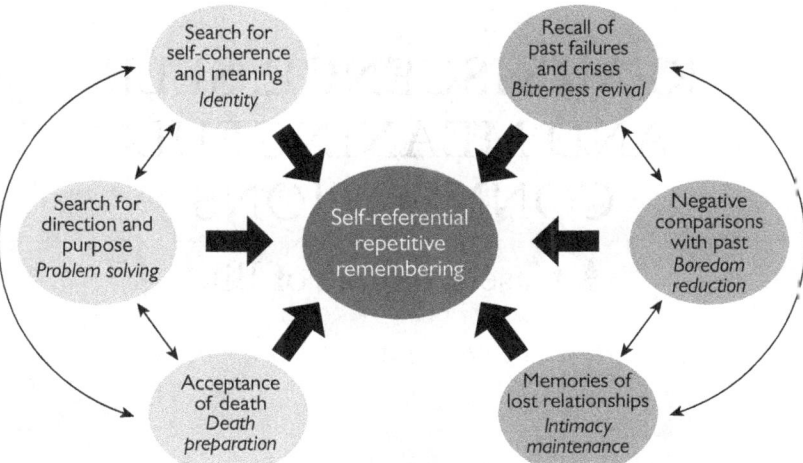

Figure 12.1: Cycles of reminiscences in late life depression

In conclusion, self reminiscences, both negative and positive, are particularly active in depression in late adulthood. They reflect a continuing struggle to find meaning and personal worth in one's life. Figure 12.1 illustrates the operations of these vicious cycles of reminiscences in depression. These findings draw the attention of mental health professionals engaged in reminiscence-based interventions to the need to help distressed older adults disengage from this perpetuating pattern of self-referential remembering.

Acknowledgments

Support for completion of the research program on reminiscence was provided by the Social Sciences and Humanities Research Council of Canada (SSHRC 410-2006-0124 and 410-2005-2328 to Dr Cappeliez and Dr O'Rourke, respectively) and by the Canadian Institutes of Health Research (CIHR 127915 and 136727 both to Dr O'Rourke).

Chapter 13

REMINISCENCE, SELF AND MEANINGFUL CONNECTIONS

A Case Example of Bill

Kate de Medeiros and Sara Stemen

An important function of reminiscence is its ability to help one create present meaning by remembering and reinterpreting moments from the past (Gibson 2011). Group reminiscence and autobiographical writing workshops for older persons continue to gain in popularity, as both worthwhile activities and topics of research. While there is a body of excellent work covering topics such as types and functions of reminiscence (Bohlmeijer and Westerhof 2011; Brooker and Duce 2000; Cappeliez *et al.* 2008; Webster and Haight 2002), the listener's role in shaping stories (Cohler and Cole 1996; Pasupathi and Billitteri 2015; Rappaport 1995), and the role of the life review (Burnside 2004; Butler 1963a, 1963b; de Vries, Birren and Deutchman 1990), there is still much to be learned about reminiscence as a social process. We use an illustrative case example of Bill[1] to explore the way he uses recollections from his past, various storytelling genres, and group members' input to shape a meaningful present and future.

We begin with a brief overview of the concepts of self, reminiscence, autobiographical memory and remembering to clarify terms and to ground our position in the existing literature. We then consider some components of self and identity, paying close attention to ways in which self may be internally interpreted, reinterpreted and externally confirmed, and the role of meaning in the context of selves. Using the case example, we examine transcripts from and pieces

---

1 Pseudonyms used throughout

created during an eight-week Self Stories workshop (de Medeiros 2014) to highlight the different ways that Bill and the group negotiate meaning. Deeper insight into the social nature of such groups may lead to better strategies to promote social inclusion and understanding among groups of older persons.

Self, reminiscence, autobiographical memory and remembering

Self, reminiscence, autobiographical memory and remembering are all interrelated terms used in the context of recalling the past. We note here some places where they overlap and places where they converge.

Self

The first concept, self, has long been acknowledged as complex and difficult to define (Baumeister 1987, 2010; de Medeiros 2005; Goffman 1959; Westerhof, Whitbourne and Freeman 2012). Baumeister (2010) suggests that there is not a single construct of self but rather an 'aggregate self schema' (p.687). He proposes three root phenomena of self, each of which may take slightly different shape and meaning depending on the cultural context:

- Reflexive consciousness or the ability to be aware of one's self as unique.
- Interpersonal being or the self in interaction with others.
- Self as actor/entity, making decisions and choices as well as assuming responsibility.

Baumeister's construct therefore encompasses the individual and social aspects of self which are important in the context of reminiscence, autobiographical memory and remembering and which we will explore in greater detail in the case example.

Westerhof *et al.* (2012, p.52) also note the challenges with the concept of 'self' and create a definition for the aging self specifically. They describe the aging self as: 'the conception of one's own aging process, a process related to but distinct from people's concepts about their bodies (physical self), their psychological qualities (personal identity) and their social relations (social self)'. Their definition recognizes that awareness of the advancement of time may require a different type of reflexive consciousness, one that might be more centered on reinterpreting past events in light of present and future goals, whatever those may be, which links to Baumeister's (2010) first root phenomenon, and the social relations (the third root phenomenon). They do not refer to Baumeister's 'self as actor' but instead mention age in the context of personal identity, which they further develop through identity process theory. Briefly, identity process theory, a way to think about how individuals incorporate their experiences into their self-concept, has three processes: identity assimilation or maintaining continuity of self, identity accommodation or reconciling discrepancies of one's self schema based on new experiences, and identity balance or maintaining self-continuity while including age-relevant experience. Overall, self and identity have the perception of being fixed, but are arguably fluid depending on experience and context. We return to these key ideas later when examining Bill's case study.

Reminiscence

Cappeliez and Webster (2011, p.188) define reminiscence as 'a personal memory that has an emotional impact'. Others describe reminiscence as the act or process of actively recalling past memories about the self (Haslam *et al.* 2014; Sherman 1991). Rather than a recall of facts, reminiscence involves a reinterpretation of past events relative to one's self; events and experiences are recalled and interpreted in relation to an 'I' (Cappeliez *et al.* 2005; Rathbone, Moulin and Conway 2008). Consequently, reminiscence does not exist without the revelation of some aspect of self (de Medeiros 2005; Rathbone *et al.* 2008).

Also important is the role that reminiscence plays in the stable maintenance or continuity of self discussed earlier when faced with discrepancies (Baumeister 2010; Rathbone *et al.* 2008; Westerhof *et al.* 2012). The maintenance function can perhaps be most clearly seen in the concept of the life review, which Butler (1963a, p.66) described as 'a naturally occurring, universal mental process characterized by the progressive return to consciousness of past experiences, and, particularly, the resurgence of unresolved conflicts; simultaneously, and normally, these revived experiences and conflicts can be surveyed and reintegrated'. Butler and others have argued that reminiscence can serve an important function of allowing a person to revisit a past memory from the present and, through reinterpretation (e.g. seeing the situation as a reflective, experienced adult rather than as a child who lived through the event), one may potentially reconcile such discrepancies from the past and arrive at a new understanding.

Another important component of self and reminiscence is the social component (Baumeister 2010; Reese and Farrant 2003). Although focused on children, Reese and Farrant (2003, p.29) note that:

> A primary function of reminiscence is social. We talk with others about our past to highlight events that were meaningful to those involved, as well as to illustrate our own personality characteristics. Thus, reminiscing is inherently social as well as a means of self-presentation.

Telling others about our past is important to self-maintenance. They also describe such reminiscence and self-narrative as practices enculturated in children to teach them how to make sense of themselves by sharing with others, an idea that can apply to older persons as well.

Autobiographical memory

Closely related to reminiscence is autobiographical memory. Brewer (1986) defines autobiographical memory as 'memory for information related to the self' (p.26) and self as 'the complex mental structure that includes the ego ["the conscious experiencing entity that is the focus of our phenomenal experience"]' (p.27), 'the self-schema, and portions of long-term memory related to the ego-self' (p.27). Fivush (2011) presents a similar definition but adds that autobiographical memories become linked in a way that brings the past, present and future together to form a life narrative and that autobiographical memory guides present and future conceptions of self and identity. Again, self and identity are central. See Chapter 5 by Fivush and Booker.

Remembering

If autobiographical memories are the 'what', 'remembering' is the 'how' or what occurs when autobiographical memories are retrieved. Rajaram (1993) distinguishes between 'remembering' being one's ability to recall having an association with an item or event, and 'knowing', being an awareness of an item or event without having a personal connection to it. Remembering differs from reminiscence in that remembering may only involve brief personal recall whereas reminiscence implies an emotional connection with the past memory and a sense of revisiting or re-experiencing at least a portion of the past event.

Meaning, life stories and social connections

Having considered components and related concepts to reminiscence we can now look to meaning, reminiscence and social connection.

Meaning

For Butler (1963a, 1963b), who drew from Erikson's (1963) developmental stages, reminiscence and the life review were tied to the ability to find meaning in life, especially as we age and come to terms with our impending mortality (e.g. the aging self). Meaning-making is therefore an important goal of reminiscence. As such, Gibson (2011, p.26) describes reminiscence as:

> a search for meaning – a search for understanding of our past. It is a re-tracing of where we have come from – a process for discovering and re-discovering who we are by making linkages between disparate aspects of our lives, our families and our communities. We come to understand as if for the first time, or to understand in different ways, the values, people and places which have shaped us and made us what we have become and are still becoming.

Again, the links between continuity, resolving discrepancies and reinterpreting are clear.

Also, important to meaning is the social context through which meaning takes place (Krause 2012). Although meaning may differ within individuals, people live within larger social organizations and are therefore shaped by them. Baumeister (1987) identified four needs or aspects of meaning: purpose, moral justification, self worth and efficacy. The first, purpose, speaks to the ideal that each individual has a reason for living. Specifically, past experiences are building blocks for reaching a life that is fulfilled. The second, moral justification, maintains that people desire to be looked at as virtuous. The third, self-worth, describes that people feel compelled to achieve because it results in self-respect and the earning of respect from others. The fourth, efficacy, is described as the need for people to feel in control of their lives. The following section will explore more deeply how life story narratives can function in meaning-making.

Life stories

In the context of reminiscence, meaning can be made through the act of recall itself or through sharing moments from one's past with others, as addressed earlier in the sections on self and identity. We note a substantial literature on the importance of putting one's experience into words (written or verbal) and sharing those stories with others (Fivush and Haden 2003; Kenyon *et al.* 2011; McAdams 1993; Randall 1995) The term 'life story' as defined by Cohler and Cole (1996, p.63) describes 'a narrative of a particular kind, one which unites disparate elements of a presently experienced life within a text which is coherent and at least potentially followable by others'. Life stories can be oral or written and can include a variety of literary genres such as memoirs, poetry or letters, although first-person memoirs are the most common approach (de Medeiros 2007, 2013). Regardless of whether they are written or spoken, life stories are shaped by both the teller and the listener. The teller selects events based on knowledge of the listener (e.g. how well does the teller know the listener, how personal are the details to be disclosed). If the listener is an unknown reader, then the teller/writer may try to anticipate what the listener/reader's reactions will be. In turn, the listener's reaction will shape the teller's future disclosures (Cohler and Cole 1996; de Medeiros 2005; Pasupathi and Billitteri 2015). In a verbal interchange, this may happen immediately. The speaker may change details based on observed or heard responses from the listener. In writing, the response may be delayed. Even a lack of response could be perceived by the speaker or writer as a response, positive or negative. As mentioned earlier in the context of selves and the social, listeners shape the content in narrative and the teller's sense of self. This joint construction between teller and listener is therefore an important aspect of reminiscence.

Social connections

An important way that meaning and life stories come together is in the social way in which stories are shared. As Bluck *et al.* (2013, p.82) have written:

sharing life stories serves several important social functions including (i) developing and maintaining intimacy (ii) teaching and informing others, and (iii) eliciting and expressing empathy. Sharing autobiographical memories may elicit an empathic response from a listener if the speaker's memory engages the listener, and if the listener responds with an autobiographical memory that relates to the experience of the speaker.

Looking back at Baumeister's four aspects of meaning, we argue that sharing stories provides the building blocks from the past that can point to reasons for living; that people can tell stories in a way that presents themselves as 'virtuous' in the sense of being 'good'; that stories can result in earning others' respect; and that telling or writing the story of one's experience can give the individual a sense of control over events. These aspects are explored in fuller detail through the following case example.

METHODS: SELF STORIES WORKSHOP

Bill's case example was drawn from a larger randomized control trial of autobiographical writing and its potential effect on autobiographical memory (see de Medeiros 2011b for specific details). Bill had been randomly assigned to participate in an eight-week, 90 minutes per week, writing workshop, 'Self Stories' (de Medeiros, 2007, 2011a, 2011b). His case was selected because, as Yin (2011) describes, Bill's experience highlights some essential components of the phenomena (reminiscence, self and social connection) being discussed and provides unique insights into the group process.

To be eligible for the study, participants had to be at least 65 years of age, able to communicate in English, able to participate in a writing workshop through either physically writing or dictating their stories using a recorder, and could not have a diagnosis of dementia or mild cognitive impairment. Institutional review board approval was provided by the first author's institution. All participants agreed, through written informed consent, to have the workshops audiotaped for use in research and teaching. All work cited in this chapter is taken from the audiotape transcripts. In addition, all identifying information, such as proper nouns and dates, has been changed to protect the participants' identities.

The goal of the writing workshop was to introduce participants to different literary genres as mediums for writing and sharing stories about their past. The genres in order of presentation were:

- Weeks one to three: First-person memoirs (any story about a past event told from the subject's perspective using the first-person pronoun 'I').

- Week four: Letter (a story by the subject written to a specific person who is named in the salutation).

- Week five: Poems (loosely defined as a collection of brief thoughts on a given topic written in stanza form but with optional rhythm, meter or rhyme).

- Week six: Third-person stories (autobiographical stories by and about the subject, but narrated from an outsider's point of view — with 'he' or 'she' instead of 'I').

- Weeks seven to eight: Participants were asked to rewrite a story from a previous assignment using a different genre.

Along with weekly assignments, participants were also given a sheet of basic literary concepts or aspects of writing to consider such as 'plot' (an ordered structure of actions, designed to achieve a particular emotional and or/artistic effect) to help 'demystify' the writing process and make the idea of writing accessible to people who may have had little experience with it.

The rationale behind using different genres was the idea that genres develop within cultures over time and that people bring their own interpretation to what is an appropriate subject for a particular genre. As such, people will likely select stories that they believe fit within that genre. Different genres, therefore, could potentially allow people to tell different kinds of stories about their past or, in the case of rewriting a story using a different genre, to re-imagine, rethink or even re-experience a past event (de Medeiros 2007, 2013).

Written stories rather than oral reminiscence was chosen since writing over the course of a week allowed people to think about what story they would like to tell, as well as details to include or omit (de Medeiros 2011b). Having a week to think about and create a piece for the next meeting provided several opportunities for participants. They could have time to think about what story or stories they'd like to tell, they had the opportunity to craft their message rather than spontaneously telling, and they could keep whatever they wrote private.

During the first meeting, participants were given an overview of the life story process. To familiarize them with workshop format, the facilitator read sample pieces from previous workshop participants and asked the group to discuss them. Each subsequent week, participants were invited to read their work aloud if they so choose (no one was required to read) to receive and provide oral feedback.

Week one

The group began with nine members – six women, three men. All described themselves as 'white'. One woman withdrew after week two. On the first day of the workshop meeting, the facilitator (de Medeiros) provided an overview of the workshop format and read a previous workshop participant's story entitled 'Good Morning, Miss Keithly' about the author's experience during a military inspection in the Second World War. The women in her barracks were instructed to say, 'Good morning, Miss Keithly' when the inspecting office arrived. However, unbeknown to the women, Miss Keithly was ill that day. A different officer, Miss Harris, conducted the inspection instead and was annoyed at being called 'Miss Keithly'. After reading the piece, the facilitator asked the group for their reactions to the story.

In general, the groups' comments were positive. For example, one participant said, 'I think she described everything. You know? You could see everything they were talking about.' Another person added, 'I could picture the room very well.' Some were not as positive. One member, Julie, for example said she thought the story was wordy and said that the writer went 'into detail that was not at all necessary to the story'.

Bill, a retired physician, was one of the last participants to comment. He began by criticizing both the story's topic and the author's writing style. He said, 'By contrast, I think there's errors in the first sentence… all the people had "Miss" titles rather than military titles and this was a military setting and it was a captain's inspection. It should have been a person with the captain's rank rather than a "Miss". And then the whole thing is, it's not a story…it's a non-event for me.' Bill's comment about the story being a 'non-event' links back to the earlier idea that people bring their own thoughts to a genre, including what 'counts' as something worth telling. For Bill, the complicating action of the story – the mistake in identity – did not 'count'.

The first workshop wasn't limited to only critiquing writing. The stories also provided opportunities for the group members to engage in reminiscence. For example, the second sample story read was selected by the facilitator since it described how a former participant's mother made angel food cake and mayonnaise from scratch, something that the group members may have identified with. The writing in this story wasn't particularly compelling (e.g. 'Everyone liked Mom's angel food cake. It was the one that rose the highest and was the lightest and tastiest of all… the whites were put in the large enamel bowl then whipped with a wire whip'). However, the details were likely to be familiar to many group members. Comments on this story included statements like, 'It made me think of my grandmother' or 'We made vinegar that way [as described in the story]. We never bought vinegar.' Bill did not comment on the second piece specifically but did ask a question regarding the purpose of the research study, asking the facilitator to reiterate the hypotheses and providing his professional medical opinion about dementia, which he erroneously thought was part of the research study. After answering Bill's questions, the facilitator ended the session by explaining the assignment for the following week – to write at least one page or four paragraphs about something from your 'past'.

Week two
At the start of week two, the facilitator asked for volunteers to read their story aloud. One person, Annie, read a story that she titled, 'Have You Ever Had a Playhouse?' This was a short first-person story about a playhouse her father built her when she was 5 years old. During the discussion of the story, most participants complimented Annie on creating a vivid image of the playhouse and shared some of their own similar experiences. When asked by the facilitator about whether the title was effective, one participant commented, 'I think it's a good title because it makes you think about playhouses and, um, kind of wish you had one.' Bill, however, disagreed. There then followed an interaction between Bill and Annie:

> Bill: But it's a feminist title. It doesn't…since boys didn't usually have playhouses. I don't identify.
>
> Annie: You're a man. I'm a woman.
>
> Bill: No, I'm just saying that a title that was more embracing would be one that wouldn't chop the boys out.

Annie: I didn't care about the boys.

Bill: Well, that's your privilege.

Annie: Not at 5 anyway.

Bill expressed feeling disconnected or purposefully excluded from the story given the topic and title. His comments seemed self-focused on what Annie's story meant to him rather than on what Annie's story meant to her.

Later in the same session, Bill read his piece, 'One Hundred Miles on the Appalachian Trail'. He brought along a special travel insert from the local paper that ran a feature that weekend on the Appalachian Trail, complete with a map. His story began with a paragraph of family background (he grew up speaking French at home) and then a description of the summer camp he attended where the counselors made fun of him by calling him 'Frenchie'. As Bill was the youngest camper in the group on the Appalachian Trail hike, he fell behind the others. The counselors first offered him a ride back to camp, which he refused, and then later to transport his bag, which he also refused. Bill described himself as tearful but determined. He wrote, 'The assistant director pulled away, but he never called me Frenchie again.'

The group responded, unprompted, with positive comments such as, 'Great ending', 'Very well written' and 'Very beautifully written'. They also asked him questions about the trail, and about Bill's reaction to the counselor, with some group members validating Bill's decision to hike without the help. For example, one person said, 'It got the message across to your counselor.' Another person added, 'And doing it in a way that was respectful.' Although people spoke about the quality of the writing, the comments for Bill's piece were more about validating Bill's actions than his writing techniques. Unlike Bill himself, who had been rather critical of others' writing, the group members focused more on the moment that Bill was communicating – overcoming a bullying situation. This group validation set an important tone that would have an effect on Bill during subsequent meetings.

Week three

For this week (the assignment was a first-person narrative), Bill wrote a piece, 'Lessons for Life', where he recalled his experiences during one class at an elite boarding school. Bill complained to his teacher that a particular decision was unfair, to which his teacher responded, 'Young man, if you learn nothing more in my class than the fact that life is not fair, you will have learned a great deal.' Bill then applies this lesson in his piece to some later hardships he experienced in more recent years, including cancer diagnoses for both him and his wife (his wife's prognosis at the time of the workshop was poor), being disowned by his parents when he married his wife some 60 years earlier, and other examples of hardship. The closing line in his story was, 'In the final analysis, it is how one deals with life's adversities. One can overcome even what seems to be not fair.' The group responded with resounding enthusiasm: 'Here, here', 'That's beautiful', 'That's an excellent point', 'That's a beautiful, beautiful story.' As with the previous week, the responses weren't about Bill's writing, but about what Bill conveyed about himself through his writing.

The group's reactions to Bill arguably had an effect on how Bill reacted to others. For example, when Julie read a story about meeting her mother-in-law for the first time, she concluded by writing, 'In the ensuing years, I practiced lessons when I became a mother-in-law, four times over. Be warm, non-judgmental, and most of all, have a sense of humor.' This was in response to the negative reaction she described in her story that she received from her mother-in-law. After Julie read her concluding lines, Bill commented, 'It sounds like Mrs Smith (her mother-in-law) didn't quite make it.' When Julie responded, 'Mrs Smith was very... She was an extraordinary woman. She had her grandchildren call her ma'am. She was not grandma, she was ma'am.' Bill pushed her a little further by asking, 'What made her extraordinary?' He also asked other questions such as, 'Did she (Mrs Smith) have a professional career?' He also asked Julie to further explain a sentence she had written that described Mrs Smith as a 'professional widow in every sense of the word'. He did so with humor, laughing as he explained, 'I have no idea what a professional widow in any sense of the word is, so you need to fill that out.' Although Bill's comments were somewhat dry and direct as in the first weeks' comments about 'Good Morning, Miss Keithly' or Annie's playhouse story, his comments now seemed to be shifting away from how he saw himself relating to a given person's story toward trying to understand the given person's story from that person's perspective.

Week four

The assignment from the previous week was to write a letter to someone, living or dead, about something from the past. Topics from participants' letters included one letter by a woman to her friend reinventing herself after the loss of her spouse, a man who became reconnected (and later friends with) a bully from his younger days, a man who wrote a letter to his brother (now deceased) as if it were 1949, and a woman whose teacher was accused of being a spy during the Second World War. Bill took an unusual direction for this assignment and rewrote a letter to the editor of the local paper regarding an article on Congressional misunderstanding of the use of mammography for breast cancer screening. The original article to which his letter responded appeared some 11 years earlier. In his letter, Bill provided a detailed argument of the need to enhance scientific understanding of Congress members to ensure appropriate allocation of research and healthcare dollars. He wrote, 'Limited healthcare resources should be spent on basic research to understand breast cancer disease – that's science – rather than on funding a screening procedure in an age group where there is no scientific consensus of its efficacy. That's politics.'

From a group standpoint, Bill's letter was clearly a departure from the other members' interpretation of the assignment (as well as the assignment's intention). Other participants' letters had been deeply personal, yet Bill's seemed curiously distant and disengaged. Rather than asking Bill about his choice of subject, something Bill himself might have done to others earlier in the workshop, the group responded positively. The first person to comment told Bill, 'That is very thoughtful.' Another person told Bill about her granddaughter who was pursuing her doctorate in biophysics and that she was hoping to do research on cancer in women. Bill was enthusiastic and asked Sue more about her granddaughter. Sue was able to make a connection between Bill's letter and someone in her personal life, which in turn made a connection between Bill and Sue. Throughout the discussion, no one questioned why Bill wrote about such a technical issue but instead seemed to 'meet him where he was' by providing positive and encouraging feedback.

Week five

This week participants were asked: 'Write a poem of at least 15 lines about an incident you remember. You may try writing a formula poem, starting each line or each group of lines with the phrase, "I remember".' Examples from participants' poems include a poem about Kenya, where Annie wrote:

> Could we be aliens, arrived from another planet?
> The Masai Mara stretches endlessly around our little plane.

Only the thin purple line of an escarpment to the west
Marks any end to the flat beige plain.

Here, Annie experimented with rhyme and figurative language to describe her trip in 1986. Another poem by Rodney, called 'Relatives in Rhyme', started as follows:

[Joseph], born in Pennsylvania in 1842, was my great-grandfather on my maternal grandmother's side.
In the Civil War, he fought for the Union at Bull Run, was wounded,
Run over by an artillery carriage, and almost died.

Rather than drawing from personal memory, Rodney used the poem to create a story about his family. Bill wrote a formula poem which he called 'Recollections'. Here is an excerpt:

I remember going to kindergarten at the International School in [Brussels, Belgium].
I remember coming to America on board an ocean liner in [1933].
I remember attending the [Washington] Elementary School in [Chicago, Illinois].
I remember during my four years at the [Brindell] School in [Boston, Massachusetts] being surrounded by the important moulding forces in my early life.
I remember majoring in chemistry at [Northeastern University] in [Boston] and my first effort in academic research, an honors paper which brought me distinction in chemistry when I graduated in [1952] with honors in general scholarship.
I remember my two years at the [University of Minnesota] where I graduated with a Master of Science Degree in [1955].
I remember mountain climbing in the Teton National Park in Wyoming where I climbed several lesser peaks but also the 13,768 foot Grand Teton.
I remember my early years as a graduate student at the [University of Maryland] where I married [Shirley] of the [Oberlin] College Class of [1953] in a small chapel on the edge of campus.

He began by recalling some of his earlier experiences, many that he had written about in earlier assignments. Midway through his poem, however, he shifted his focus to his wife, explaining how he was able to finish medical school and his wife, her doctoral degree, before they both were given faculty positions at the same university. It is important to note that the medical school decision is a key idea that comes up in subsequent writings, especially with regards to the 'unfairness' in having to have made the decision based on gendered opportunities, which he increasingly acknowledges in his writings. As with his other pieces, the group responded positively, saying, 'Very impressive' and 'I want to say wow'. Bill explained, 'I hope that the collaborative effort has come through this because without that collaboration, we had no children, uh, but we're very close and we argue furiously. I believe in reincarnation. It's very important to my whole idea of spirituality. [My wife] doesn't believe in reincarnation and we stopped arguing about it.' He went on to tell the group that his wife was diagnosed with terminal cancer a year ago and that the illness had brought them closer together. He added that he referred to the retirement community where they lived as the 'finishing school'. One of the participants asked, 'You call this place the finishing school?' 'Yes', he responded. 'We came here to finish.' As the group continued to talk about his poem and the accomplishments he highlighted, Bill became tearful at times describing how his wife had to constantly battle sexist attitudes in the workplace, especially as a female scientist. He also said he felt some regret at having pursued his own interest in medicine at the expense of his wife, who had wanted to complete medical school as well. Overall, when asked if he was pleased with his poem, Bill responded, 'Yeah. I'm pleased with it. It certainly caused me to do a lot of reflection that I would never had done.'

Bill wasn't able to attend week six, but was given the assignment for week seven.

Weeks seven and eight

During the seventh session, participants were asked to rewrite a piece from a previous session using a different genre. The purpose, as previously stated, was to have participants think about how and why their story or its details changed by virtue of the genre through which they were narrating. At the beginning of week seven, the facilitator asked the group for their reactions to that week's assignment. Julie, who rewrote her first-person story about meeting her mother-in-law (Mrs Smith) as a third-person story, commented:

> I did not find it enjoyable. I found it difficult to write in the third person. Um, I think I'm better at first person memoir-type writing and, as a

> consequence, I don't like what I wrote. I feel it is, it's stiff, and I don't know whether I got my point across. But that's not for me to say I guess.

As she read her piece, she paused periodically and added her own evaluations such as 'now that sounds awkward'. Although Julie was unsatisfied with her revised piece, very little had changed in the writing. For example, her conclusion was quite similar (except for the pronouns) to the conclusion in her original piece in week three. In her revised version, Julie wrote, 'In the ensuing years, she practiced those lessons when she became a mother-in-law. Be warm, non-judgmental, and most of all have a sense of humor.'

When the group was asked to respond to the piece, Bill said, 'I think that's pretty good. I don't know why you denigrated it. I think it's wonderful... See, we're all perfectionists is what the problem is.' He also added, 'The descriptions are great.' Unlike his earlier critical feedback which was directed at technical aspects of the writing, his reactions to others' work in the later weeks began to focus more on the overall point of what was being said rather than how it was being written. His comments also suggest Bill's willingness to connect with others in the group in a way he hadn't before. For example, he commented to Julie:

> You know, Julie, you read that originally and I don't have a copy of your first one, so at some point when you have a chance, I'd love to have a copy of that because since it's a redo I want to be able to compare them.

In this instance, Bill was trying to demonstrate to Julie that he was deeply interested in her work and that he was a careful and supportive listener.

Bill volunteered to read his piece next. Interestingly, he had rewritten his formula poem 'I Remember' from week 5 as a rhyming poem that he titled 'Poem'. He told the group:

> Well, this is week seven and because I was not satisfied with just having said 'I remember', I decided I really had to try and write a poem. This was a struggle because I don't usually write poetry and poetry has two challenges, uh, one is to get the meter right and if you have any kind of rhyme scheme, then you have to deal with the rhyme scheme. I had hoped to be able to use A, B, C, A, uh, but it didn't work that way, so I just ended up doing the best that I could with the rhymes. And this makes only sense if you know the whole story because it's three little fragments of the story and since you know the whole story, you may be able to appreciate what I was trying to do.

In a similar style to some of the other participants who read their rhyming poems in the previous weeks, Bill's new poem used more figurative language and had a basic rhyme scheme. Before reading, he laughingly told the group, 'And so to prove that I could write some poetry, I wrote three quatrains in rhyme.' He then read the following poem.

> My dad was Yankee through and through
> My mother French born all the way.
> Together they a family made.
> I never learned to blend the two.
>
> For many years, we went to school
> to earn the doctorates required.
> My wife and I did not give up.
> We made it by the Golden Rule.
>
> In later life, we learned anew
> That health may not be guaranteed.
> But docs and prayers have done their best
> And we're alive with more to do.

After reading his poem, Bill told the group, 'I don't usually write poetry, so it was a little bit of a struggle.' He added, 'And if you're writing poetry and bother to rhyme, the rhyme pushes the story in directions that you then have to justify one way or the other', to which one of the participant's responded, 'You did a good job.' Toward the end of this discussion, Annie told Bill:

> And to make another point, the very fact that you read it in front of, well, we're not strangers, but we're not intimate friends, and some of this stuff is very private and you're telling something to someone you don't know very well.

Annie's comments pointed to Bill's vulnerability and to the trust that had built up among the members. Someone mentioned that they liked how his wife was included in the poem. Bill responded, 'Well, there are not very many men feminists, but I count myself as one of those.' Bill's statement here is an interesting contrast to his comment to Annie early in the workshop about not relating to her story about the playhouse because it was 'feminist'.

Discussion

There are several key components related to reminiscence, self and meaningful connections illustrated in Bill's case example: processes Bill used to reinterpret past and current events from his life, potentially for self-maintenance and identity balance in the face of change (Westerhof *et al.* 2012); the social component of reminiscence (Reese and Farrant 2003); and ways in which meanings are made. Bill began as an unhelpful critic of others' work but then gradually became more positive towards others through their responses to his writing and personal revelations, at first through the connections that others made to him, then gradually through connections that he made to his own experiences and those of the others.

As mentioned earlier, reminiscence is very much a search for meaning, making sense of the past, and perhaps even reconciling unresolved conflicts. Bill wrote about several past conflicts including being bullied by camp counselors, realizing that life is not fair, and coming to terms with the choices he and his wife had made throughout their lives, such as choosing his medical education over hers, but being supportive of her work as a scientist in the face of adversity. In his final piece – a rewrite of his formula poem – he concluded with the lines, 'And we're alive with more to do.' This is in contrast to his comment from a few weeks earlier when he referred to the retirement community as a 'finishing school', since he and his wife would be finishing their lives there. Even though his wife had a poor medical prognosis, his poem seemed to take on a hopeful tone. In many ways, the revised poem is illustrative of Baumeister's (2010) root three phenomena of self. Bill was able to consciously reflect on his experience and recognize himself as unique from other selves; he was a self, interacting with others through the creation and reading of his poem; and he was a self as actor, both through the decisions he made to write his experiences down and also through his desire to accomplish more in life, to have a purpose.

The revised poem is also interesting to consider with regards to Baumeister's (1987) four aspects or needs of meaning. The poem demonstrates a purpose ('and we're alive with more to do'), moral justification ('My wife and I did not give up/We made it by the Golden Rule'), self worth (which is referenced in many lines including those about his family, his career and his present situation) and efficacy (similar to self as actor, mentioned in the previous paragraph).

He described how changing the poem from a formula poem (I remember) to a rhyming one pushed the story in different directions – including Bill's identification as a male feminist. It's as if the reflection on his past and the support he received from the group allowed him to directly consider his accomplishments in different ways, shifting from an 'I' only approach to recognizing the role that his wife played.

Another interesting change in Bill was the shift from what he considered a past event worth telling about. During the first session, he criticized the story about Miss Keithly as being a 'non-event' since the complicating action was the mistake in identity. However, as Bill's reactions to others gradually demonstrated through the course of the workshop, he seemed able to remove himself from the actual written story and see more of the person writing it. Specifically, in the last group meeting, Bill responded positively to Julie's piece, which had only been slightly revised from the beginning of the workshop when he was much more critical. When Julie read her revised piece, Bill complimented her while also pointing out that 'they' (the group) were perfectionists, which was why she shouldn't be unhappy with her piece. For Bill, this marked a change in not only his own work, but in how he related to others.

Overall, the social component was an important part of the reminiscence process. Having peers who were willing to listen carefully to what was being read, to provide supportive feedback, and act as a sounding board for ideas was a strong component in Bill's change over time. Annie's comment at the end about his sharing such private thoughts with people he didn't know very well speaks to the importance of the social context of meaning. The group participants undoubtedly shaped what stories were written. However, the group setting also created a need for participants to tell a coherent story, to convey to others something about the experience they wanted to share. These acts of sharing went beyond portraying a person's life as 'good' or 'interesting' but instead allowed a space for shared frailties and doubts. Overall, such sharing contributes to shaping a meaningful present and future from the past.

Acknowledgements

Funding for this work was provided by the Brookdale Foundation, New York.

Chapter 14

SHARING MEMORIES BUILDING COMMUNITIES THROUGH AN ARTS-BASED REMINISCENCE PROJECT

Marian Ferguson and Geraldine Gallagher

The Sharing Memories Building Communities (SMBC) Project was a partnership project undertaken by the Reminiscence Network Northern Ireland (RNNI), a charitable organisation which has since ceased to operate, and the Northern Health and Social Care Trust (the Trust), a statutory authority. The project was funded by the UK Big Lottery Fund's Reaching Out – Connecting Older People programme and ran from 2012 to 2016 with additional funding awarded for the fifth year. It fitted well with the Lottery Fund's priorities, which included improving mental health services for people with disabilities and encouraging older people to live independently. This chapter recounts the implementation of the project and its outcomes.

RNNI, the lead partner responsible for project management, was formed in 1999 as a membership organisation with a mission to be a catalyst for reminiscence work development and to encourage good practice through networking, training, demonstration, advice, information and knowledge development. Its vision was of a society where people valued themselves and others by recalling, valuing, sharing and preserving their personal memories. The Northern Trust is one of five integrated health and social care trusts providing primary, secondary and tertiary health services and social services to residents in the north eastern and mid-Ulster areas of Northern Ireland.

The project complemented and provided progression for older people with a disability who had already undertaken a Trust's 16-week reablement programme that aimed to assist older people to achieve their optimum level of independence, build their confidence and lessen loneliness by supporting their social engagement. The SMBC Project sought to enhance the mental health and emotional wellbeing of older people with disabilities who were in danger of social isolation by securing their active participation in group-based creative reminiscence workshops or individual life story work in order to improve quality of life, increase confidence and develop each person's abilities to learn new skills.

The need for the SMBC Project

This project represented the culmination of several years of research and development by the partners concerned with reminiscence and life story work with older people with disabilities. An evaluation report by Wallace Consulting (2010) on the views of older people involved in an earlier RNNI-led reminiscence project found that 92 per cent of informants stated reminiscence work helped them to appreciate their memories more; 97 per cent found sharing their reminiscences let others know more about them; 81 per cent felt closer to others as a consequence; 94 per cent found reminiscence activities enjoyable; and 88 per cent believed that being involved in reminiscence work made them feel good about themselves. The Trust, with assistance from RNNI, had produced a template Life Story Book (2009) and established evidence of a high demand from vulnerable older people for opportunities to be supported in completing their life stories. This work had also pinpointed a shortage of staff time as the biggest constraint in terms of continuation and expansion of life story work, not only with individuals residing in aged care facilities but also with people living in their own homes in the community.

To establish the need for the SMBC Project in the Trust's geographic catchment area the partners undertook a questionnaire survey and focus groups with potential service users. This showed that 60 per cent of older people in a convenience sample stated they wanted to take part in life story work; 75 per cent wished to join the proposed SMBC Project; and 85 per cent of the Trust's day centre staff surveyed believed the proposed Project could help to meet the social and emotional needs of disabled older isolated people.

Project objectives

The project aimed to:

- enhance the mental health and emotional wellbeing of older people with disabilities
- enable active participation in life story work and group-based creative reminiscence activity
- engage family members and carers in improving the social inclusion of older people with disabilities
- promote the acquisition of new skills
- improve the quality of life of older people living with disabilities
- produce artistic products encapsulating recalled memories that could become valued legacies for families, friends and carers (Stratford & Associates 2016).

The areas of concern articulated by many of the older people, day centre staff and family members were:

- social isolation leading to loneliness and depression
- low self-esteem and low self-confidence
- being perceived in terms of current circumstances and present disabilities without regard to lifetime achievements
- reliance on a few key relationships for support and social interaction
- being seen as a burden to society and feeling redundant within their families and local communities
- poor mental health and wellbeing impacting on physical health and threatening to reduce the likelihood of being able to sustain living at home.

Management and staffing

The operation of the project was overseen by a steering group comprising representatives from both partner organisations. The manager of RNNI served as project manager, and project activities were delivered by three part-time reminiscence workers supported by volunteers and staff from seven Trust day centres. The project recruited 27 volunteers and provided opportunities for them and day centre staff to acquire new transferable skills and to obtain an Open College Accredited Certificate in Reminiscence Work.

Structure and recruitment

Trust social workers and other staff identified, encouraged and referred older people with disabilities living in the community, either alone or with families, considered to be at risk of loneliness or social isolation. The project had two strands – creative reminiscence workshop groups held in the Trust's day centres, and individual life story work undertaken in people's own homes.

Creative reminiscence workshop groups

A series of small group workshops, meeting weekly for two hours for 10–16 weeks provided a programme of varied reminiscence activities and the creation of multifarious art works encapsulating the reminiscences shared. The programme varied from group to group, with each group's completed work culminating in a celebratory event attended by friends, families and Trust staff which showcased the artistic products created by participants. Reminiscence conversations led on to active engagement in the creation of tangible products utilising a wide range of artistic media.

Activities included sharing memories on agreed themes prompted by multi-sensory triggers consisting of varied memorabilia, such as old objects, sounds, smells, tastes, photographs, reading of stories, reciting poems, dressing up, singing, spontaneous enactments and dancing, were all used as well as occasional theme-related trips. These included visiting a local spade mill, a sweet factory and a trip to the seaside to stimulate memories and encourage their portrayal in innumerable creative ways. Another key element of the programme afforded opportunities for participants to learn new skills or rekindle old skills. Wood turning and wood carving, for example, prompted memories of handling tools but also taught new skills, while hat making brought back the excitement of getting dressed up for special occasions but also required old skills to be revived, extended and applied in new ways.

Life story work

This involved six to eight weekly visits to individuals in their own homes by a project worker who provided the support and guidance needed to complete a chronological record of the person's life story from early childhood up to the present. The Trust's life story template was often used but other approaches including audio life story books incorporating personalised playlists linked to a series of annotated photographs were also developed with great success.

Participants' characteristics

In the first four years of the project, a total of 504 older people with disabilities who were in danger of social isolation were involved. Women predominated (64%). Ages ranged from 60 to 100+, with 18 per cent aged 60–69; 30 per cent aged 70–79; 43 per cent aged 80–89; 8 per cent 90–99 and 1 per cent being 100+. All participants experienced current disabilities, with 49 per cent having multiple disabilities which for many included depression. Over a quarter (26%) had been diagnosed with dementia and equally many had impairments arising from stroke or serious heart conditions. This very wide range of disabilities, including 13 per cent of participants with sensory impairments, posed considerable challenges for project staff, who needed to be imaginative and inventive in devising ways of effectively involving everyone in fulfilling reminiscence-related activities. Having regard to people's medical conditions was essential for the effective planning and delivery of both the group and individual work.

The project focused on what each participant could still do, on individuality and potential to develop new interests and acquire new skills. For the workshop groups, additional support from day centre staff and volunteers was required, while sometimes family members assisted with the life story work in people's own homes. The Project workers supported older people to overcome impairments and limited concentration to encourage and enable optimal participation. It was especially important to build on what the participants could manage, to focus on what they had done in the past and what they could learn or re-learn to do in the present, despite diminished physical and mental health, so as to sustain them in the future.

Project processes and activities
Illustrations from creative group workshops
EXAMPLE 1

The group consisted of eight men and women aged between 80–90, most with multiple medical conditions, including anxiety, stroke, depression, dementia and heart disease, and all were at risk of loneliness and social isolation. The workshop met for 16 weekly two-hour sessions, which included a much-valued tea break. It was facilitated by a project worker, a volunteer and a day centre staff member, with other staff assisting from time to time.

It emerged that a majority of members had been bereaved and the group agreed to engage in a simple activity that would enable each participant to discuss aspects of their deceased partner or alternatively a living relative, usually a son or daughter. One exercise used a collection of old magazines and newspapers with group members being invited to visualise an individual who held a significant place in their life. They were then asked to look through the magazines and choose words that described or illustrated their chosen person. This exercise stimulated a lively discussion as each older person was paired with a staff member or a volunteer for an initial discussion and then each person, in turn, shared with the whole group the words chosen to describe their 'special' person. Much camaraderie developed as words were chosen and shared. In a subsequent session, personal photographs of the special person, or in their absence, pictures from the magazines reminiscent of the chosen person's interests or associations were scanned and scaled to fit on to an image of a tree representing a 'tree of life', which was then printed and framed to symbolise the lives of the significant people.

EXAMPLE 2

Another productive strategy to build confidence and encourage active participation was to invite group members to mime their jobs, which was always good fun, with animated discussion about work easily developing. A group reminiscing on the theme of work discovered that all the members of the group had been employed in the linen industry, so a trip to the Lisburn Linen Museum was arranged. Here the group shared their first-hand working knowledge of the linen industry and demonstrated how various pieces of equipment on display were used. The museum guide was delighted to learn directly from the older people who felt their expertise had been valued and their experience appreciated.

EXAMPLE 3

Exploring the theme of home and family life, a group member was asked to volunteer to stand up and 'physically' walk the facilitator around their childhood house. For example, specific questions were asked like 'How many steps were there leading up to your house?' The facilitator would then take the required number of steps to reach the front door with questions following about the door's colour, bell or knocker and suchlike. At every opportunity, the other group members would be encouraged to recall the colour of their front doors or to walk themselves in their imaginations through the various rooms of their childhood homes and then draw a picture or a plan of the house.

Many different strategies were utilised to encourage socialisation and to build confidence. In the early weeks, group members were encouraged to 'tell their stories' in very small groups, supported and encouraged by a project worker, day centre staff member or volunteer. Members might be asked to bring photographs of their younger selves to share with the other members. Each week a different theme would be introduced to guide discussion, but the programme was always flexible and responsive to the interests of the members. As trust and confidence grew, around week eight the idea of a celebratory exhibition was floated, and its possibility discussed. As members told their stories they discovered they could hold the attention of an audience that valued the stories being told. Participants were introduced to a large number of artistic ways of capturing and portraying the memories recounted, and opportunities abounded for participating in creating art works. At the end of each workshop session an essential 15-minute debriefing, trouble shooting, and forward planning meeting of the team ensured that all parties were working well together.

Illustrations of life story work

Individual life story work in people's own homes provided rich opportunities to help isolated older people develop an appreciation of the lives they had lived, obstacles they had overcome, achievements they had made in the face of challenges, and to reframe negative memories. Cappeliez (2002) maintained that reminiscence could have a significant impact on older adults suffering from depression and he suggested that in the act of reminiscing, a person's projections of low self-esteem and negative thinking can be reframed and given 'alternative perceptions and interpretations' (p.303). These outcomes were visibly demonstrated in the life story work undertaken.

Slavney and McHugh (1984) recognised the close connection that can evolve between a reminiscence facilitator and a participant during the various stages of producing a life story, while Cartwright and Limandri (1997) maintained that relevant data could only be obtained by encouraging an authentic relationship developed through familiarity, engagement, honest verbal exchanges and mutual self-disclosure. Such research recognises the primacy of the informant as controller of the storytelling process in which the teller is encouraged to recognise personal triumphs and the challenges faced during their life. In the SMBC Project, participants chose their own preferred methods of weaving their story together, prompted by personal photographs, personal artefacts, favourite music and cumulative recalled memories. Their stories projected their personalities, values and identities. Each, in their own unique ways portrayed a vivid picture of who they once were and still were. Butler (1963a, 1963b) described such evaluative life review as a kind of stocktaking in which meaning and continuity with one's past are found, while Wong and Watt (1991) suggested that creating a life story gives a person permission to work through feelings of 'guilt, failure and depression' (p.44). Similarly, Smith (2000) maintained that creating a life story enables the teller safely to revisit internalised trauma.

EXAMPLE 4

Engaging in the life story process proved empowering and cathartic for Sarah, now in her nineties. It provided her with an opportunity for self-reflection and emotional healing. Part of her story was not included in her book, due to the repercussions it could have caused within the family, yet seizing her opportunity to speak about a long held secret burden she was motivated to change her thinking and to move on (Coleman 1974). The project provided Sarah with a time to speak and a time for healing.

Sarah's religious beliefs and practice were central in her life. She had a large family who loved and adored her husband, their father, who many years before had had an affair with her best friend. They had moved to another country to start afresh but later returned to live in their original country. Many years later, Sarah discovered that all the time they had been away her husband had remained in contact with the friend and on returning the affair continued. She felt guilty because she hated her husband when she discovered his infidelity but could never tell anyone about it because of her family's adulation of him. The life story sessions allowed her to unburden herself and re-evaluate her husband's behaviour; she was comforted to know that her feelings were reasonable in the circumstances. She was able to contextualise and verbalise her thoughts for the first time and finally forgive her husband fully and honestly, as her faith required her to do.

EXAMPLE 5

In another example, Mary's recall and creation of her life story book illustrated Watt and Wong's (1991) classification of reminiscence as fulfilling integrative and narrative functions. Mary recalled attending school and attaining a good level of education. Her teacher wanted her to go to university, but Mary admitted she was young and bored. She was aching to earn a living and to make a financial contribution to her family. She also disclosed she was in love and wanted to get married at 18 years of age. In later years, she attained numerous business qualifications. She proudly showed the reminiscence worker her certificates and a reference from her former manager extolling her managerial skills and ability to encourage others to study to achieve further qualifications. Through reflection she came to see that declining the opportunity to go to university had been the right decision for her at the time. She also demonstrated through the production of her certificates and her references that she was able to use her abilities later in life to achieve her potential. The items were scanned and included in her life story book, a process that promoted feelings of self-worth and evidence of life lessons she wanted to pass on to her grandchildren.

The project encouraged participants to value and record their positive memories and not to include anything in their life story books that reflected negatively on other people, alive or dead. Coleman (1974) stressed the importance of helping people to focus on positive memories, while also helping them to deal with difficult memories by recognising when to challenge ways of remembering that are unhelpful in their relationship with others. This was not, however, always achieved.

EXAMPLE 6

Joe was very keen to produce a life story book. He owned a number of mementos which traced his family history back to the early days of the Ulster plantation and he had many early photos of family members. He recalled the impact and devastation of a Spanish flu epidemic when his father contracted the flu and died when Joe was still quite young, leaving his mother to raise him. He recalled the fondness of his granny who taught him all he knew about gardening. His memories of his father were also consistently loving and positive but memories of his mother were quite negative. He was persuaded to leave much of the negativity out of his book as other relatives would be likely to read it.

Joe suffered from severe mental health problems. A positive strategy was suggested to help him feel more relaxed and less stressed. He was persuaded to undertake drawing and painting to illustrate his fondness for flowers, and these illustrations were included in his book. In the act of drawing he was reminded of the positive memories of gardening with his granny and the illustrations demonstrated his skill in both gardening and painting. His narrative moved on to other more positive aspects of his life and, in the end, he was very pleased and proud of his book. However, despite the overriding joy and pride in his life story book, Joe did not manage to relinquish his negative memories of his mother which remained with him after his book was finished. For further exploration of the implications of reminiscence with older people who are depressed see Chapter 12 by Cappeliez.

Innovative methodology

At first, the project workers found it overwhelming to be welcomed into the home of an older person and to be met with a lifetime of photograph albums and personal effects gathered over many years.

How to choose what photographs were the most valuable in terms of triggering memories and illuminating the person's life story was a huge challenge. Gallagher, one of the project staff, decided to adopt a Desert Island Discs format borrowed from a popular long-running BBC Radio programme in which people are asked to select eight pieces of music which help to map the story of their lives. Accordingly, the number of photographs selected was to be limited to eight to ten, although in practice some pages contained a montage of several related photographs. Suggested sections were: grandparents and parents; childhood and school; teenage years and romance; marriage; children and family life; work; hobbies; holidays; and retirement.

The inclusion of grandparents, if memories and/or photographs existed, was considered important to situate a participant's life within their social, historical and economic context. Not all sections were included in all books, but a framework, together with a 200-word description of each photograph or montage, enabled the story to become focused. The book was designed to be pocket sized (12 x 12 cm), allowing it to fit in a handbag or jacket pocket. It was finally professionally bound, with the name of the owner set in gold lettering.

During the first meeting, previous examples of completed books were shown as exemplars and the 'contract' of eight to ten photographs to be scanned into the project worker's laptop and 200 words of related text to be jointly written over the coming weeks was agreed. Assistance of family members in locating photographs, or in their absence generic substitutes, was often essential. In preparation for the narrative composition, a template with the participant's chosen photographs and headings was prepared.

The narrative was written collaboratively week by week during the reminiscence process, stimulated by jointly discussing the chosen photographs and then rereading and redrafting until the participant was satisfied and the word limit achieved. This process reinforced that the participant was in control. Sometimes people realised that a photograph did not generate associated memories and so it would be replaced. Relevant music was located and recorded on a MP3 player. Flexibility within the framework was an important element in reassuring the participant that their opinion and their decision making were respected.

The participants were revisited six months after receiving their book and MP3 player to establish if they were being used regularly.

The evaluation process revealed that while the book was found to be used regularly, the MP3 players were temperamental and difficult to use despite enlarged instructions being supplied. Through follow-up research, an existing commercial A5-sized book shaped like an ordinary photograph album but including an extra element of clickable pages that triggered embedded audio files and holding 20 transparent pockets was found and successfully used.

EXAMPLE 7

John had moderate to severe dementia. He was unable to converse or recognise family photographs during the life story sessions, although he could read aloud. The project worker collaborated with his wife, Ella, to build a joint life story within the 20 pages of text and 20 audio files embedded in the audio book. Each page was created to fit the plastic inserts. The written narratives and accompanying photographs were linked with personally significant songs and hymns.

When the book was completed, audio feedback from the participant and his wife was included in the book. Remarkably, John, who had never spoken a word throughout the whole life story process, stated on the recording how they had 'sat up late at night choosing their favourite songs'. The worker filmed John as he flicked through the book, and as he played the songs. He began to sing along to each song, word perfect. The book had brought him out of his world of silence.

Ella remarked how at first the task seemed insurmountable and overwhelming, but with the help of the facilitator who broke down the process in to small, sequential, manageable steps, a book that she, her husband and other family members greatly treasured had been created. She said, 'It brought a tear but also smiles. Certainly, go ahead and use us as an example. May it encourage others to make a journey into the past and put it in a book for the present and future generations.'

This case study confirms the view of McKeown (2011) who found that people with dementia and their family members valued the life story process because it restored the 'personhood' of their family member whose dementia had denied them the ability to communicate verbally. It helped both the participant and their carers to engage with their shared family history in the here and now. It recovered seemingly lost memories and assisted in preserving relationships.

Involving carers

In the fifth year of the project, greater efforts were made to enlist family carers as co-helpers as poor information flow and limited support from some carers at times had hampered the project's work in earlier years. (Bob Woods in Chapter 3 writes of the complex reactions of carers and how essential meeting their needs can be in dementia care provision.) Possibly as Hannan *et al.* (2013) suggested, carers sometimes find it difficult to negotiate a satisfactory role for themselves when they have relinquished some caring responsibilities to others. Sometimes too, professional carers may fail to appreciate the 'expertise by experience' that family carers accumulate. Due to the many demands on them and a reluctance to encroach on their scarce 'free' time and multiple responsibilities, a strategy was designed to engage carers, staff and the reminiscence facilitators in a collaborative process (Phillips, Bernard and Chittenden 2002). An innovative method of welcoming carers and prospective participants to an introductory project workshop or family day was introduced and the prospect of becoming involved in creating a personal piece of art work served to increase regular attendance by the older people. One of the introductory techniques used at these workshops was hand painting (see Figure 14.1).

The facilitator welcomed each participant and carer. Each couple was asked to choose two of their favourite colours of acrylic paint. They were supplied with a crib sheet which contained questions covering each period of their life. The crib sheet contained an illustration of a hand print and described how the answers to the questions should be divided into two life zones.

The left hand should represent childhood, for example brothers and sister's names, favourite subjects at school, teachers, best friends, favourite TV programmes and so on. The right hand should represent adult life such as marriage, starting a family, work, retirement, holidays, hobbies. The narrative should start at the bottom of the left hand, at the wrist, for example write the names of the participant's parents under the title 'Mum' and 'Dad'. The answers to the crib sheet questions should form a continuous line which frames each individual finger and ultimately encircles each hand. The participant and carer were also supplied with a piece of white card, paint brushes, water and kitchen-roll. The facilitator demonstrated the process with a volunteer by painting her hands with the selected colours and then making a hand print on the card. It is important to establish whether the participant has hot or cold hands. Hot hands mean that a liberal amount of water should be applied to the hands to ensure the paint does not dry on the hand before a print is possible. The facilitator, day care workers and volunteers circulated during this process and offered help when needed. When the participant's handprints were completed, the paint could be initially wiped off with kitchen-roll and hands then washed and dried. Many of the hand prints were framed, and the information recorded on them was used to stimulate further discussion in subsequent weeks.

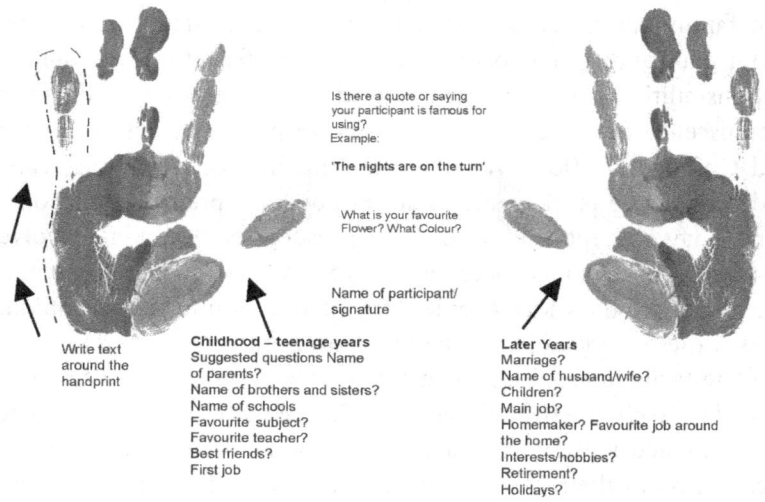

Figure 14.1: An example of a multi-sensory life story picture

This initial day also aimed to introduce carers to each other so as to contribute to decreasing the isolation that so frequently is a consequence of caring, particularly caring for people with dementia (Age UK 2010; Connelly, Carnahan and Vandervoort 2000; Seamark *et al.* 2014). Activity associated with art work, it has been established, can help people to concentrate, exchange ideas, link with others and experience satisfaction and a sense of achievement (Miller *et al.* 2016; Wenborn *et al.* 2016).

Day centre staff development and the challenges for the project's reminiscence workers

A very significant outcome of the project's work was the influence it exerted on the knowledge, attitudes and skills of long-established participating day centre staff. Some of the participants in this project had been attending the day centres for many years but engagement in the creative reminiscence workshops revealed much new information previously unknown by centre staff. Early in the project, a number of staff indicated they were hesitant to engage in any form of reminiscence for fear of upsetting the older people in their care. Some staff had been distressed when in earlier reminiscence sessions they had witnessed people sometimes crying and it seemed they had little preparation for or understanding of the challenges and opportunities involved in skilled reminiscence work with either groups or individuals. Their reluctance was gently challenged by project workers who encouraged day centre staff to join in the workshops and to develop their skills by means of sympathetic mentoring and team participation. Day centre staff were rotated so they could have first-hand experience of group process, share in creating art works and be enabled to extend their capacity for sharing other's pain with growing empathy and increased understanding. For these Trust staff, the project provided invaluable opportunities to develop new skills in safe, supportive surroundings by working side by side with knowledgeable, experienced, skilled project workers. In year five, this training element was further enhanced with extensive training and mentoring opportunities provided for 296 staff and volunteers in a series of specially designed workshops.

Being entrusted as the carriers of other people's memories exerts an emotional cost on those who have the responsibility of hearing about not only people's happy memories but unsurprisingly, also painful stories of harm endured, or even harm inflicted. Over time, as the number of participants increased, so too, inevitably, did the burden of painful stories recounted (Dickson-Swift *et al.* 2006; Lipson 1991). Although managerial supervision was provided by the RNNI, after a time, project workers were also provided with support through a confidential telephone counselling service. It is not known to what extent they used this service, but both partner organisations learned that the provision of adequate care and support for staff and volunteers engaged in such work should be planned, resourced and provided from the outset, either in-house or by being contracted out.

Project outputs

Fifty-four creative reminiscence groups were run during the five years of the project, comprising a total of 707 sessions involving 426 older people. Forty-three celebratory events were held. Such events were sometimes shared between two groups. A conference attended by 100 health and social care professionals drawn from across Northern Ireland very effectively disseminated lessons learned from the project.

In excess of 130 different artistic products were created as well as 78 life story books. These products included personal memory boxes containing artefacts of significance to the individual owners. Twelve themed memory boxes were also created and made available on loan to aged care facilities and schools. Memory maps, scrapbooks, family trees, textile products including memory quilts and photo cushions, greeting and Christmas cards, collages, calendars, art prints, decorated flower pots, self-portraits, music, DVDs and videos were also produced. An independent evaluation report (Stratford & Associates 2016), a celebratory booklet (Reminiscence Network Northern Ireland 2016) and a best practice manual (Reminiscence Network Northern Ireland 2017) were also published.

Celebration events

Throughout the life of each group, a cumulative record of activities, conversations and engagement was created by means of written comments and oral and video recordings so that this record of evidence of participation was available for presentation at each group's celebratory event. These books are now kept in the day centres and are being used to encourage similar ongoing work. During the project, the framed pieces of art work created by group members remained on display in the day centres for the following 16 weeks and were then replaced by a new exhibition, in one form or another, created by a subsequent group.

These events honoured the long lives of each individual participant as well as demonstrating their achievements in the project to families, carers, day centre and other Trust staff, friends and their local communities. The exhibitions and presentations challenged common stereotypes of ageing and elderly people and they also provided positive publicity and recognition of the work of the day centres. They also marked the end of each group's work. In myriad ways, they demonstrated that notwithstanding having dementia, heart disease, stroke or other chronic conditions, older people could still learn new skills and master new artistic ways of representing their long lives. Endings were a difficult time as participants, project staff, volunteers and care staff had all emotionally invested much in each other.

A final afternoon tea dance attended by 200 people marked the formal end of the project. Exhibitions of the work produced appeared in local museums and art galleries as well as in the Trust's day centres, and a consolidated exhibition travelled to the Ulster Hall in Belfast as part of the Imagine Arts Festival visited by over 20,000 people during October 2015 and was later further publicised via the RNNI website and a digital PDF distributed to interested people.

Outcomes and evaluation

Independent evaluators who used direct observation of group creative workshops and individual life story work sessions, questionnaires completed by participants at the end of each celebration event, semi-structured interviews with some participants, family carers and Trust day centre managers and care staff reported the following outcomes (Stratford and Associates 2016):

- Increased social interaction leading to enhanced mental health and emotional wellbeing among vulnerable older people with disabilities living in the community.

- Vulnerable older people with disabilities being recognised as valuable contributors to their immediate family, social circle and local community.

- Greater feelings of self-confidence and self-worth among community-dwelling vulnerable older people with disabilities.

- Creation of life story books that continued to be used by participants and their families and professional carers to improve self-esteem and enrich conversation. These books would also be available to ease any future transitions should the owners be admitted to hospital or to residential care.

- Families and friends regarded the life story books as cherished possessions which would provide a valued record of family history in future years.

Questionnaires also included comments which demonstrated how participants had 'enjoyed the group experience from start to finish'. Many wished they could attend further sessions and when asked if there was anything they would change to make the workshops better, 99 per cent answered 'no'. Most said they were sad the workshops had come to an end and they wished they could have been extended for a longer period.

Conclusion

The evaluation report for the SMBC Project clearly demonstrated that the project overall was successful in meeting its objectives. The techniques described in this chapter were not the only art forms used to generate, celebrate and preserve people's life stories. They illustrate, however, the pleasures shared, the loneliness dissipated, the skills learned and the justifiable pride in accomplishment that this innovative project achieved by engaging older people in creative reminiscence workshops and individual life story work. The varied art works and the life story books that embraced text, photographs, personal playlists and audio recordings provide tangible evidence of the effectiveness of engaging older people in learning new skills and benefiting from undertaking creative reminiscence and life story work.

The friendships that developed during the workshops addressed issues of loneliness, isolation and depression. The participants' questionnaires together with their regular workshop attendance and successful completion of valued art works and life story books testify to the success of the project. It lessened boredom. It reduced loneliness. Old skills were revived and new skills acquired. It helped people to value their past and enriched their present lives.

Chapter 15

REMINISCENCE ARTS
Creative Exploration of the Past in the Present

Pam Schweitzer

In this chapter, I should like to take the reader on a journey around a number of very different locations where we can see reminiscence in action and observe the relationships and attitudes that underlie reminiscence in all its various forms. I shall follow a route through the 35 years of my own reminiscence experience, picking places to visit along the way, which represent key stages on my own journey of exploration and turning points in the development of reminiscence practice more generally. My hope is to demonstrate that wherever reminiscence occurs, it is a means of building personal confidence and competence, enriching interpersonal understanding and promoting social cohesion. These will not necessarily be the ostensible or explicit purposes of the very varied activities described but as we journey from location to location, these functions will underpin each example and ultimately may be the criteria by which such recall of the past can be judged.

Early experience of reminiscing

First come with me into a room in a sheltered housing unit in southeast London for older people in 1982. Eight women in their 80s and 90s are remembering that part of their lives between leaving school at 14 and getting married. The discussion is led by a community worker with a nursing background. He does not need to say much, but his (and my) obvious interest in what the women have to say, and some gentle prompting, are crucial to the gathering's success. The participants agree about the desirability of speaking one at a time, but this is difficult as their memories keep bubbling spontaneously to the surface, one person's flash of recall stimulating a matching or contrasting memory from another. The long-forgotten scraps of memory and some more developed stories, which perhaps have been more recently brought to mind and 'rehearsed', release a tremendous amount of energy in the room. Recalled are long days of hard work in shops, other people's houses, factories and offices, but also dressing up, going to the pictures, going dancing and meeting young men. Together, the women remember a period from their own past, depicting it with detail, wit and clarity. They have tapped into a 'shared community of experience' (Buchanan 1996). It is a past in which they were active, healthy, daring, competent and even a bit wicked! This is a powerful group identity to bring to life! Their earlier selves are present in the room, made alive through energetic discussion. These very frail old women become increasingly animated, surprised and delighted by the way they, as a group, have succeeded in evoking an important part of their lives and building a bridge between past and present. What is more, they have learned things about one another that they did not know, despite living in close geographic proximity; things they have experienced in common and things unique and interesting about each of them as individuals.

For me, watching and listening and asking the odd question, this was a revelation. Coming myself from a theatre background, I found scenes forming naturally in my head as I listened, scenes which could use the colourful language of the speakers. I would have liked to hear more detail from some people, but the time had to be shared out and I wondered if some of those present would also enjoy giving me a one-to-one interview in the future. I noticed that some people spoke in the present tense, especially when reporting what they or someone else had said: for example, 'So I goes up there and I says, "Alright then, I will." That shocked 'em!' This way of 'roughly reproducing' what had been said gave a punchy quality to the stories, and I realised what excellent dramatic dialogue the stories could generate. This was for me the beginning of what was to become 35 years of writing and directing reminiscence theatre, based entirely on the recorded memories of older people.

Founding a professional reminiscence theatre company

Now let us look in on another meeting in another sheltered housing unit in 1983 where a group of five slightly nervous professional actors in their 30s, members of my newly established reminiscence theatre company, are going to test-run some scenes we have been developing in rehearsal out of the stories collected in this room on our first visit. A group of 20 residents in their 80s are assembled, not sure what to expect and perhaps even a little sceptical. The actors are dismayed because the key contributor to one of the scenes they have prepared has not appeared as she is feeling rather low. With some cajoling, she eventually agrees to join us just for a little while. The actors play her scene and ask for a reaction. It is immediate. She corrects factual errors, gives a lot more detail, embellishing the story with apparently remembered dialogue. In this way, she reclaims the story and gives it back to the actors. She is the acknowledged expert. She is pleased that her experience will feature in a play and she sees it will be a good play because the actors replay the scene with flair and humour, using her new input to sharpen their performance. Others in the lounge have heard and enjoyed her story. Her depression has evaporated and even been forgotten. She says, 'I'll always join in things like that', even though, as I am informed later by the warden of the sheltered housing complex, she seldom does. The resident's self-perception has changed, her self-esteem and sense of her own potential are raised. She feels validated by the process, and her recognition by the actors lifts her mood and brings her into positive contact with fellow residents. She remains in the room when others' stories are played out and discussed, now engaged herself in the dramatisation process. The warden has learned something important about the life of this resident and how her spirits can be lifted through involvement in the reminiscence process.

As for the theatre company, we have recognised that this is a special kind of collaboration: the older people can make an invaluable contribution even during the normally sacrosanct rehearsal period, their presence giving the ultimate production an essential authenticity. Our task when the show goes on the road, playing to different audiences every day and travelling all over the country, is to bring the older people's stories to life in action, gesture, speech and song.

When we get it right, it will be as though the actors are holding up a mirror for their audiences, reflecting their pasts too and enabling them to re-connect with their younger selves.

Three key decisions emerged from this encounter, and others like it around the same time, which were to affect the creative process and artistic product of the theatre company, Age Exchange, for many years to come:

- The performances must be followed by a reminiscence session in which the audience shares, either formally with a discussion leader or informally over a cup of tea, the memories evoked for them by the show. This enables the reminiscence process to continue beyond the performance and gives the audience their chance to become participants themselves.

- There was a realisation that the stories were too good to lose, so we must find a way to publish them as an integral part of the production. This decision had financial implications, as separate money needed to be raised, and extra time made available, but it would mean that after every performance, the memories would continue to flow between cast, audience and readers, prompted by similar stories and accompanying photos collected by the theatre company during the research period. This was also important for the original storytellers, who all received copies of the book, of which they were very proud (Schweitzer 1983).

- By transcribing the stories collected for the book, we had realised that the style of speaking and turns of phrase of the original storytellers were important to retain, as they would in all likelihood ring true (and ring bells) for audiences of a similar vintage. We decided that, from henceforth, all the scripts must be in the original verbatim language of the storytellers. This affects the playing style significantly as the mode of the play is a series of stories addressed directly to the audience and intercut with dialogue between the actors, this also to be delivered in the original style and words of the interviewees (Schweitzer 2006).

Across the Irish Sea – a play about migration memories

It is 1989. *Across the Irish Sea* (BBC 1989; Schweitzer 1989) is on the road. Three gifted and experienced Irish professional actors and a multi-instrumentalist have joined Age Exchange Theatre Company and rehearsed a new show built entirely from interviews with older Irish pensioners living in London. This is part of a policy to reflect in our theatre productions the multi-cultural and multi-ethnic make-up of London. A Jewish East End show was staged the year before and an Indian show in English and Punjabi is planned for the following year. The Irish show is playing in the Donmar Warehouse Theatre in Covent Garden, but not to the Donmar's usual intelligentsia evening audience. Camden Community Services have booked a matinee for the very active Irish Elders group. This is the last stop in a long tour which has taken the actors all over the country, playing in church halls, pensioners' clubs, aged care facilities, cultural centres, day centres, arts centres in London, Liverpool, Birmingham and several venues in Northern Ireland. Playing in a theatre is an unusual bonus for the actors. Their agents are more likely to attend than when they are performing in a church hall or care environment.

The audience clearly enjoy and identify with the stories in the show. They vocalise spontaneously their responses to the action on the stage, a phenomenon the actors are used to now, and of course they sing quietly along with all the songs which, for them, are laden with memories. The play explores childhood in rural Ireland, the constant battle to keep large families fed and clothed and the need for many young people to seek work in England. It reflects the resilience and enterprise of the young Irish men and women, taking whatever tough jobs they could get, coping with racist jibes, their meetings at the Irish dance halls and their weddings in London, Liverpool or 'back home'. The play explores powerfully the tensions arising from settling down in England, while always feeling the pull of Ireland, with family left behind, and how this tension lasts a lifetime and beyond. The BBC (1989) broadcast at the time an award-winning documentary including interviews with the Irish pensioners, the actors and the audience, featuring our process and extracts from the show (BBC 1989; Reminiscence Theatre Archive 2014).

Reminiscence theatre such as this is built on recorded lengthy individual and group interviews and retraces the ups and downs of real lives. It evokes laughter and tears in the same measure as any powerful production, but more than most, it is finely tuned to its audience. The high level of identification, supported by the set, costumes and music, helps the audience to see their individual experience within a broader socio-historical context – one in which they were active participants in periods of great change, not just passive recipients or victims of events. This powerful stimulus releases much personal exchange between the audience members, as well as between the audience and the actors (now out of role and costume) as they chat together after the show. The effect of hearing stories so similar to their own, powerfully delivered, in a play with characters, plot and action, is very stimulating and has the effect of validating their experience.

Many of the audience buy the accompanying book of stories recorded during the research period of the production (Schweitzer 1989). Reading those stories they heard during the show, and many others, reproduced verbatim in the book, so that the character of the storytellers shines through, generates a strong sense of belonging to a time and a place and an almost tangible community of memory. 'I was there. I was part of it all'; this is an affirmation of the experience of the Irish people growing old in England, and its impact on the audience is positive and invigorating. There were further tours of this popular show, including performances in Ireland, where it had a strong impact on audiences who thought again about the young men and women they had lost to England, and pondered how tough their struggle must have been to make a success of their lives while also keeping contact with 'home'.

The Reminiscence Centre Blackheath

Now let us move forward and visit a very different location in 1990. It is the Reminiscence Centre in Blackheath, London, which has been open for three years. The large room we enter contains a three-dimensional exhibition (nowadays probably called an installation) created by a talented theatre designer. A mural on one wall evokes the countryside and there are real bales of straw to sit on. On another wall, a huge train-load full of wartime evacuees is painted, based on a photograph of the time. A large map on another wall has lots of pins and threads in it indicating the journeys London children made to safety in the countryside, and reflecting the journeys made by the people who had been childhood evacuees we interviewed for the project. There is also a village post office and a letterbox as part of the installation, and a sound-track of stories from our interviewees which can be played by visitors.

A class of 30 children, aged 9–10, enter the exhibition, carrying improvised cardboard gas-mask boxes of the type supplied to the entire population at the outbreak of war. They are welcomed by the billeting officer, played by the actress as a brisk county lady feeling rather overwhelmed by this flood of evacuees who have, according to her, arrived six hours later than scheduled. The children are told they must spruce up and stand in line 'for inspection' by a group of pensioners playing country folk who will choose who they wish to take to live with them. The children have already spent an hour in another room furnished to look like a 1939 classroom, with an actor playing their teacher. They have been learning about the impending outbreak of war and the government's evacuation scheme to save them by sending them off to safety in the countryside. They have also spent time in an improvised cramped dark air raid shelter with scary explosive noises around them, getting a feel for the dangers they would face if they stayed in London. They have been talked through their train journey from London, with all its delays and halts, so that munitions supply trains could have priority, until it is announced that they have finally arrived 'in the safety of the countryside'.

Now the children meet the pensioners, about eight of them, who were themselves real live evacuees, in role as billet hosts. They go up and down the lines of children, picking one here and one there, asking them to show their muscles and checking them for lice, in much the same way they were treated as childhood evacuees. Once the older people have each collected a small number of children, they take them aside and share with them their own experience of being evacuees. The children visit different corners of the installation with 'their' pensioner and learn what life as an evacuee was like for them. The children then work with 'their' pensioner, preparing short scenes conveying the older people's childhood experience, usually including the older people in the performance. They perform these scenes for one another, with additional explanation and detail supplied by the older people. So eventually all the children hear all the stories, by playing themselves, by watching other scenes and by listening to more stories from the older people, which have been stimulated by the scenes. Dorothy Barton, a pensioner who participated in this process said:

> If the children act out the story themselves, I think it gives them a good idea as to what the child, say it was an evacuee, what it must have felt like at the time, being taken away from home. It gives them more of an insight into what the child had felt than if they had just read about it. (Schweitzer 1993, p.54)

Intergenerational work places the older people as important storytellers, as transmitters of history, linking with each other, but also with another generation through memories shared of their own childhoods. In every aspect of this project, they were the experts and felt appreciated by all at the Reminiscence Centre, the actors, the director, the teachers and, above all, the children. Their stories appeared in a book of memories and photos accompanying the production and used by the schools for preparation and follow-up work (Schweitzer 1990). For the children, listening to and playing out the elders' stories was exciting and unusual. Some children had had normally very little contact with older people, their grandparents having died or remained behind in their countries of origin, or living far away, and some of the older people had had very little contact with children, since their grandchildren had grown up or moved away. So, these encounters were highly valued by young and old alike (Schweitzer 1993).

Training in reminiscence

Let us visit another room. It is 1994 and there are no actors or older people in sight. This room is reserved for training. In the 1990s, reminiscence was being increasingly professionalised in the UK, with people employed in the social care and health sectors seeking ideas and advice on how to improve the quality of life of their elderly clients and residents and attempting to increase their own job satisfaction. The care homes, community halls and day centres where my theatre company performed were increasingly asking for staff training. In response, we had produced our first handbook on reminiscence (Osborn and Schweitzer 1993) and established a project involving an element of training, followed by a series of practical reminiscence sessions in the trainee's venue where our suggested reminiscence activities and approach could be demonstrated with their own client group, with a view to building up staff confidence in running such sessions themselves.

In this training room, there are no pens or notepads in use, no complicated transparencies shown on overhead projectors, only small groups or pairs of trainees (about 16 in all, from a wide range of health and social care backgrounds) who are sharing and exploring together their personal memories, using tried and tested reminiscence exercises relating to common topics or themes introduced by the course leader. A period of reflection and discussion follows, in which we raise awareness of the effects of participating in reminiscence and the requirements for a successful session. Some are practical matters such as using reminiscence resources, desirable seating arrangements, room to move about, attention to physical comfort, audibility, accessibility, availability of refreshments, organisation and record keeping. Other requirements explore the quality of the relationships fostered through the reminiscence work, and how these are determined by such things as the facilitator's capacity to listen to and remember what has been said, their ability to draw together common strands from different contributors, a genuine curiosity about another's experience, and a sense of humour to help the group surmount any awkward moments.

The thinking informing this training session is that the best form of preparation for reminiscence work is to practise on oneself. The pleasurable surprise of recovering a long-forgotten moment, the reassurance of finding someone with a similar experience, the sharp emotion when one suddenly remembers someone who was once close, or when some long-standing regret is awakened: all of these reactions need to be consciously experienced in order to understand the impact reminiscence work can have on older participants. There are sometimes even tears in a training session, leading to questions regarding the risk and potential danger of reminiscence work. Such anxiety is usually allayed by sharing ways of giving support to a distressed person, while enabling the group to continue. There is often discussion too about the responsibility involved in evoking a powerful mixture of emotions. Again there is reassurance when someone in the group points out the pleasure as well as pain associated with strong feelings, even crying, and how such feelings, when shared in a group of older people, who in all likelihood will have experienced similar challenges, can bring them closer to one another. The facilitator must be confident and sufficiently skilled to handle emotions in the group, since no one has led an untrammelled existence and no subject or topic can be considered completely 'safe'. Nevertheless, we all agree that the participants must feel that the group is a safe and trustworthy place, that their stories are valued, and people are respected.

The Good Companions

The next visit is to a large marquee in a country town in south-west England in 2002. There is a big community event for older people to celebrate the Queen's Golden Jubilee. You will see rows of seats filling up fast as about a hundred older people gather for a performance. The 12 performers (one man and 11 women, known as The Good Companions) have come from London and all are in their 70s or 80s. They are an older people's theatre company, a relatively new concept in the UK at this time. None of these people have performed in their earlier lives. They had participated in reminiscence groups, got to know each other, and then reluctantly allowed themselves to be persuaded to give theatre 'a go'. After their first experience of performing to highly appreciative audiences in 1992, there was no going back. The group decided to call themselves 'The Good Companions', after the book by J.B. Priestley about a rather chaotic travelling theatre company, and they worked together with me for the next 12 years, producing a new show each year, all of them based on their apparently inexhaustible supply of memories.

So back to 2002 and the time of the Queen's Golden Jubilee. At first, as The Good Companions began to work on the new play to mark the occasion, everyone claimed to remember very little about that period. In the early 1950s, Britain was still slowly recovering after the war, and the group considered those years to be a rather flat grey period when nothing much happened. However, as they began to reflect together about their own lives in those years, more and more detail emerged. Over a number of weeks, they told one another and me a great many stories about what was happening in their lives in 1951–53 at the time of the Queen's coronation. The play was of course going to be about them, not about the Queen.

One woman had moved from inner London to one of the many new housing estates in outer London and was missing her family, especially as she had just had her first child. Another had a fiancé in the forces whom she was missing very much. One woman was stationed in an Arab country where her husband was working as an engineer and regaled us with hilarious 'ex-pat' stories of petty snobbery and plain bad behaviour, but also of beautiful desert skies and camel trains on the horizon. Another was trying to get used to the new responsibility of being a mother, even admitting she once left the pram (and the baby in it) behind at the shops and only remembered when she got off the bus near home. The only man in the group was serving in the British army of occupation in Germany and falling for a local Fraulein. One woman spent the day of the coronation in tears and pregnant while her husband got drunk in the pub and flirted with the local barmaid. A Caribbean woman decided to follow her soldier husband to England and remembered her first impressions, so different from what she had expected. Most memorably, one woman had just been left by her husband and she found herself, though the innocent party, completely socially isolated and 'dropped' by her so-called friends, who perhaps feared the competition she might now possibly provide. And of course, everyone remembered watching the coronation on tiny television screens, usually in a neighbour's front room.

All of these stories were gradually played out and brought to life by the group. Everyone had ideas so we scripted and rescripted as we went along. Retrieving this largely forgotten post-war period and the group members' direct and sometimes painful experience of it was a creative challenge. This time the published illustrated book also includes the script of the play and an account of how we moved from story to scene (Schweitzer 2002).

After the show in the marquee, there is plenty of informal discussion between The Good Companions and the audience, most of whom are about the same age as the performers. They are highly appreciative, both of the stories heard and the courage of the actors to publicly play out remembered parts of their own lives. There had initially been a lot of discussion about including the divorce story, but this was the scene that frequently produced the most audience feedback. On this occasion, the performer is thanked for sharing her difficult experience and an audience member reciprocates with her own story. The Good Companions love being celebrated performers and they have certainly gained in personal confidence and social competence. Their ability to remember the script has improved with every show and they are rarely unwell. Having the adrenaline produced by an impending performance really seems to keep them healthy, mentally and physically. Above all, they have such a strong sense of group cohesion, and recognise that making such close friends so late in life is a very significant gain.

Here are some reflections by the players themselves concerning the making of the play and performance, recorded at the time (Schweitzer 2002, p.82).

> *Joan:* The tension drives me up the wall. I take Rescue Remedy all the time, so I relax. But I feel so proud when I've done it! My husband sees me walking up and down with the script and he says, 'I'm sorry, it's awful!' And another thing, I didn't know I could sing before. At home, I just get 'Shut up!'
>
> *Margaret:* I enjoy it. I like the workshops, and I like the preparation, you know, writing the script, talking. And I enjoy doing it, but only when I've learned the lines. Sometimes, it seems as though the lines get muddled up, or you have a mental block. You know it, and you're out there, and then all of a sudden, pssshhh! It goes!
>
> *Hilda:* For me, it's not a problem of stagefright. I'm raring to go. It doesn't bother me one bit. I'm not nervous. I can't wait to get there, and I enjoy every minute of it. And I love all the girls. And Ralph. We're like a family.
>
> *Kathy:* I thought, 'Yes, I could work with these women', and I've not regretted it. And when I had my accident and was stuck indoors, that phone didn't stop, and they rang and rang and rang. My sister was looking after me at home and she couldn't believe it.

The European Reminiscence Network

Come with me now to a conference hall in south-east London. We travel back a few years to May 1997 and the event is organised by the European Reminiscence Network, which came into existence five years earlier as a way of raising the profile of reminiscence of all kinds, including theatre festivals, intergenerational work and intercultural festivals bringing together ethnic minority elders' groups from different European countries. The conference we are visiting is called Widening Horizons in Dementia Care. The conference papers are held in the Reminiscence Theatre Archive, University of Greenwich (Schweitzer 1988). There are 250 people and they have come to this event from all over the world, including USA, Japan, Australia, India, Africa, Brazil and of course many European countries. Some delegates come from the world of reminiscence, with a background in the arts, museums, education, oral history and community work. Others come from the world of dementia, with a background in health, social care, residential and nursing homes. There are academics, researchers and 'coal face' project leaders. We meet with the blessing of the World Health Organization and the financial support of the European Union.

Two very significant shifts are taking place at this time. The European Union (EU) is reaching out to an ever-widening range of organisations from all member countries, encouraging them to set up partnership projects with EU funds to work together to explore common issues. The other shift is the ever-greater awareness that the challenge of our time is the exponential growth in every corner of the world of the number of people developing dementia. As we are living longer, dementia is a growing epidemic that so far defies pharmacological remedies. Lars Rasmussen, Principal Administrator to the European Commission, Directorate of Public Health, warns the conference:

> The ageing of the population will mean a rapid increase in the number of Alzheimer's sufferers and an increased burden on informal caregivers. There are 40,000 new cases in the world every month. Unless we change our attitude towards ageing, we shall very soon reach the point where we see the ageing of the population only as a burden and forget that older people may also be an asset. This development is going to put a serious strain on the solidarity between generations. (Rasmussen 1998, p.7)

Rasmussen urges us to recognise the impossibility and undesirability of providing residential care for all, and the consequent need to support family carers, many of them retired or close to retirement, to help them continue caring at home.

Tom Kitwood speaks too about the importance of maintaining personhood, of respecting and supporting the sense of self of people with dementia and the important role reminiscence could play in this regard. He shows, through a very graphic role-play, what a difference it makes when care staff know something about the life story and the personal likes and dislikes of the people in their care, and how this improves the job satisfaction of staff and the quality of care they are able to give. He also shows how failure to recognise and respond to individual needs leads to distressing behaviour on the part of the person with dementia and increased frustration on the part of carers (Kitwood 1998, p.105).

Three priorities emerge:

- The need to support family carers, to affirm their relationship with their relative and to give them insights and tools that will help them in their often demanding and lonely task.

- The need to recognise the person with dementia as an individual and to encourage communication, including non-verbal communication, using creative approaches.

- The need to extend and deepen the role of creative reminiscence (whether on a one-to-one basis or in groups) as a means of building self-esteem, social confidence and a sense of belonging.

Remembering Yesterday, Caring Today

This conference generated much excitement and led to a successful funding application by the European Reminiscence Network to the European Commission for a trial project to test the hypothesis that reminiscence can enable people with dementia to tap into their long-term memory and by so doing rebuild their sense of identity. The project, named Remembering Yesterday, Caring Today, came into being in ten European countries.

Let us now visit the project in action in its first year. Come with me to a room at the Reminiscence Centre in London where the group are going to discuss their memories of starting work. There are ten people with dementia, ten family carers, eight volunteers, three group leaders and four mental health nurses from the local Memorial Hospital, who know the families through home visits and hospital-based carers' education groups. So, the room, though large, is crowded – 35 people altogether – and the session will run for two hours. This goes against all the rules, which suggest that reminiscence with people with dementia should be conducted with a small group of four or five or less, a quiet room, for a duration of 45 minutes. So, how could this possibly work?

One of the volunteers is a pianist and plays as people arrive by bus or hospital transport. There are warm welcomes for each individual, including hugs and kisses where it feels right. It is session number four, so we are getting to know one another well. Objects related to the theme are on display and people with dementia are encouraged by volunteers to handle them. When everybody has arrived, we sit in a big circle. The theme of the previous week, schooldays, is briefly revisited and we then prepare for the new theme. Everyone is asked to work in pairs and think of an action connected to their first job. Then we go around the circle looking at each action as it is silently portrayed, copying it and guessing what it is. If someone has difficulty thinking of an action or remembering the action they had thought of a moment ago, working in pairs ensures that no one will fail in this task. And it doesn't require any words. Anyone coming into the room at this point would not be able to tell you who had dementia and who did not. In fact, they would probably think they had come to the wrong room, as there seems to be some kind of slightly anarchic party going on.

After this warm-up, people work in small groups to share 'first job' stories. They are asked to choose one story from each group and prepare a short scene arising from it, rehearse it and then perform it to the rest of the group, to much applause, with questions from those watching as to what exactly was going on, which then leads to more stories surfacing. One lady enjoys using the old typewriter in an office scene. She is the only person in the room who can make the carriage return work. It is extraordinary to see a frail little lady in her 90s striking those keys with a strength conjured up from what we have come to call 'body memory'. She shows a photo of herself in her office which was taken 70 years ago and which her daughter has recently found. The photo has been enlarged and she is able to name every one of her colleagues. A man mimes measuring a customer in the gents' outfitters where he is working, including chest and inside leg measurements. One group have recreated a scene in Siemens Factory involving pulling on long cables; another group have made a docklands scene with one person miming carrying heavy timbers on his shoulder, and another demonstrating and explaining how to pick up a hundred-weight sack of sugar with a docker's hook. A 90-year-old lady demonstrates putting curlers in a client's hair, beautifully miming the rolling mechanism when the client sits with her back to her, as if looking in the mirror. Another scene is set in a box-making factory where the staff are planning to go on a work 'beano', or annual outing.

After tea, there is a quieter session in which people draw for themselves or for one another a memory that has surfaced in the session. It could be of a boss or a work pal, or of the tools of the trade or the uniform worn. These images are shared and discussed, and the session ends with work-related songs played by Olive, the 80-year-old volunteer pianist, while the group sing along. A plan for the following week is announced and everyone has a personal farewell. The balance of large group, small group and one-to-one work has ensured that people with dementia get the chance to participate in a variety of activities, and the overriding feeling is one of celebration.

Over a period of one year, all the partners in the Remembering Yesterday, Caring Today project (now known for short as RYCT) ran the project twice and shared experiences in regular meetings hosted by different partner countries. By November 1998, we were able to hold our project conference in Vienna and report on our findings. The conclusions of the evaluators, Gibson and Bruce (1998), based on qualitative reports submitted by the partners, in summary, were as follows:

- The Remembering Yesterday, Caring Today approach offered new, positive, enjoyable ways to communicate and to discover or rediscover shared mutual enjoyment.

- People with dementia were stimulated to communicate in conversation, but also in drama, music, drawing and other activities.

- Reminiscence was successfully introduced to participants and valued by them.

- Carers felt better about the way they were coping after the project and some were able to achieve changes in their behaviour, becoming more positive.

- They experienced the project as an antidote to 'carer burn-out'.

- There were high levels of enjoyment and important social gains for people with dementia and their carers.

- Leaders and volunteers enjoyed the project too, saying that learning about the fascinating lives of the participants had been an 'eye-opener'.

The cross-country findings, despite contextual and regional differences, were very similar.

Looking back 20 years to the early years of RYCT, I believe that we had a very strong sense of ourselves as Europeans, responding to what had been put to us at our 1997 conference in London as the issue of our times, and that we had worked effectively together to develop a shared philosophy and a vital role for creative reminiscence sessions at the heart of positive dementia care. Overcoming our language divides had been relatively straightforward, as what we were doing in our sessions was essentially practical and visible. The videos of the project, produced in different countries, were evidence of our shared approach, with special qualities deriving from the personalities and personal styles of the group leaders and the particular make-up of each group of project participants. We received further funding from the European Commission to continue this work and to publish its findings. The resulting book in English, but reflecting the experience of all partners, was launched at our Stockholm conference in 1999, and was translated into Danish, French, German, Swedish, Spanish and Catalan (Bruce, Hodgson and Schweitzer 1999; Schweitzer and Bruce 2008).

Making Memories Matter: My Life in a Box

It is 2005. Let us open the door to a busy room full of large wooden boxes and a group of older people busy with hammers, nails, paints, old photographs and small personal mementos. Each person has been paired with an artist, who is working with them over eight weeks. The artists' task is to help the older people create memory boxes that will reflect and communicate key experiences in their lives. Everyone is paying attention and is focusing on practical tasks. This is definitely a present-day activity, in the here and now, drawing out and sharing memories.

Making Memories Matter is a visual arts project of the European Reminiscence Network, supported by the European Commission and involving artists and older people from seven countries. The boxes are disused ammunition boxes supplied by the armies of each partner country as symbols of peace in Europe after a century dominated by war. We are making a joint exhibition of 70 of the boxes, ten from each partner country, to tour each of these countries.

Two Nigerian women, Grace and Theresa, both in their 80s, are making beautiful boxes, working with a young Caribbean artist. The artist is showing Grace how to make and paint three-dimensional blue waves from curled sculpted paper that represent her childhood memories of the village in Nigeria where she grew up and the river where she loved to swim. A recent photograph contrasts with a childhood photograph showing her standing in the water amidst bright orange fish. Grace says she could stay under water a long time as a child and was called the mermaid. This, she says, is the mermaid's box. An oddly daring stroke is the positioning high up in the box of a piece of hand-knitted woollen baby-wear. She insists it has a place there, and how right she is. It represents her now as a contented granny in cold, grey London. Theresa is working beside Grace with the same artist. She is papering her box with an arresting digitally produced background made with the artist and featuring an African fabric design. The two Nigerian women are singing a song from 'home' as they work, and they keep moving to the rhythm as they paint and fold. From time to time they visit each other's boxes and admire progress.

A Chinese lady in her 80s, Sui Lan Voong, is making a box about growing up in Vietnam as part of an oppressed ethnic minority. When young, she had a fine singing voice. She wished to be a singer, but her parents would not hear of this. Working with a Finnish artist to convey her story, she wants the centrepiece of her box to be a microphone stand and a model of herself singing one of her favourite folk songs. She also wants cherry blossom, as that is the meaning of her name, so with the artist's help she is making blossoms from tissue paper and fixing them to a real branch. A map of her country and her wedding photo grace the box, and some miniature Chinese lanterns light the interior. In 1978, the Chinese were expelled from Vietnam and she remembers escaping in a small boat in buffeting winds, empty-handed except for her children. This critical journey is symbolised by the boat, which the artist helps her to make from card. They decide to make a raised stage within the box on which the microphone and the model singer stand. I watch her work with hammer and nails and paint this little stage. She too is singing, and the artist records this. When her box is exhibited, the recording on a concealed CD player can be listened to on earphones.

Her friend, Choi Wah Liu, is recreating the silkworm farm where she grew up. The little white feather-light fabric things she is making are the butterflies and she has constructed a miniature spinning wheel from balsa wood. The back of the box shows a portrait of Choi as a beautiful young woman, and the lid design is composed of 40 tiny copies of this same photo on silk squares sewn together, but with many of the faces painted yellow. This, she explains, signifies the need to paint your face to look dangerously ill so you could avoid being raped by the Japanese occupiers during the war.[1]

Each box tells a remarkable story which would never otherwise have been heard. The boxes are the tangible end product of an in-depth reminiscence process lasting many weeks. A text attached to each box explains the story within. These texts are in seven languages, so that when the boxes travel to Romania, Spain, Germany, Finland, the Czech Republic, Poland and the UK, viewers will be able to understand their creator's stories. The project is very different from the reminiscence work described earlier, yet it too encourages older people to reflect on their lives, assisted by an active and creative listener – an artist – to work together finding the best way to share the life story and to value the uniqueness of each person's own lived experience. Although this is not a theatre-based activity, the end result is surprisingly theatrical. When all the boxes are assembled in an international touring exhibition, each box with its own little spotlight, they look like stage set models. Writing about the effect of seeing the exhibition when it travelled to Germany, Eva Schulz-Jander writes:

> Although each box is a stage of remembrance, and reminiscence is always linked to the past, it became clearer and clearer to me that these stories and dramas are not prisoners of the past, they are not caught in sealed vessels, but reach into the present and alter it. ... Many of the people and places whose stories are told here have now disappeared, so that we need these small travelling stages and their narratives to save them from oblivion and inscribe them in the big book of European Memory. (Schweitzer and Trilling 2005, p.22)

---

1 See Making Memories Matter Project, accessed on 02/01/2018 at www.european reminiscencenetwork.org

A 20-year celebration of RYCT

Twenty years on from the start of the RYCT project described above, come with me to our most recent room. It is 2017 and we are celebrating the project's 20th anniversary at a conference at the University of Greenwich, London, which has provided a base for the European Reminiscence Network for the past six years. The RYCT project has developed over the years, including the establishment of a two-day training course and apprenticeship scheme, which is operating in partner countries across Europe. Two hundred and fifty Europeans have completed assessed apprenticeships and become accredited RYCT facilitators.[2] For information on other forms of reminiscence training see Chapters 6 by Kuo, 7 by MacKinlay, 14 by Ferguson and Gallagher and 20 by Shellman, Yancura and Gieschen.

The conference is attended by project leaders from our European partnership countries, past and present, and delegates from non-EU countries who wish to establish the project in their countries. Twelve apprentices and ten family carers from recent RYCT projects in London share their very positive experiences. Long-standing dementia supporters attend and speak. Delegates represent a wide range of disciplines: arts, art, dance, music and occupational therapies, care home management, libraries, museums, psychology, psychotherapy and social work.

Two days of talks and practical workshops culminate in five short plays prepared by University of Greenwich drama students for whom Reminiscence Theatre forms part of their studies. The plays have drawn their inspiration from the memory boxes described earlier. The boxes have been travelling Europe for the last 12 years, spawning many new memory box projects, and the Greenwich conference is their last exhibition. The students have worked with some of the older people who created the boxes in 2005 and who had not seen them since. Two 90-year-olds, Helen Aronson who survived the Lodz Ghetto, and Gwen Sewell who came to London from the Caribbean, have travelled across London to the University of Greenwich in recent weeks to help the students develop their plays. The students have responded wholeheartedly to this unusual challenge, creating theatre pieces of great sensitivity. Helen and Gwen have come to the conference to

---

2 For further details, see www.rememberingtogether.eu and www.reminiscencetheatrearchive.org.uk

see the premiere of the students' shows based on their stories. They and the entire audience are immensely moved by the plays presented in the university theatre. This is a persuasive demonstration of solidarity between the generations and between cultures. It sets a high value on people's lived experience as a key to personal identity and the promotion of social cohesion.

The RYCT project has been running since 1997 and over the years has worked with hundreds of families in the UK and across Europe. It has been the subject of major studies, including randomised control trials (discussed elsewhere in Chapters 2 and 3 by Pierce and Elliott, and Woods), qualitative evaluations and, most recently, an evidence briefing prepared for the November 2017 conference by Woodhead (2017). It has attracted funding from a range of sources, including the English Department of Health, the Medical Research Council, National Lottery funds, research bodies, charitable trusts, local authorities and, above all, the European Commission. Over the years, deep friendships and great mutual respect have developed between the European partners involved. The conference coincides with Britain leaving the European Union and for so many of us this is experienced as a wanton severing of important connections and an inevitable reduction in our combined strength. Whatever else this means, it is certain that the UK will no longer be the lead applicant for any future funding for RYCT projects and this will break a productive 20-year history. We have, however, committed ourselves to meeting every two years and to continuing as best we can to deliver the project in our own countries. Why should we do this? What is so special about it? I shall let the family carers speak for themselves below.

ROBBIE WICK, WHO CARES FOR HER HUSBAND CYRIL

Dementia/Alzheimer's is very isolating both for the carer and the person with it. We have attended several groups but cannot sufficiently emphasise enough how immensely superior and beneficial we found RYCT. It was a total revelation to us. Enlightening, challenging, engaging, inclusive and most of all – great fun! My husband became animated, chatty, anecdotal and gregarious. This was all gently, tactfully and intelligently coaxed out of him. For the carers also, it seemed such a light-hearted and enjoyable experience – reminiscing together and feeling like carefree children once again. If the NHS could take this scheme nationwide, I am sure it would be extremely beneficial for lonely people with dementia. Thank you for giving us an unforgettable, educational and heart-warming experience.

JOY MURPHY, WHO CARES FOR HER MOTHER JOYCE

This course has been a wonderful adventure of discovery about my mother. Everyone involved in the project has been so kind and attentive to my mother who is in the early stages of Alzheimer's. She really looks forward to her 'club' and I have never seen her flourish with so much confidence. This must be credited to the structure of the course and the skill and kindness of all the people involved. Each week is planned but one never feels that if the discussion wanders a little, there is no space for creativity and change. The use of role-play and drama are introduced carefully so that one finds oneself fully immersed in whatever topic is being remembered. In another group, we go to we were asked by a student doctor what would be the ideal care for Alzheimer's. This would be it!

ANGELA RUBENS, WHO CARES FOR HER HUSBAND KENNETH

The RYCT project has been the most enjoyable activity we have been involved in. Although my husband Kenneth has dementia and I am his carer, it has been of great value to be treated as a couple of equal importance once again. The reminiscence work has been very enjoyable for us both. It has been extremely interesting to see Kenneth recover some of his abilities to talk and socialise, albeit with the professionals and the apprentices, all of whom have been so encouraging and patient with him. The miming and acting out have been a revelation. There has been a lot of laughter, which is so good for all of us. We have unearthed a lot of vivid memories, which have enriched our present lives. We are so sorry, as with all good things, it will soon come to an end and we shall miss it.

This brings our journey to an end for the time being. In visiting all these different rooms, the reader will sense the great variety of ways in which reminiscence can assist people, including those with dementia. Reminiscence always requires attentive listening, genuine interest, willingness to make interpersonal connections, time for personal reflection and a degree of creativity. It rewards participants with recognition, a stronger sense of identity and validity, a reaffirmation of closeness and a sense of belonging. I hope that I have shown how these elements are common and essential in all the groups we have visited along the way, from reminiscence theatre at one end of the spectrum to reminiscence in dementia care at the other, and all stages between. For me personally, it has been a hugely rewarding 35-year journey of discovery, with future visits scheduled to explore dementia in a digital world, the prophylactic use of reminiscence and who knows what else?

Chapter 16

THE STRUCTURED LIFE REVIEW

Juliette Shellman and Julia McNeil

Reminiscence and life review can take different forms that may serve different functions and have different outcomes. The structured life review is one type of reminiscence that occurs between a trained therapeutic listener and a life reviewer or reminiscer. Erickson's theory of psychosocial development (1959) provides the theoretical underpinnings for the structured life review. The theory describes life stages that individuals pass through from infancy to older adulthood. Erickson identified the eight life stages as: a) trust vs. mistrust, b) autonomy vs. shame/doubt, c) initiative vs. guilt, d) industry vs. inferiority, e) identity vs. role confusion, f) intimacy vs. isolation, g) generativity vs. stagnation, and h) integrity vs. despair. According to Erickson (1959), each stage builds on the preceding stages and prepares the way for the subsequent periods of development. Erickson asserts that individuals experience a psychosocial conflict at each stage. Individuals who resolve the conflict are able to move forward. But an individual who is unable to resolve a conflict such as trust vs mistrust, for example, will repeatedly face problems related to mistrust throughout their life. A key point of this theory that has implications for the structured life review is that these conflicts can be resolved at any point in the lifespan. The assumption behind the structured life review is that the process of guiding the reviewer through the eight life stages from early childhood to the present using the life review form (Haight and Dias 1992) can assist individuals to resolve past conflicts and attain integrity, the final stage of Erickson's theory of human development.

Since Butler proposed life review and reminiscence in the early 1960s (1963a, 1963b), there has been a great deal of investigation into the unique characteristics that differentiate the structured life review from other reminiscence modalities. As interest grows in the use of therapeutic reminiscence and life review interventions to improve the mental health and wellbeing of older adults, it is should be mandatory that clear definitions are utilized to differentiate among the various types. In this chapter, we will identify characteristics unique to the structured life review, summarize findings from the most recent literature, and present recommendations for future research.

Characteristics of the structured life review

Haight (1998b, p.86) defines structured life review as:

> A short-term structured reminiscing intervention conducted on a one to one basis with an older person. The person who conducts the process acts as a therapeutic listener who guides the older individual in his or her recall of memories and helps that individual to reframe troubled events and to move on in their thinking.

The goal of the structured life review (SLR) using the life review form (LRF) is to assist the reviewer to attain integrity, the last stage of psychosocial development as presented by Erickson (1959). Researchers have studied the impact of SLR on outcomes such as depression, life satisfaction, ego integrity and wellbeing. A meta-analysis conducted by Pinquart and Forstmeier (2012) showed small to moderate improvements in these outcomes. However, the authors noted limitations among the studies such as variations in theory-based reminiscence interventions, samples, and the characteristics of the settings in which the participants lived and where the sessions took place.

Recommendations have been made for researchers to define the type of reminiscence or life review process employed, identify the basis of the intervention, and replicate studies to strengthen the methodology and form a solid evidence base of life review and reminiscence research (Bohlmeijer *et al.* 2007; Pinquart and Forstmeier 2012). For the purpose of this chapter, we define SLR according to the criteria established by Haight and Dias (1992), who, through their research, identified four specific characteristics that differentiate the SLR process from other types of reminiscence. These are a) structure, b) duration, c) individuality and d) evaluation. *Structure* is established by the listener guiding the reviewer through all eight of Erickson's stages of development using the LRF.

The *duration* for a successful SLR consists of six to eight one-hour visits. The first visit assists the therapeutic listener to conduct pre-intervention assessments and to begin developing a trusting relationship with the reviewer. The actual SLR process occurs during the next six visits. Closure of the process takes place during the last visit, with measurement of outcomes, referrals if necessary, and bringing the relationship to an end.

The third characteristic, *individuality*, consists of the SLR process taking place in private and only between a therapeutic listener and a reviewer. *Evaluation* is the fourth unique characteristic, where the reviewer is guided to reflect on and assess the past in order to make sense of the present. During the evaluation session, the reviewer is assisted to come to terms with difficult past experiences and to talk about any regrets they may have. In this way, they are encouraged to value past achievements, come to understand the meaning of their lives and to attain integrity as described by Erickson.

According to Haight and Haight (2007), anyone can become a therapeutic listener with training and practice. Key skills needed for conducting a successful SLR with a reviewer include therapeutic listening, counseling techniques, and an understanding of variations between different kinds of reviewers or reminiscers. *The Handbook of Structured Life Review* (Haight and Haight 2007) provides instructions for educators, practitioners, and others interested in learning the steps to conducting a successful SLR.

A review of studies reporting the use of structured life review and published during the past ten years revealed inconsistencies in SLR definitions, procedures and outcomes. These inconsistencies did not allow us to conduct a comprehensive assessment of the state of the science of SLR research. Consequently, we changed the focus of the literature review to answer the following question – how has the SLR been defined and utilized in published studies over the past ten years?

Literature review method

The search for this literature review began with using Boolean terms in several electronic databases, including: PubMed, CINAHL, psycINFO,

Sociological Abstracts, Social Work Abstracts and the Cochrane Library. The topic (SLR) encompasses many disciplines; therefore, several databases were searched in an attempt to retrieve all relevant literature. Keyword searches included: reminiscence, life review, reminiscence therapy, life review therapy, life review intervention, structured reminiscence, structured life review, SL and 'therapeutic' life review. The search also included consideration of reviews and meta-analyses to identify possible studies, and references to the articles cited were also cross-checked for any studies that were missed in the Boolean search.

The inclusion criteria covered studies:

- including reminiscence or life review in a structured format according to the specific criteria as identified by Haight and Haight (2007)
- written in English
- published within the last ten years.

Studies were excluded if reminiscence was performed in a group format or the study was a one-time intervention. Initially, eight studies were found that met the inclusion criteria. In addition, seven other studies met all criteria except one. These seven studies were also included so that a larger sample could be examined.

Sample and settings

The final sample included 15 studies that scrutinized life review using a variety of methods of intervention, description and analysis of outcomes, and case studies. Sample sizes of participants within the studies ranged from one to 107 with an age range within each study of 63–88. Characteristics of the sample ranged from terminally ill cancer patients, war veterans, those with dementia, clinically depressed patients and community-dwelling older women. The studies were conducted in a variety of international and national settings, including senior health centers, hospice units, dementia care homes and other community settings. Interventionists in the experimental studies were identified as therapists, clinical psychologists, psychology students and homecare workers.

Results

The main objective of this review was to examine how structured life review was defined and utilized in published studies over the past ten years. The 15 studies identified all conducted structured life review or reminiscence in the form of a one-on-one interview. Among these 15 studies, three labelled the intervention used as a structured life review. The three studies that identified their life review process as a structured life review had similar but abbreviated definitions as compared to Haight and Haight (2007). For example, Ando, Tsuda and Morita (2007, p.226) use the definition 'type of reminiscence therapy that includes various activities of reminiscence, evaluation and reconstruction of one's life'. Morgan and Woods (2010, p.46) define structured life review as, 'a therapeutic approach that involves an in-depth, structured, evaluation of the lifespan, and is usually conducted on a one to one basis'. Ando, Morita and O'Connor (2007, p.266) refer to a definition cited from Haight, 'reviewers look back at their lives along developmental stages similar to those outlined by Erikson' (Haight 1998b, p.225). Among these three studies, two of them used all four of Haight and Haight's (2007) unique characteristics of a structured life review. Six other studies followed all four of the characteristics; however, they did not identify their process as a structured life review. These studies used other labels to identify structured life review, such as therapeutic life review, life review, life review intervention, reminiscence, individual reminiscence therapy and autobiographical retrieval (Binder *et al.* 2009; Latorre *et al.* 2015; Maercker and Bachem 2013; Serrano *et al.* 2012; Sok 2015; Tanaka *et al.* 2007).

A full structured life review (SLR) requires a systematic review of memories of all of Erickson's developmental stages. Haight and Haight (2007) operationalize the SLR process by using the life review form (LRF) to guide the sequence of interviews and the content within each interview. Four studies in this review specified using or adapting the LRF (Ando, Tsuda and Morita 2007; Latorre *et al.* 2015; Morgan and Woods 2010; Subramaniam *et al.* 2014). Some studies did not state whether the LRF was utilized as a guide for the life review interview. For example, Xiao *et al.* (2011) and Deng *et al.* (2015) reported their life review interventions were based on Erickson's theory, but did not clarify whether or not the LRF form was utilized. The remaining six studies that used a life review process that had the potential to meet all criteria for Haight and Haight's (2007) structured life review were examined to identify specific criteria not met. The studies met three of the four characteristics including:

- providing structure for reviewing the client's life
- conducting the process on a one-to-one basis
- assisting the client in the evaluation process.

The one characteristic not met was the duration of the life review process of six to eight one-hour sessions over eight weeks. Studies identified as not using the specified duration characteristic of Haight and Haight (2007) reported time intervals spanning anywhere from three to 24 interview sessions with a timeframe ranging from 10 to 90 minutes. Some variations in the length of sessions were justified because of the cognitive status of some members of the sample. For example, in a study that utilized Haight's SLR process with older adults with mild to moderate dementia, an average of 12 sessions (range 11–16) were needed to complete the process (Subramaniam et al. 2014).

Overall, the literature revealed that although Haight identified a label for this specific type of reminiscence and four unique characteristics critical to the process, researchers are using many other terms for the structured life review. Additionally, researchers seemed to follow most of the criteria set forth by Haight, but not duration, although Haight had identified time as an important characteristic to be able to 'forge trust, establish a relationship, and recall a life' (Haight and Haight 2007, p.25).

Keeping in mind the variation in sample sizes, types of interventions and sample characteristics, in general, the studies did report positive findings in areas such as depression, quality of life, autobiographical memory retrieval and life satisfaction. However, the variations in rigor in the various research methodologies used cast doubt on the veracity of the results. Qualitative data reported also revealed positive results about the experience of using the SLR. For example, in a study examining older women's experiences of participation in a life review intervention, Binder et al. (2009) reported the following themes:

- Someone was there to listen to my story.
- It was a special time.
- A valued interaction with the home care worker developed.

- Remembering was meaningful and pleasurable.
- Integration with one's lived experiences was healing.

Many variations of reminiscence and life review have been utilized over the years since Butler first proposed the importance of life review in the early 1960s. Both processes of reminiscence and life review are being used across various disciplines and settings with the goal of improving the lives of older adults. Numerous problems were identified through this literature review. They include variations in the definitions of structured life review, use of reminiscence and life review terms used interchangeably, lack of rigor and variations in methodology employed, including length and number of sessions, differences in application of the SLR process as defined by Haight and Haight, differences in outcome measures utilized, and inconsistencies in the preparation of the interventionist.

Recommendations

In order to move forward in developing the scientific basis of the structured life review, researchers need to pay close attention to the definition of the phenomenon and clearly explicate their theoretical framework and research methodology. More research needs to be conducted with clearly defined interventions using experimental designs, including the possible use of control groups. In addition, it is imperative that when researchers use the term structured life review that they refer to the four elements as determined by Haight and Haight (2007). Unless there is a consistent use of the SLR, there will never be clarity regarding its efficacy. At this time, the literature provides a confusing mix of terminology that leads to lack of precision and thus the inability to compare studies effectively. The second recommendation is that Erickson's theory of human development should provide the theoretical foundation for the structure and process of conducting SLR and operationalizing this theory by use of the life review form developed by Haight and Haight (2007).

A further recommendation relates to research design. Most of the studies reviewed had small sample sizes, limiting the generalizability of the findings. In addition, the majority of the studies lacked experimental designs using control groups, which weakened the results. After reviewing the studies, we are left with a provocative question that requires further thought and exploration. Since all of the studies reviewed demonstrated positive outcomes, did these result from the intervention used or from the social interaction that occurred between the therapeutic listener and reviewer dyad? This question cannot be answered without following the above recommendations in future research.

Chapter 17

LIFE REVIEW

Lifespan Development, Meaning Processes and Interventions

Gerben J. Westerhof

Life review refers to a process of recollecting and attributing meaning to one's personal memories across all phases of life. Nowadays, it is accepted that life review serves as a process for the developmental regulation of mental health and wellbeing across the lifespan. Insights into life review have also been applied in interventions that aim to support people in promoting their mental health and wellbeing. In the first part of this chapter, the historical roots of the concept will be described and some empirical research on life review as a naturally occurring lifespan process will be explored. Second, the meaning processes that are involved in life review will be elaborated. Third, the relation of life review to mental health and wellbeing will be discussed. Last, the application of life review in interventions will be described.

Life review and lifespan development

The concept of life review was first used by psychiatrist-gerontologist Robert Butler (1963a, 1963b) and lifespan psychologist Erik Erikson (1959). Butler (1963a, 1963b) distinguishes life review from reminiscence. Whereas reminiscence refers to the recollection of personal memories, life review includes the process of evaluation and integration of both positive and negative memories from different phases of life. Next, Butler distinguished between pathological and successful life reviews. Some older adults have difficulty in coming to terms with mistakes or missed opportunities in their lives – they continue to feel guilty or have regrets about their lives. As a result, they maintain a fear of death. Other older adults succeed in evaluating and integrating their memories into a larger whole. They are able to resolve problems and conflicts from the past and thereby come to accept life's end.

Erikson (1959) similarly distinguishes between despair and ego integrity. People have reasons to despair in later life: problems from their past, present and future life might be difficult to integrate into a meaningful whole. However, they may also be able to resolve such issues and come to experience a sense of ego integrity, i.e. a sense of coherence and wholeness that can be characterized as 'the acceptance of one's one and only life cycle as something that had to be' (Erikson 1959, p.268). Most people oscillate between despair and integrity as two states that need to be balanced. A successful resolution of the duality of ego integrity and despair results in the virtue of wisdom.

Although Butler and Erikson have somewhat different views on the process of life review, they would both agree that a successful life review results in an integrated view of one's past life cycle, including positive memories and achievements alongside the reconciliation of failures and disappointments. Similarly, both see life review as an important developmental task in later life. They describe life review as a naturally occurring process that is sparked by approaching death. Hence, they see a return to the past as functional in accepting that one's life must end.

The evidence that life review is a naturally occurring process in later life is somewhat limited. Some older studies have shown that only about half of older people are involved in a more or less systematic review of their past (Coleman 1986a, 1986b; Merriam 1993; Wink and Schiff 2002). Although older adults often have a more past-oriented time perspective, some may also have a future-oriented perspective (Webster, Bohlmeijer and Westerhof 2014). A smaller group might even want to avoid looking back in order to escape the confrontation with past problems (Coleman 1986a, 1986b).

Other studies have shown that reminiscence is not only distinctive for old age. People reminisce about and review their lives throughout the lifespan (Merriam and Cross 1982; Pasupathi and Carstensen 2003; Webster and Gould 2007). Young children already learn to share and elaborate on their memories with their parents (Fivush 2008), although it is generally granted that a fuller integration of one's personal memories in a more encompassing life story only starts in young adulthood (Habermas and Bluck 2000; see also Chapter 5 by Fivush and Booker). Some studies found higher levels of ego integrity (Domino and Affonso 1990) or lower levels of regret (Timmer, Westerhof and Dittmann-Kohli 2005) in older compared to younger adults. However, most empirical studies have shown that the levels of ego integrity and despair are unrelated to chronological age (Domino and Affonso 1990; Hannah *et al.* 1996; Ryff and Heincke 1983; Webster 2003; Westerhof, Bohlmeijer and McAdams 2017). A longitudinal study also did not find evidence that ego integrity increases with age (Sneed, Whitbourne and Culang 2006; Whitbourne, Sneed and Sayer 2009).

Last, there are some interesting nuances concerning the function of life review; for example, is the process of life review necessary to come to accept death? A meta-analysis of 20 studies found a moderate relation between ego integrity and death acceptance (Fortner and Niemeyer 1999). Although ego integrity is related to death acceptance, the moderate relation suggests that there are older adults who accept death without a process of life review and, vice versa, people who engage in a process of life review do not necessarily accept death. Alternatively, it has also been argued that reminiscence serves different functions beyond death acceptance (Webster 1993; see also Chapter 12 by Cappeliez): identity construction, problem solving, reducing boredom, bitterness revival, intimacy maintenance, conversation or teaching/informing others. Some of these functions belong more to reminiscence as a process of recollecting personal memories, whereas the functions of identity construction, problem solving and bitterness revival involve a more or less successful process of life review. These have also been described as integrative functions that serve to answers question like 'who am I?' and 'what is of value in my life?' (Westerhof and Bohlmeijer 2014).

Although Butler and Erikson argued that life review is a natural occurring developmental task in later life, it is nowadays accepted that life review is a process that takes place throughout the lifespan and serves important functions for the regulation of personal development (Fivush *et al.* 2011; Pasupathi, Weeks and Rice 2006; Westerhof and Bohlmeijer 2014). (See also Fivush and Booker, Chapter 5.)

Meaning processes: evaluation, identification, reasoning and integration

We have seen that life review involves not only the retrieval of memories, but also the process of attributing meaning to these memories. Several concepts have been used that refer to processes of meaning construction, including but not limited to evaluation, elaboration, acceptance, reasoning, identification, integration, importance and meaning. In this section, an attempt to order and classify these different aspects of meaning construction is made, based on overviews of studies on life review (Webster *et al.* 2010; Westerhof *et al.* 2010; Westerhof and Bohlmeijer 2014), autobiographical memory (Conway 2005; Singer *et al.* 2013), and life stories (Adler *et al.* 2016).

The attribution of meaning to one's memories goes back to the human ability to reflect on oneself. As William James (1890) mentioned, the 'I' as an intentional subject is able to reflect on and construct a 'Me', the aspect of one's own person that the 'I' reflects on. A further distinction can be made in terms of the self-memory system that distinguishes between episodic memories of particular events in one's life and semantic memories about oneself as a person across different situations (Conway 2005). Episodic memories are about specific one-time events in one's life, whereas semantic memory concerns the more abstract social-cognitive schemas about oneself as a person. Episodic memories differ in a number of qualities, such as content, vividness, emotional valence and frequency of rehearsal. Similarly, the more abstract social-cognitive schemas about oneself as a person may also differ in a number of qualities, like themes, level of self-esteem or complexity. The 'I' plays an important role in the attribution of meaning to the memories, a process in which specific episodic memories and semantic memory are linked. The following processes can be distinguished: evaluation, identification, reasoning, and integration.

Evaluation refers to the positive or negative valence that is attributed to a memory. The meaning attached does not transcend the specific memory but relates to the evaluation of the specific memory as a nice, beautiful, pleasant, sad or troubling memory. One basically appraises the positive or negative value of the memory, although the value might also be more mixed or ambiguous. Some examples: 'My wedding day was a beautiful day', 'I feel proud of my graduation day',

'My daughter's accident was a shocking event', 'The death of my father was a very sad, but intimate moment'.

Identification refers to the strength of the relation between the episodic memory and the semantic system. One might also say that the specific episodic memory is more or less meaningful, important or central to the semantic self-schema. On the one hand, people may distance themselves from a specific memory or dismiss that the memory is characteristic of their person. On the other hand, people may identify with a particular memory as they see it as characteristic for themselves. Between dismissal and identification, there might be memories that are not related to the self: there is no connection between the episodic memory and the semantic self-knowledge. These would be more transient or mundane memories that people do not attach a special value to in terms of their identity. Identification may best be seen as a continuum rather than as concrete categories. It may range, for example, from a realization that a particular memory is important and reveals a certain aspect of the self to self-defining memories that reflect a person's most enduring concerns and aspects of the self. Some examples are: 'The mistake I made at work was really not who I am', 'I could have made another decision, but that did not influence who I am now', 'I missed that opportunity, but that doesn't matter to me', 'The memory of my first ride in my own car is very important to me', 'I stood up in class for a fellow student who was treated unfairly: this shows my concern for justice', 'My first experience with classical music was overwhelming, it made me who I am now'.

Whereas identification is more a matter of degree, *autobiographical reasoning* relates to the quality of the relationship between an episodic memory and the conceptual self (Pasupathi and Mansour 2006; Thorne, McLean and Lawrence 2004). Autobiographical reasoning transcends the particular memory by attaching a meaning that is relevant to the semantic self. One might compare this to making the moral of the story explicit: what does this particular memory say or teach me about myself? The process of reasoning might differ as a memory might reveal, explain, cause, give insight or provide a lesson learned about oneself. The meaning attributed in the process of autobiographical reasoning may also be more positive or more negative. Examples are: 'I helped people escape from a fire: I discovered how helpful I am', 'I failed in this one important football game that could have made us champions – that shows that I am a loser in life',

'I comforted my friend – this reveals that I believe it is important to be there when it matters', 'I really worked hard for this exam and passed – that taught me that perseverance pays off'.

Autobiographical integration refers to the links that are made between different episodic memories. This is the level of life stories that integrate past, present, and future and help to find coherence and purpose in life. The meaning of particular life events is construed by ordering them in a narrative plot. Habermas and Bluck (2000) described four different ways of ordering life events in a plot. First, the ordering might be purely temporal as when listing several jobs in a curriculum. Second, the ordering might also be more causal by drawing links between different events in one's life. A third way of ordering is thematic. In a process that has been called magnification, people order events by similarity or analogy to broader themes that recur in their lives. Last, events are ordered in relation to cultural expectations about the life course.

Life stories include processes of continuity and change (Brockmeier 2000). Several similar events may sum up a particular self-view or self-schema. Some people see their lives as a continuous repetition of the same kind of events or they may describe how a particular traumatic event blocked their further development. People may also describe how certain events brought change in their lives for the good or for the bad. This has also been described as redemption and contamination (McAdams and McLean 2013). In a redemption sequence, an initially negative experience is salvaged by the good that follows it. For example, people see what they learned from a difficult experience, how they grew from it, or how it strengthened their social relations. A contamination sequence refers to a plot where an emotionally positive experience becomes negative, as it is ruined or spoiled: a marriage is followed by divorce, success in one's work by failure. These negative consequences often come to dominate the life story.

To conclude, processes of evaluation, identification, reasoning and integration all refer to distinct aspects of the process of life review. Although these processes can be distinguished from the quality of specific memories that are recollected in a process of reminiscence, it should be noted that they are not independent of each other. Memories are not simply retrieved from an archive of memories but are always reconstructed in relation to current concerns and goals or one's current working self (Conway 2005). In hindsight (Freeman 2011) or by rereading their lives (Randall and McKim 2008), people may attribute new meanings to events. This involves both processes of assimilation (in which memories are interpreted in line with existing self-schemata) and accommodation (in which self-schemata are changed as a result of a process of life review; Westerhof 2009, 2010). These processes of life review may also be blocked. This has been described as narrative foreclosure (Bohlmeijer *et al.* 2011; Freeman 2011): the conviction that no new experiences and commitments from both the past and the future are possible that can substantially change the meaning of one's life as it is told now.

Life review and mental health and wellbeing

The process of life review is important for mental health and wellbeing across the lifespan (Westerhof *et al.* 2010).

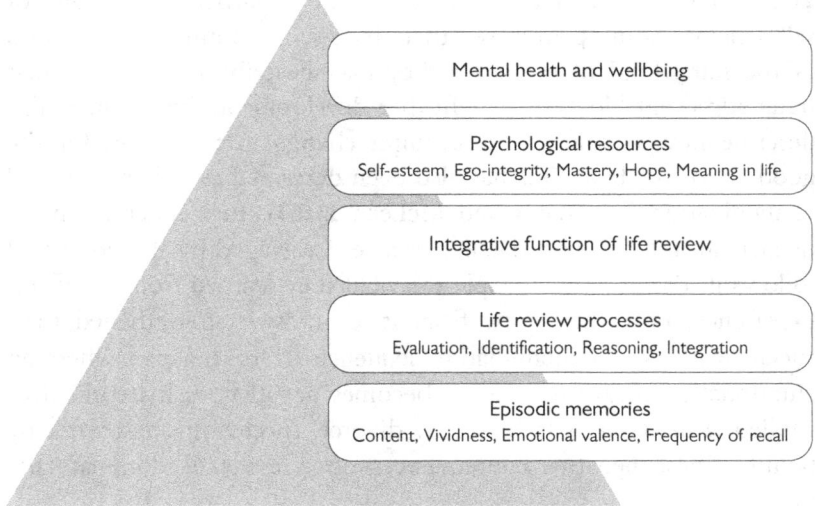

Figure 17.1: Relation of life review to mental health and wellbeing

Figure 17.1 presents a heuristic model that relates life review to mental health and wellbeing. The episodic memories themselves are at the bottom. The process of recollecting them can be described as reminiscence. The meaning attributed to a specific memory may be more important than the remembered event itself (Adler *et al.* 2016).

The meaning may be changed in a process of life review in order to support a person's mental health and wellbeing (Westerhof 2017b). The different processes of life review are distinguished in Figure 17.1. They help to attribute meaning to the memories and thereby fulfill the integrative function of life review. The integrative function of life review supports the accumulation of psychological resources like self-esteem, ego integrity, mastery, hope and meaning in life that are in turn related to mental health and wellbeing (Liao, Bluck and Westerhof 2018; Scogin *et al.* 2005; Westerhof and Bohlmeijer 2014).

There is little research concerned with the *evaluation* of memories. Studies on the fading affect bias have shown that the emotional valence of a memory may change over time and even flip from negative to positive and vice versa (Walker and Skowronski 2007). However, these are the affects that are immediately associated with the memory and not its explicit evaluation. A recent study showed that a more positive evaluation of memories mediated the longitudinal relationship between the emotional valence of a memory and self-esteem one year later (Liao *et al.* 2018).

There has been some work on the *identification* with memories, in particular with regard to regrets. Some studies showed that disengaging from regrets is related to lower levels of depression (Wrosch, Bauer and Scheier 2005; Wrosch and Heckhausen 2002). Disengagement was assessed as a less internal attribution of control or as a dissociation from goals related to regrets. These findings support the lifespan theory of control (Schulz and Heckhausen 1996), that holds that secondary control, i.e. changing oneself and one's goals, is important when primary control, i.e. changing the world according to one's own self-views and goals, is not possible. Furthermore, there has been some work on the sense of closure, the idea that difficult memories are resolved and belong to the past and are therefore less relevant to the current self. Closure is related to greater wellbeing and less psychological distress (Adler and Poulin 2009; King *et al.* 2000; Pals 2006). The experienced time distance from an event may also be seen as an indicator of identification (Wilson and Ross 2003): events that seem to be more remote in time are less related to wellbeing than events that are experienced as closer in time.

The link between the process of *autobiographical reasoning* and mental health and wellbeing has been studied in some detail. Autobiographical reasoning, i.e. connecting episodic memories to broader semantic meanings of the memories to one's own person, is important for mental health and wellbeing (Singer *et al.* 2013). Both people with depression and people with trauma often fail to connect specific episodic memories to more general meanings. Depressed people tend to have an overgeneralized autobiographical memory – they have difficulties in retrieving specific episodic memories (Williams *et al.* 2007). This prevents them from relating their self-schema to these specific episodic memories. Conversely, people with post-traumatic stress disorder have difficulty in integrating specific traumatic memories with their self-concept (Pillemer 1998). Studies on expressive writing have shown that people who describe traumatic events in detail and express their emotions about the event are better able to attribute meaning to the events (Pennebaker and Chung 2011) and thereby support their mental health and wellbeing (Frattarolli 2006). The study by Liao *et al.* (2018) found that drawing a positive meaning out of episodic memories also contributes to self-esteem over time.

As we have seen, people may *integrate* different episodic memories into a more overarching life story. The narrative identity that they construct in their own story plays an important role in psychological adaptation and development (McAdams and McLean 2013). Whereas the evidence for the relation of coherence of life stories with mental health and wellbeing is mixed, a recent review of narrative studies concluded that there is solid evidence from cross-sectional and longitudinal studies that redemption stories are related to wellbeing, even when controlling for other variables of individual differences like personality traits (Adler *et al.* 2016).

Last, life review was described as a *continuous process* across the lifespan. However, sometimes, people may experience a sense of foreclosure that stops the process of life review. In a recent study, it was shown that narrative foreclosure is related to depressive symptoms and wellbeing in a general as well as a clinical sample (Bohlmeijer, Westerhof and Lamers 2014). Although these studies show that the attribution of meaning to personal memories is generally good for one's mental health and wellbeing, there has also been some discussion with regard to the benefits of meaning-making. It has been argued that not all people in all contexts can attribute positive meanings to all life events (Cappeliez and Robitaille 2010; Greenhoot and McLean 2013).

Life review interventions

The important role of life review for mental health and wellbeing has inspired many practical applications (Westerhof *et al.* 2010). Life review interventions need to be distinguished from reminiscence interventions (Haight and Burnside 1993; Westerhof *et al.* 2010). *Reminiscence interventions* stimulate the recollection and sharing of positive memories, most often from childhood, youth and young adulthood. Their main goals are improving mood and social bonding. *Life review interventions* ask people to recollect both positive and negative memories from all phases of life, from childhood to old age. An important aspect of life review interventions is that participants are also stimulated to attribute new meanings to the recollected memories. Counselors in reminiscence and life review interventions need good general counseling competencies such as active listening, open questioning, reflection on feelings, and structuring conversations. More specific competencies for life review interventions are helping participants to attribute new meanings to past events and to link past events to each other and to the present. This asks for some more professional distance as well as motivating participants to search for alternative meanings of their memories. Professionals in healthcare and social work will generally be able to deliver life review interventions after a specific training that includes knowledge and insight in processes of reminiscence and life review as well as skills in guiding the processes of reminiscence and life review.

The life review and experiencing form (LREF; Black and Haight 1992) and guided autobiography (Birren and Cochran 2001) are two of the most used forms of life review (see also Chapter 16 by Shellman and McNeil). Life review interventions tend to consist of some six to ten sessions that most often follow the life course but can also be thematically arranged (e.g. a session on love and friendship and one on study and work). Life review interventions exist in individual formats as well as in group formats. Individual interventions have the advantage that the intervention can be adapted to personal needs and allows for discussion of sensitive issues (Haight, Coleman and Lord 1995). Group interventions make use of social processes that benefit social exchange and learning from others (Birren and Deutchman 1991; Watt and Cappeliez 2000). A qualitative study showed that most participants in a face-to-face group intervention were positive about the peer support they received (Korte *et al.* 2014). They mentioned a good group atmosphere, disclosing to peers and relating to others as important social processes in the intervention. However, some also mentioned that they had difficulties with sharing in a group, were anxious or did not experience the group as supportive and encouraging recognition.

There have been several developments in life review interventions in recent years. Whereas life review interventions originated in gerontology and focused on older adults, they are nowadays also used in younger age groups, such as middle-aged people (Lamers *et al.* 2015) and younger adults (Hallford and Mellor 2016a, 2016b). These applications also emphasize the relation of life review to the present and future somewhat more than interventions for older adults (Lamers *et al.* 2015). A specific method that has been used here is to write a letter from a flourishing future point in time to the current self (Sools, Triliva and Filippas 2017). Furthermore, life review interventions have been tailored to specific groups, like African Americans (Shellman *et al.* 2009), people with cancer (Zhang, Xiao and Chen 2017) or life threatening illness (Chen *et al.* 2017), people with depressive symptomatology (Korte *et al.* 2012a), people with post-traumatic stress disorder (Daniels, Boehnlein and McCallion 2015) or people with mental illness and intellectual disability (Westerhof *et al.* 2016). The focus on people with mental illness has also stimulated the combination of life review interventions with other forms of therapy, like cognitive behavioural therapy (Watt and Cappeliez 2000), creative therapy (Pot *et al.* 2010), and narrative therapy (Bohlmeijer *et al.* 2008). The modes of delivery have also been broadened to include internet use (e.g. Lamers *et al.* 2015).

An example of life review therapy is The Stories We Live By (Bohlmeijer and Westerhof 2010). This intervention integrates life review therapy with narrative therapy. It has been studied as a face-to-face group intervention (Korte *et al.* 2012a), a self-help book with online counseling (Lamers *et al.* 2015) and as a fully digital platform with counseling by peers or a trained counselor (Westerhof *et al.* 2017). It is tailored to middle-aged and older people with depressive symptoms.

Table 17.1: Overview of the intervention The Stories We Live By

	Youth and family	Adolescence and becoming an adult	Work and care	Love and friendship	Old and new goals	Reading your life
Start	What to expect?	Look back on week 1	Look back on week 2	Look back on week 3	Look back on week 4	Look back on week 5
Theory	Alternative stories	Your shadow	The plot your life	Your own wisdom	Life goals	Reading your life
Tip	Physical condition	More positive memories	Pleasant activities	Mood scan living room	Self-compassion	Focusing your senses
Creative exercise	A short poem	Haiku	Using your senses	Phantasy	The life course of your hands	Letter from the future
Examples	Personal stories	Personal stories	Personal stories	Personal stories	Personal stories	Personal stories
Autobiographical recollection	Open questions	Open questions	Open questions	Open questions	-	-
	Positive memories	Positive memories	Positive memories	Positive memories		
Autobiographical reasoning	Difficult memory	Difficult memory	Difficult memory	Difficult memory	-	-
	Alternative stories	Alternative stories	Alternative stories	Alternative stories		
	Meaning	Meaning	Meaning	Meaning		
Autobiographical integration	-	-	-	-	Balanced goals	Chapters of your life

Three life review processes provide the basis for the intervention: autobiographical recollection of vivid positive memories, autobiographical reasoning about negative memories, and autobiographical integration of memories across different phases of the lifespan. There are six modules that can be carried out at home during a period of 12 weeks: Younger years and family; Adolescence and becoming an adult; Work and care; Love and friendship; Old and new goals; Reading your life. The first four modules focus on life themes across the life course from birth to present. These modules have the same structure. First, assignments are provided for reminiscence about the life theme, based on open questions. Second, there is an exercise on autobiographical recollection of positive memories. Third, there are assignments for autobiographical reasoning about difficult memories, by providing alternative stories and addressing new meaning found in the difficult memories. The last two modules focus on the entire life course from the past to the near future, i.e. they have a focus on integration. Module 5 has a focus on disengagement and (re)engagement with old and new goals, whereas module 6 focuses on the common theme through the chapters of one's life stories, ending with the chapter on envisioning the future.

Evidence of the effects of life review interventions

The evidence for the effectiveness of life review interventions has accumulated with the publication of a number of different systematic reviews and meta-analyses. Some studies focused on both reminiscence and life review interventions and were not only limited to life review interventions. Others reported findings for reminiscence and life review interventions separately or focused on life review interventions only. Bohlmeijer, Smit and Cuijpers (2003) conducted a meta-analysis of studies on reminiscence and life review interventions that also included a control group. Nine studies using a life review intervention showed a mean effect size of .92 (Cohen's d) on depressive symptoms. Bohlmeijer *et al.* (2007) also conducted a meta-analysis on wellbeing. The mean effect size of seven studies on life review interventions was 1.04 (Cohen's d). Pinquart and Forstmeier (2012) distinguished between reminiscence interventions, life review interventions and life review therapy. The mean effect of 27 studies on life review interventions was 0.31 for depressive symptoms and 0.38 for wellbeing

(Hedges g). The mean effect of life review therapy was larger: 1.28 for depressive symptoms and 1.02 for wellbeing (Hedges g). Lan, Xiao and Chen (2017) conducted a meta-analysis of 11 studies that were either randomized controlled trials (RCT) or controlled clinical trials (CCT). They focused on life review interventions among older adults and found a standardized mean difference of 0.57 for depressive symptoms, and 0.54 for wellbeing.

There have also been some studies on more specific target groups. Chen *et al.* (2017) conducted a meta-analysis of nine studies (RCTs and CCTs) on life review for people with life-threatening illness. They found an effect of 0.78 for depressive symptoms and 2.21 for quality of life (standardized mean difference). Zhang *et al.* (2017) focused on RCTs and CCTs on life review interventions for cancer patients. They did not conduct a meta-analysis but found that most of the 15 studies found significant effects on depression and quality of life.

Overall, the evidence shows that life review interventions are effective in diminishing depressive symptoms and in improving wellbeing and quality of life. Effect sizes can be classified as at least moderate for life review interventions, but strong for life review therapy. Interestingly, there is not much overlap in the studies that were included in the different systematic meta-analyses, with the exception of the meta-analyses by Bohlmeijer *et al.* (2003, 2007) and the one by Pinquart and Forstmeier (2012). However, most reviews conclude that not all studies were of sufficient quality, even though most of them were RCTs or CCTs.

An important question is how life review interventions contribute to mental health and wellbeing. Besides the overall effects on depressive symptoms and wellbeing or quality of life there were a number of other significant effects of life review interventions, such as those on ego integrity, purpose in life, hope, self-esteem, mastery and death preparation (Lan *et al.* 2017; Chen *et al.* 2017; Pinquart and Forstmeier 2012; Wang, Chow and Chan 2017). As Figure 17.1 illustrates, these can be seen as psychological resources that support mental health. A number of studies have also shown that such resources indeed mediate the effects of life review interventions (Korte *et al.* 2012a; Lamers *et al.* 2015; Westerhof *et al.* 2010). Although some studies also report effects on autobiographical memory (Lan *et al.* 2017), there is less evidence for how the actual process of life review contributes to the effects on mental health and wellbeing.

Conclusion

We have seen that life review is a process that occurs throughout the lifespan. It consists of different processes that are related to the attribution of meaning to personal memories: evaluation, identification, reasoning and integration. These processes serve an integrative function to answer questions like 'who am I?' and 'what is of value in my life?' Studies have shown that life review processes are related to the accumulation of psychological resources that are in turn related to mental health and wellbeing. Life review interventions stimulate the processes of life review and are effective in alleviating depressive symptoms and improving wellbeing in older adults as well as in people with life-threatening illness and cancer. Further research could focus on the different relations that were visualized in Figure 17.1. Although there is some evidence for these relations, the specific relations between different kinds of memories with different life review processes to particular psychological resources and particular aspects of mental health can be further studied. These studies will also inform the further development of life review interventions.

Part 4

TECHNOLOGY IN REMINISCENCE PRACTICE, TRAINING AND DEVELOPMENT

Chapter 18

MEMOIR WRITING
The Challenge of Leaving a Legacy

Mary O'Brien Tyrrell

While I was in graduate school at the University of Minnesota in 1979, Dr Norman Craig, the director of the program in community health education, alerted me to the impending upsurge in services for the elderly that statisticians were predicting as the cohort of baby boomers aged. Given those needs, he strongly suggested that after completing my program I consider concentrating on gerontology, and I'm greatly indebted to him for his foresight. Gerontology did become my focus and led to a challenging and rewarding career that took a final twist which I could never have imagined at the time.

Following two-and-a-half decades of experience as a nurse and gerontologist with a background in community health education, I began using reminiscence work to help elders narrate their life stories and to honor them by publishing those stories in limited-edition hardbound books that could be shared with family members and others interested in their stories. By the time I retired two decades later, I had helped almost three hundred clients in 17 states capture their life stories in the form of a cherished book and family heirloom. My original inspiration for the business I created to make this work possible came from observing the way that elders were honoured in the Native American community in Minneapolis, Minnesota.

Here's how it happened. In 1992 I was hired as coordinator of a National Institute of Health (NIH) grant conducted at the Hennepin County Medical Center (HCMC) in Minneapolis. The goal of the grant was to test an intervention intended to increase the rate of breast cancer screening for low-income, elderly minority women living in large American cities. The historical rate of screening among American

Indian women was especially low, and it was postulated that such a program could decrease their morbidity and mortality rates.

From my training in community health, I knew that my first step would be to find a way to observe the normal mores and acceptable behavior of one of our target populations, the American Indian community in Minneapolis, within their regular environment. HCMC was the first US hospital to hire a full-time American Indian advocate, whose name was Lorraine Rivera. When I met Lorraine on one of my first days on the project, she encouraged me to attend several cultural events held by the community, including powwows, honouring ceremonies and sweat ceremonies. Lorraine had been diagnosed with kidney cancer several years earlier, but unlike so many of the elderly patients I had worked with, she seemed at peace with knowing her time was limited and had even already purchased her own casket, which she stored in her garage. She invited me to attend her honouring ceremony, where she was feted in the hospital basement with drummers, smudging (an ancient ritual) and community members singing and dancing in full regalia. Many dozens of staff members attended along with Lorraine's relatives and friends. During the ceremony, she received gifts for her 'passing-on', such as new moccasins, her favourite foods, handmade quilts, and a dress from her tribe in northern New York State – items intended to make the trip to her new life comfortable. It was a wonderful and happy community occasion, a real celebration of life.

Following Lorraine's advice, I also volunteered to serve food for the elderly Native American people in the Phillips Neighbourhood at their monthly feast, a lovely meal served by community volunteers, which was an experience that was new to me. Each month, I was particularly impressed by a specific behavior – whenever an elder spoke during those meals, the whole room went quiet as everyone listened. It was startling and very impressive! I had never before observed such group behavior and mused about how that value might be emulated in mainstream culture. If they could do it, why couldn't mainstream communities revere elders in a similar manner?

But most Americans aren't proficient at honouring by silence. We talk a lot. So, what might be a comparable behavior of honouring elders in mainstream American culture? It occurred to me that one of the ways we do honour our heroes in mainstream US society is to produce and read accounts of their life story. Libraries and bookstores contained shelves of biographies of famous people, and the advent of affordable home computers at the time would make the production of books in small quantities easier. After visiting several printing and bindery shops in the Minneapolis Warehouse District, it became clearer to me that it might be possible to write the life stories of ordinary elderly people through a small home business and have the document bound at a short-run bindery.

An opportunity to test my theory came soon after, when I was asked by a college friend living out of state to provide emotional support to her 52-year-old sister, Geri, who was dying of breast cancer in Minneapolis. Although several medical interventions had been attempted for Geri, none had been successful. I asked Geri if she would like to have me help her write her life story by interviewing her for several hours and crafting the information she shared with me into in a memoir published in a few bound copies to be given to her family and friends. She immediately agreed, and the prospect of this impending project seemed to provide her a new energy.

As we began our interviews, I learned that Geri had experienced considerable heartbreak and difficulty in her life, including two divorces and rearing her daughter as a single parent. In the midst of the third interview, however, Geri suddenly and unexpectedly declared, 'I realize now that I had a wonderful life!' This statement reflected a dramatic change in her mood and a reframing of her understanding of her life. We proceeded to have several more interviews, and at one point again reviewed the results, which by then also included family photos. About two weeks later, she telephoned to ask that we review the document for the final time. It was a Saturday night, and although she was still living alone at home, she was quite weak. On my arrival, she asked if I would read the document to her, which I did. Announcing her final approval, she clutched the document to her chest saying, 'That's me. That's Geri!' The following morning, I received a phone call asking that I come to see her at the hospital. She died that day. Geri's life story was posthumously published and distributed as promised, and Geri's daughter later told me that she would read the book whenever she wanted to hear her mother's voice.

At work a while later, the secretary from across the hall asked me about the copy of Geri's book on my desk. After explaining it to her, she picked it up, hugged it to her chest (just as I'd seen Geri do to the manuscript) and asked, 'Would you do this for my grandpa? He has the most wonderful stories.' Recognizing this was a great opportunity for me to test and time the process I had developed in working with Geri, I told her that I would be willing to do the work if her family was willing to pay for the printing and the hardcover binding. Thus George, a 92-year-old Wisconsin farmer, became my second narrator. At his birthday party a few months later, as George was unwrapping his books and distributing his life story to about 75 members of his family in front of his barn, he stopped to announce to me, 'This is the best day of my life!' Again, I was stunned by his excitement. Could this, I wondered, be a replicable model for honouring elders, and a new way for me to follow my calling as a nurse and gerontologist? Six months later, with my responsibilities for the grant and my research job complete, I decided to take the proverbial plunge and dive in headfirst. Having just turned 50 years old, I was about to enter what Gene Cohen (2005) describes as the second phase of aging – experimentation – and to create a new business and advance a new profession.

Turning a mission into a business

Because I didn't know anyone else who was doing such work and had received mostly sceptical responses from the colleagues with whom I had shared my ideas, in 1996 I wrote to Dr Robert N. Butler to see if he would be willing to meet with me for ten or fifteen minutes while in town to give the keynote speech for the Minnesota Gerontological Association. He agreed to meet me in the hallway before his address, and I showed him a few of the books I had produced with clients. To my relief, he agreed that my business was a 'great' idea and called over another attendee and introduced us. 'I want you to meet John Kunz', he said. 'You two should work together.' John was the founder of the International Institute for Reminiscence and Life Review (IIRLR), located not far away at the University of Wisconsin–Superior, and as a result of that introduction we did work closely together for years.

In early December 2000, John contacted me to tell me that Metropolitan Life Foundation had awarded him a grant to produce materials for public education about older adults having their life story recorded and to ask for my help. Sitting at my dining room table in St Paul, Minnesota, the two of us developed a select list of elders from my clients who exemplified some typical scenarios I had observed, a description of what issues those clients presented, and educational principles for a video that became *The Joys and Surprises of Telling Your Life Story* (Kunz 2002). So, with Dr Butler's assurance and moral and practical support from John Kunz, I proceeded to expand my business.

Given that I had never established a business before, I needed to learn many new skills. Thankfully, due to my past responsibilities for the NIH grant, I had become computer literate and was proficient with interview techniques because of my nursing background. My training in gerontology and public health also provided knowledge of a wealth of principles on family and social issues and on working with elderly people. But it certainly was a mixed bag of skills and experiences, and an outsider looking at my situation probably would not have placed any bets on my success.

The first thing I needed if I was to make a real business out of this work was to figure out how the production of these books could be funded. I'd hoped that my experience as treasurer of the Minnesota Gerontological Society for several years might prove helpful, but I knew nothing about accounting, marketing, sales or publishing books. And because I wanted the elders with whom I worked to have power to control the outcome of the book – one of the most important goals of this process – I didn't want to pursue the path of seeking funds through grants that would have to be tailored to the goals or interests of the funding organization. So somehow I would have to find a replicable model that would also make the final product affordable for individual clients. Through careful record keeping and financial projections, I eventually developed a model that included a set number of hours of interviewing, three rounds of client review of the manuscript, a set range of pages and family photographs, a standard binding, and a set number of final copies. Over the years, I came to offer a broader range of options at various price points, but it was always important to me to be able to offer a product that middle-income families could afford.

Because I wanted the books to become a treasured family heirloom and to meet the same expectations as any published book, I also chose to fold into the price the cost of a round of professional editing and design by a book designer. The price also had to cover office overhead, travel expenses and the services of a lawyer and certified public accountant. And because I wanted to be able to pursue this new profession for the rest of my career, I also factored in the cost of savings for retirement. I learned from the many good small-business 'how to' books that I consulted, for instance, that if I needed to make an annual income of $50,000, I would have to bill almost twice that, as half of my income would have to be used for business expenses and to cover the benefits most people receive from their employers. Once I knew how much I needed to earn each year and how many clients I could reasonably expect to serve, I was able to set my pricing and develop a strategic plan.

From those small-business books, I learned how to write an annual business plan for my company that would include the objectives and goals of the company; describe the type of business, products and services; identify how and where the service would be sold and how long it would take to produce a book; specify the quality and average price of the memoirs; analyse the market environment and competition; and outline plans for the future. Suddenly my business and marketing plans were going to dictate and measure my future and my future income. Eventually I created tools to monitor my goals (including income) and forecast those annually. On my desk or bulletin board, I kept a month-by-month goal for the number of client contracts (usually two per month) that needed to be signed. In my first business plan, my goal for that year was to sign contracts with 20 new clients.

So how would I find those clients? My first big learning experience on that front came when my nephew Greg Weinberger, who was taking a marketing class at St Thomas University in St Paul, generously gifted me with a marketing plan for my new company, Memoirs, Inc. I had never before heard of a marketing plan, but I could immediately see its similarity to a community health education plan in which, among other things, one identifies key informants and develops ways to build a bridge between one's own goals and theirs. As that plan made clear to me, marketing is simply the means by which one informs the community, 'I'm available'. I quickly learned that, however much the world needed what I had to offer, I couldn't expect it to beat a path to my door without my doing everything I could to get the word out. For about three years, I spent time every day thinking about how I could get my name and business into the newspaper, on television and radio and online. As uncomfortable as it seemed at first, I came to understand that this was not bragging – this was about the future of my business and profession. My first big marketing break came about a year into my business when a feature writer for the local newspaper wrote an article about me. When my phone started ringing, I was ready with a model book, contract and price sheet. I was on my way.

At first, I expected that I would develop clients by giving presentations to groups of older people at churches, libraries and senior centers, but I soon found out that did not work, for several reasons – most ordinary elders don't think their story is important or interesting, and they generally do not want to pay thousands of dollars to preserve it. As I began to field emails and phone enquiries, it turned out that in most cases I was contacted by a family member, most often the eldest daughter or granddaughter, and the two of us would have a conversation to discuss the process, length of time from start to finish, where the interviews would take place, and such other relevant issues as the narrator's hearing ability, cognition and conversational ease. I would explain to the family member that I preferred to interview the elder in the comfort of their own home with an audio recorder running and only the narrator and I present. If all those conditions were agreeable, we would sign a contract and set an appointment and I received a down payment of the first half of the agreed-on cost.

The heart of the process

I came to my new work aware that the heart of the process was the interview, which would eventually become the manuscript. Instead of peppering clients with a list of questions, I learned to ask one leading question: 'What is your earliest memory?' That usually caused a pause, after which the narrators would begin to describe important memories and occasions from their childhood, adolescence, adulthood and old age. Even clients who started the process thinking they didn't have much to talk about or who worried about how much they would be able to remember soon were able to tap into a deep well of memories, many of which they might not have recalled for a long time and some that even their spouses might not have heard about. Typically, I would meet with a narrator for five two-hour tape-recorded interviews. Then I would transcribe the tapes to try to capture the elder's inflections and figures of speech as we metaphorically learned to dance together, which I would then craft into a coherent and intelligible narrative. The end result was not a word-for-word transcription of the interviews but rather a series of vignettes that flowed together. My goal was always to produce a manuscript that would capture the client's voice and that they and their family would recognize as sounding just like them. The narrator was given three opportunities to review the drafts as they developed and always had the final say over phrasing and what was included. The full process typically took four months, which also provided clients with the opportunity to reflect on the contents of the manuscript and make additions, adjustments or deletions before the final version was bound and distributed.

Although it was not possible for every client to distribute copies of the finished book at a family book-signing party, from the beginning I saw this honouring ceremony as a central element of the process I was devoted to making possible for elders. Imitating the idea of the Native American honouring ceremonies I had witnessed, I had initiated the book-signing party for family and friends as a recommended capstone to the memoir publication process with my second narrator, George, who had declared it the best day of his life, and the book-signing parties to which I was invited validated this decision over and over again. A year after George's party, for instance, I attended the 49th wedding anniversary party of the first couple I had interviewed together, who had kept the writing of their double memoir a secret from their children right up to the party at the same hotel where they had honeymooned. The other guests' puzzlement as to who I was and why I was there was resolved when, after dinner, the wife sprung the surprise on all gathered, telling them, 'In all of our 49 years of marriage, we've never had so much fun as we did this year working together with Mary to publish our memoirs.' Her testimony and the positive response of the gathered family members once again cemented for me the value of this formal celebration.

But I was also on the lookout for ways in which the honouring of elders' experiences and wisdom could be expanded to the larger society. Early on, for instance, I also often recommended to my Minnesota narrators and their families that they consider donating a copy of their book to the Minnesota Historical Society (MHS). I soon learned, however, that despite good intentions, family members tended to get busy and not follow through on my suggestion. So, I queried the MHS library staff directly as to whether they were interested in receiving donated memoirs for their collection and discovered that not only were they very interested, but they would welcome the opportunity to meet the narrators and evaluate each book for its significance to the MHS collection. Thus, for many of my Minnesota clients, the visit to the MHS became the conclusion of our process and professional relationship. The MHS building has a lovely dining area, and so I would make an appointment to present the finished book to the MHS staff, who would examine the volume and thank the narrator for their contribution, and then to treat the narrator and family members to lunch in a symbolic parting gesture. That innovation resulted in 69 books currently catalogued at the MHS.

I have also urged narrators to consider donating copies of their book to their local libraries or historical societies, church or synagogue, or other organizations to which they belong. Other clients have donated their memoirs to the Veterans History Project at the Library of Congress or the Women in Military Service for America Memorial Foundation. An example of a book that has had an especially large reach was by an American Indian woman, Miscobineshii, who had spoken only her native tongue until she was six, when she enrolled in school to learn English. Because the oral tradition was so central to her Chippewa heritage, she had originally hesitated in having her story written down and published but also felt strongly that her story needed to be recorded so as not to be forgotten. After its completion, she was invited to contribute a copy for the grand opening of the Smithsonian's National Museum of the American Indian in Washington, DC, and, on the recommendation of the staff there, also donated a copy to the National Museum of American History. Back home in Luck, Wisconsin, her tribal leaders also voted to provide funds to publish an additional two hundred copies of her book.

First, do no harm

Although my own observations and those of other researchers in the field leave little doubt that such reminiscence work can have considerable and lasting benefits for the elderly, it also includes some risks. For that reason, I adopted several practices and ethical principles in my work to protect clients and their families from possible harm.

One of these was that I would initially screen potential clients for conditions or situations that might create problems. Given my ten years' experience working in psychiatric nursing at Minnesota's St. Cloud Veterans Medical Center, I was aware that recalling memories of long-ago events could have negative as well as positive effects on certain individuals. By searching the literature and quizzing as many gero-psychiatrists as were available at meetings of the IIRLR conferences, I developed a list of behaviors that might predict a bad outcome.

As a result, I decided not to work with persons with a history of multiple psychiatric hospitalizations. I would also not accept individuals who were reluctant or ambivalent about being interviewed even though their family was pressuring them to agree. And I decided not to work with people who had recently experienced a serious personal loss. After the death of a parent, some families coax the remaining parent into immediately recording his or her life story, but after a couple of experiences with clients who over-rode my hesitations and then were unable to finish the process, I finally developed a stronger backbone and suggested that instead I put them on a waiting list and they could contact me in a couple of years if they were ready.

The scant literature that I found was in agreement with those cautions. Not wanting to cause harm to someone who already had a history of severe trauma, I always asked about such issues when interviewing the initial contact person and remained alert for that possibility during the interview process. In working with Holocaust survivors and former prisoners of war, for instance, I made a verbal agreement with the narrators that should certain symptoms emerge, we would pause the process while they sought appropriate counseling. Over the years, three of my clients did develop symptoms of depression, and each of them, after receiving appropriate treatment, returned to finish their memoir with good results.

To enable the trust, control, and freedom necessary for my elderly clients fully to engage in the reminiscence work we did together, I assured them of total confidentiality. I would inform narrators that if at any time they wanted to tell me something that they didn't want recorded, to let me know and I would turn off the recorder, or if they slipped and told me something that they didn't want recorded, it would be erased. I also told them that if they didn't want their family to have a copy of the recorded interviews after the book was completed, I would honour their request. A 91-year-old woman, for instance, once asked me to turn off the recorder and then told me that as an adolescent, she had been abused by her family's physician and had kept it a secret. After finishing the story, she said she felt relieved just to be able to say that aloud to another human being whom she could trust to keep it confidential. She wasn't the only one who did that. Those were the kind of lessons that indicated to me that performing this service of assisting an elder to write a life story is an important profession that requires special training and that we're working not just with others' memories but with their 'souls'.

I also made clear to the elders I worked with that we would make choices later about what would be included in the final book and thus not everything we talked about necessarily needed to be shared with other people. I was always very mindful that the written version was intended to be shared with the client's family and careful to guide them away from including material or information that was likely to cause avoidable pain or strains within the family. For instance, although it didn't happen often, I would warn narrators against trying to settle old scores, nurse old wounds, or reveal painful family secrets in their memoirs. I also stipulated in my contract for service that I refused to publish negative descriptions of others. This was in part a legal matter, as I didn't want the client or my company to end up being sued for libel, but it was primarily an ethical issue, as causing harm to the elder or their family threatened the very purpose of the memoir writing and sharing process. Even more subtle criticisms or insidious comparisons also had potential to create hard feelings among family members. A frequent occurrence, especially among narrators from large families, were such comparisons as, 'I was the only one in the family to graduate from high school.' In such cases, I would make a suggestion such as, 'This book is going to be treasured by family members for many future generations. How about if we phrase it, "I was so delighted to have graduated from high school"?' I was also scrupulous about making sure that the narrator's children got as equal treatment as possible in the finished version. Because I stressed that the purpose of the book was to tell the narrator's story, I asked few questions about their children and kept the focus on the narrator's experiences. Most of the completed books included just a paragraph about each child's birth within the larger narrative and one about their current life in the final chapter.

As a quality assurance measure and as a safety check to make sure that the memoir was not creating family problems over something we'd included, I would usually contact clients a few months after its completion to see how the book-signing event had gone or what kind of feedback they'd received from recipients of the books. In one such call, I learned that after giving the book to her son, the narrator had stopped distribution of her memoirs because the son had been upset because he believed that one of the words used to describe another person was not accurate. So, I offered to remove that one word from all the copies, which was accomplished by having the bindery 'rip and tip' (replace) just that page. That accomplished, she successfully distributed her memoir to what she described as great acclaim. To avoid such problems, I often recommended that clients ask one trusted family member to read the next-to-final draft before sending it to be typeset, so as to alert us to any potential problems we had not anticipated.

My legacy

In a survey conducted by mail with 50 former narrators or their survivors (Tyrrell 2007), I learned that of the half who had held a book-signing party, two-thirds considered it an important event in their life; that more than three-quarters had recommended the memoir-writing process to others; and that more than 80 per cent enjoyed rereading their own memoir. My files contain numerous thank-you notes from clients and their families and programs from funerals and celebration-of-life ceremonies to which I've been invited. At many of those services, family members or clergy have read passages from the client's book. It was great work, and I considered these connections part of my paycheck, as they brought considerable joy to my life.

Though I never became financially rich as a result of my work, I managed to make a comfortable living and my life and friendships have been enormously enriched. When I first started, I had no mentors in how to do this work as an independent memoirist and business owner. In fact, some of my professional colleagues thought I was taking a step backwards by moving from involvement in important medical research to a new and unknown occupation that to many of them appeared to be little more than transcribing other people's words. Over the years, however, I found new colleagues and insights through my work with the IIRLR and with the now-defunct Association of Personal Historians. Now, more than two decades later, there is a much greater awareness within the profession and the general public about the value and benefits of reminiscence work among elderly people. My question as to whether there was enough need and interest in this service to make it possible to earn a living from it has been answered.

From the beginning of this work, I kept notes on the lessons I was learning in terms of principles I might share with other people interested in becoming a memoirist. To that end, I published several articles describing my work (Hecht and Tyrrell 2007; Tyrrell 2003, 2008) and produced a book, *Become a Memoirist for Elders: Create a Successful Home Business* (Tyrrell 2012), to help others create similar businesses. In addition, I developed a five-session workshop, *Jumpstart Your Memoir Writing Business*, that I have presented at St Catherine University in St Paul and at Bridgewater State University, Cape Cod, Massachusetts. During my retirement, I have continued to plant seeds for the next generation of memoirists by teaching that course, selling my textbook, writing articles such as this one, and giving talks in the community on the benefits of writing one's life story (Tyrrell 2013). Doing so has continued to provide what Dr Cohen described as food for my soul.

My wish for the future of this profession is that universities with gerontology programs will develop standards, training courses and credentials in reminiscence work and memoir writing for master's-level students based on best knowledge and measureable results to ensure benefits and safety for the public. If the popularity of writing memoirs for elders increases at the rate I have witnessed in my time in the field, I hope a more stable and institutional means for training will become standard and include coursework in gerontology, psychology of aging, small business and marketing training, qualitative interviewing, ethics, narrative writing and a semester practicum.

Steeped in the joy this profession has brought to my life and the families I've been privileged to serve, I remain humbled and hopeful for the future. May we remember what Dr James E. Birren once told me in a personal conversation: if we knew each other's individual life stories, world peace might actually be possible.

Chapter 19

THE CONTRIBUTION OF INFORMATION TECHNOLOGY TO REMINISCENCE, LIFE REVIEW AND LIFE STORY WORK

The Perspective of People Living with Dementia and their Families

Assumpta Ryan

Prior evaluations of reminiscence have typically relied on static material such as photographs and personal items as triggers or prompts (Lazar 2014; O'Rourke *et al.* 2011). It is now recognised that technology-based applications have the potential to provide a more dynamic reminiscence experience (Lazar, Thompson and Demiris 2014). Technology-based reminiscence activities can be rapidly downloaded and ready for use or quickly personalised to the individual and family. Smaller mobile devices and a wider availability of wireless networks have also increased portability. Studies have shown that computer use by people living with dementia is highly rated by participants, families and staff (Astell *et al.* 2010; Tamura *et al.* 2007). However, a review of technology-based interventions has indicated that, although the use of technology for reminiscence, life review and life story work is an area of significant interest, a need remains to explore the types and content of media beneficial to individuals at different stages of dementia (Astell, Purves and Phinney 2011; Lazar *et al.* 2014). See also Chapters 2 by Pierce and Elliott, 3 by Woods and 17 by Westerhof.

Information technology and dementia

Kerssens *et al.* (2015) tested the usability, feasibility and adoption of the *Companion* in a study involving seven people living with dementia and their caregivers. The *Companion* was designed to mitigate neuropsychological symptoms and cue daily health and wellness routines. It is a touch-screen computer with no keyboard or mouse, that delivers psychosocial interventions such as reminiscence, simulated presence and orientation to place and person. Interventions were personalised and delivered in the home for a minimum of three weeks. Post-intervention measures indicated that the technology was easy to use, significantly facilitated meaningful and positive engagement and simplified carers' daily lives. Participants living with dementia used the system independently but were limited by cognitive and physical impairments. The authors concluded that the *Companion* can help manage some of the neuropsychiatric symptoms associated with dementia and offer support to carers. The findings of Kerssens *et al.* (2015) are consistent with the work of other researchers using technology to promote reminiscence and quality of life (Astell *et al.* 2010) and confirmed that psychosocial interventions can be delivered using computer-based tools.

Lorenz *et al.* (2017) conducted a literature review to explore technology-based tools and services for people living with dementia and their carers and concluded that, despite the wide range of technologies available for this client group, there was little evidence of widespread practical application. On the contrary, it appeared that people living with dementia and their carers frequently relied on everyday technologies re-purposed to meet their needs. Consistent with other studies, the review identified the role of technology in supporting the delivery of therapeutic interventions, including home-based reminiscence, to reduce caregiver burden and stress (Carers UK 2017; O'Shea *et al.* 2014). While Lorenz *et al.* (2017) acknowledged the significant role technology can play in supporting connection, communication and independent living, it also highlighted the challenges posed by the ever-changing cognitive status of users. This was supported by a host of other studies which recommended that technologies for older people and their caregivers need to be accessible at the right time, adaptable to changing needs, easy to use and inexpensive to buy (Karlsson *et al.* 2014; Mulvenna *et al.* 2011; Ryan and McKenna 2013).

Technology facilitated reminiscence

For people living with dementia, their ability to present rational ideas and to reason lucidly is diminished (Wayman 2017). However, it has been demonstrated that these individuals can participate in research and provide useful feedback on information technology (IT) solutions (Kerssens et al. 2015). The development of new treatments for dementia has become a UK government priority (Department of Health 2016). The use of digital systems to facilitate reminiscing has been shown to be beneficial for people living with dementia (Lazar et al. 2014). Reminiscence systems have been defined as 'the use of technology to support reminiscence work' (Mulvenna et al. 2011, p.58). Technology that facilitates reminiscence increases opportunities for people living with dementia to participate in conversations and to enhance their social interactions (Subramaniam and Woods 2016)

Many existing software systems, apps and online social networking websites provide opportunities to gather, browse and share multimedia resources (Lorenz et al. 2017). However, there is very little research into the usability of these systems for the purpose of reminiscing among people with deteriorating cognitive function. Thiry (2013) discovered that many older people do not use social networking sites or online communities because there is 'too much going on'. Consistent with the findings of other studies (Cosley et al. 2009; Good et al. 2012), Thiry's research indicated a need for software systems which were simpler and minimalistic and which required only the most basic support for content creation and management.

Recent advances in information and communications technology (ICT) have enabled increased opportunities for supportive interventions, such as reminiscence, to be conducted in the home (Karlsson et al. 2014). However, ICT-facilitated reminiscence has posed documented challenges, as it usually relies on caregiver willingness to participate and to source appropriate memorabilia or stimuli (Sarne-Fleischmann and Tractinsky 2008). Despite this, research into technology-facilitated reminiscence has shown that it can provide opportunities for people living with dementia to retain an empowered role in their conversations, interactions and relationships (Lazar et al. 2014).

Lazar et al. (2014) carried out a systematic review of literature surrounding the use of technology in reminiscence therapy using the ACM Guide to Computing Literature, PubMed and psychINFO databases. Forty-four papers were selected for review and, although limited by the small sample size of some of the selected papers, the authors concluded that there are benefits to using ICT for reminiscence interventions. Some of these benefits have been reported elsewhere and include access to rich and engaging multimedia reminiscence materials (Astell *et al.* 2010; Elfrink *et al.* 2017), opportunities for people with dementia to participate in social interactions and take ownership of conversations (Hamel *et al.* 2016; Kerssens *et al.* 2015) and a reduction of barriers due to motor deficits during interactions with media (Kerssens *et al.* 2015; Mulvenna *et al.* 2011). The authors recommended that future studies should explore the types and content of media beneficial to individuals at different stages of dementia. Additionally, Lazar *et al.* (2014) proposed that technology can reduce the burden of the delivery of reminiscence as it provides opportunities for remote therapy, thereby reducing travel and time commitments for carers.

A study by Mulvenna *et al.* (2011) examined the attitudes of older people (n=19) to using a device to reminisce as opposed to a card-based approach. Participants in the study were randomly allocated to reminisce using either an iPad or more traditional images and cards. The results from the study indicated that participants enjoyed using the iPad. Using a parallel convergent mixed methods design, the feasibility of *Memory Matters* (*MM*), a mobile device application developed to promote reminiscence, was evaluated by Hamel *et al.* (2016). Eighteen people living with dementia and eight family carers were asked to use *MM* for four weeks. Consistent with the findings of other studies exploring similar devices (Haesner *et al.* 2015; Lazar *et al.* 2014), Hamel *et al.* reported that family and staff perceived *MM* favourably. Family participants enjoyed discussing the early years with their relative and on several occasions, residents shared memories in a direct response to prompts provided by *MM*. People living with dementia who had only interacted minimally, or who had never spoken before, interacted and supported each other while playing the application. The authors concluded that these findings support the social engagement potential of mobile devices that include stimulating interactive content (Bleakely *et al.* 2015; Delello and McWhorter 2015). However, Mulvenna *et al.* caution that the risk in adopting such technologies is that the essence and richness inherent in such a human activity as reminiscing are lost in translation and that older people may be expected to use technology as a proxy for interaction with other people (Mulvenna *et al.* 2011).

User engagement in technology research

As the use of computer applications (apps) and ubiquitous devices is fast becoming an integral part of everyday existence, there is a need to design digital systems that can be used by all, regardless of physical or cognitive abilities or impairments. The need to involve all stakeholders in systems design and to undertake usability testing of the user interface is imperative and is widely accepted as good practice (Carroll and Rosson 2007; O'Connor et al. 2016; Span et al. 2013). As a result, researchers into human-computer-interaction have proposed standard instruments, protocols and metrics for measuring 'usability' as a construct (Gibson et al. 2016; Sauro 2016). However, where the target user group has diminished cognitive abilities and perhaps also physical impairments, issues can arise that pose problems when using these standard methods for usability testing (Astell et al. 2009; Riley, Alm and Newell 2009). There is widespread agreement in the literature that developments must take into account the needs, abilities and desires of the intended users, especially in respect of those with cognitive impairments which can interfere with both their ability to participate in the development process and their ability to utilise the technology once created (Astell et al. 2009; Robinson et al. 2009; Span et al. 2013). It is therefore important that the design and development of digital systems and apps should formally involve the intended target user group, and that their contribution should be evidenced in usability protocols (Brankaert and Ouden 2015; Sauro and Dumas 2009).

Span et al. (2013) conducted a systematic review on the involvement of people living with dementia in the development of supportive IT applications. Consistent with other studies, the methods most frequently used to involve participants were interviews (Gibson et al. 2016; Hamel et al. 2016; O'Connor et al. 2016), observations (Hamel et al. 2016; Mulvenna et al. 2011) and usability tests (Gibson et al. 2016; Sauro and Dumas 2009). In most studies, participants were objects of study and informants. The authors concluded that involving people living with dementia in developing supportive IT applications is limited and a fairly recent phenomenon. People living with dementia were mostly involved in the explorative and technical development phases. Only a few publications describe their involvement in all stages (Astell et al. 2007; Hanson et al. 2007; Riley et al. 2009). However, their involvement improved the usefulness and acceptability of the device and may have had an empowering effect on the individuals.

Usability is measured in terms of how easily a system can achieve its goals and how efficiently a user can interact with the system through its user interface. Standard protocols to measure these attributes can be classified into three main approaches: observational-based approaches, questionnaire-based approaches and task completion-based approaches. These methods in turn provide metrics that are used by researchers to determine the usability of the user interface. Together with seven couples comprising a person living with dementia with their family caregiver, Gibson *et al.* (2016) co-designed and tested an app, *InspireD* to support personalised reminiscence. The complete project life cycle from requirements gathering, through testing, refinement of specifications, amendments, additional functionality and final working version of the app occurred over an eight-month period. The *InspireD* app enables users to compile and store selected personalised memorabilia (photographs, videos, sounds, music) and provides easy access to these visual and audio-visual cues to support personalised reminiscence. As part of their study, Gibson and colleages investigated the appropriateness of several common usability testing methods in evaluating the usability of the *InspireD* app. The tests and metrics for investigation in this study comprised: concurrent think-aloud protocol (Lewis 1982), video recording and audio recording devices (Lewis 1982; Sauro and Lewis 2012), task completion rates (Bangor, Kortum and Miller 2008), task completion times (Bangor *et al.* 2008), single ease questions (Sauro and Lewis 2012) and the Systematic Usability Scale (Sauro and Lewis 2012).

The value of the tests and metrics was examined in a series of five workshops during a six-week period. Results indicated that observation and recording of task completion rates and times produced the most reliable results. The think-aloud methodology was difficult for people living with dementia and did not produce any reliable data. Thinking-aloud while doing a task was perhaps a distraction since it requires a higher cognitive load. The Systematic Usability Scale (SUS) score which is derived from a post-test instrument was not reliable, as it had no association with the task completion times. The authors reported that common usability testing protocols such as the SUS instrument, think-aloud protocols and external mobile macro cameras attached to the mobile testing device were not adequate for evaluating apps whose target users had been diagnosed with a progressive cognitive disease such as dementia. This suggests that there is a research opportunity to design new protocols or to optimise existing protocols to improve the data collected from usability testing of devices and apps in these contexts.

In the UK, O'Connor *et al.* (2016) explored the barriers experienced when co-producing a memory and reminiscence app. A focus group and interviews were conducted with four dyads, comprising a person living with dementia and their family carer, and personnel involved in the design of the app. Consistent with the findings of other studies, the researchers recommended that co-producing digital applications with people living with dementia and their carers needs to be well thought out, planned and executed to address poor attitudes and inaccurate perceptions (Lorenz *et al.* 2017), lack of digital literacy, knowledge and skills (Kerkhof, Bergsma and Graff 2017; Span *et al.* 2013) and to ensure that any compromises made in the design are justified and add value for money (Gibson *et al.* 2016; Nijhof, van Gemert-Pijnen and Burns 2013).

A Dutch study by Kerkhof *et al.* (2017) used eight focus groups involving people with mild cognitive impairment or dementia and informal carers. The aim of the study was to explore users' requirements for the development of a tool for selecting usable apps in the domain of self-management and meaningful activities. Findings highlighted the importance of enhancing the navigation experience of people living with dementia by minimising the need for scrolling, providing an easy and intuitive user experience, minimising the use of excessive screens and clicks and presenting clear instructions on a step-by-step basis. Both people living with dementia and their carers found entering codes and passwords annoying. Informal carers considered the apps built for Android more difficult to operate than those built for Apple. Studies into the use of touch-screen technology by people living with dementia have shown that the Apple iPad and its apps were primarily used because of the intuitive interface and user-friendliness (Groenewoud and deLange 2014; Kerkhof *et al.* 2017; Upton, Upton and Jones 2011) and because less instructions were needed for independent use of easy-to-operate apps (Astell, Joddrell and Groenewoud 2016; Lim, Wallace and Luszcz 2013). This suggests a general preference for Apple as a platform for people living with dementia. Recognising the limitations of the small sample size, the authors recommended that tools should be designed and developed in close cooperation with intended users and other stakeholders such as family carers and experts to ensure user-friendliness (McCormack 2015).

Barriers to user engagement

The reasons for lack of involvement of older people, including those living with dementia, in the development of technology are many and have been explored in the literature. The stigma associated with old age and dementia and the paternalistic attitudes of some professionals have been identified as contributing factors (Span *et al.* 2013; Werner and Heinik 2008). The distress caused to people living with dementia when devices are in the early stage of development or do not work have also been highlighted as barriers to user engagement (Orpwood *et al.* 2007; Riley *et al.* 2009). While the lack of involvement of people living with dementia in application development may be partly explained by this phenomenon of anticipated stress, other researchers have not reported any such distress (Hanson *et al.* 2007; Robinson *et al.* 2009). It is important to note that, despite the possibility of distress, Span *et al.* (2013) found that many participants enjoyed taking part in research and believed that their wellbeing seemed to increase as a result of their contribution. This confirms the assertions of Hellstrom *et al.* (2007) and Whitlatch and Menne (2009) concerning the importance of involving people living with dementia in all aspects of dementia research, including usability testing of technology support systems.

Other factors such as cognitive impairment and frailty have been identified as barriers to user engagement by people living with dementia. Several studies have included recommendations to overcome these barriers, such as prioritising the wellbeing of participants, allowing sufficient time, providing active and continuous support and ensuring that the study location is dementia friendly (Hanson *et al.* 2007; Riley *et al.* 2009). Many authors have described the learning potential of people with dementia (Deschamps *et al.* 2011; Hanson *et al.* 2007; van Tilborg, Kessels and Hulstijn 2011), whereas, Riley *et al.* (2009) refer to the inability of people with dementia to learn new skills. It is noteworthy that in their review of the literature on involving people living with dementia in the development of supportive IT applications, Span *et al.* (2013) concluded that cognitive impairment is no reason to exclude potential research participants. Nevertheless, it is important to ensure that ethical issues are carefully considered in light of the potential vulnerability of this population group.

Multimedia

The use of multimedia in reminiscence was arguably the first stage in the growth of use of technology in reminiscence systems and there are a significant number of research projects and publications highlighting such work (Astell *et al.* 2010; Hamel *et al.* 2016; Subramaniam and Woods 2016). It is natural, perhaps, that the reminiscence process, which uses visual and hearing senses (as well as others) could be enriched with multimedia material encompassing photographs, videos, audio recordings and music as well as historical material such as newspapers. The multimedia paradigm also lends itself to extending the concept of memory books, used in traditional reminiscence activities, where a carer or family member compiles a personal story book with images and pictorial mementos of a person's life. Using multimedia, technology-based reminiscence can animate the material thus making it more appealing than the paper-based alternative. However, since the process of creating a memory book provides rich reminiscing opportunities, care must be taken not to replace this type of work with a less user-centred approach.

It is noteworthy that there is evidence to suggest that older people experience no negative effect when using touch-screen devices such as tablet devices versus paper for reminiscing (Upton *et al.* 2011; Wright and Mulvenna 2012). It could be argued that viewing photographs on modern screens may not recreate the same tactile experience as holding and touching them. However, with the advent of higher resolution screens, recent studies have shown that older adults aged 60 and above found reading and viewing images easier when using backlit electronic devices due to the increased contrast between the text/images and the background (Kretzschmar *et al.* 2013).

In recent years, a major development in computer-assisted reminiscence has been the *Computer Interactive Reminiscence Conversation Aid* (*CIRCA*), designed to support people living with dementia and the people who care for them. *CIRCA* is an interactive multimedia touch-screen system that contains a wide range of stimuli to prompt reminiscing. The program highlights the significance of ease of use regarding such interventions and emphasises the importance of touch-screen technology so that users can become actively involved in the process. Astell *et al.* (2010) evaluated the utility of *CIRCA* in facilitating people living with dementia (n=11) and their professional carers (n=11) to engage in mutually satisfying interactions. Although limited by the inclusion of generic rather than personal content, the authors concluded that *CIRCA* was engaging for both sets of participants, prompting long-term memories and occasional stories from people living with dementia in ways that no other type of reminiscence-based activities had previously achieved (Alm *et al.* 2009; Astell *et al.* 2010).

Building on this work, the Computer Assisted Reminiscence Therapy (CART) project in Nottingham was designed to use mobile tablet computer technology to structure reminiscence therapy sessions in care settings for people living with dementia. Pringle and Somerville (2013) explored whether using multimedia technology could develop the reminiscence process further by creating personal computer files for a group of eight care home residents. These files contained personal photographs, general photographs and a playlist of songs of significance to the people living with dementia. Pringle and Summerville compared the CART process with the existing approach to reminiscence involving structured conversation or memory books. Findings suggested that using the tablet technology increased the engagement time from ten minutes using a memory book to 20 minutes using the computer. Perhaps the most significant observation of the use of technology was the way in which it appeared to expand conversation and increase the depth of memory by adding extra details. The authors acknowledged that while many of the current generation of older people may have never interacted with a computer before, they can benefit enormously from tablet-based computer assisted reminiscence packages (Astell *et al.* 2009). Limitations of Pringle and Somerville's study have been reported elsewhere and include the small sample size (Lazar *et al.* 2014; O'Rourke *et al.* 2011), the short duration of the project (Hamel *et al.* 2016; Kerssens *et al.* 2015) and the involvement of staff in the intervention (Hamel *et al.* 2016; Kerssens *et al.* 2015).

Lazar (2014) carried out a small study to assess how a multi-functional interactive technology system, designed to facilitate engagement in activities by people living with dementia, was perceived by staff (n=7), residents (n=5) and families (n=4). Participants were observed using the system twice a week for two hours and the researcher took notes, including rating factors such as whether residents interacted with staff, each other and the system. Interviews were also held with staff on a regular basis. As reported elsewhere (Hamel *et al.* 2016; Sarne-Fleischmann and Tractinsky 2008), the findings suggested the staff and family members found benefits in using the system, such as providing residents with something to do, giving residents a sense of accomplishment and enabling conversations around new topics. People living with dementia were able to use and benefit from the system with assistance but not independently (Gibson *et al.* 2016).

Karlsson *et al.* (2014) explored the process of acceptance and integration of a digital photography diary (DPD) as a reminiscence and conversation aid. Seven couples in which one individual within the couple had Alzheimer's disease tested the DPD for six months. Data were collected on three sequences with interviews, observations and screening instruments. Factors contributing to regular use have been reported elsewhere and include:

- how the DPD matched expectations (Kerssens *et al.* 2015)
- patterns of use (Gibson *et al.* 2016)
- support (Hanson *et al.* 2007)
- experienced usefulness (Karlsson *et al.* 2011)
- reaction from family and friends (McHugh *et al.* 2012; Stenhouse *et al.* 2013).

These findings support an earlier study by Karlsson *et al.* (2011) which concluded that there is a need to consider the integration of digital devices into the daily lives of people living with dementia as a process that requires a considerable amount of time as well as active support and encouragement from the family member.

The InspireD study

A feasibility study by Ryan *et al.* (2018) investigated the outcomes of a home-based, individual specific reminiscence intervention facilitated through the use of an iPad app (*InspireD*) for people living with dementia and their family carers. The study used a quasi-experimental design whereby the app was used by a paired sample of 30 people living with mild to moderate dementia and their family carers, with each participant serving as his or her own control. Prior to the use of the *InspireD* app, participants received four reminiscence training sessions and a fifth session on compiling memorabilia for use with the app. The training was provided to each participating dyad in their own homes by a reminiscence facilitator from the Reminiscence Network Northern Ireland (RNNI). At the close of reminiscence training, an IT assistant supported the dyads to upload their personal memorabilia onto the app and then provided two one-hour sessions, in order to ensure that the person with dementia and their carer had developed sufficient confidence and skill to use the app independently. A contact phone number for further IT assistance was also provided. Participants were encouraged verbally and in writing to use the app for a minimum of three times a week for the following three months. Outcome measures were collected at three time points. These examined the impact of reminiscence on mutuality (the primary outcome measure), using the Mutuality Scale developed by Archbold *et al.* (1990). Secondary outcome measures included the WHO-5 Wellbeing Index (Bech *et al.* 2003) and the Quality of the Carer–Patient Relationship (QCPR) developed by Spruytte *et al.* (2002). At the end of the intervention, individual interviews were conducted with a sample of participants (n=32) to explore their experience of the intervention.

Ryan *et al.* (2018) reported that people living with dementia had more interactions with the *InspireD* app than their carers. Photographs, followed by music and then video, were the preferred reminiscence approaches, and personalised media was preferred over generic media. Results of the outcome measures revealed statistically significant increases in Mutuality, WHO-5 Index and QCPR scores from baseline to endpoint for participants living with dementia. Non-significant increases in Mutuality and QCPR scores and a non-significant decrease in WHO-5 scores from baseline to endpoint were observed for carers. Data from the semi-structured interviews revealed that participating dyads perceived the intervention as a positive experience which focused on gains rather than losses in the context of memory retention and learning new skills. The reminiscence and IT training and the impact of the intervention on relationships were also viewed as positive outcomes. The authors concluded that a programme of training and individual specific reminiscence supported by an iPad app can deliver positive impacts pertaining to mutuality, caregiving relationships and emotional wellbeing in the context of early to moderate dementia.

Caregiver support

In the UK, an estimated 700,000 family and friends are caring for a person living with dementia and over 24 million people know a family member or friend with a dementia diagnosis (Alzheimer's Research UK 2015). There is widespread variation in the literature on the impact of reminiscence, life review and life story work on family carers, with many studies reporting the significant challenges faced by families (Aguirre *et al.* 2011; Charlesworth *et al.* 2016; Melunsky *et al.* 2015; Woods *et al.* 2012; Woods *et al.* 2018). A consistent theme in all the studies exploring technology-facilitated reminiscence is the centrality of support provision by formal and informal carers. In an Irish study, McHugh *et al.* (2012) explored the role of ICT in supporting caregivers of people living with dementia. Interviews were conducted with 14 spousal caregivers and analysed using a grounded theory approach.

Findings revealed specific areas in which technology could alleviate caregiver burden based around three key themes; support needed, social isolation and the relationship between the person living with dementia and their caregiver. As reported in previous studies (Astell *et al.* 2011; Lazar *et al.* 2014), the authors highlighted the importance of consulting carers to ensure that technology design is grounded in an understanding of the problems being addressed. Participants expressed the need to access information about dementia and how to manage the change in their lives (McDonnell and Ryan 2014) while also requiring informal support in the context of mentorship and reassurance (McKeown *et al.* 2010). Social isolation was a key issue because of the difficulties in leaving the house and in sustaining social networks (Melunsky *et al.* 2015). The third theme related to the interaction between the caregiver and the person living with dementia. Caregivers reported a 'disappearance of the relationship' due to dementia-related personality changes and the desire to avoid distress or confrontation (Regier and Gitlin 2017). Consistent with the literature on family caregiving (McDonnell and Ryan 2014; Melunsky *et al.* 2015), McHugh *et al.* (2012) highlighted the need to encourage caregivers to protect their own mental and physical wellbeing, not least because of the positive consequences for the caregivers to continue their caring role. The study concluded that ICT can facilitate communication between people living with dementia and their carers while also supporting connectivity between carers and their family and friends. Similar to Lazar *et al.* (2014), the authors cautioned that the benefits of technology for people living with dementia must be considered in the context within which technology may place additional demands on an already strained population of family carers.

Personal versus generic memorabilia

The benefits of using personalised versus generic materials have been explored in a number of studies. Astell *et al.* (2010) found that generic photographs prompted more storytelling by individuals with dementia. In contrast, Yasuda *et al.* (2009) found that people showed more interest and less distraction while viewing personalised photos and videos than while viewing TV shows. The potential for emotional distress when a person living with dementia fails to recognise themselves or others in personal photographs has been recognised in the literature (Gowans *et al.* 2004). Similarly, discomfort or distress may arise if reminiscence materials contain disturbing images such as photographs of wartime or of deceased relatives, leading to the recommendation that decisions on whether to include potentially distressing images or videos should be based on the wishes of participants and their families as well as on their reactions to different types of media (Smith *et al.* 2009).

Sharne-Flecischmann and Tractinsky (2008) examined the effectiveness of a personalised multimedia system developed for use by people living with Alzheimer's disease (n=5) and their carers. The system was developed iteratively using the opinions and observations of people living with dementia and their carers as the primary evaluation mechanism. The results indicated high user satisfaction levels with the system and a strong tendency towards repeated use. The system was found to be effective in promoting conversations and invoking personal memories. The results showed a clear preference for personal as opposed to generic materials when both were available. Contrary findings were reported in other studies. Mulvenna *et al.* (2011) showed no difference in how participants (n=11) viewed three types of images (personal, generic and shared experience). There was also no evidence that participants spent longer viewing and discussing images that were not personal, as suggested by Astell *et al.* (2010). An American study by Boyd and Shenk (2014) used personal and generic videos to engage people living with dementia (n=11) and concluded that both personal and generic videos can be used by minimally trained individuals to engage this client group. Participants showed a slight, though not significant, preference for looking first at personalised videos, although in keeping with the findings of Astell *et al.* (2010), the generic videos generated more diverse comments on a broader range of topics.

Life stories

Storytelling about a life is a way for people living with dementia to construct and express meaning in their lives and has an important impact in helping people identify themselves. According to Hardy and Summer (2010), narrating the story of one's life can be seen as a way to sustain a sense of self. There are many tablet and smartphone apps that can be used to create a digital personalised story including *My Story Book Creator*, *Story Maker* or *Book of You*. While there is evidence of the potential benefits of multimedia and personalisation for people living with dementia, Alm *et al.* (2009), Stenhouse *et al.* (2013) and Subramaniam and Woods (2016) caution that too many stimuli can overwhelm people living with dementia and therefore a judicious balance between engagement and over stimulation needs to be sought.

Digital storytelling is a generic term used to describe the use of new media technologies to create innovative narrative forms. Still images usually drawn from the storyteller's personal photograph albums are combined with a recorded voiceover scripted by the storyteller, and sometimes music is added. In reflective digital storytelling, this results in a rich tapestry that is at once effective, affective and reflective (Hardy and Summer 2010). The process is person centred with participants retaining control over the story that is told.

Digital life story books have three main advantages. First, it is easy to document and retrieve personal memories that match the idiosyncrasies of individual life stories. Second, technology provides multimedia for the storage and retrieval of memories. Sound, music, photos and movies can be easily added beside anecdotes and verbal cues. Third, technology makes it possible to use the life story book in an interactive way. Informal caregivers and family members and friends can add new memories or remarks on memories that were especially vivid to them. Of particular significance is the ability to update and adjust the life story book even when the dementia progresses.

Stenhouse *et al.* (2013) conducted a study whereby digital stories were made with seven people with early stage dementia as part of a learning package for student nurses. The authors reflected on their experience and observation from facilitating the four-day digital story-making workshop. Despite considerable challenges in developing a story and anxiety about using the technology, all participants engaged in creating their own digital stories. During the workshop, a number of positive changes were observed among participants, including increased confidence, improved speech, a sense of purpose and increased connection. These improvements appeared to be the product of the person-centred facilitation and the creative process which supported self-expression and a sense of identity. Consistent with the findings of other studies (Kelly 2010; Peisah, Lawrence and Reutens 2011), the authors concluded that participation in the workshop engendered some improvements in participants' social interactions.

Subramanian and Woods (2016) designed a study to establish an evidence base for the acceptability and efficacy of using multimedia digital life story books in comparison with conventional life story books. Participants included six people living with dementia in care homes, their relatives and care staff. A participatory design was used to create a life story movie based on previously completed conventional life story books. Data was collected using quantitative and qualitative approaches. The results indicated that five of the six participants showed additional improvements in measures of quality of life and autobiographical memory. All participants showed improvement or stability in depression scores. Thematic analysis revealed that participants, relatives and care home staff viewed digital life story books as a very useful tool for triggering memories and generating positive emotions. Savage (2016) reported similar findings with regard to the *Book of You*, a web app that uses digital media to facilitate people living with dementia to complete a profile of their memories and life stories. As previously highlighted, the accessibility of the app on a tablet computer or other mobile devices was important (Ancient *et al.* 2011; Lim *et al.* 2013), as was its portability, which meant that it could remain with the individual, regardless of location (Astell *et al.* 2016; Kerkhof *et al.* 2017).

Despite the many potential benefits of integrating technology into life story work for individuals with dementia, there are barriers (Palmer *et al.* 2012). Research has shown that iPads are preferred over Android devices by people living with dementia (Kerkhof *et al.* 2017).

However, iPads are expensive. In addition, the completion of life story work can be a time-consuming process. Smith *et al.* (2009) developed multimedia life stories for individuals with Alzheimer's disease or mild cognitive impairment. This necessitated the gathering of photographs, videos, audio-clips and music, which were subsequently complied into a digital video format. The success of the study was measured by the completion of the multimedia biography and caregiver interviews at various stages, from completion of the multimedia biography to one year later. Although positively evaluated, the authors reported that it took an average of 130 hours over five to six months to create the biographies and that the success of similar ventures will therefore require a significant amount of training and support for people living with dementia and their carers (Palmer *et al.* 2012). The need for further research in this area has been recognised by Elfrink *et al.* (2017) who have published a study protocol to examine the effects of an online life story book on neuropsychiatric symptoms. Their study will investigate the impact of the intervention on carers and provide a preliminary health economic evaluation. (See Chapter 14 by Ferguson and Gallagher for other examples of multimedia use in life story work.)

Summary

This chapter has reviewed the evidence around the positive and negative effects of technology in facilitating reminiscence, life review and life story work from the perspective of people living with dementia and their families. Most of the studies reported the benefits of technology from the perspective of the person living with dementia. These included positive effects on mood and social engagement. It is recognised that positive outcomes for people living with dementia can have a secondary impact on family caregivers. Seeing improvements in the person living with dementia can decrease the anxiety and distress experienced by formal and informal caregivers. However, few studies have explored the long-term benefits of technology-facilitated reminiscence, life review and life story work, acknowledging that it may be difficult to quantify given the progressive nature of dementia.

The reported benefits of reminiscence, life review and life story work for families are somewhat varied. Some studies indicate positive outcomes whereas others report that family members experience increased stress. The impact of reminiscence on caregiver burden and on the relationships between the family caregiver and the person living with dementia has identified some conflicting findings, with some studies reporting a reduction in caregiver burden whereas others highlight the key role of already overburdened families in supporting the reminiscence process.

Relative to other interventions, reminiscence-related activities are not considered expensive, but support is still required to enable family members to engage in joint reminiscence activities. Although limited by the small sample size of most of the cited studies, this chapter has highlighted the need for greater user engagement throughout the research process and for studies to take note of the need to support people living with dementia to engage in technology-facilitated reminiscences without adverse consequences for their carers.

Chapter 20

INCREASING THE USE OF REMINISCENCE AND LIFE REVIEW

Experiences with the Development, Implementation, and Evaluation of an Online International Certificate Course

Juliette Shellman, Loriena Yancura and Esther Gieschen

The overlapping fields of reminiscence and life review have grown exponentially over the past three decades. In correspondence with this growth has come a parallel need to educate professionals to safely conduct reminiscence and life review. Scholars and researchers in the field interact with each other through various professional organizations such as the Gerontological Society of America, American Geriatrics Society, International Institute for Reminiscence and Life Review (IIRLR) and others. However, as the interest in the use of reminiscence and life review grew, so too did the need for additional forums to exchange ideas and standardize practice for practitioners who come from various professions such as personal historians, nursing home administrators, social workers, counselors, nurses, and the like. Of particular need was an easily accessible, structured educational program to train new professionals in the field to increase their understanding of the benefits and risks, theoretical underpinnings and ethical considerations important to conducting successful reminiscence and life review. This chapter describes the historical development, implementation, and evaluation of the online Certificate in Reminiscence and Life Story Work (R&LSW) offered by the University of Wisconsin–Superior (UWS) Center for Continuing Education (CCE).

History

All of this work began with the development of the IIRLR founded by John Kunz while he was Program Manager with the CCE at UWS. Under his supervision, the CCE sponsored the premier National Reminiscence and Life Review Conference in 1995. Major leaders in the field formed the IIRLR as a follow up to that conference. Originally named the International Society for Reminiscence and Life Review, the name was changed following the 1999 conference. The IIRLR is a membership organization that has operated as a program of UWS since 1997. Its mission is to define and further develop the interdisciplinary field of reminiscence and life review through discussion and collaboration in practice, research, education, volunteer and individual applications across the lifespan. Members of the IIRLR and the CCE maintain the website[1] and coordinate the International Conference for Reminiscence and Life Review, generally held on a biennial basis. Currently, the IIRLR has a membership of 70 individuals from around the globe. Members have access to educational resources, a newsletter and opportunities to set up a personal web page to promote their work. Leadership of the IIRLR consists of an elected advisory board, which meets at the biennial conference, and the executive committee, which meets periodically throughout the year to discuss current issues and conduct strategic planning with UWS-CCE. One of the major accomplishments of the IIRLR is the publication of the online peer-reviewed *International Journal of Reminiscence and Life Review*, coordinated by members of the Institute.[2]

> Since 1996, when James Atlas, editor of the *New York Times Magazine* proclaimed this to be the 'Age of Memoir', the practice of ordinary people recording their life stories has steadily increased. It is a common experience to many who stumble upon the powerful tools of reminiscence and life review to think they are the first to think of the idea. As a result, many individuals naively proceed to apply these concepts in their classrooms, clinical and research settings, and even in their own businesses without being adequately prepared to do so, sometimes resulting in devastating outcomes. (John Kunz, personal communication)

---

1 http://reminiscenceandlifereview.org/welcome-2
2 Open source and available at http://143.95.253.101/~radfordojs/index.php/IJRLR/issue/current

The paragraph above is how John Kunz drafted his proposal to develop an online certificate in life story work. The proposed program would prepare participants from wide-ranging backgrounds to engage in life story work in a variety of settings by teaching them about the intricacies of doing such work, including the rewards, challenges and dangers. Those who earn the certificate, he said, 'should be confident in their knowledge base and be able to ethically proceed to engage in life story work in their own settings'. Unfortunately, John Kunz did not live to see the program become a reality. But after his death in 2011, others from the University of Wisconsin–Superior, the IIRLR and the Association of Personal Historians collaborated in developing an online certificate program that includes much of Kunz's vision.

The process of course development began with an enthusiastic group of experts from various professional organizations providing advice and recommendations. For example, leaders from the field of reminiscence and life review advised UWS-CCE staff regarding key concepts they felt needed to be included in the training program. Experts from the Association of Personal Historians shared the core competencies and learning objectives they identified as critical for a program for those aspiring to be personal historians. Faculty staff from the UWS psychology and social work departments also contributed to the structuring of the program, utilizing the Desire2Learn Course Management System.[3]

Working in conjunction with staff members of the UWS-CCE program, the groups came together via email, in person at meetings at annual conferences, and through phone conferences to begin the course planning. Logistical issues such as course format (asynchronous vs live webinar format), naming the course, marketing strategies and recruiting instructors were discussed first. After several meetings, the group came to a consensus that an asynchronous, online, cohort module would better accommodate participation from any time zone, offer greater flexibility for students with already busy schedules, and facilitate the recruitment of experts in the field who already have full-time teaching loads to teach the courses. Results from The Global Survey of Reminiscence and Life Review conducted by the IIRLR in July 2013 indicated that the majority of respondents felt that life story work was the best label for their work, with many others

---

3   www.d2l.com

preferring 'reminiscence'. Thus, it was decided that calling the program a Certificate in Reminiscence and Life Story Work would be the most appropriate. Marketing strategies such as developing a brochure, advertising at professional conferences, contacting organizations, and reaching out to professionals and students from various disciplines ranging from history and gerontology to the arts and music were conducted to recruit potential students. Fees sufficient to cover the costs of offering the course were determined by UWS-CCE, and instructors were recruited by the UWS program manager and through the IIRLR.

Certificate in Reminiscence and Life Story Work course content

There was strong agreement among the experts that all courses needed to emphasize ethical considerations and that regardless of the field and setting of their practice, graduates should have an interdisciplinary background in history, theory and research in reminiscence and life review, and be aware of the many ways reminiscence, life review and related disciplines are applied in a variety of professional fields to meet widely varying client needs. Furthermore, individuals receiving a certificate should engage in at least one hands-on reminiscence activity under the guidance of a practitioner. Because it was anticipated that many participants in the program would be new to the field, it would be important to their future professional success to have at least one completed project they could include in a resume or portfolio and that completing a project with the help of someone experienced in their intended area of practice would build their skill and confidence. It was decided the certificate would comprise four modules: three course modules and one capstone practicum module.

By autumn 2014, instructors had been identified to develop and teach the three courses. Each asynchronous course runs approximately for eight weeks. The courses each contain eight learning units that include required readings, discussion questions and a written assignment pertaining to the topic of the week. The instructors use a variety of online educational techniques such as discussion boards, videos, online group meetings, and *PowerPoint* presentations of current issues and topics in reminiscence and life story work. Course assignments include weekly takeaways where students reflect on what they learn and areas where they feel they need assistance in meeting course objectives. The course descriptions are provided below.

Module 1: Fundamentals of reminiscence and life review: Theory and research

The first module is designed to provide students with a solid background in the fundamentals of reminiscence and life review. There are two required textbooks. Haight and Webster's (1995) *The Art and Science of Reminiscing: Theory, Research, Methods and Applications* covers the historical and theoretical foundations of reminiscence work, and Gibson's (2011) *Reminiscence and Life Story Work: A Practice Guide* covers practical considerations. By the end of this module, students are expected to:

- appreciate the various definitions and approaches to reminiscence work
- identify major contributors to the field of reminiscence and life review
- identify different uses for reminiscence and life review work and how they've evolved
- understand age-related changes and how those may impact reminiscence and life review work
- recognize reasons for setting objectives for planned reminiscence work in both individual and group settings.

These objectives are obtained through a variety of activities and assignments such as readings summaries, exploration activities (e.g. browsing through current online issues of the *International Journal of Reminiscence and Life Review*, developing ideas for the use of themes and props in reminiscence work, examining the influence of cohort on adult development through consideration of various timelines that document political/sociohistorical events, art, music and popular culture). Students also read evidence-based research on various outcomes of reminiscence and discuss the practical and ethical boundaries between reminiscence work and therapy. The main paper, due at the end of this module, requires students to consider how they will apply what they have learned in the course to their future work.

Most students' plans change substantially over the 16 months after this initial draft, but this early focus on the final project serves to stimulate students' creativity and resourcefulness, pointing them toward their capstone projects, and ensures that they maintain focus on theories and scholarship as they develop their plans through future modules.

Module 2: Practice and application of reminiscence and life review

The goal of the second module is to prepare students to facilitate integrative reminiscence with an older adult. In this course, students are introduced to the knowledge, skills, and principles for conducting successful and safe reminiscence and life review sessions. For this course, *The Handbook of Structured Life Review* (Haight and Haight 2007) is added to the students' library of resources. Additional articles written by experts in the field are provided on the course website. Interview techniques, strategies for conducting individual and group sessions, and cultural considerations are examined and discussed. By the end of the course students are expected to be able to:

- differentiate between the types of reminiscence and life review
- examine effective communication skills for facilitating reminiscence and life review with individuals and groups
- identify strategies for safe and effective reminiscence and life review sessions
- discuss cultural considerations when conducting reminiscence and life review sessions
- apply effective communication skills and safe practice techniques by conducting a reminiscence or life review session with an older adult.

These objectives are measured by assessing how well students apply the concepts learned in the course by conducting reminiscence or life review sessions with a volunteer using a structured format outlined in one of the learning units. The final assignment is a paper that requires students to describe a summary of the reminiscence session, observations made during the session and a self-evaluation of their use of facilitator skills.

Module 3: Reminiscence and life review or life story work as a business

Initially this module was titled 'Developing a personal history practice', because the pilot cohort in 2015 primarily targeted aspiring or practicing personal historians. This module is currently transitioning into 'Developing a reminiscence/life story work practice' to be more inclusive of those who will be doing other life story work such as community-based or other group or individual reminiscence activities as independent contractors or as a staff member of a senior center or other institution. This module introduces participants to specific competencies required to launch and operate a personal history or life story work practice. The material covered corresponds with business management education but does not replicate what is available through college course work, small-business development centers, Service Corps of Retired Executives (SCORE) or other resources, which students are encouraged to explore. Required readings consist of a series of essays written by the instructor with four other readings strongly suggested: Campbell's (2001) *Start and Run a Personal History Business*; Tyrrell's (2012) *Become a Memoirist for Elders*; Stahel's (2013) *Listen Up: The Art of Interviewing for Personal History*; and Kadel Taras's (2013) *Mountain Girls, Time Pieces, Personal Biographies*. By the end of this module, students will be able to:

- demonstrate understanding of the personal history/life story work professional landscape
- articulate what type of life story work they intend to practice
- describe a potential business model for their work.

During each week of this eight-week course, students are required to submit a reflection paper, and post and reply to others' posts on topic-specific critical thinking questions. During the first couple of weeks of the course, they are instructed to take a field trip in their own communities to explore resources that are relevant to their potential projects. Students must produce a final paper that identifies basic elements of their proposed business plans, including a business model, target consumers, a marketing plan, description of how their product or service will be produced and delivered, as well as projected banking, business and legal needs.

Module 4: Capstone practicum

The fourth module is a hands-on capstone practicum in which each student plans and completes a project within their chosen area of reminiscence and life story work. The purposes of the capstone are:

- for students to demonstrate that they can effectively apply what they learned in the course work to actual practice
- to ensure that students have at least one hands-on completed project for their portfolio or resume.

The capstone practicum is completed with mentoring and oversight from an experienced professional in an area of reminiscence and life story work matching the student's intended area of practice. Program staff within the CCE and UW–Superior developed the criteria and steps for successful completion of the capstone project with the assistance of the course faculty.

The capstone practicum projects have been creative, ranging from personal endeavors to professional projects. For example, one student created a memory cookbook with her mother who has memory loss. The student gathered the stories from her mother while they cooked or baked her mother's favourite recipes. She created a book with the recipes, the stories behind the recipes, and family photos. Copies were made for her mother to keep and give to family members. The student commented that her mother's copy was already covered with food stains because she kept it on her kitchen counter and read it over and over as she ate breakfast. This project is an excellent example of a project that provided benefits for the student and project participant. While the project originated as a personal endeavor to help her mother with memory loss, making memory cookbooks has the potential to become a viable business. Another student, an established professional journalist, entered the course with the goal of building a foundation for a personal history branch of her own business. For her capstone project, she interviewed a woman who created a non-profit to provide music as therapy. It was two projects at once – a history of the non-profit and a personal/family history. She ran into many complicated, painful childhood experiences and unexpectedly interviewed one family member on her death bed. This project turned out to be different from the expected project, but a very powerful experience for the student, who described it as follows:

I made a decision during the course that dealing with the elderly who were dying was NOT on my list of things I wanted to do. Well it didn't work out that way, as I ended up interviewing my first client's mother over the course of five days while she was literally on her death bed. In fact, through that project, I encountered just about every issue discussed during that course for the certificate. It was a wonderful experience.

Outcomes

At the time of this writing, three cohorts of students have participated in the Reminiscence and Life Story Work Certificate program. The pilot cohort started the program in spring 2015 with 13 students registering for the course. Ten of the original cohort completed the program and earned their certificates by autumn 2016. The second cohort of students started the program in Spring 2016, and six of nine students in that cohort have completed their capstone practicum projects. In March 2017, nine more students started as the third cohort. Because the course is taught in English, the majority of participants have come from various regions in the United States. Yet, in keeping with the international intent of the course, several have come from other countries, including the UK, Canada and Austria.

Students come to the program with a variety of backgrounds and goals. So far, all have at least BA/BS degrees, and many have master's degrees or higher. They have come from a variety of professions: journalists, authors, social workers, occupational therapists, counselors, graduate students and educators. Some students are currently personal historians while others plan to become personal historians; others are using (or want to use) reminiscence in their work with older adults, adults in life transitions and people with serious or terminal illnesses.

Course evaluations

Formative and summative evaluations are conducted for each course. Program staff and faculty utilize the data to identify program strengths and areas in need of improvement. For example, students requested more online group discussions. As a result, the program manager and faculty implemented virtual class meetings as part of the certificate experience to promote collegiality and interaction among the students.

Overall, students have been very positive about their experiences on the certificate course. The following section reflects results from a qualitative analysis of student evaluations gathered from open-ended questions on formative and summative evaluations over the three-year period. Using Borkan's Immersion/Crystallization (1999) technique to analyse the data, the following themes emerged from the students' responses:

- gaining confidence
- professional skill development
- unexpected discoveries.

The following section describes the themes with quotes representing each theme.

Theme 1: Gaining confidence

> Through the coursework and this capstone project, I feel more confident as I move forward. I now have a better understanding and knowledge of the many components of reminiscing and life story work. I have a sample activity and soon will have more, just in time for a presentation next week and an upcoming life story workshop next month. I have been waiting to finish this course to approach retirement facilities. Now, I feel that I can walk in with confidence, that I have something of value to offer them.

Other participants expressed this confidence in terms of being able to foster more effective interactions with their clients. Another participant in the pilot cohort, a personal historian for several years before enrolling in the certificate program, conducted a reminiscence session at an assisted living facility for her capstone project. She reported feeling more confident in working with groups:

> I felt a sense of accomplishment in that there was increased mutual understanding by the residents and family members, particularly for Mr A who can no longer verbalize and for Mrs M and Ms J who have very different backgrounds from the others.

Theme 2: Professional skill development

Graduates of the program report that they have been able to use the skills that they gained in a wide variety of professional venues. As anticipated during the design phase of the certificate program, many are using these skills as the foundation for small businesses as personal historians. Some participants have focused on business ventures designed to educate the public, such as one participant who has focused on group presentations, 'I am beginning to market a life story presentation informing people about the different ways they can tell their stories and the benefits of life story work.' Other participants report that they are using skills to enhance the effectiveness of products they offer through their existing businesses, such as one graduate who has incorporated reminiscence and life story work activities into assisting clients in retirement planning and/or establishing ethical wills. Incorporation of skills learned in the certificate program has not been limited to those in small businesses, one graduate, who works as an ombudsman, noted that she uses what she learned:

> When conversing with residents of nursing homes and rehabilitation centers, to rather quickly break the ice and learn about them as people with a whole life behind them and within them. And I have encouraged the facilities I cover as ombudsman to learn about their residents – *more* than is typical.

Active listening as a skill emerged in the students' writings. Some reported listening as difficult, especially during emotional reminiscences, while others developed a deep appreciation of the importance of listening to others. This student reported:

> As I learned about my clients' lives in greater detail, going through their various life stages, a colourful life mosaic emerged that reflected on all these different elements. I have a whole new appreciation for good listening practices: if we know what a person's circumstances were in the past, we can begin to understand this person in the present.

Learning the challenges associated with conducting successful and safe reminiscences assisted the students with analyzing their own skill level and putting things in perspective for the benefit of the client. This student recognized how easy it is to cross boundaries in this line of work and was working to overcome this challenge:

> Completing this project was a great experience for me, personally and professionally. I truly enjoyed the time I spent with my narrator and felt like it was an honour to be trusted with her story. My favourite part of the process, without a doubt, was the interview; I found myself wishing we could spend more time together after it was over. One difficulty I had and continue to have is knowing that my visits with her relieved some of her loneliness, but the limits of my scope of work prevent me from visiting her in the future; I wish I could continue to be a presence in her life, both for her sake and my own. I anticipate this will be an ongoing occupational 'hazard' of working with pleasant and interesting older adults who are often lonely, but it also suggests that I'll most likely continue to enjoy this work.

Theme 3: Unexpected discoveries

The students discovered many things about themselves and their clients as a result of taking the course. It is interesting to note that student expectations were as varied as their educational and professional backgrounds and geographic locations. One student through participation in the certificate course discovered the following:

> I thought the certification course would be a breeze – an easy credential. Wrong! The course opened my very narrow view of this field and I was exposed to the theories and history behind it. This included explanations about the many forms reminiscence can take in a variety of settings. Yes – I chafed (more than a little) because the first module used an academic approach and I've been out of that scene for a long, long, long time. To say I was 'rusty' as a student would be an understatement, yet it was a real eye opener. In the end, I decided that the Association of Personal Historians' philosophy/ approach was the best 'fit' for me, but now I'm aware of other options. That's valuable.

Evaluations of the hands-on experiences in the course revealed that students were somewhat surprised at the degree of intimacy that occurs during a reminiscence session as well as their client's positive responses to their interactions. This particular student conducted an integrative reminiscence session with an older woman and expressed the following:

I left in awe of an amazing experience and was drained in the way of watching an emotional roller-coaster movie. I needed quiet time to process what had just happened. I felt gifted by her sharing very deep and personal memories. The reviewer had the opportunity to recall memories that she didn't know she had. She said the questions I asked triggered memories. This made her happy and I felt pleased about helping her.

Discussion and future directions

This chapter describes the development, implementation, and evaluation of the Reminiscence and Life Story Work Certificate course envisioned by John Kunz from the University of Wisconsin–Superior. Data gathered from students and faculty reveal that the course does prepare students confidently to engage in reminiscence and life story work in a variety of settings. The four separate modules provide theoretical perspectives and methods, introduce students to the challenges and rewards of conducting this type of work while broadening their network to include experts from the field in their learning experiences. While UWS and IIRLR are pleased that we have carried on John Kunz's vision, we realize we must continue to strengthen the program. Based on student and faculty feedback and enquiries from interested prospective students, future goals include broadening the scope of Module 3 better to meet the needs of a wider range of reminiscence/life story work professionals; adding an optional module focused on working with individuals who have cognitive impairment/dementia, especially those residing in long-term care settings or receiving in-home healthcare or other services; and increasing opportunities for students and faculty to meet 'face to face' virtually via web conferencing.

Acknowledgements

Special thanks to Donna Sislo, Program Associate at the UWS-CCE, for her assistance in the description of the historical development of the IIRLR and John Kunz for his vision which provided the impetus for the development of the online certificate course. Finally, we are grateful to our students for participating in the evaluation process. Their comments have been instrumental in the continued implementation and success of the Certificate in Reminiscence and Life Story Work course.

Chapter 21

AFTERWORD

Faith Gibson

If Butler's seminal article is taken as the beginning, though not really the beginning of reminiscence, what of the future? People are story. No nation, family or individual exists without their story, whether talked about or not – actual, revised and in part imagined. These stories are dynamic. They provide the very bedrock, the foundation and guarantee of our existence. To know me it is important to know something of my story – not in its entirety as it will always be incomplete, a work in progress within our lifetime and in some ways, beyond our death. Our story will continue to be revised in the retelling by others who knew us, or thought they knew us, and by many who may be connected through family ties, friendship, work, other networks or perhaps by published or spoken word. Without a knowledge of our past we are adrift in the present. Without a knowledge of our present, we cannot hope to contemplate the future with equanimity.

The varied contents of this book and the wide-ranging sources cited and reviewed are tangible evidence of how the study and practice of reminiscence, life review and life story work have steadily progressed in the last 20 or so years, both in terms of the diverse facets being researched and the growing sophistication of methodologies employed and variety of persons engaged.

Publisher's limitations have inevitably meant that some topics, many potential authors and some geographic regions of the world are unrepresented in this book. This does not mean they are less important or less relevant but simply that word limits inevitably imposed restrictions. Some readers will be disappointed to see that Africa, parts of Asia, Eastern Europe, Russia and South America are not represented, although reminiscence is known to be used in these countries. Prisoners, except for a brief mention, and refugees, among many other topics, are also under-represented. Rural and predominantly oral societies, more the territory of anthropologists than narrative methods theorists are also largely absent. Some readers may think dementia receives too much attention but as this is such an urgent worldwide public health issue and a major growing cause of expense, distress and death, such attention is wholly justified.

It has long been known that reminiscence does not suit everyone, as Coleman, Cappeliez and Westerhof and others suggested many years ago, a view re-confirmed here. This established finding is still too often ignored by some over-zealous reminiscence enthusiasts. The meticulous reported research helps us to understand why for some people who are contending with depression and anxiety it may actually be unhelpful. The need for clinicians and reminiscence workers to exercise great sensitivity, skill and discipline in selecting participants to engage in reminiscence either in small groups or individually is paramount. They need to be alert to and aware of underlying personality traits and clinical manifestations of repetitious obsessional preoccupation with negative past events that some people seem unable to accept, surmount or leave behind.

It is customary for many edited volumes such as this to end with wise words by the editor who seeks to foreshadow future directions and possible or probable developments in the field of work encompassed by the book. Many of the contributors to this volume have already concluded their chapters with such suggestions. There is scarcely need to add more. What they all, in their own way, have done is to write with considerable conviction, founded on their own scholarship and experience of narrative methods, and have identified what has been accomplished since the early 1960s. Neuroscience is increasingly skilled in charting brain activity activated by the cognitive tasks inherent in retrieving memories, so closely allied to imagination, and given form either as private or public thoughts, or potentially made accessible to others through being translated into various tangible formats. Researchers with diverse backgrounds continue to examine the effects of this intricate dynamic process on human emotions and behavior, and clinicians and creative artists study the visible representations of these processes and their effects on interpersonal interactions and behavior in people living in varied contexts. Still, many questions remain to be explored and understood but as Pierce and Elliott remark in Chapter 2, 'translations of widely used measuring instruments now make it possible to compare patterns of reminiscence use across participants from different cultural and language groups'.

We still seem more skilled at producing the bricks of reminiscence than we have been so far in developing the theoretical mortar essential to erect these bricks into a sturdy wall. As the pile of bricks grows ever larger, so does the task of creating the intellectual cement of building theory grow more urgent. The cry for 'evidence-based practice' grows ever more insistent. While the phrase may be relatively new, the idea is old. Clinicians are expected to engage only in those practices that are supported by proven empirical research findings. Funders and policy makers insist on supporting only those interventions, projects and applications that are founded on such evidence – this is something of a vicious circle. Yet, increasingly there are critical voices being raised about the validity and reliability of, or indeed, the very legitimacy of much that passes as 'evidence'. Devisch and Murray (2009), Every-Palmer and Howick (2014), Harris (2016) and Pincus (2014), for example, offer stringent criticism of much peer-reviewed published accounts of randomized controlled trials, considered the gold standard of evidence, albeit in reference to the biological sciences, medicine and surgery, that social scientists would be wise to heed.

Practitioners, including those drawn from the several health and human services professions represented in this volume, need to be alert to the shortcomings of much that passes as research-based evidence and not underestimate the evaluative expertise they possess as experienced clinicians and practitioners. Pincus (2014) argues, as do Pierce and Elliott in Chapter 2 and Woods in Chapter 3, for using both quantitative and qualitative methodologies in researching bio/psycho/social aspects of human functioning. Pincus suggests that, 'a contemporary view of evidence-based medicine recognizes limitations of clinical trials and that in some instances, observational studies and case series may provide "best evidence"' (p.207). Perhaps we should remind ourselves of Einstein's salutary advice that not everything that can be counted, counts, and not everything that counts can be counted.

Let everyone interested in the process, content, outcomes and impact of the various narrative approaches explored in this book become their own stringently critical researcher as they scrutinize their work and its impact on the people of all ages who engage with them in exploring their personal pasts. Let us be neither blind to nor ignorant of the potentially distorting effects of over-enthusiasm, nor feel obliged to apologize for how relatively little, despite all efforts so far exerted, and as is so well documented in this collection of writings, remains to be known about the effectiveness of reminiscence.

Rather, let us be glad of the enlarged understandings and profit from the work assembled here from many countries that has been undertaken with people of varied abilities, ages and circumstances. These accounts document the enormous pleasure, enhanced communication, enriched relationships, therapeutic impact and enlarged understanding of life's meaning and value that reminiscence, life review and life story work make possible for many people. This is not to minimize or excuse past or contemporary methodological shortcomings, nor to be dismissive of criticism but rather to encourage further exploration of the profound, sometimes even life-changing, outcomes arising from such interventions and to build a comprehensive theory or theories that illuminate this work and define, replicate and inform best practice.

This book has brought together the thinking, research and writing of many people. Both individually and collectively they represent a continuing commitment to exploring and explaining multiple aspects of the seemingly so simple yet infinitely complex nature of reminiscence, its varied functions and its utility. I hope that it will encourage a new generation of scholars, clinicians and practitioners to contribute in the years to come. Over time, ideas evolve and understanding grows. And different approaches attract their enthusiastic disciples and supporters. For example, reality orientation has evolved into cognitive behavioral stimulation; validation therapy has alerted us to the continuing need for empathetic understanding of the feelings, translated into behavior of people with dementia. Oral history and reminiscence continue to be inextricably entwined and each nourishes the other. Our life experience, wrapped up in memories and made present through innumerable acts of remembering, informs our daily lives. In that sense, we are what we once were and tomorrow we will be both the same and different from what we are today. The processes of creating memories and recreating and rehearsing them in the present by means of reminiscence provide us with a rich reservoir on which to draw to inform both our own and others' understanding. This is everyone's heritage and what each person makes of it will be absolutely unique yet serve to connect them to people, places and other times. For as Glover (2014) says '…as he looked back upon a place but also upon his life he knew that the truth of a life was not an isolated narrative, but the confluence of all the stories it had created in the lives of others' (p.371).

The purposes, pitfalls, pains and rewards involved from utilizing reminiscence processes have been well covered in this book. Seeking to develop and consolidate personal identity and striving to make sense of our lives or to find meaning in our lives have emerged as two salient, contemporary, recurring themes throughout many chapters. It is left for each of us, in ways uniquely idiosyncratic to explore, reflect, appropriate and build on the deliberations of the authors and what they have written.

Having developed an enduring fascination with gerontology, and in particular the functions and dysfunctions of memory arising from experiences within my personal and professional life, for me, reminiscence and life review, captured in tangible visible 'products' or representations such as life story books and other artistic formats, provides a reassurance. We are not alone; we are connected within the long story of our families and the even longer sweep of public history. Although I still only partially understand the complexities of memory, I do know that reminiscence is a way into the worlds of myself and other people. It brings understanding of the long and varied roads by which people have travelled from past to present; the heroic efforts expended to make the most of what life has thrown at us, both good and ill, and the values which inform the final stage of the life cycle. Now, as an actual inhabitant of this time and space, I have even greater opportunities to learn about the complexities of this phase of life and how I and my elderly travelling companions are coping with the demands and rewards of our long journeys.

Here is presented ample evidence of an increasing sophistication in conceptualizing and writing about reminiscence. Understanding the differential functions served by engagement in reminiscence is essential in terms of both the type of intervention used and the people it is intended to benefit. A fuller appreciation of the dynamic nature of memory and the complexities involved in stimulating, encoding, retrieving, reconstructing and reinterpreting memories concerning personal life experience have all been considered.

It seems reasonable to conclude from the work presented in this volume that Pear's (1922) suggestion that the mind never photographs but rather paints pictures is vindicated. For mind and memory are dynamic, changing imperceptibly with every memory recalled to consciousness, reviewed, revised and re-presented in an assortment of tangible and intangible ways, and held potentially available for re-activation in the future. Pear's artistic metaphor amply encapsulates the approaches encompassed by the various contributors to this book. They have critically reviewed a vast amount of relevant literature, discussed the outcomes of much meticulous research and enthusiastically shared the infectious engagement that occurs in reminiscence and life review projects. They have urged the next generation of researchers and practitioners to be more precise in their use of terminology, more rigorous in their definition of the objectives of specific interventions undertaken with defined subjects, and more willing to use both conventional and creative approaches for gathering, analyzing and reporting results, both positive and negative. This collection of writings will have accomplished its purpose if a new generation of scholars and practitioners find it informs their understanding of earlier work and inspires them to engage in further efforts to explore how recollection of the past informs their own and other people's appreciation of how such functions and processes may enrich the present and inform the future.

This book is but the next stepping stone in a field of scholarship and practice, endlessly fascinating and richly rewarding, but still in its relative infancy. This is a fruitful field of engagement for clinicians, practitioners and researchers and for those people whose intellectual curiosity, work and leisure activities provide opportunities that encompass narrative enquiry and engagement. For in remembering we are not alone but connected to others, in encouraging others to remember, we too, for a time may be remembered.

Unremembered in the Heartland of Iowa

I read the name on the marker that I had read before;
'Stella Garrett', who died at age 4 in 1876
Out in the heartland of Iowa
And was buried in a now abandoned cemetery.

She was neither the oldest nor the youngest in her family,
But she was the first of the children to die
Out in the heartland of Iowa
And to lie buried in an abandoned cemetery.

Her parents must have mourned their loss,
Her siblings, too young to remember her death
Where out in the heartland of Iowa
She lay buried in an abandoned cemetery.

The other children had children and moved on.
Only the parents could be the memory keepers of Stella
Where out in the heartland of Iowa
She lay buried in an abandoned cemetery.

Robert and Catherine became grandparents and more
Having nothing but fading memories of Stella
Where out in the heartland of Iowa
She lay buried in an abandoned cemetery.

But the parents died, too, passing into the lingering memory
Of children and friends who lived for a while longer.
But Stella could not be remembered anymore by anyone;

I read the name I had read before;
'Stella Garrett', who died at age 4 in 1876.
But reading a name is not the same as remembering.
I can't remember what I never knew of those
Who out in the heartland of Iowa
Lie buried in an abandoned cemetery.

I wonder how long
Before I become unremembered, too,
Like Stella
Out in the heartland of Iowa?

Craig R. Garrett (2015)

Mum Now

tapestry
threads of colour weft
back and forth
yarns unravel slowly
loosening the seams of memory
but holding the intricacies of its
pattern
sketch
your pen tracks its way across
the desert of the page
wispy lines plotted in sand are visible
in a moment
then dusted away with a puff of breeze
Watercolour
faded was of memory layered on
memory
a palimpsest of your experience
with each brush stroke
voice
your voice whispers stories
deep thoughts drift on air
dandelions parachute and tumble
earth moon and stars
in an altered world
stories
words fashioning stories
are the tapestries of your past
images of life's textures
that cannot wither
Twilight
I miss you most when I am with you.

Margaret McClintock (2016)

In researching and writing about memory, its functions and dysfunctions, we enlarge our understanding. May the readers join us on this journey, working to extend their own and others' reminiscence knowledge, skills and understanding of this absorbing field of scholarship and its creative, versatile, rewarding practice applications. It is an omnicultural field with active national and trans-national research programs in many countries.

Reinforced by the research and writings represented in this book, four abiding practical convictions remain with me. First, reminiscence, life review and life story work have wide applications, are immensely interesting, and evidence suggests they can contribute to the wellbeing of people of varied ages, cultures, states of health and ill-health and social circumstances. Second, despite this wide acceptability, reminiscence does not suit everyone, and care needs to be taken in inviting people to participate, and reluctance to do so should be respected. Third, if we invite people to share the stories of their lives with us, we must do them the courtesy of devoting the time and attention required to truly listen. Finally, should we come to share closely in the lives of people who have memory and recall disabilities, in either personal or professional ways, or possibly in both, we need to become what Bryden calls 'narrative care-partners', privileged memory keepers and memory holders for others, and hope that if we too should one day require such assistance ourselves, there will be someone able and prepared to do the same for us.

References

Abraham, R. (2016) 'Reflections on narrative in pastoral theology.' *Pastoral Psychology*, 65, 727–742.

Adler, J.M. (2012) 'Living into the story: Agency and coherence in a longitudinal study of narrative identity development and mental health over the course of psychotherapy.' *Journal of Personality and Social Psychology*, 102, 367–389.

Adler, J.M. and Poulin, M.J. (2009) 'The political is personal: Narrating 9/11 and psychological wellbeing.' *Journal of Personality*, 77, 4, 903–932.

Adler, J.M., Lodi-Smith, J., Philippe, F.L. and Houle, I. (2016) 'The incremental validity of narrative identity in predicting wellbeing: A review of the field and recommendations for the future.' *Personality and Social Psychology Review*, 20, 142–175.

Age UK (2010) *Loneliness and Isolation: Evidence Review*. London: Age UK.

Affleck, G., Allen, D.A., Tennen, H., McGrade, B.J. and Ratzan, S. (1985) 'Causal and control cognitions in parents' coping with chronically ill children.' *Journal of Social and Clinical Psychology*, 3, 367–377.

Aguirre, E., Spector, A., Streater, A., Burnell, K. and Orrell, M. (2011) 'Service users' involvement in the development of a maintenance cognitive stimulation therapy (CST) programme: A comparison of the views of people with dementia, staff and family carers.' *Dementia*, 10, 4, 459–473.

Alea, N. and Bluck, S. (2003) 'Why are you telling me that? A conceptual model of the social function of autobiographical memory.' *Memory*, 11, 165–178. doi:10.1080/741938207

Alea, N. and Bluck, S. (2007) 'I'll keep you in mind: The intimacy function of autobiographical memory.' *Applied Cognitive Psychology*, 21, 1091–1111. doi:10.1002/acp.1316

Alea, N. and Bluck, S. (2013) 'When does meaning making predict subjective wellbeing? Examining young and older adults in two cultures.' *Memory*, 21, 1, 44–63. doi:10.1080/09658211.2012.704927

Alea, N., Bluck, S. and Ali, S. (2015) 'Function in context: Why American and Trinidadian young and older adults remember the personal past.' *Memory*, 1, 55–68. doi:10.1080/09658211.2014.929704

Allé, M.C., Manning, L., Potheegadoo, J., Coutelle, R., Danion, J. and Berna, F. (2017) 'Wearable cameras are useful tools to investigate and remediate autobiographical memory impairment: A systematic PRISMA review.' *Neuropsychology Review*, 27, 1, 81–99.

Allen, R.S., Hilgeman, M.M., Ege, M.A., Shuster, J.L. and Burgio, L.D. (2008) 'Legacy activities as interventions approaching the end of life.' *Journal of Palliative Medicine*, 11, 1029–1038. doi:10.1089/jpm.2007.0294

Alm, N., Astell, A.J., Gowans, G., Dye, M. *et al.* (2009) 'Engaging multimedia leisure for people with dementia.' *Gerontechnology*, 8, 236–246.

Alwin, D.F. (2012) 'Integrating varieties of life course concepts.' *Journals of Gerontology, Series B: Psychological Sciences and Social Sciences*, 67B, 1–15.

Alzheimer's Disease International (2000) *Annual Report 1999/2000*. Accessed on 08/08/18 at www.alz.co.uk/adi/pdf/annrep00.pdf. London: Author.

Alzheimer's Research UK (2015) *The Power to Defeat Dementia. Dementia in the Family: The Impact on Carers*. Cambridge: Alzheimer's Research UK.

Amano, K., Morita, T., Tatara, R., Katayama, H. *et al.* (2015) 'Association between early palliative care referrals, inpatient hospice utilization, and aggressiveness of care at the end of life.' *Journal of Palliative Medicine,* 18, 270–273. doi:10.1089/jpm.2014.0132

Ancient, C., Good, A., Wilson, C. and Fitch, T. (2011) 'Can ubiquitous devices utilising reminiscence therapy be used to promote wellbeing in dementia patients? An exploratory study.' Accessed on 3/10/2017 at https://researchportal.port.ac.uk/portal/files/209627/HCI_international_Ancient_et_Al.pdf

Ando, M., Morita, T., Akechi, T. and Takashi, K. (2012) 'Factors in narratives to questions in the short-term life review interviews of terminally ill cancer patients and utility of the questions.' *Palliative and Supportive Care,* 10, 2, 83–90.

Ando, M., Morita, T. and O'Connor, S. (2007) 'Primary concerns of advanced cancer patients identified through the structured life review process: A qualitative study using a text mining technique.' *Palliative and Supportive Care,* 5, 265–271.

Ando, M., Tsuda, A. and Morita, T. (2007) 'Life review interviews on the spiritual wellbeing of terminally ill cancer patients.' *Support Care Cancer,* 225–231. doi:10.1007/s00520-0060121-y

Andrews, J., Zaman, W., Merrill, N., Duke, M. and Fivush, R. (2015) 'Gender differences in adolescent birth narratives.' *Journal of Applied Research in Memory and Cognition,* 4, 356–362.

Archbold, P.G., Stewart, B.J., Miller, L.L., Harvath, T.A. *et al.* (1990) 'Mutuality and preparedness as predictors of caregiver role strain.' *Research in Nursing and Health,* 13, 375–384.

Astell, A.J., Alm, N., Gowans, G., Ellis, M., Dye, R. and Vaughan, P. (2009) 'Involving older people with dementia and their carers in designing computer-based support systems: Some methodological considerations.' *Universal Access in the Information Society,* 8, 49–58.

Astell, A.J., Ellis, M., Bernardi, L., Alm, N. *et al.* (2007) 'Developing Technology to Support the Relationship between People with Dementia and Caregivers. Proceedings of the 22nd Conference of Alzheimer's Disease International, Berlin (pp.30–33).

Astell, A.J., Ellis, M., Bernardi, L., Alm, N. *et al.* (2010) 'Using a touch screen computer to support relationships between people with dementia and caregivers.' *Interacting with Computers,* 22, 267–275.

Astell, A.J., Joddrell, P. and Groenewoud, H. (2016) 'Does familiarity affect the enjoyment of touchscreen games for people with dementia?' *International Journal of Medical Informatics,* 1–3. doi:10.1016/j.ijmedinf.2016.02.001

Astell, A.J., Purves, B. and Phinney, A. (2011) 'Story of my life? The contents and functions of reminiscing.' CHI. ACM 978-1-4503-0268-5/11/05.

Attig, T. (2000) *The Heart of Grief: Death and the Search for Lasting Love.* New York: Oxford University Press.

Ba, Amadou Hampaté (2017) QuoteLand. Accessed on 10/08/2017 at http://forum.quoteland.com/eve/forums/a/tpc/f/99191541/m/963102526.

Baars, J. (2011) 'Concepts of time and narrative temporality in the study of aging.' *Journal of Aging Studies,* 4, 11, 283–295.

Baars, J. (2012) 'Critical turns of aging, narrative and time.' *International Journal of Ageing and Later Life,* 7, 2, 143–165.

BBC (1989) Sony Award documentary film *Across the Irish Sea.* Accessed on 06/03/2018 at www.reminiscencetheatrearchive.org.uk/page/tour_schedule_media_press_and_feedback?path=0p138p139p.

Baddeley, A. (1988) 'But What the Hell Is It For?' In M.M. Gruenberg, P.E. Morri and R.N. Skyes (eds) *Practical Aspect of Memory: Current Research and Issues* (pp.3–18). Chichester: Wiley. doi:10.1002/acp.1614

Baddeley, J.L. and Singer, J.A. (2008) 'Telling losses: Personality correlates and functions of bereavement narratives.' *Journal of Research in Personality,* 42, 421–438. doi:10.1016/j.jrp.2007.07.006

Baddeley, J.L. and Singer, J.A. (2009) 'A social interactional model of bereavement narrative disclosure.' *Review of General Psychology*, 13, 202–218. doi:10.1037/a0015655

Baddeley, J.L. and Singer, J.A. (2010) 'A loss in the family: Silence, memory, and narrative identity after bereavement.' *Memory*, 18, 198–207. doi:10.1080/09658210903143858

Baldwin, C. and Estey, J. (2015) 'The self and spirituality: Overcoming narrative loss in aging.' *Journal of Religion and Spirituality in Social Work: Social Thought*, 34, 2, 205–222.

Balk, D.E. (1997) 'Death, bereavement and college students: A descriptive analysis.' *Mortality*, 2, 207–220. doi:10.1080/713685866

Baltes, P.B. (1987) 'Theoretical propositions of life-span developmental psychology: On the dynamics between growth and decline.' *Developmental Psychology*, 23, 611–626.

Bangor, A., Kortum, P.T. and Miller, J.T. (2008) 'An empirical evaluation of the System Usability Scale.' *International Journal of Human-Computer Interaction*, 24, 6, 574–594.

Basting, A. and Killick, J. (2003) *The Arts and Dementia Care: A Resource Guide*. New York: Center for Creative Aging.

Baumeister, R.F. (1987) 'How the self became a problem: A psychological review of historical research.' *Journal of Personality and Social Psychology*, 52, 1, 163.

Baumeister, R.F. (2010) *'The Self.' Advanced Social Psychology. The State of the Science.* (pp.139–175). Oxford: Oxford University Press.

Bech, P., Olsen, L.R., Kjolle, M. and Rasmussen, N.K. (2003) 'Measuring wellbeing rather than the absence of distress symptoms: A comparison of the SF-36 Mental Health subscale and the WHO-Five Wellbeing Scale.' *International Journal of Methods Psychiatric Research*, 12, 85–91.

Beck, A., Rush, A.J., Shaw, B.F. and Emery, G. (1979) *Cognitive Therapy of Depression*. New York: Guilford Press.

Beekman, A.T., Deeg, D.J., Van Limbeek, J., Braam, A.W., De Vries, M.Z. and van Tilburg, W. (1997) 'Criterion validity of the Center for Epidemiological Studies Depression scale(CES-D): Results from a community-based sample of older subjects in the Netherlands.' *Psychological Medicine*, 27, 1, 231–235. doi.10.1017/S0033291796003510

Bell, G. and Gemmell, J. (2009) *Total Recall: How the e-Memory Revolution Will Change Everything*. New York: Dutton.

Bennett, K.M. and Vidal-Hall, S. (2000) 'Narratives of death: A qualitative study of widowhood in later life.' *Ageing and Society*, 20, 413–428. doi:10.1017/S0144686X99007813

Berntsen, D. (2008) 'Involuntary Memories: What are the Important Questions?' In J. Mace (ed.) *Involuntary Memory* (pp.4–40). Chichester: Wiley. doi:10.1002/9780470774069

Berry, E., Kapur, N., Williams, L., Hodges, S. *et al.* (2007) 'The use of a wearable camera, SenseCam, as a pictorial diary to improve autobiographical memory in a patient with limbic encephalitis: A preliminary report.' *Neuropsychological Rehabilitation*, 17, 4–5, 582–601.

Bible, New Revised Standard Version (1989) Nashville, TN: Thomas Nelson Inc.

Binder, B., Mastel-Smith, B., Hersch, G., Symes, L., Malecha, A. and McFarlane, J. (2009) 'Community-dwelling, older women's perspectives on therapeutic life review: A qualitative analysis.' *Issues in Mental Health Nursing*, 30, 5, 288–294.

Birren Center for Autobiographical Studies (2017) Courses-Online GAB Instructor Training. Accessed on 24/08/2017 at http://guidedautobiography.com/classes-1.

Birren, J.E. and Cochran, K. (2001) *Telling the Stories of Life through Guided Autobiography Groups*. Baltimore, MD: Johns Hopkins University Press.

Birren, J.E. and Deutchman, D.E. (1991) *Guiding Autobiography Groups for Older Adults*. Baltimore, MD: Johns Hopkins University Press.

Birren, J.E., Kenyon, G., Ruth, J.E., Schroots, J.J. and Svensson, T. (eds) (1996) *Aging and Biography: Explorations in Adult Development*. New York: Springer Publishing.

Birren, J.E. and Schroots, J.J. (2006) 'Autobiographical Memory and the Narrative Self Over the Life Span.' In J.E. Birren and K.W. Schaie (eds) *Handbook of the Psychology of Aging* (6th ed). Burlington, MA: Academic Press.

Birren, J.E. and Svensson, C.M. (2009) 'Anticipated and actual evaluation of the components of guided autobiography.' Paper presented at the Life in the Past Lane: Reflections in a Review Mirror. Symposium, 62 Annual Scientific Meeting of the Gerontological Society of America, Atlanta, Georgia.

Birren, J.E. and Svensson, C.M. (2013) 'Reminiscence, life review, and autobiography: Emergence of a new era.' *The International Journal of Reminiscence and Life Review*, 1, 1–6.

Black, J. and Haight, B.K. (1992) 'Integrality as a theoretical framework for the life review process.' *Holistic Nursing Practice*, 7, 7–15.

Bluck, S. (2003) 'Autobiographical memory: Exploring its functions in everyday life.' *Memory*, 11, 113–123. doi:10.1080/741938206

Bluck, S. (2009) 'Baddeley revisited: The functional approach to autobiographical memory.' *Applied Cognitive Psychology*, 23, 1050–1058. doi:10.1002/acp.1609

Bluck, S. and Alea, N. (2002) 'Exploring the Functions of Autobiographical Memory: Why Do I Remember the Autumn?' In J.D. Webster and B.K. Haight (eds) *Critical Advances in Reminiscence Work: From Theory to Application* (pp.61–75). New York: Springer Publishing.

Bluck, S. and Alea, N. (2009) 'Thinking and talking about the past: Why remember?' *Applied Cognitive Psychology*, 23, 1089–1104. doi:10.1002/acp.1612

Bluck, S. and Alea, N. (2011) 'Crafting the TALE: Construction of a measure to assess the functions of autobiographical remembering.' *Memory*, 19, 5, 470–486. doi:10.1080/09 658211.2011.590500

Bluck, S., Alea, N. and Demiray, B. (2010) *You Get What You Need: The Act of Remembering*. Malden, MA: Wiley-Blackwell. doi:10.9781444328202

Bluck, S., Alea, N., Habermas, T. and Rubin, D.C. (2005) 'A tale of three functions: The self-reported uses of autobiographical memory.' *Social Cognition*, 23, 1, 91–117. doi:10.1521/ soco.23.1.91.59198

Bluck, S., Baron, J., Ainsworth, S., Gesselman, A. and Gold, K. (2013) 'Eliciting empathy for adults in chronic pain through autobiographical memory sharing.' *Applied Cognitive Psychology*, 21, 81–90.

Bluck, S. and Levine, L.J. (1998) 'Reminiscence as autobiographical memory: A catalyst for reminiscence theory development.' *Ageing and Society*, 18, 185–208.

Bluck, S. and Liao, H.W. (2013) 'I was therefore I am: Creating self-continuity through remembering our personal past.' *The International Journal of Reminiscence and Life Review*, 1, 7–12.

Bluck, S. and Mroz, E.L. (2018) 'The end: Death as part of the life story.' *International Journal of Reminiscence and Life Review*, 5, 1, 6–14. Accessed on 24/06/2018 at http://143.95.253.101/~radfordojs/index.php/IJRLR/issue/current.

Blustein, J. (1999) 'Choosing for others as a continuing life story: The problem of personal identity revisited.' *Journal of Law, Medicine and Ethics*, 27, 20–31.

Boerner, K. and Heckhausen, J. (2003) 'To have and have not: Adaptive bereavement by transforming mental ties to the deceased.' *Death Studies*, 27, 199–226. doi:10.1080/07481180302888

Bohanek, J., Fivush, R., Zaman, W., Thomas-Lepore, C. *et al.* (2009) 'Narrative interaction in family dinnertime interactions.' *Merrill-Palmer Quarterly*, 55, 488–515.

Bohlmeijer, E.T., Roemer, M., Cuijpers, P. and Smit, F. (2007) 'The effects of life-review on life-satisfaction and wellbeing: Results of a meta-analysis.' *Aging and Mental Health*, 11, 291–300.

Bohlmeijer, E.T., Smit, F. and Cuijpers, P. (2003) 'Effects of reminiscence and life review on late-life depression: A meta-analysis.' *International Journal of Geriatric Psychiatry*, 18, 1088–1094.

Bohlmeijer, E.T., Valenkamp, M., Westerhof, G.J., Smit, F. and Cuijpers, P. (2005) 'Creative reminiscence as an early intervention for depression: Results of a pilot project.' *Aging and Mental Health*, 9, 4, 302–304.

Bohlmeijer, E. and Westerhof, G. J. (2010) *Op Verhaal Komen: Je Autobiografie als Bron van Wijsheid* [*The Stories We Live By: Your Autobiography as Source of Wisdom*]. Amsterdam: Boom.

Bohlmeijer, E.T. and Westerhof, G.J. (2011) 'Reminiscence Interventions: Bringing Narrative Gerontology into Practice.' In G. Kenyon, E. Bohlmeijer and W.L. Randall (eds) *Storying Later Life: Issues, Investigations and Interventions in Narrative Gerontology* (pp.273–289). New York: Oxford University Press.

Bohlmeijer, E.T. and Westerhof, G.J. (2013) 'Life review as a way to enhance personal growth in midlife: A case study.' *International Journal of Reminiscence and Life Review*, 1, 1, 13–18.

Bohlmeijer, E.T., Westerhof, G.J. and Emmerik-de Jong, M. (2008) 'The effects of integrative reminiscence on meaning in life: Results of a quasi-experimental study.' *Aging and Mental Health*, 12, 5, 639–646.

Bohlmeijer, E.T., Westerhof, G.J. and Lamers, S.A. (2014) 'The development and initial validation of the narrative foreclosure scale.' *Aging and Mental Health*, 18, 7, 879–888.

Bohlmeijer, E.T., Westerhof, G.J., Randall, W.W., Tromp, T.T. and Kenyon, G.G. (2011) 'Narrative foreclosure in later life: Preliminary considerations for a new sensitizing concept.' *Journal of Aging Studies*, 25, 364–370.

Bonanno, G.A. (2004) 'Loss, trauma, and human resilience: Have we underestimated the human capacity to thrive after extremely aversive events?' *American Psychologist*, 59, 20. doi:10.1037/0003-066x.59.1.20

Booker, J.A. and Dunsmore, J.C. (2017) 'Affective social competence in adolescence: Current findings and future directions.' *Social Development*, 26, 3–20. doi:10.1111/sode.12193

Borkan, J. (1999) 'Immersion/Crystallization.' In B. Crabtree and W. Miller (eds) *Qualitative Research* (2nd ed) (pp.179–184). Thousand Oaks, CA: Sage.

Bornat, J. (1994) *Reminiscence Reviewed: Perspectives, Evaluations and Achievements*. Berkshire: Open University.

Bornat, J. (2001) 'Reminiscence and oral history: Parallel universes or shared endeavours.' *Ageing and Society*, 21, 2, 32–35.

Bowlby, J. (1969) *Attachment and Loss, Vol. 1 Attachment*. New York: Basic Books.

Boyd, H.D. and Shenk, D. (2014) 'Beyond reminiscence: Using generic video to elicit conversational language.' *American Journal of Alzheimer's Disease and Other Dementias*, 1–8. doi:10.1177/1533317514534759

Brankaert, R. and Ouden, E.D. (2015) 'Design of a Mobile Interface: Reflections on an In-context Evaluation.' Proceedings of Participatory Innovation Conference 2015. The Hague, The Netherlands.

Brassai, L., Piko, B.F. and Steger, M.F. (2015) 'A reason to stay healthy: The role of meaning in life in relation to physical activity and healthy eating among adolescents.' *Journal of Health Psychology*, 20, 473–482.

Breen, A.V., McLean, K.C., Cairney, K. and McAdams, D.P. (2016) 'Movies, books, and identity: Exploring the narrative ecology of the self.' *Qualitative Psychology*, 4, 3, 243–259. Accessed on 21/06/2018 at http://dx.doi.org/10.1037 qup 0000059.

Brewer, W.F. (1986) 'What is Autobiographical Memory?' In D.C. Rubin (ed.) *Autobiographical Memory?* (pp.25–49). New York: Cambridge University Press.

Brinker, J. K. (2013) 'Rumination and reminiscence in older adults: Implications for clinical practice.' *European Journal of Ageing*, 10, 223–227. doi:10.1007/s10433-013-0271.y

Brockmeier, J. (2000) 'Autobiographical time.' *Narrative Inquiry*, 10, 1, 51–73.

Brooker, D. and Duce, L. (2000) 'Wellbeing and activity in dementia: A comparison of group reminiscence therapy, structured goal-directed group activity and unstructured time.' *Aging and Mental Health*, 4, 4, 354–358. doi:10.1080/713649967

Brown-Shaw, M., Westwood, M. and de Vries, B. (1999) 'Integrating personal reflection and group-based enactments.' *Journal of Aging Studies*, 13, 109–199.

Bruce, D. (1989) 'Functional Explanations of Memory'. In L.W. Poon, D.C. Rubin and B.A. Wilson (eds) *Everyday Cognition in Adulthood and Late Life* (pp.44–58). Cambridge: Cambridge University Press. doi:10.1017/cbo9780511759390.005

Bruce, E., Hodgson, S. and Schweitzer, P. (1999) *Reminiscing with People with Dementia: A Handbook for Carers*. London: Age Exchange.

Bruner, J. (1990) *Acts of Meaning*. Cambridge, MA: Harvard University Press.

Bryan, J. (2016) *Human Being. Insights from Psychology and the Christian Faith*. London: SCM Press.

Bryden, C. (2002) 'A person-centred approach to counselling, psychotherapy and rehabilitation of people diagnosed with dementia in the early stages.' *Dementia*, 1, 2, 141–156.

Bryden, C. (2005) *Dancing with Dementia*. London: Jessica Kingsley Publishers.

Bryden, C. (2012) *Who Will I Be When I Die?* (Revised edition). London: Jessica Kingsley Publishers.

Bryden, C. (2015a) *Before I Forget*. Melbourne: Penguin Random House.

Bryden, C. (2015b) *Nothing About Us, Without Us*. London: Jessica Kingsley Publishers.

Bryden, C. (2016) 'A spiritual journey into the I-Thou relationship: A personal reflection on living with dementia.' *Journal of Spirituality, Religion and Aging*, 28, 1–2, 7–14.

Bryden, C. and MacKinlay, E. (2002) 'Dementia – A Spiritual Journey towards the Divine: A personal view of dementia.' In E. MacKinlay (ed.) *Mental Health and Spirituality in Later Life*. New York: Haworth Pastoral Press.

Buchanan, K. (1996) 'Talk and identity in reminiscence groups' *Reminiscence Magazine*, 13, 3.

Buchsbaum, B.C. (1996) 'Remembering a Parent Who Has Died: A Developmental Perspective.' In D. Klass, P.R. Silverman and S. Nickman (eds) *Continuing Bonds: New Understandings of Grief* (pp.113–124). New York: Taylor & Francis.

Burnside, I. (1978) *Working with Older Adults: Group Process and Techniques*. Sudbury: Jones and Bartlett (with M.G. Schmidt 1986, 1994).

Burnside, I. (2004) 'Life Review and Reminiscence in Nursing Practice.' In J.E. Birren, G. Kenyon, J.E. Ruth, J.F. Schroots and C.M. Svensson (eds) *Aging and Biography: Explorations in Adult Development* (pp.248–264). New York: Springer Publishing.

Burton, N. (2012) 'Our Hierarchy of Needs.' *Psychology Today*. Accessed on 20/02/2018 at www.psychologytoday.com/gb/blog/hide-and-seek/201205/our-hierarchy-needs.

Butler, R.N. (1963a) 'The life review. An interpretation of reminiscence in the aged.' *Psychiatry*, 26, 65–76. doi: 10.1521/00332747.1963.11.023339

Butler, R.N. (1963b) 'The Life Review: An Interpretation of Reminiscence in the Aged.' In B.L. Neugarten (ed.) (1968) *Middle Age and Aging: A Reader in Social Psychology*. Chicago, IL: The University of Chicago Press.

Butler, R.N. (1995) 'Foreword.' In B. Haight and J. Webster (eds) *The Art and Science of Reminiscing*. Washington, DC: Taylor & Francis.

Butler, R. and Lewis, M.I. (1977) *Aging and Mental Health*. St. Louis, MO: C.V. Mosby & Co.

Byrne, L and MacKinlay, E. (2012) 'Seeking meaning: Making art and the experience of spirituality in dementia care.' *Journal of Religion, Spirituality and Aging*, 24, 1–2, 105–119.

Caldwell, R.L. (2005) 'At the confluence of memory and meaning: Life review with older adults and families: Using narrative therapy and the expressive arts to re-member and re-author stories of resilience.' *The Family Journal: Counselling and Therapy for Couples and Families*, 13, 172–175.

Calhoun, L.G. and Tedeschi, R.G. (1998) 'Beyond recovery from trauma: Implications for clinical practice and research.' *Journal of Social Issues*, 54, 357–371.

Campbell, J. (2001) *Start and Run a Personal History Business*. Vancouver: Self Counsel Press.

Cappeliez, P. (2002) 'Cognitive-Reminiscence Therapy for Depressed Older Adults in Day Hospital and Long-term Care.' In J.D. Webster and B.K. Haight (eds) *Critical Advances in Reminiscence Work* (pp.300–313). New York: Springer Publishing.

Cappeliez, P. (2013) 'Characteristic Reminiscence Patterns of Depressed, Anxious and Bereaved Older Adults.' Paper at the International Reminiscence and Life Review Conference, New Orleans, LA.

Cappeliez, P. (in press) 'Distinct processing of emotional contents in prosocial reminiscences.' *International Journal of Reminiscence and Life Review*.

Cappeliez, P., Guindon, M. and Robitaille, A. (2008) 'Functions of reminiscence and emotional regulation among older adults.' *Journal of Aging Studies*, 22, 266–272. doi:10.1016/j.jaging.2007.06.003

Cappeliez, P. and O'Rourke, N. (2002) 'Personality traits and existential concerns as predictors of the functions of reminiscence in older adults.' *The Journals of Gerontology, Series B: Psychological and Social Sciences*, 57B, 116–123. doi:10.1093/geron/57.2.116

Cappeliez, P. and O'Rourke, N. (2006) 'Empirical validation of a model of reminiscence and health in later life.' *The Journals of Gerontology, Series B: Psychological and Social Sciences*, 61B, 4, 237–244. doi:10.1093/geronb/61.4.p.237

Cappeliez, P., O'Rourke, N. and Chaudhury, H. (2005) 'Functions of reminiscence and mental health in later life.' *Aging and Mental Health*, 9, 295–301. doi:10.1080/13607860500131427

Cappeliez, P. and Robitaille, A. (2010) 'Coping mediates the relationships between reminiscence and psychological wellbeing among older adults.' *Aging and Mental Health*, 14, 807–818. doi: 10.1080/13607861003713307

Cappeliez, P. and Webster, J.D. (2011) 'Mneme and Anamnesis: The Contribution of Involuntary Reminiscences to the Construction of a Narrative Self in Older Age.' In G. Kenyon, E.T. Bohlmeijer and W.L. Randall (eds) *Storying Later Life: Issues, Investigations, and Interventions in Narrative Gerontology* (pp. 177–194). New York: Oxford University Press.

Cappeliez, P. and Webster, J.D. (2017) 'Reminiscence through a cultural lens.' *International Journal of Reminiscence and Life Review*, 4, 2, 46–47.

Carers UK (2017) *Making Life Better for Carers*. Accessed on 21/06/2018 at www.carersuk.org/help-and-advice/technology-and-equipment.

Carroll, J.M. and Rosson, M.B. (2007) 'Participatory design in community informatics.' *Design Studies*, 28, 3, 243–261.

Cartwright, J. and Limandri, B. (1997) 'The challenge of multiple roles in the qualitative clinician researcher-participant client relationship.' *Qualitative Health Research*, 7, 2, 223–235.

Caserta, M., Lund, D., Utz, R. and de Vries, B. (2009) 'Stress-related growth among the recently bereaved.' *Aging and Mental Health*, 13, 463–476. doi:10.1080/13607860802534641

Chambers Coxsey, A. (1996) 'Keep my memory.' Accessed on 28/10/2017 at www.allisonsheart.com/keepmemory/keepmemory.html.

Chao, S.Y., Liu, H.Y., Wu, C.Y., Jin, S.F. *et al.* (2006) 'The effects of group reminiscence and therapy on depression, self-esteem, and life satisfaction of elderly nursing home residents.' *Journal of Nursing Research*, 14, 1, 36–45.

Charlesworth, G., Burnell K., Crellin, N., Hoare, Z. *et al.* (2016) 'Peer support and reminiscence therapy for people with dementia and their family carers: A factorial pragmatic randomized trial.' *Journal of Neurology, Neurosurgery and Psychiatry*, 87, 11, 1218–1228. doi:10.1136/jnnp-2016-31373

Chen, Y., McAnally, H.M., Wang, Q. and Reese, E. (2012) 'The coherence of critical event narratives and adolescents' psychological functioning.' *Memory*, 20, 667–681. doi:0.1080/09658211.2012.693934

Chen, Y., Xiao, H., Yang, Y. and Lan, X. (2017) 'The effects of life review on psycho-spiritual wellbeing among patients with life-threatening illness: A systematic review and meta-analysis.' *Journal of Advanced Nursing*, 73, 1539–1554.

Chiang, K., Chu, H., Chang, H., Chung, M. *et al.* (2010) 'The effects of reminiscence therapy on psychological wellbeing, depression, and loneliness among the institutionalized aged.' *International Journal of Geriatric Psychiatry*, 25, 380–388.

Chippendale, T. and Bear-Lehman, J. (2012) 'Effect of life review writing on depressive symptoms in older adults: A randomized controlled design.' *The American Journal of Occupational Therapy*, 66, 4, 438–446.

Chochinov, H.M., Hack, T., Hassard, T., Kristjanson, L.J., McClement, S. and Harlos, M. (2005) 'Dignity therapy: A novel psychotherapeutic intervention for patients near the end of life.' *Journal of Clinical Oncology*, 23, 5520–5525. doi:10.1200/JCO.2005.08.391

Chochinov, H., Hack, T., McClement, S., Kristjanson, L. and Harlos, M. (2002) 'Dignity in the terminally ill: A developing empirical model.' *Social Science and Medicine*, 54, 433–443. doi:10.1016/S0277-9536(01)00084-3

Chonody, J. and Wang, D. (2013) 'Connecting older adults to the community through multimedia: An intergenerational reminiscence program.' *Activities, Adaptation and Aging*, 37, 79–93. doi:10.1080/01924788.2012.760140

Choy, J.C. and Lou, V.W. (2016) 'Effectiveness of the Modified Instrumental Reminiscence Intervention on psychological wellbeing among community-dwelling Chinese older adults: A randomized controlled trial.' *American Journal of Geriatric Psychiatry*, 24, 1, 60–69.

Clandinin, D.J. (2006) 'Narrative inquiry: A methodology for studying lived experience.' *Research Studies in Music Education*, 27, 44–54.

Clandinin, D.J. and Roziek, J. (2006) 'Mapping a Landscape of Narrative Inquiry: Borderland Spaces and Tensions.' In D.J. Clandinin (ed.) *Handbook of Narrative Inquiry: Mapping a Methodology*. Thousand Oaks, CA: Sage.

Cohen, G.D. (2005) *The Mature Mind: The Positive Power of the Aging Brain*. New York: Basic Books.

Cohen, G.D. (2006) 'Research on creativity and aging: The positive impact of the arts on health and illness.' *Generations* 30, 1, 7–15.

Cohen, G.D. (2009) 'New theories and research findings on the positive influence of music and art on health with aging.' *Arts and Health*, I, 1 48–62.

Cohler, B.J. and Cole, T.R. (1996) 'Studying older lives: Reciprocal acts of telling and listening.' *Aging and Biography: Explorations in Adult Development*, 61–76.

Coleman, P.G. (1974) 'Measuring reminiscence characteristics from conversation as adaptive features of old age.' *International Journal of Aging and Human Development*, 5, 281–294.

Coleman, P.G. (1984) Assessing self-esteem and its sources in elderly people.' *Ageing and Society*, 4, 117–135.

Coleman, P.G. (1986a) *Ageing and Reminiscence Processes*. Chichester: Wiley.

Coleman, P.G. (1986b) 'Issues in the Therapeutic Use of Reminiscence with Elderly People.' In I. Hanley and M. Gilhooly (eds) *Psychological Therapies for the Elderly* (pp.41–64). London: Croom Helm.

Coleman, P.G., Ivani-Chalian, C. and Robinson, M. (2015) *Self and Meaning in the Lives of Older People: Case Studies Over Twenty Years*. Cambridge: Cambridge University Press.

Connelly, D.M., Carnahan, H. and Vandervoort, A.A. (2000) 'Motor skill learning of concentric and eccentric isokinetic movements in older adults.' *Experimental Aging Research*, 26, 209–222.

Conway, M.A. (2005) 'Memory and the self.' *Journal of Memory and Language*, 53, 594–628.

Cooney, A., Hunter, A., Murphy, K., Casey, D. *et al.* (2014) 'Seeing me through my memories: A grounded theory study on using reminiscence with people with dementia living in long-term care.' *Journal of Clinical Nursing*, 23, 23–24, 3564–3574.

Cosley, D., Akey, K., Alson, B., Baxter. J. *et al.* (2009) 'Using Technologies to Support Reminiscence.' *Proceedings of the 23rd British HCI Group Annual Conference on People and Computers: Celebrating People and Technology* (pp.480–484).

Cosley, D., Sosik, V.S., Schultz, J., Peesapati, S.T. and Lee, S. (2012) 'Experiences in designing tools for everyday reminiscing.' *Journal of Human-Computer Interaction*, 27, 1–2.

Coyle, S.M. (2014) *Uncovering Spiritual Narratives: Using Story in Pastoral Care and Ministry*. Minneapolis, MN: Fortress Press.

Crites, S. (1971) 'The Narrative Quality of Experience.' *Journal of the American Academy of Religion*, 3, 291–311. Also in S. Hauerwas and L.J. Jones (eds) (1997) *Why Narrative? Readings in Narrative Theology* (pp.293–302). Grand Rapids, MI: W.B. Eerdmans Publishing.

Cully, J.A., La Voie, D. and Gfeller, J.D. (2001) 'Reminiscence, personality and psychological functioning in older adults.' *The Gerontologist*, 41, 89–95. doi:10.1093/geront/41.1.8

Currier, J.M., Irish, J.E., Neimeyer, R.A. and Foster, J.D. (2015) 'Attachment, continuing bonds and complicated grief following violent loss: Testing a moderated model.' *Death Studies*, 39, 201–210. doi:10.1080/07481187.2014.975869

Damasio, A.R. (2010) *Self Comes to Mind*. New York: Pantheon Books.

Dambrun, M. and Ricard, M. (2011) 'Self-centeredness and selflessness: A theory of self-based psychological functioning and its consequences for happiness.' *Review of General Psychology*, 15, 138–157. doi:10.1037/a0023059

Daniels, L.R., Boehnlein, J.K. and McCallion, P. (2015) 'Life-review and PTSD community counseling with two groups of Vietnam War veterans.' *Traumatology*, 21, 3, 161–171.

Davis, C.G., Nolen-Hoeksema, S. and Larson, J. (1998) 'Making sense of loss and benefiting from the experience: Two construals of meaning.' *Journal of Personality and Social Psychology*, 75, 2, 561–574. doi:10.1037/0022-3514.75.2.561

Davison, E.H., Kaiser, A.P., Spiro, A., Moye, J. *et al.* (2015) 'From late-onset stress symptomatology to later-adulthood trauma reengagement in aging combat veterans: Taking a broader view.' *The Gerontologist*, 56, 1, 14–21.

Deschamps, A., Fasotti, L., Jungheim, J., Leone, E., Dood, E. and Allioux, A. (2011) 'Effects of different learning methods for instrumental activities of daily living in patients with Alzheimer's dementia: A pilot study.' *Journal of Alzheimer's Disease and Other Dementias*, 26 273–281.

Degroot, J.M. (2012) 'Maintaining relational continuity with the deceased on Facebook.' *OMEGA: Journal of Death and Dying*, 65, 195–212. doi:10.2190/om.65.3.c

Delello, J.A. and McWhorter, R.R. (2015) 'Reducing the digital divide: Connecting older adults to iPad technology.' *Journal of Applied Gerontology*. doi:10.1177/0733464815589985

de Medeiros, K. (2005) 'The complementary self: Multiple perspectives on the aging person.' *Journal of Aging Studies*, 19, 1, 1–13. doi:10.1016/j.jaging.2004.02.001

de Medeiros, K. (2007) 'Beyond the memoir: Telling life stories using multiple literary forms.' *Journal of Aging, Humanities and the Arts*, 1, 3–4, 159–167. doi:10.1080/19325610701 638052

de Medeiros, K. (2011a) 'Self stories in older age: Crafting identities using small moments from the past.' *Amerikastudien/American Studies*, 53, 1, 103–122.

de Medeiros, K. (2011b) 'Telling Stories: How Do Expressions of Self Differ in a Writing Group Versus a Reminiscence Group?' In G. Kenyon, E. Bohlmeijer and W.L. Randall (eds) *Storying Later life: Issues, Investigations, and Interventions in Narrative Gerontology* (pp.159–176). New York: Oxford University Press.

de Medeiros, K. (2014) *Narrative Gerontology in Research and Practice*. New York: Springer Publishing.

de Medeiros, K., Mosby, A., Hanley, K.B., Pedraza, M.S. and Brandt, J. (2011) 'A randomized clinical trial of a writing workshop intervention to improve autobiographical memory and wellbeing in older adults.' *International Journal of Geriatric Psychiatry*, 26, 8, 803–811. doi:10.1002/gps.2605

Demiray, B., Mischler, M. and Martin, M. (2017) 'Reminiscence in everyday conversations: A naturalistic observation study of older adults.' *Journals of Gerontology: Psychological Sciences*. doi:10.1093/geronb/gbx141

Deng, D., Deng, Q., Liu, X., Xie, C.H. *et al.* (2015) 'Expectation in life review: A term of spiritual needs easily understood by Chinese hospice patients.' *American Journal of Hospice and Palliative Medicine*, 32, 7, 725–731. doi:10.1177/1049909114539727

Denham, S.A., Bassett, H.H. and Wyatt, T. (2007) 'The Socialization of Emotional Competence.' In J.E. Grusec and P.D. Hastings (eds) *Handbook of Socialization: Theory and Research* (pp.614–637). New York: Guilford Press.

Dennis, M.R. (2008) 'The grief account: Dimensions of a contemporary bereavement genre.' *Death Studies,* 32, 801–836. doi:10.1080/07481180801928980

Department of Health (2016) *O'Neill launches dementia learning and development framework.* Accessed on 29/04/2017 at www.health-ni.gov.uk/news/oneill-launches-dementia-learning-and development-framework.

Devisch, I. and Murray, S. (2009) '"We hold these truths to be self-evident": Deconstructing "evidence-based" medical practice.' *Journal of Evaluation in Clinical Practice,* 15, 950–954.

de Vries, B., Birren, J.E. and Deutchman, D.E. (1990) 'Adult development through guided autobiography: The family context.' *Family Relations,* 39, 1, 3–7.

de Vries, B., Blando, J., Southard, P. and Bubeck, C. (2001) 'The Times of Our Lives.' In G. Kenyon, P. Clark and B. de Vries (eds) *Narrative Gerontology: Theory, Research, and Practice.* New York: Springer Publishing.

de Vries, B., Bluck, S. and Birren, J.E. (1993) 'The understanding of death and dying in a life-span perspective.' *Gerontologist,* 33, 366–372. doi:10.1093/geront/33.3.366

de Vries, B. and Rutherford, J. (2004) 'Memorializing loved ones on the World Wide Web.' *OMEGA: Journal of Death and Dying,* 49, 1, 5–26. doi:10.2190/dr46-ru57-uy6p-newm

de Vries, B. and Thornton, J.E. (2018) 'Research on guided autobiography: A review of content, process, and outcome.' *International Journal of Reminiscence and Life Review,* 5, 1, 22–27.

Dickson-Swift, V., James, E.L., Kippen, J.E. and Liamputtong, P. (2006) 'Blurring boundaries in qualitative health research on sensitive topics.' *Qualitative Health Research,* 16, 6, 853–871.

Diener, E., Emmons, R.A., Larsen, R.J. and Griffin, S. (1985) 'The satisfaction with lifescale.' *Journal of Personality Assessment,* 49, 1, 71–75.

Disch, R. (1988) *Twenty-Five Years of the Life Review: Theoretical and Practical Considerations.* New York: Haworth Press.

Dittmann-Kohli, F. (1990) 'The construction of meaning in old age: Possibilities and constraints.' *Ageing and Society,* 10, 279–294.

Dobrof, R. (1984) 'Introduction: A Time for Reclaiming the Past.' In M. Kaminsky (ed.) *The Uses of Reminiscence: New Ways of Working with Older Adults* (pp.xvii–xix). New York: Haworth Press.

Domino, G. and Affonso, D.D. (1990) 'A personality measure of Erikson's life stages: The Inventory of Psychosocial Balance.' *Journal of Personality Assessment,* 54, 3–4, 576–588.

Duke, M.P., Lazarus, A. and Fivush, R. (2008) 'Knowledge of family history as a clinically useful index of psychological wellbeing and prognosis: A brief report.' *Psychotherapy Theory, Research, Practice, Training,* 45, 268–272.

Dunlop, W.L. and Tracy, J.L. (2013) 'Sobering stories: Narratives of self-redemption predict behavioral change and improved health among recovering alcoholics.' *Journal of Personality and Social Psychology,* 104, 576–590.

Dunsmore, J.C. and Karn, M.A. (2001) 'Mothers' beliefs about feelings and children's emotional understanding.' *Early Education and Development,* 12117138. doi:10.1207/s15566935eed1201-7

Eisenberg, N., Cumberland, A. and Spinrad, T.L. (1998) 'Parental socialization of emotion.' *Psychological Inquiry,* 9, 241–273.

Eisenberg, N., Fabes, R.A. and Murphy, B.C. (1996) 'Parents' reactions to children's negative emotions: Relations to children's social competence and comforting behavior.' *Child Development,* 67, 2227–2247. doi:10.2307/1131620

Elfrink, T.R., Zuidema, S.U., Kunz, M. and Westerhof, G. (2017) 'The effectiveness of creating an online life story book on persons with early dementia and their informal caregivers: A protocol of a randomized controlled trial.' *BMC Geriatrics,* 17, 95. doi:10.1186/S12877-017-0471-Y

El Haj, M. and Antoine, P. (2016) 'Death preparation and boredom reduction as functions of reminiscence in Alzheimer's disease.' *Journal of Alzheimer's Disease*, 54, 2, 515–523. doi:10.3233/JAD-160497

Eliot, T.S. (1969) *Four Quartets. The Complete Poems and Plays*. London: Faber and Faber.

Erikson, E.H. (1959) 'Identity and the life cycle: Selected papers.' *Psychological Issues*, 1.

Erikson, E.H. (1963) *Childhood and Society* (2nd ed). New York: W.W. Norton and Company. (Original work published 1950).

Erikson, E.H. (1968) *Identity Youth and Crisis*. New York: W.W. Norton and Company. (Original work published 1959).

Erikson, E.H. (1978) 'Reflections on Dr Borg's Life Cycle.' In E.H. Erikson (ed.) *Adulthood*. New York: W.W. Norton and Company.

Erikson, E.H. and Erikson, J. (1997) *The Life Cycle Completed: Extended Version*. New York: W.W. Norton and Company.

Erikson, E.H., Erikson, J.M. and Kivnick, H.Q. (1986) *Vital Involvement in Old Age*. New York: W.W. Norton and Company.

Eritz, H., Hadjistavropoulos, T., Williams, J., Kroeker, K. *et al.* (2016) 'A life history intervention for individuals with dementia: A randomised controlled trial examining nursing staff empathy, perceived patient personhood and aggressive behaviours.' *Ageing and Society*, 36, 10, 2061–2089.

Eschenbruch, N. (2007) '"The good life is not beyond suffering": Narrative reflections on old hospice patients.' *Journal of Aging, Humanities and the Arts*, 1, 3–4, 169–176. doi:10.1080/19325610701638060. Published online 23 October 2007.

European Reminiscence Network's Projects and RYCT Training. Accessed on 06/03/2018 at www.europeanreminiscencenetwork.org.

Evans, G.E. (1906) 'The Women of the West.' In *The Secret Key and Other Verses*. The Australian Poetry Library. Accessed on 10/03/2018 at www.poetry/library.edu.au/Poems-book/ the secret key-and-other-verses-0015000.

Every-Palmer, E. and Howick, J. (2014) 'How evidence-based medicine is failing due to biased trials and selective publication.' *Journal of Evaluation in Clinical Practice*, 20, 6, 1–12. doi.org/10.1111/jep.12147

Fagerstrom, K.M. (2002) 'The Effects of Life Review on Wellbeing in The Elderly.' Master's thesis for California State University, San Bernadino.

Field, N.P., Nichols, C., Holen, A. and Horowitz, M.J. (1999) 'The relation of continuing attachment to adjustment in conjugal bereavement.' *Journal of Consulting and Clinical Psychology*, 67, 212. doi:10.1037/0022-006X.67.2.212

Fiese, B.H., Hooker, K.A., Kotary, L., Scwagler, J. *et al.* (1995) 'Family stories in the early stages of parenthood.' *Journal of Marriage and the Family*, 57, 763–770.

Fivush, R. (2007) 'Maternal reminiscing style and children's developing understanding of self and emotion.' *Clinical Social Work*, 35, 37–46.

Fivush, R. (2008) 'Remembering and reminiscing: How individual lives are constructed in family narratives.' *Memory Studies*, 1, 49–58.

Fivush, R. (2011) 'The development of autobiographical memory.' *Annual Review of Psychology*, 62, 559–582.

Fivush, R., Berlin, L.J., Sales, J.M., Mennuti-Washburn, J. *et al.* (2003) 'Functions of parent-child reminiscing about emotionally negative events.' *Memory*, 11, 179–192. doi:10.1080/09658210244000351

Fivush, R., Bohanek, J.G. and Duke, M. (2008) 'The Intergenerational Self: Subjective Perspective and Family History.' In F. Sani (ed.) *Individual and Collective Self-Continuity* (pp.131–144). Mahwah, NJ: Lawrence Erlbaum Associates.

Fivush, R., Bohanek, J.G. and Zaman, W. (2010) 'Personal and Intergenerational Narratives in Relation to Adolescents Wellbeing.' In T. Habermas (ed.) *The Development of Autobiographical Reasoning in Adolescence and Beyond: New Directions in Child and Adolescent Development*, 4, 131, 45–57.

Fivush, R., Booker, J.A. and Graci, M.E. (2017) 'Ongoing narrative meaning-making within events and across the lifespan.' *Imagination, Cognition, and Personality*, 37, 127–152.

Fivush, R. and Graci, M.E. (2017) 'Autobiographical Memory.' In J. Wixted (ed.) *Learning and Memory: A Comprehensive Reference* (2nd ed). Amsterdam: Elsevier.

Fivush, R., Habermas, T., Waters, T. and Zaman, W. (2011) 'The making of autobiographical memory: Intersections of culture, narratives and identity.' *International Journal of Psychology*, 46, 5, 321–345.

Fivush, R. and Haden, C.A. (2003) *Autobiographical Memory and the Construction of a Narrative Self: Developmental and Cultural Perspectives*. Mahwah, NJ: Lawrence Erlbaum Associates.

Fivush, R., Haden, C.A. and Adam, S. (1995) 'Structure and coherence of preschoolers-personal narratives over time: Implications for childhood amnesia.' *Journal of Experimental Child Psychology*, 60, 32–56.

Fivush, R., Haden, C.A. and Reese, E. (2006) 'Elaborating on elaborations: The role of maternal reminiscing style in cognitive and socioemotional development.' *Child Development*, 77, 1568–1588.

Fivush. R. and Merrill, N. (2016) 'An ecological systems approach to family narratives.' *Memory Studies*, 9, 305–314.

Fivush, R. and Sales, J.M. (2006) 'Coping, attachment and mother-child narratives of stressful events.' *Merrill-Palmer Quarterly*, 52, 125–150.

Fivush, R. and Zaman, W. (2013) 'Gender and Autobiographical Consciousness.' In P.J. Bauer and R. Fivush (eds) *The Handbook of Children's Memory Development*. New York: Wiley-Blackwell.

Flaskerud, J.H. (2017) 'Individual and dynamic: Western views of a good death.' *Issues in Mental Health Nursing*, 38, 1–4. doi:10.1080/01612840.2017.1295492

Folstein, M.F., Folstein, S.E. and McHugh, P.R. (1975) '"Mini Mental State": A practical method for grading the cognitive state of patients for the clinician.' *Journal of Psychiatry Research*, 12, 189–198.

Ford, D.F. (1985) 'The best apologetics is good systematics: A proposal for the place of narrative in systematic theology.' *Anglican Theological Review*, LXVI 11, 3, 232–254.

Fortner, B.V. and Neimeyer, R.A. (1999) 'Death anxiety in older adults: A quantitative review.' *Death Studies*, 23, 5, 387–411.

Frank, A. (2013) *The Wounded Story Teller: Body, Illness and Ethics* (2nd ed). Chicago, IL: University of Chicago Press.

Frankl, V.E. (1984) *Man's Search for Meaning* (2nd ed). New York: Washington Square Press. (Original work published 1963).

Frattaroli, J. (2006) 'Experimental disclosure and its moderators: A meta-analysis.' *Psychological Bulletin*, 132, 823–865.

Freeman, M. (2011) 'Narrative Foreclosure in Later Life: Possibilities and Limits.' In G. Kenyon, E. Bohlmeijer and W.L. Randall (eds) *Storying Later Life: Issues, Investigations, and Interventions in Narrative Gerontology*. New York: Oxford University Press.

Freeman, M. (2016) 'The Gift of Giving: A Case Study in Narrative Care.' Keynote lecture conference on Changing the Conversation about Serious Illness: The Future of Palliative Care, Collaborative for Palliative Care, White Plains, NY.

Freud, S. (1953) 'Mourning and Melancholia.' In J. Strachey (ed.) *Standard Edition of the Complete Psychological Works of Sigmund Freud* (vol. 14). London: Hogarth. (Original work published 1917).

Gabrian, M., Dutt, A.J. and Wahl, H.W. (2017) 'Subjective time perceptions and aging well: A review of concepts and empirical research: A mini review.' *Gerontology*. doi:10.1159/000470906

Garland, J. and Garland, C. (2001) *Life Review in Health and Social Care*. Philadelphia, PA: Taylor & Francis.

Garner, P.W., Dunsmore, J.C. and Southam-Gerrow, M. (2008) 'Mother-child conversations about emotions: Linkages to child aggression and prosocial behavior.' *Social Development,* 17, 259–277. doi:10.1111/j.1467-9507.2007. 0042

Garrett, C.R. (2015) 'Unremembered in the heartland of Iowa.' (Unpublished).

Genevro, J.L., Marshall, T., Miller, T. and Center for the Advancement of Health (2004) 'Report on bereavement and grief research.' *Death Studies,* 28, 491–491. doi:10.1080/07481180490461188

Gibson, A., McCauley, C.O., Mulvenna, M.D., Ryan, A.A. *et al.* (2016) 'Assessing Usability Testing for People with Dementia.' REHAB-2016 Workshop-4th Workshop on ICTS. Improving Patients' Rehabilitation Research Techniques, ACM Digital Library.1-58113-000-0/0010.

Gibson, F. (1989) *Do You Mind the Time? Northern Ireland Recall.* London: Help the Aged.

Gibson, F. (1994) 'What Can Reminiscence Contribute to People with Dementia?' In J. Bornat (ed.) *Reminiscence Reviewed: Perspectives, Evaluations and Achievements* (pp.46–60). Berkshire: Open University.

Gibson, F. (2000) *The Reminiscence Trainer's Pack.* London: Age Concern.

Gibson, F. (2004) *The Past in the Present: Reminiscence in Health and Social Care.* Baltimore, MD: Health Professions Press.

Gibson, F. (2011) *Reminiscence and Life Story Work: A Practice Guide* (4th ed). London: Jessica Kingsley Publishers.

Gibson, F. and Bruce, E. (1998) Evaluators' Report. European Reminiscence Network Conference Papers, Remembering Yesterday, Caring Today. London: Age Exchange.

Gillies, J. and Neimeyer, R.A. (2006) 'Loss, grief, and the search for significance: Toward a model of meaning reconstruction in bereavement.' *Journal of Constructivist Psychology,* 19, 31–65. doi:10.1080/ 10720530500311182

Glover, M. (2014) *A House Called Askival.* Glasgow: Freight Books.

Goffman, E. (1959) *The Presentation of Self in Everyday Life.* London: Penguin Books.

Gomes, B. and Higginson, I.J. (2008) 'Where people die (1974–2030): Past trends, future projections and implications for care.' *Palliative Medicine,* 22, 33–41. doi:10.1177/0269216307084606

Good, A., Wilson, C., Ancient, C. and Sambhanthan, A. (2012) 'A Proposal to Support Wellbeing in People with Borderline Personality Disorder: Applying Reminiscent Theory in a Mobile App.' In *The ACM Conference on Designing Interactive Systems.* New York: ACM Press.

Gottschall, J. (2012) *The Storytelling Animal: How Stories Make Us Human.* Boston, MA: Houghton Mifflin, Harcourt.

Gowans, G., Campbell, J., Alm, N., Dye, R. *et al.* (2004) 'Designing a Multimedia Conversation Aid for Reminiscence Therapy in Dementia Care Environments.' In *CHI'04 Extended Abstracts on Human Factors in Computing Systems (CHI EA 04)* (pp. 825–836). New York: ACM Press.

Grace, L., Dewhurst, S.A. and Anderson, R.J. (2016) 'A dysphoric's TALE: The relationship between the self-reported functions of autobiographical memory and symptoms of depression.' *Memory,* 24, 9, 1173–1181. doi:10.1080/09658211.2015.1084009

Granek, L. (2010) 'Grief as pathology: The evolution of grief theory in psychology from Freud to the present.' *History of Psychology,* 13, 46. doi:10.1037/a0016991

Greenberg, M.A. and Stone, A.A. (1992) 'Emotional disclosure about traumas and its relation to health: Effects of previous disclosure and trauma severity.' *Journal of Personality and Social Psychology,* 63, 75–84.

Greenhoot, A.F. and McLean, K. (2013) 'Introduction to this special issue: Meaning in personal memories: Is more always better?' *Memory,* 21, 2–9.

Groenewoud, J.H. and de Lange, J.J. (2014) *Evaluation of Personalised Happy Games on the iPad for People with Dementia.* Rotterdam: Kenniscentrum zorginnovatie.

Grusec, J.E. (2002) 'Parental Socialization and Children's Acquisition of Values.' In M.H. Bornstein (ed.) *Handbook of Parenting: Practical Issues in Parenting* Vol. 5 (pp.143–168). Mahwah, NJ: Lawrence Erlbaum Associates.

Gulotta, R., Odom, W., Forlizzi, J. and Faste, H. (2013) 'Digital Artifacts as Legacy: Exploring the Lifespan and Value of Digital Data.' *Proceedings of the SIGCHI Conference on Human Factors in Computing Systems*, 1813–1822. doi:10.1145/2470654.2466240

Gudex, C., Horsted, C., Jensen, A.M., Kjer, M. and Surensen, J. (2010) 'Consequences from use of reminiscence – A randomised intervention study in ten Danish nursing homes.' *BMC Geriatrics*, 10, 33. doi:org/10.1186/1471-2318-10-33

Haber, D. (2006) 'Life Review: Implementation, theory, and therapy.' *The International Journal of Aging and Human Development*, 63, 2, 153–171.

Habermas, T. and Bluck, S. (2000) 'Getting a life: The emergence of the life story in adolescence.' *Psychological Bulletin*, 126, 748–769.

Habermas, T. and Reese, E. (2015) 'Getting a life takes time: The development of the life story in adolescence, its precursors and consequences.' *Human Development*, 58, 3, 172–201.

Haesner, M., Steinert, A., O'Sullivan, J.L. and Weichenberger, M. (2015) 'Evaluating an online cognitive training platform for older adults: User experience and implementation requirements.' *Journal of Gerontological Nursing*, 41, 8, 22–31.

Hagman, G. (1995) 'Mourning: A review and reconsideration.' *The International Journal of Psycho-analysis*, 76, 909–925.

Haight, B. (1992) 'The Structured Life-review Process: A Community Approach to the Ageing Client.' In G.M. Jones and B.M. Miesen (eds) *Caregiving in Dementia* (pp.277–292). London: Routledge.

Haight, B.K. (1998a) 'The therapeutic role of a structured life review process in homebound elderly subjects.' *Journal of Gerontology*, 43, 40–44.

Haight, B.K. (1998b) 'Use of Life Review and Life Story Books in Families with Alzheimer's Disease.' In. P. Schweitzer (ed.) *Reminiscence in Dementia Care*. London: Age Exchange.

Haight, B.K. and Gibson, F. (eds) (2005) *Burnside's Working with Older Adults: Group Process and Techniques* (4th ed). Sudbury, MA: Jones and Bartlett.

Haight, B.K., Bachman, D., Hendrix, S., Wagner, M. *et al.* (2003) 'Life review: Treating the dyadic family unit with dementia.' *Clinical Psychology and Psychotherapy*, 10, 3, 165–174.

Haight, B. K. and Burnside, I. (1993) 'Reminiscence and life review: Explaining the differences.' *Archives of Psychiatric Nursing*, 7, 2, 91–98.

Haight, B.K., Coleman, P. and Lord, K. (1995) 'The Linchpins of a Successful Life Review: Structure, Evaluation, and Individuality.' In B.K. Haight and J.D. Webster (eds) *The Art and Science of Reminiscing: Theory, Research, Methods, and Applications* (pp.179–192). Philadelphia, PA: Taylor & Francis.

Haight, B.K. and Dias, J. (1992) 'Examining key variables in selected reminiscence modalities.' *International Journal of Psychogeriatrics*, 4, (Sup. 2), 279–290.

Haight, B.K., Gibson, F. and Michel, Y. (2006) The Northern Ireland life review/life story book project for people with dementia.' *Alzheimer's and Dementia*, 2, 56–58.

Haight, B.K. and Haight, B.S. (2007) *The Handbook of Structured Life Review*. Baltimore, MD: Health Professions Press.

Haight, B.K. and Hendrix, S. (1995) 'An Integrated View of Reminiscence.' In B.K. Haight and J.D. Webster *The Art and Science of Reminiscing* (pp.3–21). Washington, DC. Taylor & Francis.

Haight, B.K., Michel, Y. and Hendrix, S. (1998) 'Life review: Preventing despair in newly relocated nursing home residents: Short- and long-term effects.' *International Journal of Aging and Human Development*, 47, 2, 119–142.

Haight, B.K. and Webster, J.D. (1995) *The Art and Science of Reminiscing: Theory, Research, Methods and Applications*. Washington, DC: Taylor & Francis.

Halberstadt, A.G., Denham, S.A. and Dunsmore, J.C. (2001) 'Affective social competence.' *Social Development,* 10, 79–119.

Hallford, D.J. (2016) 'Autobiographical memory-based intervention for depressive symptoms in young adults: A randomized controlled trial of cognitive-reminiscence therapy.' *Psychotherapy and Psychosomatics,* 85, 4, 246–249.

Hallford, D.J. and Mellor, D. (2015) 'Autobiographical memory and depression: Identity-continuity and problem-solving functions indirectly predict symptoms of depression over time through psychological wellbeing.' *Applied Cognitive Psychology,* 30, 2, 152–159. doi:10.1002/acp.3169

Hallford, D.J. and Mellor, D. (2016a) 'Autobiographical memory and depression: Identity-continuity and problem-solving functions indirectly predict symptoms over time through psychological wellbeing.' *Applied Cognitive Psychology,* 30, 2, 152–159.

Hallford, D.J. and Mellor, D. (2016b) 'Brief reminiscence activities improve state wellbeing and self-concept in young adults: A randomised controlled experiment.' *Memory,* 24, 10, 1311–1320. doi: 10.1080/09658211.2015.1103875

Hallford, D.J. and Mellor, D. (2017) 'Development and validation of the Awareness of Narrative Identity Questionnaire (ANIQ).' *Assessment,* 24, 3, 399–413.

Hallford, D.J., Mellor, D. and Cummins, R.A. (2013) 'Adaptive autobiographical memory in younger and older adults: The indirect association of integrative and instrumental reminiscence with depressive symptoms.' *Memory,* 21, 4, 444–457. doi: 10.1080/09658211.2012.736523

Hamel, A.V., Sims, T.L., Klassen, D., Harvey, T. and Gaugler, J.E. (2016) 'Memory Matters: A mixed-method feasibility study of a mobile aid to stimulate reminiscence in individuals with memory loss.' *Journal of Gerontological Nursing,* 42, 7, 15–24.

Hannah, M., Domino, G., Figueredo, A.J. and Hendrickson, R. (1996) 'The prediction of ego integrity in older persons.' *Educational and Psychological Measurement,* 56, 6, 930–950.

Hannan, R., Thompson, R. and Worthington, A. (2013) *The Triangle of Care. Carers Included: A Guide to Best Practice in Dementia Care in Scotland.* London: Carers Trust and Royal College of Nursing.

Hanson, E., Magnusson, L., Arvidsson, H., Claesson, A., Keady, J. and Nolan, M. (2007) 'Working together with persons with early stage dementia and their family members to design a user-friendly technology-based support service.' *Dementia,* 6, 3, 411–434.

Hardy, P. and Summer, T. (2010) 'Humanizing Health-Care.' In J. Lambert (ed.) *Digital Storytelling: Capturing Lives, Creating Community* (3rd ed) (pp.143–156). Berkeley, CA: Digital Diner Press.

Harris, I. (2016) *Surgery: The Ultimate Placebo.* Sydney: Newsouth Books.

Harris, C.B., Rasmussen, A.S. and Berntsen, D. (2014) 'The functions of autobiographical memory: An integrative approach.' *Memory,* 22, 5, 559–581. doi: 10.1080/09658211.2013.806555

Haslam, C., Haslam, S.A., Ysseldyk, R., McCloskey, L.G., Pfisterer, K. and Brown, S.G. (2014) 'Social identification moderates cognitive health and wellbeing following story- and song-based reminiscence.' *Aging and Mental Health,* 18, 4, 425–434. doi:10.1080/13607863.2013.845871

Haug, F. (1999) *Female Sexualization: A Collective Work of Memory.* New York: Verso.

Huang, H.C., Chen, Y.T., Chen, P.Y., Hu, S.H. *et al.* (2015) 'Reminiscence therapy improves cognitive functions and reduces depressive symptoms in elderly people with dementia: A meta-analysis of randomized controlled trials.' *Journal of the American Medical Directors Association,* 16, 12, 1087–1094.

Hecht, A. and Tyrrell, M. (2007) 'Life Stories as Heirlooms: The Personal History Industry.' In J. Kunz and F. Soltys (eds) *Transformational Reminiscence: Life Story Work.* New York: Springer Publishing.

Heintzelman, S.J. and King, L.A. (2014) 'Life is pretty meaningful.' *American Psychologist*, 69, 561–574.

Hellstrom, I., Nolan, M., Nordenfelt, L. and Lundh, U. (2007) 'Ethical and methodological issues in interviewing persons with dementia.' *Nursing Ethics*, 14, 608–619.

Help the Aged (1981) *Recall.* London: Help the Aged.

Hendrix, S. and Haight, B.K. (2002) 'A Continued Review of Reminiscence.' In J.D. Webster and B.K. Haight (eds) *Critical Advances in Reminiscence Work: From Theory to Application* (pp.3–29). New York: Springer Publishing.

Henkel, L.A., Kris, A., Birney, S. and Krauss, K. (2017) 'The functions and value of reminiscence for older adults in long-term residential care facilities.' *Memory*, 25(3), 425–435. doi:10.1080/09658211.2016.1182554

Hepper, E.G., Wildschut, T., Sedikides, C., Ritchie, T.D. *et al.* (2014) 'Pan cultural nostalgia: Prototypical conceptions across cultures.' *Emotion*, 14, 4, 733–747. doi:10.1037/a0036790.supp

History Alive (2018) Accessed on 22/02/2018 at http://historyalive-tw.com.

Hofer, J., Busch, H., Šolcová, I.P. and Tavel, P. (2017) 'When reminiscence is harmful: The relationship between self-negative reminiscence functions, need satisfaction and depressive symptoms among elderly people from Cameroon, the Czech Republic and Germany.' *Journal of Happiness Studies*, 18, 389–407. doi:10.1007/s10902-016-9731-3

Hsiang Shang Culture and Education Foundation (2018) Accessed on 14/02/2018 at www.carelove.org.tw.

Hsu, H. (2015) 'Introduction of Active Aging Index.' *The Journal of Long-Term Care*, 19, 4, 109–115.

Hu, Y. and Chou, Y. (1996) 'Women and three generation dwelling: An exploration of old women's finance dependency and living arrangement problems.' *Journal of Women and Gender Studies*, 7, 27–57.

Hunter, E.G. and Rowles, G.D. (2005) 'Leaving a legacy: Toward a typology.' *Journal of Aging Studies*, 19, 327–347. doi:10.1016/j.jaging.2004.08.002

Ingersoll-Dayton, B., Spencer, B., Campbell, R., Kurokowa, Y. and Ito, M. (2016) 'Creating a duet: The Couples Life Story Approach.' *Dementia*, 15, 4, 481–493.

International Institute for Reminiscence and Life Review (2013) *The Global Survey of Reminiscence and Life Review.* Superior: University of Wisconsin: IIRLR.

International Journal of Reminiscence and Life Review (2018) *Special Issue: In Honor of James Emmett Birren (1918–2016).* Accessed on 23/06/2018 at http://143.95.253.101/~radfordojs/index.php/IJRLR/issue/current.

Istvandity, L. (2017) 'Combining music and reminiscence therapy interventions for wellbeing in elderly populations.' *Complementary Therapies in Clinical Practice*, 28, 18–25.

James, W. (1981) *The Principles of Psychology.* Cambridge, MA: Harvard University Press. (Original work published 1890).

James, D.T., Gibson, F., McCauley, G. and McCauley, J. (1995) 'Teaching Older People to Use Computers: Evolution and Evaluation of a Course.' In C.A. Robertson (ed.) *Ergonomics* (pp.262–267). London: Taylor & Francis.

Janoff-Bulman, R. and McPherson F.C. (1997) 'The Impact of Trauma on Meaning: From Meaningless World to Meaningful Life.' In M. Power and C.R. Brewin (eds) *The Transformation of Meaning in Psychological Therapies: Integrating Theory and Practice* (pp.91–106). New York: Wiley.

Jenkins, D. (2004) 'Geriatric Burden or Elderly Blessing?' In A. Jewell (ed.) *Ageing, Spirituality and Wellbeing* (pp.197–202). London: Jessica Kingsley Publishers.

Johnson, C.W., Singh, A.A. and Gonzalez, M. (2014) '"It's complicated": Collective memories of transgender, queer, and questioning youth in high school.' *Journal of Homosexuality*, 61, 3, 419–434.

Johnson, M.L. (1976) 'That Was Your Life: A Biographical Approach to Later Life.' In V. Carver and P. Liddiard (eds) *An Ageing Population: Reader and Source Book*. London: Hodder and Stoughton.

Jung, C.G. (1933) *The Stages of Life: Modern Man in Search of a Soul*. Orlando, FL: Harcourt Brace.

Kadel Taras, S. (2013) *Mountain Girls. Time Pieces, Personal Biographies*. Accessed on 10/03/2018 at http://timepiecesbios.com.

Kaminsky, M. (ed.) (1984a) *New Ways of Working with Older Adults*. New York: Haworth Press.

Kaminsky, M. (1984b) 'All That Our Eyes Have Witnessed: Memories of a Living History Workshop in the South Bronx.' In Disch, R. (ed.) *Twenty-Five Years of the Life Review: Theoretical and Practical Considerations* (pp.101–109). New York: Haworth Press.

Karlsson, E., Axelsson, K., Zingmark, K., Fahlander, K. and Savenstedt, S. (2014) '"Carpe Diem": Supporting conversations between individuals with dementia and their family members.' *Journal of Gerontological Nursing*, 40, 2, 38–46.

Karlsson, E., Axelsson, K., Zingmark, K. and Savenstedt, S. (2011) 'The challenge of coming to terms with the use of a new digital assistive device: A case study among two persons with mild dementia.' *Open Nursing Journal*, 5, 102–110. doi:10.2174/1874434601105 0100102

Kastenbaum, R.J. (2015) *Death, Society, and Human Experience* (11th ed). Upper Saddle River, NJ: Pearson.

Katz, L.F., Maliken, A.C. and Stettler, N.M. (2012) 'Parental meta-emotion philosophy: A review of research and a theoretical framework.' *Child Development Perspectives*, 6, 417–422. doi:10.1111/j.1750-8606.2012.00244.x

Keal, R.M., Clayton, J.M. and Butow, P.N. (2015) 'Therapeutic life review in palliative care A systematic review of quantitative evaluations.' *Journal of Pain and Symptom Management*, 49, 4, 747–761.

Keck, D. (1996) *Forgetting Whose We Are. Alzheimer's Disease and the Love of God*. Nashville, TN: Abingdon Press.

Kelly, F. (2010) 'Recognising and supporting self in dementia: A new way to facilitate a person-centred approach to dementia care.' *Ageing and Society*, 30, 103–124.

Kemp, M. (1978) *Audio-visual Reminiscence Aids for Elderly People Including the Mentally Frail*. London: Department of Health.

Kenyon, G.M. (2003) 'Telling and listening to stories: Creating a wisdom environment for older people.' *Generations*, 27, 3, 30–33.

Kenyon, G. (2011) 'On Suffering, Loss, and the Journey to Life: Tai Chi as Narrative Care.' In G. Kenyon, E. Bohlmeijer and W.L. Randall (eds) *Storying Later Life: Issues, Investigations, and Interventions in Narrative Gerontology*. New York: Oxford University Press.

Kenyon, G., Bohlmeijer, E. and Randall, W.L. (eds) (2011) *Storying Later Life: Issues, Investigations, and Interventions in Narrative Gerontology*. New York: Oxford University Press.

Kenyon, G. and Randall, W.L. (2001) 'Narrative Gerontology: An Overview.' In G. Kenyon, P. Clark and B. de Vries (eds) *Narrative Gerontology: Theory, Research, and Practice* (pp.3–18). New York: Springer Publishing.

Kerkhof, Y.J., Bergsma, A. and Graff, M.J. (2017) 'Selecting apps for people with mild dementia: Identifying user requirements for apps enabling meaningful activities and self-management.' *Journal of Rehabilitation and Assistive Technologies Engineering*, 4, 1–21.

Kerssens, C., Kumar, R., Adams, A., Knott, C. *et al*. (2015) 'Personalized technology to support older adults with and without cognitive impairment living at home.' *American Journal of Alzheimer's Disease and Other Dementias*, 30, 1, 85–97.

Kevern, P. (2012) 'Community without memory? In search of an ecclesiology of liberation in the company of people with dementia.' *International Journal for the Study of the Christian Church*, 12, 1, 44–54.

Killick, J. and Craig, C. (2012) *Creativity and Communication in Persons with Dementia: A Practical Guide*. London: Jessica Kingsley Publishers.

Kim, Jinsoo J. (2008) 'Spiritual Development Through Guided Autobiography Group Among Elderly Korean American Immigrants.' Doctoral thesis, Claremont School of Theology, Claremont, CA.

King, D.B., Cappeliez, P., Carmel, S., Bachner, Y.G. and O'Rourke, N. (2015) 'Remembering genocide: The effects of early life trauma on reminiscence functions among Israeli holocaust survivors.' *Traumatology*, 21, 3, 145–152. doi: 10.1037/trm0000040

King, D.B., Cappeliez, P., Canham, S.L. and O'Rourke, N. (2017) 'Functions of reminiscence in later life: Predicting change in the physical and mental health of older adults over time.' *Aging and Mental Health*. doi:10.1080/13607863.2017.1396581

King, L.A., Heintzelman, S.J. and Ward, S.J. (2016) 'Beyond the search for meaning: A contemporary science of the experience of meaning in life.' *Current Directions in Psychological Science*, 25, 4, 211–216. doi:10.1177/0963721416656354

King, L.A., Scollon, C.K., Ramsey, C. and Williams, T. (2000) 'Stories of life transition: Subjective wellbeing and ego development in parents of children with Down Syndrome.' *Journal of Research in Personality*, 34, 4, 509–536.

Kinoshita, H., Maeda, I., Morita, T., Miyashita, M. *et al.* (2014) 'Place of death and the differences in patient quality of death and dying and caregiver burden.' *Journal of Clinical Oncology*, 33, 357–363. doi:10.1200/jco.2014.55.7355

Kitwood, T. (1997) *Dementia Reconsidered*. Maidenhead, Berkshire: Open University Press.

Kitwood, T. (1998) 'Life History and its Vestiges.' In P. Schweitzer (ed.) *Reminiscence in Dementia Care* (pp.103–107). London: Age Exchange.

Kivnick, H.Q. (1991) *Living with Care, Caring for Life: The Inventory of Life Strengths*. Minneapolis, MN: University of Minnesota.

Klass, D., Silverman, P.R. and Nickman, S.L. (1996) *Continuing Bonds: New Understandings of Grief*. Washington, DC: Taylor & Francis.

Kober, C. and Habermas, T. (2017) 'Development of temporal macrostructure in life narratives across the lifespan.' *Discourse Processes*, 54, 143–162.

Korte, J., Bohlmeijer, E.T., Cappeliez, P., Smit, F. and Westerhof, G.J. (2011a) 'Life review therapy for older adults with moderate depressive symptomatology: A pragmatic randomized controlled trial.' *Psychological Medicine*, 42, 6, 1163–1173.

Korte, J., Bohlmeijer, E.T., Westerhof, G.J. and Pot, A.M. (2011b) 'Reminiscence and adaptation to critical life events in older adults with mild to moderate depressive symptoms.' *Aging and Mental Health*, 15, 5, 638–646. doi: 10.1080/13607863.2010.551338

Korte, J., Cappeliez, P., Bohlmeijer, E.T. and Westerhof, G.J. (2012a) 'Meaning in life and mastery mediate the relationship of negative reminiscence with psychological distress among older adults with mild to moderate depressive symptoms.' *European Journal of Ageing*, 9, 4, 343–351. doi: 10.1007/s0433-012-0239-3

Korte, J., Drossaert, C.C., Wester, G.J. and Bohlmeijer, E.T. (2014) 'Life review in groups? An explorative analysis of social processes that facilitate or hinder the effectiveness of life review.' *Aging and Mental Health*, 18, 3, 376–384.

Korte, J., Westerhof, G.J. and Bohlmeijer, E.T. (2012b) 'Mediating processes in an effective life-review intervention.' *Psychology and Aging*, 27, 1172–1181. doi:10.1037/a0029273

Krause, N. (2012) 'Meaning in Life and Healthy Aging.' In P.T. Wong (ed.) *The Human Quest for Meaning: Theories, Research and Applications* (pp.409–432). Abingdon: Routledge.

Kretzschmar, F., Pleimling, D., Hosemann, J., Füssel, S. *et al.* (2013) 'Subjective impressions do not mirror online reading effort: Concurrent EEG-eyetracking evidence from the reading of books and digital media.' *PloS ONE* 8, 2: e56178. https://doi:org/10.1371/journal.pone.0056178

Krok, D. (2017) 'When is meaning in life most beneficial to young people? Styles of meaning in life and wellbeing among late adolescents.' *Journal of Adult Development*. doi:10.1007/s10804-017-9280-y

Kross, E., Ayduk, O. and Mischel, W. (2005) 'When asking "why" does not hurt: Distinguishing rumination from reflective processing of negative emotions.' *Psychological Science*, 16, 9, 709–715. doi:10.1111/j.1467-9280.2005.01600.x

Kübler-Ross, E. and Kessler, D. (2005) *On Grief and Grieving*. New York: Scribner.

Kuhl, D.R. and Westwood, M.J. (2001) 'A narrative approach to integration and healing among the terminally ill.' In G. Kenyon, P. Clark and B. de Vries (eds) *Narrative Gerontology: Theory, Research, and Practice* (pp.311–330). New York: Springer Publishing.

Kulkofsky, S., Wang, Q. and Koh, J.B. (2009) 'Functions of memory sharing and mother-child reminiscing behaviors: Individual and cultural variations.' *Journal of Cognition and Development*, 10, 92–114.

Kunz, J. (2002) *The Joys and Surprises of Telling Your Story*. Video film. Metropolitan Life Foundation.

Kunz, J. (2010) *Proposal to IIRLR and UWS-CCE for a Certificate Course*. Superior, WS: University of Wisconsin and IRLR.

Kunz, J. and Soltys, F. (2007) *Transformational Reminiscence: Life Story Work*. New York: Springer Publishing.

Kuo, T. (2015) 'The Psycho-social Impact of Life Review Groups in Taiwan.' Presentation at the Annual Conference of the Gerontological Society of America, Orlando, FL, 18–22 November 2015.

Lamers, S.A., Bohlmeijer, E.T., Korte, J. and Westerhof, G.J. (2015) 'The efficacy of life-review as online-guided self-help for adults: A randomized trial.' *The Journals of Gerontology*, 70, 1, 24–34.

Lan, X., Xiao, H. and Chen, Y. (2017) 'Effects of life review interventions on psychosocial outcomes among older adults: A systematic review and meta-analysis.' *Geriatrics and Gerontology International*, 17, 1344–1357.

Latorre, J.M., Serrano, J.P., Ricarte, J., Bonete, B. *et al*. (2015) 'Life review based on remembering specific events in active aging.' *Journal of Aging and Health*, 27, 1, 140–157.

Lazar, A. (2014) 'Using technology to increase meaningful engagement in a memory care unit. Group 14, November 9–12, Sanibel Island, FL: ACM. 978-1-4503-3043-5/14/11. http://dx.doi.org/10.1145/2660398.2660433

Lazar, A., Thompson, H. and Demiris, G. (2014) 'A systematic review of the use of technology for reminiscence therapy.' *Health Education and Behaviour*, 41, 15, 515–615.

Legacy Art Work (2018) Accessed on 14/02/2018 at http://legacyartwork.sklf.org.tw/?lang=english.

Le Guin, U. (2017) *Good Reads*. Accessed on 24/08/ 2017 at www.goodreads.com/author/quotes/874602.Ursula_K_Le_Guin?page=2.

Leming, M.R. and Dickinson, G. (2007) *Understanding Death, Dying and Bereavement* (6th ed). Belmont, CA: Thomson Wadsworth.

Lewis, C.N. (1971) 'The adaptive value of reminiscing in old age.' *Journal of Geriatric Psychiatry*, 6, 117–121.

Lewis, C. (1982) *Using the 'Thinking-aloud' Method in Cognitive Interface Design. Research Report RC 9265, 17 February*. Yorktown Heights, NY: IBM T.J. Watson Research Center.

Lewis, M.I. and Butler, R.N. (1974) 'Life-review therapy. Putting memories to work in individual and group psychotherapy.' *Geriatrics*, 29, 165–173.

Liao, H.W., Bluck, S. and Westerhof, G.J. (2018) 'The longitudinal relation between self-defining memories and self-esteem: Role of memory valence, function, and meaning.' *Imagination, Cognition and Personality*, 37, 3, 318–341.

Lilgendahl, J.P. and McAdams, D.P. (2011) 'Constructing stories of self-growth: How individual differences in patterns of autobiographical reasoning relate to well-being in midlife.' *Journal of Personality*, 79, 391–428. doi:10.1111/j.1467-6494.2010. 00688.x

Lim, F.S., Wallace, T. and Luszcz, M.A. (2013) 'Usability of tablet computers by people with early-stage dementia.' *Gerontology*, 59, 174–182.

Lin, C. and Liu, S. (2013) 'Healthy life expectancy for successful and active aging elderly in Taiwan.' *Taiwan Journal of Public Health*, 32, 6, 562–575.

Lipson, J. (1991) 'The Use of Self in Ethnographic Research'. In J.M. Morse (ed.) *Critical Issues in Qualitative Research Methods* (pp.73–90). London: Sage.

Liu-Huang, L., Chieng, K., Liu, Y., Yeh, K. and Yu, L. (2010) *Active Aging-Reminiscence and Memory Activities Guidebook*. Taiwan: Tao-Yuan Educational Volunteer Alliance.

Lopes, T.S., Afonso, R.M. and Ribeiro, O.M. (2016) 'A quasi-experimental study of a reminiscence program focused on autobiographical memory in institutionalized older adults with cognitive impairment.' *Archives of Gerontology and Geriatrics*, 66, 183–192.

Lorenz, K., Freddolino, P., Comas-Herrera, A., Knapp, M. and Damant, J (2017) 'Technology-based tools and services for people with dementia and carers: Mapping technology onto the dementia care pathway.' *Dementia*, 1–17. doi:10.1177/1471301217691617

Lou, V.W. and Choy, J.C. (2014) 'Factorial structure and psychometric properties of a brief version of the Reminiscence Functions Scale with Chinese older adults.' *Aging and Mental Health*, 18, 4, 531–536. doi: 10.1080/13607863.2013.860423

Lu, P. (2012) 'The effects of reminiscence and group intervention on wellbeing of community-dwelling older adults.' *NTU Social Work Review*, 10, 121–152.

MacIntyre, A. (1977) 'Epistemological Crises, Dramatic Narrative, and the Philosophy of Science.' *Monism*, 60, 4. Also in S. Hauerwas and L.J. Jones (eds) (1997) *Why Narrative? Readings in Narrative Theology* (pp.138–157). Eugene, OR: Wipf and Stock Publishers.

MacIntyre, A. (1981) 'The Virtues, the Unity of a Human Life and the Concept of a Tradition.' *After Virtue, Notre Dame*. University of Notre Dame Press, pp.190–2019. Also in S. Hauerwas and L.J. Jones (eds) (1997) *Why Narrative? Readings in Narrative Theology* (pp.89–112). Eugene, OR: Wipf and Stock Publishers.

Mackay, M.M. and Bluck, S. (2010) 'Meaning-making in memories: A comparison of memories of death-related and low point life experiences.' *Death Studies*, 34, 715–737. doi:10.1080/07481181003761708

MacKinlay, E. (1998) 'The Spiritual Dimension of Ageing: Meaning in Life, Response to Meaning and Well Being in Ageing.' Doctoral thesis. Melbourne: La Trobe University.

MacKinlay, E. (2001) *The Spiritual Dimension of Ageing*. London: Jessica Kingsley Publishers.

MacKinlay, E. (2006) *Spiritual Growth and Care in the Fourth Age of Life*. London: Jessica Kingsley Publishers.

MacKinlay, E. (2011) 'Creative Processes to Bring Out Expressions of Spirituality: Working with People Who Have Dementia.' In H. Lee and T. Adams (eds) *Creative Approaches in Dementia Care* (pp.212–229). UK: Palgrave Macmillan.

MacKinlay, E. (2016) 'Journeys with people who have dementia: Connecting and finding meaning in the journey.' *Journal of Religion, Spirituality and Aging*. 28, 1/2, 24–36.

MacKinlay, E. (2017) *The Spiritual Dimension of Ageing* (2nd ed). London: Jessica Kingsley Publishers.

MacKinlay, E. and Burns, R. (2017) 'Spirituality promotes better health outcomes and lowers anxiety about aging: The importance of spiritual dimensions for baby boomers as they enter older adulthood.' *Journal of Religion, Spirituality and Aging*, 29, 4, 248–265. doi:10.1080/15528030.2016.1264345, 1–18.

MacKinlay, E. and Trevitt, C. (2012) *Finding Meaning in the Experience of Dementia: The Place of Spiritual Reminiscence Work*. London: Jessica Kingsley Publishers.

MacKinlay, E. and Trevitt, C. (2015a) *Facilitating Spiritual Reminiscence for People with Dementia: A Learning Guide*. London: Jessica Kingsley Publishers.

MacKinlay, E. and Trevitt, C. (2015b) 'Spiritual Factors in the Experience of Alzheimer's Disease and Other Dementias.' In C. Dick-Muehlke, R. Li and M. Orleans (eds) *Psychosocial Studies of the Individual's Changing Perspectives in Alzheimer's Disease* (pp.230–253). USA: IGI Global Publishing.

Madori, L.L. (2007) *Therapeutic Thematic Arts Programming for Older Adults*. Baltimore, MD: Health Professions Press.

Maercker, A. and Bachem, R. (2013) 'Life review interventions as psychotherapeutic techniques in psychotraumatology.' *European Journal of Psychotraumatology*, 4, 10–16.
Malde, S. (1988) 'Guided autobiography: A counselling tool for older adults.' *Journal of Counselling and Development*, 66, 6, 290–293.
Marwit, S.J. and Klass, D. (1995) 'Grief and the role of the inner representation of the deceased.' *OMEGA: Journal of Death and Dying*, 30, 283–298. doi:10.2190/peaa-p5ak-l6t8-570C
Mather, M. and Carstensen, L.L. (2005) 'Aging and motivated cognition: The positivity effect in attention and memory.' *Trends in Cognitive Sciences*, 9, 10, 496–502. doi:10.1016/j.tics.2005.08.005
Mayseless, O. and Keren, E. (2014) 'Finding a meaningful life as a developmental task in emerging adulthood: The domains of love and work across culture.' *Emerging Adulthood*, 2, 63–73.
McAdams, D.P. (1993) *The Stories We Live By: Personal Myths and the Making of the Self.* New York: Guilford Press.
McAdams, D.P. (2001) 'The psychology of life stories.' *Review of General Psychology*, 5, 100. doi:10.1037/1089-2680.5.2.100
McAdams, D.P. (2004) 'The Redemptive Self: Narrative Identity in America Today.' In D.R. Beike, J.M. Lampinen and D.A. Behrend (eds) *The Self and Memory.* New York: Psychology Press.
McAdams, D.P. (2013a) 'The psychological self as actor, agent and author.' *Perspectives on Psychological Science*, 8, 272–295. doi:10.1177/1745691624646557
McAdams, D.P (2013b) *The Redemptive Self: Stories Americans Live By* (2nd ed). Oxford: Oxford University Press.
McAdams, D.P. and McLean, K.C. (2013) 'Narrative identity.' *Current Directions in Psychological Science*, 22, 233–238.
McClintock M. (2018) 'Mum now.' (Unpublished).
McConkey, J. (1996) *The Anatomy of Memory: An Anthology.* Oxford: Oxford University Press.
McCormack, B. (2015) 'Gaming for health: A systematic review of the physical and cognitive effects of interactive computer games in older adults.' *Journal of Applied Gerontology*, 34 NP166-NP189.
McDonnell, E. and Ryan, A. (2014) 'The experience of sons caring for a parent with dementia. *Dementia*, 13, 6, 788–802. doi:10.1177/1471301213485374
McElwain, N.L., Halberstadt, A.G. and Volling, B.L. (2007) 'Mother-and father-reported interactions to children's negative emotions: Relations to young children's emotional understanding and friendship quality.' *Child Development*, 78, 5, 1407–1425. doi:10.1111/j.1467-8624.2007.01074
McHugh, J.E., Wherton, J.P., Prendergast, D.K. and Lawlor, B.K. (2012) 'Identifying opportunities for supporting caregivers of persons with dementia through information and communication technology.' *Gerontechnology*, 10, 4, 220–230.
McKeown, J. (2011) 'It Made Me See Him in a Different Light: The Use of Life Story Work with Older People Who Have Dementia in Health and Social Care Practice.' Doctoral thesis, University of Sheffield: School of Nursing and Midwifery.
McKeown, J., Clarke, A., Ryan, T. and Repper, J. (2010) 'The use of life work with people with dementia to enhance person-centred care.' *International Journal of Older People Nursing*, 10, 1, 148–158.
McLean, K. (2015) *The Co-authored Self.* New York: Oxford University Press.
McLean, K.C. and Lilgendahl, J.P. (2008) 'Why recall our highs and lows: Relations between memory functions, age, and wellbeing.' *Memory*, 16, 7, 751–762. doi:10.1080/09658210802215385
McLean, K. and Mansfield, C.D. (2011) 'The co-construction of adolescent narrative identity: Narrative processing as a function of adolescent age, gender, and maternal scaffolding.' *Developmental Psychology*, 48, 436–447. doi:10.1037/a0025563

McLean, K., Pasupathi, M. and Pals, J. (2007) 'Selves creating stories creating selves: A process model of self-development.' *Personality and Social Psychology Review*, 11, 262–278.

McLean, K.C. and Syed, M. (2015) 'Personal, master, and alternative narratives: An integrative framework for understanding identity development in context.' *Human Development*, 58, 6, 318–349. doi:10.1159/000445817

McMahon, A.W. and Rhudick, P.J. (1964) 'Reminiscing: Adaptational significance in the aged.' *Archives of General Psychiatry*, 10, 292–298.

Meléndez, J.C., Fortuna, F.B., Sales, A. and Mayordomo, T. (2015) 'The effects of instrumental reminiscence on resilience and coping.' *Archives of Gerontology and Geriatrics*, 60, 2, 294–298.

Melunsky, N., Crellin, N., Dudzinski, E., Orrell, M. *et al.* (2015) 'The experience of family carers attending a joint reminiscence group with people with dementia: A thematic analysis.' *Dementia*, 14, 6, 842–859. doi:10.1177/1471301213516332

Merriam, S.B. (1980) 'The concept and function of reminiscence: A review of the research.' *Gerontologist*, 20, 604–609.

Merriam, S.B. (1993) 'Butler's life review: How universal is it?' *International Journal of Aging and Human Development*, 37, 163–175.

Merriam, S.B. and Cross, L.H. (1982) 'Adulthood and reminiscence: A descriptive study.' *Educational Gerontology*, 8, 275–290.

Merrill, N., Booker, J.A. and Fivush, R. (2018) 'Functions of parental intergenerational narratives told by young people.' *Topics in Cognitive Science*, Wiley Online Library. doi.org/10.111/tops.12356

Merrill, N. and Fivush, R. (2016) 'Intergenerational narratives and identity across development.' *Developmental Review*, 40, 72–92. doi:10.1016/j.dr.2016.03.001

Merrill, N., Gallo, E. and Fivush, R. (2014) 'Gender differences in family dinnertime conversation.' *Discourse Processes*, 52, 533–558.

Merrill, N., Srivanas, E. and Fivush, R. (2017) 'Personal and intergenerational narratives of transgression and pride in emerging adulthood: Links to gender and wellbeing.' *Applied Cognitive Psychology*, Wiley Online Library.

Metzger, B.M. and Murphy, R.E. (1991) *The New Oxford Annotated Bible: New Revised Standard Version*. New York: Oxford University Press.

Mezred, D., Petigenet, V., Fort, I., Blaison, C. and Gana, K. (2006) 'La réminiscence: Concept, fonctions et mesures. Adaptation française de la Reminiscence Functions Scale.' *Les Cahiers Internationaux de Psychologie Sociale*, 71, 3–14. doi:10.3917/cips.071.0003

Miller, W.L., Cohen, D.G. and Barker, T.H. (2016) *Sky Above Clouds, Finding Our Way through Creativity, Aging and Illness*. Oxford: Oxford University Press.

Miller, E.J. and Gwynne, G.V. (1972) *A Life Apart: A Pilot Study of Residential Institutions for Physically Handicapped and the Young Chronic Sick*. London: Taylor & Francis.

Moen, T. (2006) 'Reflections on the narrative research approach.' *International Journal of Qualitative Methods*, 5, 4, 56–69.

Molinari, V. and Reichlin, R.E. (1985) 'Life review reminiscence in the elderly: A review of the literature.' *International Journal of Aging and Human Development*, 20, 81–92.

Montgomery, S.A. and Asberg, M. (1979) 'A new depression scale designed to be sensitive to change.' *British Journal of Psychiatry*, 134, 382–389.

Moody, H. (1988) 'Where Are We Going?' In R. Disch (ed.) *Twenty-Five Years of the Life Review: Theoretical and Practical Considerations* (pp.7–21). New York: Haworth Press.

Moos, I. and Bjorn, A. (2006) 'Use of life story in the institutional care of people with dementia: A review of intervention studies.' *Ageing and Society*, 26, 431–454.

Morgan, S. and Woods, R.T. (2010) 'Life review with people with dementia in care homes: A preliminary randomized controlled trial.' *Non-Pharmacological Therapies in Dementia*, 1, 1, 43–60.

Moules, N.J. (1998) 'Legitimizing grief: Challenging beliefs that constrain.' *Journal of Family Nursing*, 4, 142–166. doi:10.1177/107484079800400203

Muhlert, N., Milton, F., Butler, C.R., Kapur, N. and Zeman, A.Z. (2010) 'Accelerated forgetting of real-life events in transient epileptic amnesia.' *Neuropsychologia*, 48, 11, 3235–3244.

Mulvenna, M.D., Doyle, L., Wright, T., Zheng, H. et al. (2011) 'Evaluation of card-based versus device-based reminiscing using photographic images.' *Journal of CyberTherapy & Rehabilitation*, 4, 1, 57–66.

Myers, J.E. (1989) *Adult Children and Aging Parents.* Alexandria, VA: American Counseling Association.

National Center for Creative Aging. Accessed on 29/12/2017 at www.creativeaging.org.

Negru-Subtirica, O., Pop, E.I., Luyckx, K., Dezutter, J. and Steger, M.F. (2016) 'The meaningful identity: A longitudinal look at the interplay between identity and meaning in life in adolescence.' *Developmental Psychology*, 52, 11. 1926–1936.

Neimeyer, R.A. (2001) 'Reauthoring life narratives: Grief therapy as meaning reconstruction.' *Israel Journal of Psychiatry and Related Sciences*, 38, 3–4, 171–183.

Neimeyer, R.A. (2004) 'Fostering posttraumatic growth: A narrative elaboration.' *Psychological Inquiry*, 15, 53–59.

Neimeyer, R.A., Baldwin, S.A. and Gillies, J. (2006) 'Continuing bonds and reconstructing meaning: Mitigating complications in bereavement.' *Death Studies*, 30, 8, 715–738. doi:10.1080/07481180600848322

Neimeyer, R.A., Klass, D. and Dennis, M.R. (2014) 'A social constructionist account of grief Loss and the narration of meaning.' *Death Studies*, 38, 485–498. doi:10.1080/0748118 7.2014.913454

Neisser, U. (1988) 'Five kinds of self-knowledge.' *Philosophical Psychology*, 1, 35–59. doi:10.1080/09515088808572924

Nelson, K. and Fivush, R. (2004) 'The emergence of autobiographical memory: A social cultural developmental theory.' *Psychological Review*, 111, 486–511. doi:10.1037/0033-295X.111.2.486

Neugarten, B.L. (1968) 'Adult Personality: Toward a Psychology of the Life Cycle.' In B. L. Neugarten (ed.) *Middle Age and Aging: A Reader in Social Psychology.* Chicago, IL: The University of Chicago Press.

Newman, E.J. and Lindsay, D.S. (2009) 'False memories: What the hell are they for?' *Applied Cognitive Psychology*, 23, 1105–1121. doi:10.1002/acp.1613

Niebuhr, H.R. (1941) *The Story of Our Life, the Meaning of Revelation* (pp.43–81). New York: Macmillan. Also in S. Hauerwas and L.G. Jones (eds) (1997) *Why Narrative? Readings in Narrative Theology* (pp.21–45). Eugene, OR: Wipf and Stock Publishers.

Nijhof, N., van Gemert-Pijnen, J.E. and Burns, C.M. (2013) 'A personal assistant for dementia to stay at home safe at reduced cost.' *Gerontechnology*, 11, 469–479.

Nile, E. and Van Bergen, P. (2015) 'Not all semantics: Similarities and differences in reminiscing function and content between Indigenous and non-Indigenous Australians.' *Memory*, 23, 1, 83–98.

Nolen-Hoeksema, S., Wisco, B.E. and Lyubomirsky, S. (2008) 'Rethinking rumination.' *Perspectives on Psychological Science*, 3, 400–424. doi:10.1111/j.1745-6924.2008.00088

Northern Health and Social Care Trust (2009) *My Life Story Book.* Ballymena: NHSCT.

O'Connor, S., Bouamrane, M.M., O'Donnell, C.A. and Mair, F.S. (2016) 'Barriers to co-designing mobile technology with persons with dementia and their carers.' *Nursing Informatics.* doi:10.3233/978-1-61499-658-3-1028

O'Rourke, N., Cappeliez, P. and Claxton, A. (2011) 'Functions of reminiscence and the psychological wellbeing of young-old and older adults over time.' *Aging and Mental Health*, 15, 272–281. doi:10.1080/13607861003713281

O'Rourke, N., Carmel, S., Chaudhury, H., Polchenko, N. and Bachner, Y.G. (2013) 'A cross-national comparison of reminiscence functions between Canadian and Israeli older adults.' *Journals of Gerontology Series B: Psychological Sciences and Social Sciences*, 68, 2, 184–192.

O'Rourke, N., King, D.B. and Cappeliez, P. (2017) 'Reminiscence functions over time: Consistency of self-functions and variation of prosocial functions.' *Memory*, 25, 403–411. doi:10.1080/09658211.2016.1179331

O'Rourke, J., Tobin, F., O'Callaghan, S., Sowman, R. and Collins, D.R. (2011) '"You Tube": A useful tool for reminiscence therapy in dementia?' *Age and Ageing*, 40, 6, 742–744.

Orpwood, R., Sixsmith, A., Torrington, J., Chadd, J. and Chalfont, G. (2007) 'Designing technology to support quality of life of people with dementia.' *Technology and Disability*, 19, 103–112.

Orrell, M., Yates, L., Leung, P., Kang, S. *et al.* (2017a) 'The impact of individual Cognitive Stimulation Therapy (iCST) on cognition, quality of life, caregiver health, and family relationships in dementia: A randomized controlled trial.' *PLoS Med 2017*, 14, 3, e1002269.

Orrell, M., Hoe, J., Charlesworth, G., Russell, I. *et al.* (2017b) 'Support at Home: Interventions to Enhance Life in Dementia (SHIELD) – Evidence, development and evaluation of complex interventions.' *Programme Grants Application Research 2017*, 5, 5. doi:10.3310/pgfar05050

Osborn, C. and Schweitzer, P. (1993) *The Reminiscence Handbook: Ideas for Creative Activities with Older People*. London: Age Exchange.

Orth, K. and Wetzstein, V. (eds) (2016) *Kinder im Zweiten Weltkrieg – Spuren ins Heute*. [*Children during World War II – Traces from the Past in the Present*]. Freiburg: Catholic Academy of the Archdiocese.

O'Shea, E., Devane, D., Cooney, A., Casey, D. *et al.* (2014) 'The impact of reminiscence on the quality of life of residents with dementia in long-stay care.' *International Journal of Geriatric Psychiatry*, 29, 10, 1062–1070.

O'Shea, E., Devane, D., Murphy, K., Cooney, A. *et al.* (2011) 'Effectiveness of a structured education reminiscence-based programme for staff on the quality of life of residents with dementia in long-stay care: A study protocol for a cluster randomised trial.' *Trials*, 12, 41.

Palmer, S.B., Wehmeyer, M.L., Davies, D.K. and Stock, S.E. (2012) 'Family members' reports of the technology use of family members with intellectual and developmental disabilities.' *Journal of Intellectual Disability Research*, 56, 4, 402–414.

Pals, J.L. (2006) 'Narrative identity processing of difficult life experiences: Pathways of personality development and positive self-transformation in adulthood.' *Journal of Personality*, 74, 4, 1079–1110.

Park, C.L. (2010) 'Making sense of the meaning literature: An integrative review of meaning making and its effects on adjustment to stressful life events.' *Psychological Bulletin*, 136, 257–301.

Parker-Oliver, D. (2000) 'The social construction of the "dying" role and the hospice drama.' *OMEGA: Journal of Death and Dying*, 40, 493–512. doi:10.2190/yt9d-12y2-54ly-tcmn

Pasupathi, M. and Billitteri, J. (2015) 'Being and becoming through being heard: Listener effects on stories and selves.' *International Journal of Listening*, 29, 2, 67–84.

Pasupathi, M. and Carstensen, L.L. (2003) 'Age and emotional experience during mutual reminiscing.' *Psychology and Aging*, 18, 430–442. doi:10.1037/0882-7974.18.3.430

Pasupathi, M. and Mansour, E. (2006) 'Adult age differences in autobiographical reasoning in narratives.' *Developmental Psychology*, 42, 5, 798–808.

Pasupathi, M., McLean, K.C. and Weeks, T. (2009) 'To tell or not to tell: Disclosure and the narrative self.' *Journal of Personality*, 77, 1–35.

Pasupathi, M., Weeks, T. and Rice, C. (2006) 'Reflecting on life: Remembering as a major process in adult development.' *Journal of Language and Social Psychology*, 25, 3, 244–263.

Patterson, M. and Perlstein, S. (2011) 'Good for the head, good for the soul: The creative arts and brain health in later life.' *Generations*, 2, 27–36.

Pear, T.H. (1922) *Remembering and Forgetting*. London: Methuen.

Peisah, C., Lawrence, G. and Reutens, S. (2011) 'Creative solutions for severe dementia with BPSD: A case of art therapy used in an inpatient and residential care setting.' *International Psychogeriatrics*, 23, 1011–1013.

Pennebaker, J.W. and Beall, S. (1986) 'Confronting a traumatic event: Toward an understanding of inhibition and disease.' *Journal of Abnormal Psychology*, 95, 274–281.

Pennebaker, J.W. and Chung, C.K. (2006) 'Expressive Writing, Emotional Upheavals, and Health.' In H.S. Friedman and R.C. Silver (eds) *Foundations of Health Psychology* (pp. 263–284). New York: Oxford University Press.

Pennebaker, J.W. and Chung, C.K. (2011) 'Expressive Writing: Connections to Physical and Mental Health.' In H.S. Friedman (ed) *Oxford Handbook of Health Psychology* (pp.417–437). New York: Oxford University Press.

Petrie, K.J., Booth, R.J., Pennebaker, J.W. and Davison, K.P. (1995) 'Disclosure of trauma and immune response to a hepatitis B vaccination program.' *Journal of Consulting and Clinical Psychology*, 63, 787–792.

Phillips, J., Bernard, M. and Chittenden, M. (2002) *Juggling Work and Care: The Experiences of Working Carers of Older Adults*. Bristol: The Policy Press.

Pierce, T.W. (2005) 'Evaluation Issues in Group Work.' In B. Haight and F. Gibson (eds) *Burnside's Working with Older Adults* (4th ed) (pp.469–479). Sudbury, MA: Jones and Bartlett Press.

Pierce, T.W. (2013) 'Multimedia and the practice of reminiscence and life review.' *Conference Proceedings of the Eleventh Biennial Meeting of the International Institute for Reminiscence and Life Review* (pp.36–44). Superior, WI: University of Wisconsin–Superior.

Pillemer, D.B. (1992) 'Remembering Personal Circumstances: A Functional Analysis.' In E.Winograd and U. Neisser (eds) *Affect and Accuracy in Recall: Studies of "Flashbulb" Memories. Emory Symposia in Cognition 4* (pp.236–264). New York: Cambridge University Press. doi: 10.1017/CBO9780511664069.013

Pillemer, D.B. (1998) *Momentous Events, Vivid Memories*. Cambridge, MA: Harvard University Press.

Pincus, A. (1970) 'Reminiscence in aging and its implications for social work practice.' *Social Work*, 15, 3, 47–53.

Pincus, T. (2014) 'Limitation of Traditional Randomized Controlled Clinical Trials in Rheumatology'. In H. Yazici, Yazici and E. Lesaffre (eds) *Understanding Evidence-Based Rheumatology: A Guide to Interpreting Drugs, Trials, Registries and Ethics* (pp.179–207). Cham, Switzerland: Springer Publishing.

Pinquart, M. and Forstmeier, S. (2012) 'Effects of reminiscence interventions on psychosocial outcomes: A meta-analysis.' *Aging and Mental Health*, 16, 5, 541–558. doi:10.1080/136 07863.2011.651434

Poll, J.B. and Smith, T.B. (2003) 'The spiritual self: Toward a conceptualization of spiritual identity development.' *Journal of Psychology and Theology*, 31, 2, 129–142.

Pot, A., Bohlmeijer, E.T., Onrust, S., Melenhorst, A. *et al.* (2010) 'The impact of life review on depression in older adults: A randomized controlled trial.' *International Psychogeriatrics*, 22, 572–581.

Price, B. (1992) *Family Memories: A Guide to Reminiscing*. Sydney: New South Wales State Library

Prigerson, H.G. and Jacobs, S.C. (2001) 'Caring for bereaved patients: All the doctors just suddenly go.' *Journal American Medical Association*, 286, 1369–1376. doi:10.1001/ jama.286.11.1369

Prigerson, H.G., Maciejewski, P.K., Reynolds, C.F., Bierhals, A.J. *et al.* (1995) 'Inventory of complicated grief: A scale to measure maladaptive symptoms of loss.' *Psychiatry Research*, 59, 65–79.

Pringle, A. and Somerville, S. (2013) 'Computer-assisted reminiscence therapy: Developing practice.' *Mental Health Practice*, 17, 4 (posted online 1 December 2013).

Proust, M. (1981) *Remembrance of Things Past*. New York: Alfred A. Knopf.

Radloff, L.S. (1977) 'The CES-D scale: A self-report depression scale for research in the general population.' *Applied Psychological Measurement*, 1, 385–401. doi: 10.1177/014662167700100306

Radloff, L.S. and Teri, L. (1986) 'Use of the Center for Epidemiological Studies – Depression Scale with Older Adults.' In T.L. Brink (ed.) *Clinical Gerontology: A Guide to Assessment and Intervention* (pp.119–136). New York: Haworth Press.

Rajaram, S. (1993) 'Remembering and knowing: Two means of access to the personal past.' *Memory and Cognition*, 21, 1, 89–102.

Randall, W.L. (1995) *The Stories We Are: An Essay on Self-Creation*. Toronto: University of Toronto Press.

Randall, W.L. (2001) 'Acquiring a Narrative Perspective on Aging, Identity, and Everyday Life.' In G. Kenyon, P. Clark and B. de Vries (eds) *Narrative Gerontology: Theory, Research, and Practice* (pp.31–61). New York: Springer Publishing.

Randall, W.L. (2011) 'Memory, Metaphor, and Meaning: Reading for Wisdom in the Story of Our Lives.' In G. Kenyon, E. Bohlmeijer and W.L. Randall (eds) *Storying Later Life: Issues, Investigations, and Interventions in Narrative Gerontology*. New York: Oxford University Press.

Randall, W.L. and McKim, A. (2008) *Reading Our Lives: The Poetics of Growing Old*. New York: Oxford University Press.

Rappaport, J. (1995) 'Empowerment meets narrative: Listening to stories and creating settings.' *American Journal of Community Psychology*, 23, 795–807.

Rasmussen, A.S. and Berntsen, D. (2010) 'Personality traits and autobiographical memory: Openness is positively related to the experience and usage of recollections.' *Memory*, 18, 7, 774–786. doi:10.1080/09658211.2010.514270

Rasmussen, L. (1998) 'An Overview of Ageing and Health in Europe.' In P. Schweitzer (ed.) *Reminiscence in Dementia Care* (pp.5–10). London: Age Exchange.

Rathbone, C.J., Moulin, C.J. and Conway, M.A. (2008) 'Self-centered memories: The reminiscence bump and the self.' *Memory and Cognition*, 36, 8, 1403–1414. doi:10.3758/mc.36.8.1403

Reedy, M. and Birren, J.E. (1980) 'Life Review through Guided Autobiography.' Poster session presented at the annual meeting of the American Psychological Association, Montreal, Canada.

Reese, E., Bird, A. and Tripp, G. (2007) 'Children's self-esteem and moral self: Links to parent-child conversations regarding emotion.' *Social Development*, 16, 460–478. doi:10.1111/j.1467-9507.2007. 00393.x

Reese, E. and Farrant, K. (2003) 'Social Origins of Reminiscing.' In R. Fivush and C.A. Haden (eds) *Autobiographical Memory and the Construction of a Narrative Self: Developmental and Cultural Perspectives* (pp.29–48). Mahwah, NJ: Lawrence Erlbaum Associates.

Reese, E., Jack, F. and White, N. (2010) 'Origins of adolescents' autobiographical memories.' *Cognitive Development*, 25, 352–367.

Regier, N.G. and Gitlin, L.N. (2017) 'Dementia-related restlessness: Relationship to characteristics of persons with dementia and family caregivers.' *International Journal of Geriatric Psychiatry*, 33, 1, 185–192.

Reker, G.T., Birren, J.E. and Svensson, C.M. (2012) 'Restoring, Maintaining and Enhancing Personal Meaning in Life through Autobiographical Methods.' In P.T. Wong (ed.) *The Human Quest for Meaning* (pp.383–407). New York: Taylor & Francis.

Reker, G.T., Birren, J.E. and Svensson, C.M. (2014) 'Self-aspect reconstruction through guided autobiography: Exploring underlying processes.' *International Journal of Reminiscence and Life Review*, 2, 1, 1–15.

Remembering Yesterday, Caring Today Apprenticeship Scheme. Accessed on 03/01/218 at www.reminiscencetheatrearchive.org.uk and at www.rememberingtogether.eu.

Reminiscence Network Northern Ireland (2016) *Sharing Memories: Building Communities 2012–2016 Celebratory Booklet.* Belfast: RNNI.

Reminiscence Network Northern Ireland (2017) *Best Practice Manual: Creative Reminiscence and Life Story Work.* Belfast: RNNI.

Reminiscence Theatre Archive (2014) Accessed on 04/03/2018 at www.reminiscencetheatrearchive.org.uk.

Rengade, C.E. (2016) 'De l'ennui au bore-out, une revue de la littérature.' ['From boredom to bore-out, a literature review.'] *Journal de thérapie comportementale et cognitive,* 26, 123–130. doi:10.1016/j.jtcc.2016.03.002

Ricoeur, P. (1991) Life in Quest of Narrative. In D. Wood (ed.) *On Paul Ricoeur: Narrative and Interpretation* (pp.20–33). London: Routledge.

Riley, P., Alm, N. and Newell, A. (2009) 'An interactive tool to promote musical creativity in people with dementia.' *Computers in Human Behaviour,* 25, 599–608.

Robinaugh, D.J. and McNally, R.J. (2013) 'Remembering the past and envisioning the future in bereaved adults with and without complicated grief.' *Clinical Psychological Science,* 3, 290–300. doi:10.1177/2167702613476027

Robinson, L., Brittain, K., Lindsay, S., Jackson, D. and Olivier, P. (2009) '"Keeping in Touch Everyday" (KITE) project: Developing assistive technologies with people with dementia and their carers to promote independence.' *International Psychogeriatrics,* 21, 494–502. doi:10.1080/09658211.2010.514270

Rochat, L., Billieux, J. and Van der Linden, M. (2012) 'Difficulties in disengaging attentional resources from self-generated thoughts moderate the link between dysphoria and maladaptive self-referential thinking.' *Cognition and Emotion,* 26, 748–757. doi:10.1080/02699931.2011.613917

Ros, L., Meléndez, J.C., Webster, J.D., Mayordomo, T. *et al.* (2016) 'Reminiscence Functions Scale: Factorial structure and its relation with mental health in a sample of Spanish older adults.' *International Psychogeriatrics,* 28, 9, 1521–1532. doi:10.1017/S1041610216000326

Rossetti, C. (1992) *The Complete Poems* (1979–1990). Accessed on 21/06/2018 at www.poetryfoundation.org/poems/45000/remember-56d224509b7ae.

Rubin, S.S. (1984) 'Mourning distinct from melancholia: The resolution of bereavement.' *Psychology and Psychotherapy: Theory, Research and Practice,* 57, 339–345.

Ruth, J.E., Birren, J.E. and Polkinghorne, D.E. (1996) 'The projects of life reflected in autobiographies of old age.' *Ageing and Society,* 16, 677–699.

Ryan, A.A., McCauley, C., Laird, E., Gibson, A. *et al.* (2018) *A Feasibility Study of Facilitated Reminiscence for People Living with Dementia.* Belfast: Ulster University.

Ryan, A.A. and McKenna, H. (2013) 'Familiarity as a key factor influencing rural family carers experience of the nursing home placement of an older relative: A qualitative study.' *BMC Health Services Research,* 13, 252. doi:10.1186/1472-6963-13-252

Ryff, C.D. (1989) 'Beyond Ponce de Leon and life satisfaction: New directions in the quest of successful aging.' *International Journal of Behavioral Development,* 12, 1, 35–55.

Ryff, C.D and Heincke, S. G. (1983) 'Subjective organization of personality in adulthood and aging.' *Journal of Personality and Social Psychology,* 44, 4, 807–816.

Saarni, C. (1999) *The Development of Emotional Competence.* New York: Guilford Press.

Sabat, S.R. (2001) *The Experience of Alzheimer's Disease: Life Through a Tangled Veil.* Oxford: Blackwell.

Sabat, S. (2016) 'Implicit memory and people with Alzheimer's Disease: Implications for caregiving.' *American Journal of Alzheimer's Disease and Other Dementias,* 21, 1, 11–14.

Sabat, S. (2018) *Alzheimer's Disease and Dementia: What Everyone Needs to Know.* Oxford: Oxford University Press.

Sabir, M., Henderson, C.R., Kang, S. and Pillemer, K. (2016) 'Attachment focused integrative reminiscence with older African-Americans: A randomized controlled intervention study.' *Aging and Mental Health*, 20, 5, 517–528.

Sabir, M.G., Yull, D., Jones, J. and Pillemer, K. (2017) 'Personalized generativity in the work pursuits of African Americans of the Great Migration.' *The International Journal of Reminiscence and Life Review*, 4, 1, 24–33.

Salmon, K. and Reese, E. (2016) 'The benefits of reminiscing with young children.' *Current Directions in Psychological Science*, 25, 233–238.

Salovey, P. (1992) 'Mood-induced self-focused attention.' *Journal of Personality and Social Psychology*, 62, 4, 699–707. doi:10.1037/0022-3514.62.4.699

Sarne-Fleischmann, V. and Tractinsky, N. (2008) 'Development and evaluation of a personalised multimedia system for reminiscence therapy in Alzheimer's patients.' *International Journal of Social and Humanistic Computing*, 1, 1, 81–95.

Sauro, J. (2016) *How to Conduct a Usability Test on a Mobile Device*. Accessed on 10/052016 at www.measuringu.com/blog/mobile-usability-test.php.

Sauro, J. and Dumas, J.S. (2009) Comparison of three one-question, post-task usability questionnaires. In *Proceedings of the SIGCHI Conference on Human Factors in Computing Systems (CHI 2009)*. New York: ACM. 1599–1608.

Sauro, J. and Lewis, J.R. (2012) *Quantifying the User Experience: Practical Statistics for User Research*. London: Elsevier.

Savage, C. (2016) 'Harnessing new technologies to improve mood and wellbeing.' *Care Analysis*, 18, 2, 98–100.

Sawin, L., Corbett, L. and Carbine, M. (eds) (2014) *Jung and Aging: Possibilities and Potentials for the Second Half of Life*. New Orleans, LA: Spring Journal Books.

Schiff, B. and Cohler, B.J. (2001) 'Telling Survival Backward: Holocaust Survivors Narrate the Past.' In G. Kenyon, P. Clark and B. de Vries (eds) *Narrative Gerontology: Theory, Research, and Practice* (130–136). New York: Springer Publishing.

Schroots, J.J. and van Dongen, L. (1995) *Birren's ABC: Autobiografie Cursus. Exploratief onderzoek* (pp.15–124). [*Birren's GAB: Guided Autobiography. Explorative Study*.] Assen (NL): van Gorcum.

Schulz, R. and Heckhausen, J. (1996) 'A life span model of successful aging.' *American Psychologist*, 51, 7, 702–714.

Schwab, R. (2004) 'Acts of remembrance, cherished possessions, and living memorials.' *Generations*, 28, 26–30.

Schweitzer, P. (ed.) (1983) *Fifty Years Ago: Memories of the 1930s*. London: Age Exchange.

Schweitzer, P. (ed.) (1988) 'European Reminiscence Network Conference Papers.' Greenwich: University of Greenwich Reminiscence Theatre Archive.

Schweitzer, P. (1989) *Across the Irish Sea: Memories of London Irish pensioners*. London: Age Exchange.

Schweitzer, P. (1990) *Goodnight Children Everywhere: Memories of Evacuation in World War II*. London: Age Exchange.

Schweitzer, P. (1993) *Age Exchanges: Reminiscence Projects for Children and Older People*. London: Age Exchange.

Schweitzer, P. (2002) *Jubilee: Memories, Photos, A Play and the Story of How It Was Made*. London: Age Exchange.

Schweitzer, P. (2006) *Reminiscence Theatre: Making Theatre from Memories*. London: Jessica Kingsley Publishers.

Schweitzer, P. and Bruce, E. (2008) *Remembering Yesterday, Caring Today: Reminiscence in Dementia Care: A Guide to Good Practice*. London: Jessica Kingsley Publishers.

Schweitzer, P. and Trilling, A. (2005) *Making Memories Matter*. Kassel, Germany: Euregioverlag.

Scogin, F., Welsh, D., Hanson, A., Stump, J. and Coates, A. (2005) 'Evidence-based psychotherapies for depression in older adults.' *Clinical Psychology: Science and Practice*, 12, 3, 222–237.

Seamark, D.B., Blake S., Brearley, S.G., Milligan., C. *et al.* (2014) 'Dying at home: A qualitative study of family carers' views of support provided by GPs community staff.' *British Journal of General Practice*, 64, 629: e796-803. doi:10.3399/bjgp14X682885

Seamon, J.G., Moskowitz, T.N., Swan, A.E., Zhong, B. *et al.* (2014) 'SenseCam reminiscence and action recall in memory-unimpaired people.' *Memory*, 22, 7, 861–866.

Sedney, M.A., Baker, J.E. and Gross, E. (1994) '"The story" of a death: Therapeutic considerations with bereaved families.' *Journal of Marital and Family Therapy*, 20, 287–295. doi:10.1111/j.1752-0606.1994.tb00116.x

Segal, Z.V., Williams, J.M. and Teasdale, J.D. (2002) *Mindfulness-Based Cognitive Therapy for Depression: A New Approach to Preventing Relapse.* New York: Guilford Press.

Segerstrom, S.C., Roach, A.R., Evans, D.R., Schipper, L.J. and Darville, A.K. (2010) 'The structure and health correlates of trait repetitive thought in older adults.' *Psychology and Aging*, 25, 505–515. doi:10.1037/a0019456

Serrano, J.P., Latorre, J.M., Gatz, M. and Montañes, J. (2004) 'Life review therapy using autobiographical retrieval practice for older adults with depressive symptomatology.' *Psychology and Aging*, 19, 272–277. doi:10.1037/0882-7974.19.2.272

Serrano Selva, J.P., Latorre Postigo, J.M., Ros Segura, L. Navarro Bravo, B. *et al.* (2012) 'Life review therapy using autobiographical retrieval practice for older adults with clinical depression.' *Psicothema*, 24, 2, 224–229.

Shadden, B.B., Hagstrom, F. and Koski, P.R. (2008) *Neurogenic Communication Disorders: Life Stories and the Narrative Self.* Abingdon, Oxfordshire: Plural Publishing.

Shakespeare, W. (2017) *As You Like It.* New York: Penguin Books. (Original work published 1623).

Shand, A.F. (1920) *The Foundations of Character* (2nd ed). London: Macmillan. (Original work published 1914).

Shear, K. and Shair, H. (2005) 'Attachment, loss, and complicated grief.' *Developmental Psychobiology*, 47, 253–267. doi:10.1002/dev.20091

Sheikh, J.I. and Yesavage, J.A. (1986) 'Geriatric Depression Scale (GDS): Recent evidence and development of a shorter version.' *Clinical Gerontologist: Journal of Aging and Mental Health*, 5, (1–2), 165–173.

Shellman, J., Ennis, E. and Bailey-Addison, K. (2011) 'A contextual examination of reminiscence functions in older African-Americans.' *Journal of Aging Studies*, 25, 348–354. doi:10.1016/j.aging.2011.01.001

Shellman, J.M., Mokel, M. and Hewitt, N. (2009) 'The effects of integrative reminiscence on depressive symptoms in older African Americans.' *Western Journal of Nursing Research*, 31, 772–786.

Shellman, J.M. and Zhang, D. (2014) 'Psychometric testing of the Modified Reminiscence Function Scale.' *Journal of Nursing Measurement*, 22, 3, 500–510.

Sherman, E.A. (1991) *Reminiscence and the Self in Old Age.* New York: Springer Publishing.

Shik, A.W., Sau-Chun Yue, J., Kwong-leung and Tang, Y.L. (2009) 'Life is beautiful: Using reminiscence groups to promote wellbeing among Chinese older people with mild dementia.' *Groupwork*, 19, 2, 8–27. doi:10.1921/095182410X490368

Singer, J.A., Blagov, P., Berry, M. and Oost, K.M. (2013) 'Self-defining memories, scripts, and the life story: Narrative identity in personality and psychotherapy.' *Journal of Personality*, 81, 569–582.

Slavney, P.R. and McHugh, P. (1984) 'Life stories and meaningful connections: Reflections on a clinical method in psychiatry and medicine.' *Perspectives in Biology and Medicine*, 27, 279–288.

Smith, D.L. (2000) 'The mirror image of the present: Freud's theory of retrogressive screen memories.' *Psychoanalytische Perspecktieven*, 39, 7–29.

Smith, E.E. (2017) *The Power of Meaning*. New York: Broadway Books.

Smith, K.L., Crete-Nishihata, M., Damianakis, T., Baecker, R. and Marziali, E. (2009) 'Multimedia biographies: A reminiscence and social stimulus tool for persons with cognitive impairment.' *Journal of Technology in Human Services*, 27, 4, 287–306.

Sneed, J.R., Whitbourne, S. and Culang, M.E. (2006) 'Trust, identity and ego integrity: Modelling Erikson's core stages over 34 years.' *Journal of Adult Development*, 13, 3–4, 148–157.

Sok, S.R. (2015) 'Effects of individual reminiscence therapy for older women living alone.' *Ageing and Aged Care*, 62, 517–524.

Sommer, K.L. and Baumeister, R.F. (1998) 'The Construction of Meaning from Life Events: Empirical Studies of Personal Narratives.' In P.T. Wong, P.S. Fry and S. Prem (eds) *The Human Quest for Meaning from Life Events: A Handbook of Psychological Research and Clinical Applications* (pp.143–161). Mahwah, NJ: Lawrence Erlbaum.

Sools, A., Triliva, S. and Filippas, T. (2017) 'The role of desired future selves in the creation of new experience: The case of Greek unemployed young adults.' *Style*, 51, 318–336.

Span, M., Hettinga, M., Vernooij-Dassen, M., Eefstinge, J. and Smits, C. (2013) 'Involving people with dementia in the development of supportive IT applications: A systematic review.' *Ageing Research Reviews*, 12, 535–551. doi:10.1016/j.arr.2013.01.002

Spector, A., Orrell, M., Davies, S. and Woods, R.T. (1998) 'Reminiscence Therapy for Dementia: A Review of the Evidence of Effectiveness (Cochrane Review).' In *The Cochrane Library, Issue 3*. Oxford: Update Software.

Spector, A., Thorgrimsen, L., Woods, B., Royan, L. *et al.* (2003) 'Efficacy of an evidence-based cognitive stimulation therapy programme for people with dementia: Randomised controlled trial.' *British Journal of Psychiatry*, 183, 248–254.

Spielberger, C.D., Gorsuch, R.L., Lushene, P.R., Vagg, P.R. and Jacobs, A.G. (1983) *Manual for the State-Trait Anxiety Inventory (STAI)*. Palo Alto, CA: Consulting Psychologists Press.

Spruytte, N., Van Audenhove, C., Lammertyn, F. and Storms, G. (2002) 'The quality of the caregiving relationship in informal care for older adults with dementia and chronic psychiatric patients.' *Psychology and Psychotherapy: Theory, Research and Practice*, 75, 295–311.

Stahel, P. (2013) *Listen Up: The Art of Interviewing for Personal History*. Tampa, FL: Breath and Shadows Publications.

Staudinger, U.M. (2001) 'Life reflection: A social-cognitive analysis of life review.' *Review of General Psychology*, 5, 2, 148–160. doi:10.1037/1089-2680.5.2.148

Steger, M.F., Frazier, P., Oishi, S. and Kaler, M. (2006) 'The meaning in life questionnaire: Assessing the presence of and search for meaning in life.' *Journal of Counseling Psychology*, 53, 80–93.

Steger, M.F., Kashdan, T.B., Sullivan, B.A. and Lorentz, D. (2008a) 'Understanding the search for meaning in life: Personality, cognitive style, and the dynamic between seeking and experiencing meaning.' *Journal of Personality*, 76, 199–228.

Steger, M.F., Kawabata, Y., Simai, S. and Otake, K. (2008b) 'The meaningful life in Japan and the United States: Levels and correlates of meaning in life.' *Journal of Research in Personality*, 42, 660–678.

Steinhauser, K.E. (2000) 'Factors considered important at the end of life by patients, family, physicians, and other care providers.' *Journal American Medical Association*, 284, 2476. doi:10.1001/jama.284.19.2476

Stenhouse, R., Tait, J., Hardy, P. and Sumner, T. (2013) 'Dangling conversations: Reflections on the process of creating digital stories during a workshop with people with early stage dementia.' *Journal of Psychiatric and Mental Health Nursing*, 20, 134–141.

Stratford & Associates (2016) *Sharing Memories, Building Communities*. Belfast: RNNI.

Stroebe, M. and Schut, H. (1999) 'The dual process model of coping with bereavement: Rationale and description.' *Death Studies*, 23, 197–224. doi:10.1080/074811899201046

Stroebe, M. and Schut, H. (2005) 'To continue or relinquish bonds: A review of consequences for the bereaved.' *Death Studies*, 29, 477–494. doi:10.1080/07481180590962659

Stroebe, M. and Schut, H. (2010) 'The dual process model of coping with bereavement: A decade on.' *OMEGA: Journal of Death and Dying*, 61, 273–289. doi:10.1177/0030222815598668

Su, B. (2017) *Taiwan's 400 Year History* (in traditional Chinese). Taipei, Taiwan: Avanguard Company.

Subramaniam, P. and Woods, B. (2012) 'The impact of individual reminiscence therapy for people with dementia: Systematic review.' *Expert Reviews in Neurotherapeutics*, 12, 5, 545–555.

Subramaniam, P. and Woods, B. (2016) 'Digital life storybooks for people with dementia living in care homes.' *Clinical Interventions in Aging*, 11, 1263–1276.

Subramaniam, P., Woods, B. and Whitaker, C. (2014) 'Life review and life story books for people with mild to moderate dementia: A randomized control trial.' *Aging and Mental Health*, 18, 3, 363–375. doi:10.1080/13607863.2013.837144

Svensson, C.M. (2018) *Online Guided Autobiography Training*. Accessed on 18/02/2018 at http://guidedautobiography.com.

Sweeting, H.N. and Gilhooly, M.L. (1992) 'Doctor, am I dead? A review of social death in modern societies.' *OMEGA: Journal of Death and Dying*, 24, 251–269. doi:10.2190/l0n6-p489-nr8n-jq6k

Swinton, J. (2012) *Dementia: Living in the Memories of God*. Grand Rapids, MI: Eerdmans Publishing.

Taiwan Ministry of Health and Welfare (2017). Accessed on 18/02/2018 at www.mohw.gov.tw/cp-3425-36761-2.html.

Taiwan National Development Council (2016) *Taiwan Statistical Data Book. Population Projections for R.O.C.* (Taiwan) 2016–2160. Accessed on 17/02/2018 at www.ndc.gov.tw/en/cp.aspx?n=2E5DCB04C64512CC.

Tamura, T., Ohsumi, M., Oikawa, D., Higashi, Y. et al. (2007) 'Reminiscence: A comparison of conventional therapeutic and computer-based interactive methods.' *Journal of Robotics and Mechatronics*, 19, 6, 724–726.

Tanaka, K., Yukiko, Y., Kobayashi, Y., Sonohara, K. et al. (2007) 'Improve-d cognitive function, mood and brain blood flow in single photon emission computed tomography following individual reminiscence therapy in an elderly patient with Alzheimer's disease.' *Geriatric and Gerontology International*, 7, 305–309.

Tarman, V.I. (1988) 'Autobiography: The negotiation of a life time.' *International Journal of Aging and Human Development*, 27, 3, 171–191.

Taylor, C. (1989) *Sources of the Self: The Making of the Modern Identity*. Cambridge, MA: Harvard University Press.

Tedeschi, R.G. and Calhoun, L.G. (1996) 'The posttraumatic growth inventory: Measuring the positive legacy of trauma.' *Journal of Traumatic Stress*, 9, 455–471. doi:10.1002/jts.2490090305

Tedeschi, R.G. and Calhoun, L.G. (2004) 'Post traumatic growth: Conceptual foundations and empirical evidence.' *Psychological Inquiry*, 15, 1–18. doi:10.1207/s15327965pli1501_01

Tedeschi, R.G. and Calhoun, L.G. (2008) 'Beyond the concept of recovery: Growth and the experience of loss.' *Death Studies*, 32, 27–39. doi:10.1080/07481180701741251

Testad, I., Corbett, A., Aarsland, D., Lexow, K.O. et al. (2014) 'The value of personalized psychosocial interventions to address behavioral and psychological symptoms in people with dementia living in care home settings: a systematic review.' *International Psychogeriatrics*, 26, 07, 1083–1098.

Thiry, E. (2013) 'Designing a digital reminiscing system for older adults.' *ACM SIGACCESS Accessibility & Computing*, 105, 24–28. doi:10.1145/2444800.2444805

Thomas, L. and Briggs, P. (2016) 'Reminiscence through the lens of social media.' *Frontiers in Psychology*, 7, (Article 870), 1–11.
Thompson, P. with Bornat, J. (2017) *The Voice of the Past* (4th ed). Oxford: Oxford University Press.
Thorgrimsen, L., Schweitzer, P. and Orrell, M. (2002) 'Evaluating reminiscence for people with dementia: A pilot study.' *The Arts in Psychotherapy*, 29, 2, 93–97.
Thorgrimsen, L.; Selwood, A., Spector, A., Royan, L. *et al.* (2003) 'Whose quality of life is it anyway? The validity and reliability of the Quality of Life – Alzheimer's Disease (QoL-AD) Scale.' *Alzheimer Disease and Associated Disorders*, 17, 4, 201–208.
Thorne, A., McLean, K.C. and Lawrence, A.M. (2004) 'When remembering is not enough: Reflecting on self-defining memories in late adolescence.' *Journal of Personality*, 72, 3, 513–541.
Thornton, J.E. (2008) 'The Guided Autobiography method: A learning experience.' *International Journal of Aging and Human Development*, 66, 2, 155–173.
Thornton, J.E. and Collins, J.B. (2010) 'Adult Learning and Meaning Making in Community-based Guided Autobiography Workshops.' Commissioned Report. Toronto: Canadian Council on Learning.
Thornton, J.E., Collins, J.B., Birren, J.E. and Svensson, C.M. (2011) 'Guided autobiography's developmental exchange: What's in it for me?' *International Journal of Aging and Human Development*, 73, 3, 227–251.
Timmer, E., Westerhof, G.J. and Dittman-Kohli, F. (2005) 'When looking back on my past life I regret… Retrospective regret in the second half of life.' *Journal of Death Studies*, 29, 7. doi. org/080/07481180591004660
Tornstam, L. (2005) *Gerotranscendence: A Developmental Theory of Positive Ageing.* New York: Springer Publishing.
Tõugu, P., Tulviste, T., Schröder, L., Keller, H. *et al.* (2011) 'Socialization of past event talk: Cultural differences in maternal elaborative reminiscing.' *Cognitive Development*, 26, 142–154.
Tyrrell, M. (2003) 'Memoirist of ordinary, yet extraordinary elders.' *Generations*, 27, 3, 99–102.
Tyrrell, M. (2007) 'Satisfaction Survey of Elderly Clients and Families Hiring a Memoirist.' *Selected Conference Papers and Proceedings, International Reminiscence and Life Review Conference San Francisco* (pp.429–434). University of Wisconsin-Superior: IIRLR.
Tyrrell, M. (2008) 'Stories behind life stories: Musings of a memoirist.' *Journal of Aging, Humanities and the Arts*, 2, 99–112.
Tyrrell, M. (2012) *Become a Memoirist for Elders: Create a Successful Home Business.* St. Paul, MN: Memoirs, Inc. Accessed on 2/2/2018 at www.MemoirsLLC.com.
Tyrrell, M. (2013) 'A new and growing profession: Personal historians listening to elders' life stories.' *International Journal of Reminiscence and Life Review*, 1, 1, 48–50.
Uehara, I. (2015) Developmental Changes in Memory-Related Linguistic Skills and their Relationship to Episodic Recall in Children. *PloS ONE*, 10, e0137220.
Upton, D., Upton, P. and, Jones, T. (2011) *Evaluation of the Impact of Touch Screen Technology on People with Dementia and Their Carers within Care Home Settings.* Worcester: University of Worcester.
Valentino, K., Comas, M., Nuttall, A.K. and Thomas T. (2013) 'Training maltreating parents in elaborative and emotion-rich reminiscing with their preschool-aged children.' *Child Abuse and Neglect*, 37, 585–595.
van den Hoonaard, D.K. (1999) 'No regrets: Widows' stories about the last days of their husbands' lives.' *Journal of Aging Studies*, 13, 59–72.
van den Hoven, E., Sas, C. and Whittaker, S. (2012) 'Introduction to special issue on Designing for Personal Memories: Past, present, and future.' *Human-Computer Interaction*, 27, 1–2, 1–12. doi:10.1080/07370024.2012.673451

van der Velden, A.M., Kuyken, W., Wattar, U., Crane, C. et al. (2015) 'A systematic review of mechanisms of change in mindfulness-based cognitive therapy in the treatment of recurrent major depressive disorder.' *Clinical Psychology Review*, 37, 26–39. doi:10.1016/j.cpr.2015.02.001

van Tilborg, I.A., Kessels, R.P. and Hulstijn, W. (2011) 'How should we teach everyday skills in dementia? A controlled study comparing implicit and explicit training methods.' *Clinical Rehabilitation* 25, 638–648.

van Tilburg, W.A., Igou, E.R. and Sedikides, C. (2013) 'In search of meaningfulness: Nostalgia as an antidote to boredom.' *Emotion*, 13, 3, 450–461. doi:10.1037/a0030442

Vota, R.L. and de Vries, B. (2001) 'Guided Autobiography in Cyberspace.' In G. Kenyon, P. Clark and B. de Vries (eds) *Narrative Gerontology: Theory, Research and Practice* (pp.331–351). New York: Springer Publishing.

Vowinckel, J.C., Westerhof, G.J., Bohlmeijer, E.T. and Webster, J.D. (2015) 'Flourishing in the now: Initial validation of a present-eudaimonic time perspective scale.' *Time and Society*, 26, 2, 203–226.

Vygotsky, L.S. (1978) *Mind in Society: The Development of Higher Psychological Processes*. Cambridge, MA: Harvard University Press.

Walker, W.R. and Skowronski, J.J. (2009) 'The Fading Affect Bias: But What the Hell Is It For?' *Applied Cognitive Psychology* 23, 1122–1136.

Wallace Consulting (2010) *Evaluation Report for Reminiscence Network Northern Ireland*. Belfast: RNNI.

Walter, T. (1996) 'A new model of grief: Bereavement and biography.' *Mortality*, 1, 7–25. doi:10.1080/713685822

Wang, Q. (2013) 'The Cultured Self and Remembering.' In P.J. Bauer and R. Fivush (eds) *The Handbook of Children's Memory Development*. New York: Wiley-Blackwell.

Wang, C.W., Chow, A.Y. and Chan, C.L. (2017) 'The effects of life review interventions on spiritual wellbeing, psychological distress, and quality of life in patients with terminal or advanced cancer: A systematic review and meta-analysis of randomized controlled trials.' *Palliative Medicine*, 31, 883–894.

Warnock, M. (1987) *Memory*. London: Faber and Faber.

Washington, G. (2009) 'Modification and psychometric testing of the modified Reminiscence Functions Scale.' *Journal of Nursing Measurement*, 17, 2, 134–147.

Waters, T.E. (2014) 'Relations between the functions of autobiographical memory and psychological wellbeing.' *Memory*, 22, 265–275. doi:10.1080/09658211.2013.778293

Waters, T.E. and Fivush, R. (2015) 'Relations between narrative coherence, identity, and psychological wellbeing in emerging adulthood.' *Journal of Personality*, 83, 4, 44–451.

Watkins, E. (2015) 'Over General Autobiographical Memories and Their Relationship to Rumination.' In L.A. Watson and D. Berntsen (eds) *Clinical Perspectives on Autobiographical Memory* (pp.199–220). New York: Cambridge University Press.

Watson, L.A. and Dritschel, B. (2015) 'The Role of Self During Autobiographical Remembering and Psychopathology: Evidence from Philosophical, Behavioral, Neural and Cultural Investigations.' In L.A. Watson, and D. Berntsen (eds) *Clinical Perspectives on Autobiographical Memory* (pp.335–357). New York: Cambridge University Press.

Watt, L.M. and Cappeliez, P. (1995) 'Reminiscence Interventions for the Treatment of Depression in Older Adults.' In B.K. Haight and J.D. Webster (eds) *The Art and Science of Reminiscing: Theory, Research, Methods, and Applications* (pp.221–232). Philadelphia, PA: Taylor & Francis.

Watt, L.M. and Cappeliez, P. (2000) 'Integrative and instrumental reminiscence therapies for depression in older adults: Intervention strategies and treatment effectiveness.' *Aging and Mental Health*, 4, 2, 166–177.

Wayman, L. (2017) *A Loving Approach to Dementia Care. Making Meaningful Connections with the Person who has Alzheimer's Disease or Other Dementia or Memory Loss* (2nd ed). Maryland: John Hopkins University Press.

Webster, J.D. (1993) 'Construction and validation of the Reminiscence Functions Scale.' *Journal of Gerontology.* 48, 5, 256–262. doi:10.1093/geronj/48.5.p256

Webster, J.D. (1995) 'Adult Age Differences in Reminiscence Functions.' In B.K. Haight and J.D. Webster (eds) *The Art and Science of Reminiscing: Theory, Research, Methods, and Applications* (pp.89–102). Washington, DC: Taylor & Francis.

Webster, J.D. (1997) 'The Reminiscence Functions Scale: A replication.' *The International Journal of Aging and Human Development,* 44, 2, 137–148.

Webster, J.D. (2003) 'An exploratory analysis of a self-assessed wisdom scale.' *Journal of Adult Development,* 10, 1, 13–22.

Webster, J.D. (2011) 'A new measure of time perspective: Initial psychometric findings for the balanced time perspective scale (BTPS).' *Canadian Journal of Behavioural Science,* 43, 2, 111–118.

Webster, J.D., Bohlmeijer, E.T. and Westerhof, G.J. (2010) 'Mapping the future of reminiscence: A conceptual guide for research and practice.' *Research on Aging,* 32, 4, 527–564. doi:10.1177/0164027510364122

Webster, J.D., Bohlmeijer, E.T. and Westerhof, G.J. (2014) 'Time to flourish: The relationship of temporal perspective to wellbeing and wisdom across adulthood.' *Aging and Mental Health,* 18, 1046–1056.

Webster, J.D. and Gould, O. (2007) 'Reminiscence and vivid personal memories across adulthood.' *The International Journal of Aging and Human Development,* 64, 2, 149–170.

Webster, J.D. and Haight, B.K. (1995) 'Memory Lane Milestones: Progress in Reminiscence Definition and Classification.' In B.K. Haight and J.D. Webster (eds) *The Art and Science of Reminiscing: Theory, Research, Methods, and Applications* (pp.273–286). Washington, DC: Taylor & Francis.

Webster, J.D. and Haight, B.K. (2002) *Critical Advances in Reminiscence Work: From Theory to Application.* New York: Springer Publishing.

Webster, J.D., Weststrate, N.M., Ferrari, M., Munroe, M. and Pierce, T.W. (2017) 'Wisdom and meaning in emerging adulthood.' *Emerging Adulthood.* doi:10.1177/2167696817707662

Wenborn J., Hynes, S., Moniz-Cook, E., Mountain, G. *et al.* (2016) 'Community occupational therapy for people with dementia and family carers (COTiD-UK) versus treatment as usual: Valuing Active Life in Dementia (VALID) programme: Study protocol for a randomised controlled trial.' *Trials,* 17, 65. doi:10.1186/s13063-015-1150-y

Werner, P. and Heinik, J. (2008) 'Stigma by association and Alzheimer's disease.' *Aging and Mental Health,* 12, 92–99.

Westerhof, G.J. (2009) 'Identity Construction in the Third Age: The Role of Self-narratives.' In H. Hartung and R. Maierhofer (eds) *Narratives of Lives: Mediating Age* (pp.55–69). Münster: LIT.

Westerhof, G.J. (2010) '"During my life so much has changed that it looks like a new world to me": A narrative perspective on identity formation in times of cultural change.' *Journal of Aging Studies,* 24, 12–19.

Westerhof, G.J. (2017a) 'Technologies to remember or forget? A perspective from reminiscence and life review.' *International Journal of Reminiscence and Life Review,* 4, 8–13.

Westerhof, G.J. (2017b) 'The Use of Life Story Books for People with Dementia: A Systematic Review.' In G.J. Westerhof (Chair) Innovations in Interventions for Reminiscence and Life Review. Symposium at IAGG World Congress of Gerontology and Geriatrics. San Francisco, CA.

Westerhof, G.J., Beernink-Wassink, J. and Sools, A.M. (2016) 'Who am I? A life story intervention for persons with intellectual disability and psychiatric problems.' *Intellectual and Developmental Disabilities,* 54, 173–186.

Westerhof, G.J. and Bohlmeijer, E.T. (2014) 'Celebrating fifty years of research and applications in reminiscence and life review: State of the art and new directions.' *Journal of Aging Studies,* 29, 107–114. doi:10.1016/j.aging.2014.02.003

Westerhof, G.J., Bohlmeijer, E.T., van Beljouw, I.J. and Pot, A. (2010) 'Improvement in personal meaning mediates the effects of a life review intervention on depressive symptoms in a randomized controlled trial.' *The Gerontologist*, 50, 4, 541–549.
Westerhof, G.J., Bohlmeijer, E.T. and McAdams, D.P. (2017) 'The relation of ego-integrity and despair to personality traits and mental health.' *Journals of Gerontology: Psychological Sciences*, 72, 400–407.
Westerhof, G.J., Bohlmeijer, E. and Valenkamp, M.W. (2004) 'In search of meaning: A reminiscence program for older persons.' *Educational Gerontology*, 30, 751–766.
Westerhof, G.J., Bohlmeijer, E.T. and Webster, J.D. (2010) 'Reminiscence and mental health: A review of recent progress in theory, research and interventions.' *Ageing and Society*, 30, 4, 697–721. doi:10.1017/S0144686X09990328
Westerhof, G.J., Whitbourne, S.K. and Freeman, G.P. (2012) 'The aging self in a cultural context: The relation of conceptions of aging to identity processes and self-esteem in the United States and the Netherlands.' *The Journals of Gerontology Series B: Psychological Sciences and Social Sciences*, 67B, 1, 52–60. doi:10.1093/geronb/gbr075
Westwood, M.J., McLean, H., Cave, D., Borgen, W. and Slakov, P. (2010) 'Coming home: A group-based approach for assisting military veterans in transition.' *The Journal for Specialists in Group Work*, 35, 1, 44–68.
Whitbourne, S., Sneed, J.R. and Sayer, A. (2009) 'Psychosocial development from college through midlife: A 34-year sequential study.' *Developmental Psychology*, 45, 5, 1328–1340.
Whitlatch, C.J. and Menne, H.L. (2009) 'Don't forget about me: Decision making by people with dementia.' *Journal of the American Society on Aging*, 33, 66–71.
Whittaker, S., Kalnikaité, V., Petrelli, D., Sellen, A. et al. (2012) 'Socio-technical lifelogging: Deriving design principles for a future proof digital past.' *Human-Computer Interaction*, 27, 1–2, 37–62.
Williams, J.G., Barnhofer, T., Crane, C., Herman, D. et al. (2007) 'Autobiographical memory specificity and emotional disorder.' *Psychological Bulletin*, 133, 1, 122–148.
Williams, J.M. and Broadbent, K. (1986) 'Autobiographical memory in suicide attempters.' *Journal of Abnormal Psychology*, 95, 2, 144–149.
Williams, K., Harris, B., Lueger, A., Ward, K. et al. (2011) 'Visual cues for person-centered communication.' *Clinical Nursing Research*, 20, 4, 448–461.
Wilson, A.E. and Ross, M. (2000) 'The frequency of temporal-self and social comparisons in people's personal appraisals.' *Journal of Personality and Social Psychology*, 78, 928.
Wilson, A.E. and Ross, M. (2003) 'The identity function of autobiographical memory: Time is on our side.' *Memory*, 11, 2, 137–149.
Wink, P. and Schiff, B. (2002) 'To Review or Not to Review? The Role of Personality and Life Events in Life Review and Adaptation to Older Age.' In J.D. Webster and B.K. Haight (eds) *Critical Advances in Reminiscence Work: From Theory to Applications* (pp.44–60). New York: Springer Publishing.
Wong, P.T. (1989) 'Personal meaning and successful aging.' *Canadian Psychology/Psychologie Canadienne*, 30, 3, 516–525.
Wong, P.T. and Watt, L.M. (1991) 'What types of reminiscence are associated with successful aging?' *Psychology and Aging*, 6, 2, 272–279. doi:10.1037/0882-7974.6.2.272
Woodhead, D. (2017) *Evidence Briefing: Remembering Yesterday, Caring Today: Participants' Voices*. London: European Reminiscence Network. Accessed on 22/02/2018 at www.rememberingtogether.eu/David-Woodhead-report-RYCT.pdf.
Woods, B., Bruce, E., Edwards, R., Elvish, R. et al. (2012) 'REMCARE: Reminiscence groups for people with dementia and their family caregivers, effectiveness and cost-effectiveness: Pragmatic multicentre randomized trial.' *Healthcare Technology Assessment*, 16, 48, 1–116. doi:10.3310/hta16480
Woods, R.T., Bruce, E. and Edwards, R.T., Hounsome, B. et al. (2009) 'Reminiscence groups for people with dementia and their family carers: Pragmatic eight-centre randomised trial of joint reminiscence and maintenance versus usual treatment: A protocol.' *Trials*, 10, 64.

Woods, B., O'Philbin, L., Farrell, E.M., Spector, A.E. and Orrell, M. (2018) 'Reminiscence Therapy for Dementia (Review).' *Cochrane Library Database of Systematic Reviews. Issue 3.* doi:10.1002/14651858. CD001120.pub3

Woods, R.T., Orrell, M., Bruce, E. and Edwards, R.T. (2016) 'REMCARE: Pragmatic multi-centre randomised trial of reminiscence groups for people with dementia and their family carers: Effectiveness and economic analysis.' *PLoS One*, 11, 4, e0152843. doi:10.1371/journal.pone.0152843

Woods, R.T., Nelis S.M., Martyr A., Roberts, J.L. et al. (2014) 'What contributes to a good quality of life in early dementia? Awareness and the QoL-AD: A cross-sectional study.' *Health and Quality of Life Outcomes 12*, 94. doi:10.1186/1477-7525-12-94

Woods, B., Spector, A.E., Jones, C.A., Orrell, M. and Davies, S.P. (2005) 'Reminiscence Therapy for Dementia.' *Cochrane Database of Systematic Reviews, Issue 2.* Chichester: Wiley. doi:10.1002/14651858.CD001120.pub2

World Health Organization (2008) *Active Ageing: A Policy Framework.* Accessed on 20/02/2018 at http://apps.who.int/iris/bitstream/10665/67215/1/WHO_NMH_NPH_02.8.pdf.

Wortman, C.B. and Boerner, K. (2011) 'The Myths of Coping with Loss: What the Scientific Evidence Tells Us.' In H. Friedman (ed.) *Oxford Handbook of Health Psychology* (pp.441–479). New York: Oxford University Press. doi:10.1093/oxfordhb/9780195342819.013.0019

Wright, A.A., Keating, N.L., Balboni, T.A., Matulonis, U.A., Block, S.D. and Prigerson, H.G. (2010) 'Place of death: Correlations with quality of life of patients with cancer and predictors of bereaved caregivers' mental health.' *Journal of Clinical Oncology*, 28, 4457–4464.

Wright, T. and Mulvenna, M.D. (2012) 'The Memory Game: An iPad-based interactive reminiscence programme to aid those with dementia.' *Gerontologist*, 52, 1, 274–274.

Wrosch, C., Bauer, I. and Scheier, M.F. (2005) 'Regret and quality of life across the adult life span: The influence of disengagement and available future goals.' *Psychology and Aging*, 20, 657–670.

Wrosch, C. and Heckhausen, J. (2002) 'Perceived control of life regrets: Good for young and bad for old adults.' *Psychology and Aging*, 17, 340–350.

Xiao, H., Kwong, E., Pang, S. and Mok, E. (2011) 'Perceptions of a life review program among Chinese patients with advanced cancer.' *Journal of Clinical Nursing*, 21, 564–572. doi:10.1111/j.1365-2702.2011.03842.x

Yancura, L.A. (2013) 'How to make reminiscence movies: A project-based gerontology course.' *Educational Gerontology*, 39, 11, 828–839.

Yasuda, K., Kuwabara, K., Kuwahara, N., Abe, S. and Tetsutani, N. (2009) 'Effectiveness of personalised reminiscence photo videos for individuals with dementia.' *Neuropsychological Rehabilitation*, 19, 4, 603–619.

Yin, R.K. (2011) *Applications of Case Study Research.* Thousand Oaks, CA: Sage.

Young, R., Camic, P.M. and Tischler, V. (2015) 'The impact of community-based arts and health interventions on cognition in people with dementia: A systematic literature review.' *Aging and Mental Health*, 20, 4, 337–351.

Zaman, W. and Fivush, R. (2011) 'Intergenerational narratives and adolescents' emotional wellbeing.' *Journal of Adolescence*, 21, 703–716.

Zaman, W. and Fivush, R. (2013) 'Gender differences in elaborative parent–child emotion and play narratives.' *Sex Roles*, 68, 591–604.

Zeilig, H., Killick, J. and Fox, C. (2014) 'The participative arts for people with a dementia: A critical review.' *International Journal of Ageing and Later Life*, 9, 1, 7–34.

Zhang, X., Xiao, H. and Chen, Y. (2017) 'Effects of life review on mental health and wellbeing among cancer patients: A systematic review.' *International Journal of Nursing Studies*, 74, 138–148.

Zizioulas, J.D. (1975) 'Human capacity and human incapacity: A theological exploration of personhood.' *Scottish Journal of Theology*, 28, 5, 40–44.

List of Contributors

Susan Bluck PhD is a Professor in Psychology at the University of Florida. As Director of the Life Story Laboratory, she works with her team of doctoral students and undergraduates to conduct research on the functions of autobiographical remembering across the lifespan. She teaches courses on memory, adult development and aging, and death and dying.

Jordan Booker PhD is an Assistant Professor in the Department of Psychological Sciences at the University of Missouri, Columbia, Missouri. His research focuses broadly on socio-emotional development and flourishing among youth and emerging adults.

Christine Bryden AM PhD was recently awarded her doctorate for research on the continuing sense of self in the lived experience of dementia and she is an Adjunct Research Fellow in the Public and Contextual Theology Centre of Charles Sturt University, Canberra, Australia. Diagnosed with dementia in 1995, she has become a published author and international speaker and made a member of the Order of Australia in 2016 for her national and international pioneering dementia advocacy work.

Philippe Cappeliez PhD is Emeritus Professor at the University of Ottawa, where for 30 years he taught psychology of aging and clinical geropsychology. His clinical and research interests are the functions of reminiscence for health and wellbeing, and reminiscence therapy for depression in older adulthood.

Peter Coleman PhD is Emeritus Professor of Psychogerontology and an associate member of the Centre for Research on Ageing at the University of Southampton, UK. His research relates to the mental health of older people, especially the functions of reminiscence and life review and sources of self-esteem and meaning in later life.

Kate de Medeiros PhD is Associate Professor of Gerontology at Miami University, Oxford, Ohio. Her work focuses broadly on cultural structures affecting the experience of aging and the construction of self, the role of friendships in later life, and narrative approaches to understanding the experiences of older age.

Brian de Vries PhD is Professor Emeritus of Gerontology at San Francisco State University, with adjunct appointments at Canada's Simon Fraser University, Vancouver, and the University of Alberta, Edmonton. He has co-edited several professional journals and academic books, authored and co-authored many journal articles and books on life review and reminiscence, the social and psychological wellbeing of midlife and older lesbian, gay, bisexual, and transgender (LGBT) persons.

Ann Elliott PhD is a Professor at Radford University where she is the Coordinator of the Clinical-Counseling Psychology Master's Degree Program and the Director of the Center for Gender Studies. Her doctorate in clinical psychology is from Northern Illinois University and her clinical internship was undertaken at the National Crime Victims Research and Treatment Center, Medical University of South Carolina. She currently serves on the Editorial Board of *Child Maltreatment*.

Marian Ferguson BA MEd PGCE introduced reminiscence activities into the Ulster Museum Belfast's programme and developed its reminiscence loan box service in her role as Education Officer. An experienced project facilitator and reminiscence trainer and group facilitator, she was the manager of the Reminiscence Network Northern Ireland during its Sharing Memories Building Communities project.

Robyn Fivush PhD is the Samuel Candler Dobbs Professor of Psychology at Emory University. Her teaching and research focuses on the social construction of autobiographical memory and the relations among memory, narrative, identity, trauma, and meaning-making.

Geraldine Gallagher PhD is an independent reminiscence trainer and practitioner with a research interest in intergenerational repressed trauma related to families of political ex-prisoners in Northern Ireland. Her interactive workshops train practitioners to use a range of creative artistic techniques for evoking, capturing and displaying the reminiscences of people challenged with a range of health issues, including stroke and dementia.

Faith Gibson OBE AM BA BEd is Emeritus Professor of Social Work, Ulster University, Northern Ireland. She returned to live in Australia after many years in the UK and has a long-time interest in teaching, researching, practising and writing about reminiscence and life story work.

Esther Gieschen MA coordinates the online certificate course in Reminiscence and Life Story Work offered by the University of Wisconsin at the Superior Center for Continuing Education. Prior to her position with the university she was an Alzheimer's educator and care consultant and is especially interested in the use of reminiscence to improve the quality of life of individuals living with memory loss/dementia.

Barbara Haight RNC DRPH FAAN FGSA is Professor Emeritus at the College of Nursing, Medical University of South Carolina. Involved in the process of reminiscence for many years through research in life review and publishing widely, she served as the first President of the International Institute for Reminiscence and Life Review and also helped to establish the Reminiscence and Aging Group at the Gerontological Society of America.

Christine Ivani-Chalian PhD has specialised in the study of adult development and learning, and has undertaken a master's thesis on the University of the Third Age and a doctorate on disability and open learning. She has also worked for the UK's Open University, teaching on social care and social work courses.

TsuAnn Kuo MSW MSG MHA PhD is an Assistant Professor, Department of Medical Sociology and Social Work, Chung Shan Medical University, Taichung City, Taiwan. She has a master's degree from the Davis School of Gerontology, University of Southern California and a doctorate from the University of California, Los Angeles. She heads the Hsiang Shang Culture and Education Foundation, providing training for life review group leaders and establishing evidence-based life review programmes for Taiwan's diverse elderly population.

Elizabeth MacKinlay AM PhD is a registered nurse, a priest in the Anglican Church of Australia and an Adjunct Professor in the School of Theology, Charles Sturt University, where she was the inaugural Director of the Centre for Ageing and Pastoral Studies. She has published widely on spiritual reminiscence and a second edition of her book, *The Spiritual Dimension of Ageing*, was published in February 2017.

Julia McNeil is a PhD student in nursing at the University of Connecticut. She has worked as a critical care nurse, a critical care nurse educator and an adjunct medical/surgical clinical instructor. These experiences have led her to an interest in mental health research and improving patient outcomes.

Emily Mroz MS is a doctoral student in the department of Developmental Psychology at the University of Florida. Her bachelor's degree in Psychology and Gerontology is from the University at Buffalo and her master's degree is from the University of Florida where her research primarily focuses on how memory plays a role in end-of-life experiences, palliative care and caregiving at the end of life.

Mary O'Brien Tyrrell MPH BSN designed a model to honour elderly people by founding Memoirs, Inc. (now Memoirs, LLC) in 1994. She assists people to publish their life story in limited-edition hardcover books that whenever possible are distributed at family book-signing parties. Her company has been featured in *The New York Times*, *The Wall Street Journal*, *VFW Magazine*, and *Kiplinger's Retirement Report*. Also recognised academically, her articles were the first in academic gerontological literature to describe this emerging industry of personal historians.

Thomas Pierce PhD is a Professor of Psychology at Radford University. He has a bachelor's degree from McGill University, a doctorate from the University of Maine and has held a postdoctoral fellowship in the Center for the Study of Aging and Human Development at Duke University Medical Center. He is a past President of the International Institute for Reminiscence and Life Review and currently serves as the Editor of the *International Journal of Reminiscence and Life Review*.

Maureen Robinson MPhil is a psychologist, who worked on all stages of the Southampton Ageing Project. She is an independent advocate for older people and people experiencing dementia, and is a long-standing community activist, having served over 20 years as a local councillor as well as holding non-executive posts within the UK's National Health Service and housing organisations.

Assumpta Ryan PhD is Professor of Ageing and Health, Ulster University, Northern Ireland. Her research covers aging and the care of older people, especially the needs of family carers, psychosocial approaches in dementia care and improving quality of life in care homes. She edits the *Journal of the All-Ireland Gerontological Nurses Association* and is an editorial board member of *Dementia: The International Journal of Social Research and Practice*, and *The International Journal of Older People Nursing*.

Pam Schweitzer MBE BA is an Honorary Doctor of Arts and Honorary Research Fellow at the University of Greenwich, London. She is a writer, theatre director, lecturer and trainer who founded Age Exchange Theatre and the Reminiscence Centre in Blackheath in 1983 and was its Artistic Director until 2005. She is Founder/Director of the European Reminiscence Network and is currently specialising in reminiscence in dementia care. In recognition of her work, in 2014 she received a National Dementia Award.

Juliette Shellman PhD is an Associate Professor at the University of Connecticut School of Nursing where she is involved in training healthcare professionals and students to facilitate integrative reminiscence with older adults. Her reminiscence research focuses on the development and testing of a peer reminiscence intervention for minority elders to decrease depressive symptoms. She is presently president of the IIRLR.

Sara Stemen is a doctoral student in Social Gerontology at Miami University, Oxford, Ohio. Her work focuses on the intersection of social connectedness and wellbeing, the experience of bereavement and continuing bonds in later life, and the social construction of age.

Cheryl Svensson PhD has worked in the field of aging since 1977 when she received her master's degree in Gerontology from the University of Southern California (USC) and completed a doctorate from the University of Lund, Sweden. For over 20 years she worked closely with James Birren to develop guided autobiography and is currently the Director of the Birren Center for Autobiographical Studies at USC.

Jeffrey Dean Webster PhD has taught at Langara College in Vancouver, Canada, for the past 30 years. He is the developer of the Reminiscence Functions Scale (RFS), a past President of the International Institute for Reminiscence and Life Review and was awarded the Robert Butler/Myrna Lewis award for excellence in reminiscence research in 2009. His current research interests include wisdom, time perspective and reminiscence.

Gerben Westerhof PhD is Professor of Narrative Psychology and Technology and Director of the Story Lab at the University of Twente, Enschede, the Netherlands. His work focuses on how the telling of stories and remembering one's life is related to mental health and wellbeing across the lifespan. He designs narrative and life review interventions, connecting theoretical insights, professional expertise and client values.

Bob Woods is an Emeritus Professor of Clinical Psychology of Older People at Bangor University, Wales, UK. For over 40 years he combined clinical work in the National Health Service with research that has helped to develop and evaluate psychosocial interventions for people with dementia and their carers, including cognitive stimulation and reminiscence work.

Loriena Yancura PhD is Professor and Program Coordinator for the Human Development and Family Studies Program at the University of Hawaii at Manoa. Assisted by her students, she has been doing reminiscence interviews and making movies with older adults for ten years. She is Chair of the Reminiscence, Narrative and Life Story: Research and Practice Interest Group of the Gerontological Society of America and is a board member of the *International Institute for Reminiscence and Life Review*.

Subject Index

Across the Sea (play) 285–6
adolescence, reminiscing during 119–22
Age Exchange (theatre company) 284
Aged Friendly City program (Taiwan) 127–8
art-based reminiscence programs
  Legacy Art Work 127
  life review program (Taiwan) 135–6
  My Life in a Box project 297–9
  see also theatre, reminiscence
autobiographical memory 247–8

bitterness revival function 234–5
body-mind unity 214
books
  community-based story book projects 127
  digital life story book 42, 83, 355–7
  see also Memoirs, Inc. (life story publishing)
boredom reduction function 233–4

carers
  information technology for supporting 353–4
  involving 50–2, 275
Cartesian dualism 214
Certificate in Reminiscence and Life Story Work
  capstone practicum projects 366–7
  course content 362–7
  course evaluations 367–71
  history of 360–2
  outcomes 367
children
  adolescents 119–22
  elaborative reminiscing style with 114–5, 117–8

emotion reminiscing style with 116–7, 118–9
intergenerational narratives 120–4, 187–8, 286–8
parent-child reminiscing 112–3
parental reminiscing style 114–6
parents' stories 120–2
Reminiscing and Emotion Training (RET) with 57
closure 319
Cochrane reviews of reminiscence therapy for dementia 65–71
community-based story book projects 127
Companion computer 342
Computer Interactive Reminiscence Conversation Aid (CIRCA) 349–50
computer technology *see* information technology
connections, making 27–8
continuing bonds with lost loved one 167
conversation partners 219–21
cultural differences
  in guided autobiography (GAB) 194–6
  in narrative forms of storytelling 111, 113
  recent research into 45–8
  in self-positive functions of reminiscence 202–3
  in topics for reminiscence 129–30
  see also life review program (Taiwan)

DARES program 49
death
  preparation for (function of reminiscence) 238–9
  setting of 177–9
  see also loss of a loved one

423

dementia
  Cochrane reviews of reminiscence therapy for 65–71
  deficit view of 222–3
  diagnosis as dominant story 215, 218
  evidence-based practice 62–5
  fear of 217–8
  narrative care for people with 219–21
  narrative care-partners 219–21
  narrative quest of 221–2
  narrative self and 212–5
  present moment as pivotal point 216–7
  recent research 49–52
  religious faith endures 224
  reminiscence as cognitive training in 49–50
depression
  Centre for Epidemiological Studies – Depression Scale (CES-D) 230–1
  cycles of reminiscences in 243
  functions of reminiscence in (study) 229–40
  life review therapy for 53–4
  mindfulness-based therapy for 241
difficult memories
  case studies 89–96
  resolution of uncomfortable feelings/relationships (Taiwan study) 141
digital life story book 42, 83, 355–7
digital photographs 42
directive function of reminiscence 44

elaborative reminiscing style 114–5, 117–8
emotion socialisation of children 116–7, 118–9
episodic memory 212–3
European Reminiscence Network 292–4
expressive writing 184–5

family
  intergenerational narratives 120–4, 187–8, 286–8
  see also children
functions of reminiscence
  bitterness revival 234–5
  boredom reduction 233–4
  death preparation 238–9
  in depressed adults (study) 229–40
  intimacy maintenance 235–6
  overview 172–3
  problem solving 238
  Reminiscence Functions Scale (RFS) 43, 44, 226–7, 230
  self-continuity 173–4
  self-function 44
  self-negative 44, 55–6, 228, 233–6
  self-positive 44, 55–6, 200–1, 227–8, 236–9
  social 44, 174–6, 228–9, 239–40

Good Companions, The 290–2
Gospel narratives 216
grief responses 164
  see also loss of a loved one
groups
  joint reminiscence groups 69
  self stories workshop (case example) 250–60
  Sharing Memories Building Communities (SMBC) Project workshops 266–7
  small group process (guided autobiography) 185
  vs. one-to-one work 68–9
growth, personal (through loss of a loved one) 165–6
guided autobiography (GAB)
  benefits/value of 186–9, 197–9
  confidentiality in 185–6
  content/themes in 182, 190
  expressive writing 184–5
  history of 180–1
  life themes 183
  outcomes of 183–6, 192–4
  process of 182–3, 190–2
  research into 189–94
  sensitizing questions 184
  small group process 185
  see also life review program (Taiwan)

heuristic model of reminiscence 40
history of reminiscence movement 17–24
hope, in Taiwan life review program 141–3

identity
  development in adolescence 119–22
  loss of a loved one and 173–4

as self-positive function of reminiscence 237
women's loss of (Taiwan study) 139–41
information technology
  Companion computer 342
  Computer Interactive Reminiscence Conversation Aid (CIRCA) 349–50
  computer-assisted reminiscence 127, 343–4
  and dementia 342
  digital photographs 42
  digital story books 42, 83, 355–7
  InspireD study 351–2
  Memory Matters (MM) app 344
  multimedia 349–51
  in Sharing Memories Building Communities (SMBC) Project 272–4
  for supporting caregivers 353–4
  user engagement in development of 345–9
InspireD study 351–2
instrumental reminiscence 44, 53
integrative reminiscence 44, 52–3, 317, 320
intergenerational narratives 120–4, 187–8, 286–8
International Institute for Reminiscence and Life Review (IIRLR) 359–60
intimacy maintenance function 235–6

joint reminiscence groups 69

language as basis for narrative 218–9
life review
  effectiveness evidence 324–5
  function of 314
  interventions 321–5
  and lifespan development 312–4
  meaning processes in 315–8
  and mental health/wellbeing 318–20
  Stories We Live By 322–3
  see also guided autobiography (GAB); life review therapy; structured life review
life review program (Taiwan)
  art therapy in 135–6
  evaluation/results 137–43
  guided autobiography basis of 128

hope for future 141–3
main themes emerging from 138
pride in life stories 138–9
program structure 131–2
recognition of self-achievements 139
resolution of uncomfortable feelings/relationships 141
topics chosen for 129–30
Train the Leaders program 133–7
life review therapy 48, 53–4
  see also structured life review
life stories
  digital story books 42, 83, 355–7
  meaning-making through 249
  multi-sensory life story pictures 276
  sociocultural nature of 110–2, 113
'lifelogging' 43
lifespan development 312–4
listening, in spiritual reminiscence 149–50
loss of a loved one
  continuing bonds 167
  identity and 173–4
  meaning reconstruction in 163–6
  memories of the dying days 162–3, 170–7
  personal growth through 165–6
  records left by deceased 169–70
  remembering final conversations 176–7
  remembering life of 167–70
  setting of the death 177–9
  social bonding through reminiscence 174–6
  spontaneous reminiscence after 167–8

meaning
  autobiographical integration and 317
  evaluation of memory and 315–6, 319
  identification with memory and 316, 319
  narrative as search for 147–8, 202–3
  narrative/reminiscence/meaning study 203–10
  and our sense of time 215–7
  reasoning and 316–7, 319–20
  role of memory in 163–6
  search for final 153, 155–6
  search for 248–9
  through life stories 249

mediational models 54–6
Memoirs, Inc. (life story publishing)
  background to 328–31
  book signing party 335
  donating to local library 335–6
  establishing the business 321–34
  ethical principles of 336–9
  legacy of 339–40
  process of 334–9
memorializing behaviours 168
memory
  autobiographical 247–8
  of deceased's dying days 162–3, 170–7
  episodic 212–3
  reminiscence as cognitive training for 49–50
  role in meaning reconstruction 163–6
Memory Matters (MM) app 344
mental health
  closure 319
  life review and 318–20
  reminiscence therapy for 52–6
  see also depression
methodology *see* research
mind-body unity 214
mindfulness-based therapy 241
multi-sensory life story picture 276
multimedia *see* information technology
My Life in a Box project 297–9

narrative awareness 201, 204
narrative care-partners 219–21
narrative quest (parable) 221–2
narrative research methodology 30
narrative self
  emergence of 112–3
  language as basis for 218–9
  in lived experience of dementia 213–5
  vs. factual chronology 213
narrative/reminiscence/meaning study 203–10
negative feelings towards reminiscence
  carers 81–2
  patients 79–80, 106–7
negative outcomes in reminiscence therapy 241

one-to-one vs. group work 68–9

parable (narrative quest) 221–2
parents
  parent-child reminiscing 112–3
  reminiscing style of 114–6
  telling stories to children 120–2
personal growth, through loss of a loved one 165–6
personal vs. generic memorabilia 354–5
photographs, digital 42
problem solving function of reminiscence 238
PTSD (war veterans) 57–8

qualitative vs. quantitative research 29–30, 52

redemption narrative 111
REMCARE study 74–82
Remembering Yesterday, Caring Today (RYCT) program 50–2, 71–82, 294–7, 300–2
reminiscence, definitions of 246–7
Reminiscence Centre Blackheath 286–8
Reminiscence Functions Scale (RFS) 43, 44, 226–7, 230
Reminiscence Network Northern Ireland (RNNI) 263
reminiscence/narrative/meaning study 203–10
Reminiscing and Emotion Training (RET) 57
research
  basic research 41–8
  basic vs. applied research 39
  breadth vs. depth path 41
  Cochrane reviews of reminiscence therapy for dementia 65–71
  functions of reminiscence 43–5
  future of 58–9
  heuristic model of reminiscence 40
  mediational models 54–6
  Medical Research Council (MRC) Framework 63–4
  methodology difficulties 63
  narrative methods 30
  new technologies to elicit reminiscences 42–3
  overview of 38–41
  practice-oriented research 48–58

qualitative vs. quantitative 29–30, 52
REMCARE study 74–82

self *see* identity; narrative self
self stories workshop (case example) 250–60
self-actualisation 143
self-concept 245–6
self-continuity 173–4
self-function of reminiscence 44
self-negative functions of reminiscence 44, 55–6, 228, 233–6
self-positive functions of reminiscence 44, 55–6, 200–1, 227–8, 236–9
setting
  care home vs. community 69
  of death 177–9
Sharing Memories Building Communities (SMBC) Project
  background 263–4
  carers involved in 275–6
  case examples (creative workshops) 266–7, 268–9
  case examples (life story work) 270–2
  celebration events 278–9
  life story work 267
  methodology 272–4
  objectives of 265
  outputs of 278–80
  participants 267–8
  staffing/management 265–6, 277
SHIELD programme 80–1
social functions of reminiscence 44, 174–6, 228–9, 239–40
sociocultural nature of life stories 110–2, 113
Southampton Longitudinal Study
  difficult memories (case studies) 89–96
  overview of 86–8
  review and acceptance of life story (case studies) 96–105
spiritual reminiscence
  definition of 145, 150–1
  developing a method for 150–2
  examples/case studies 156–60
  narrative and 151–2
  process of 154, 155–6
  search for final meanings 153, 155–6
  study overview 148–50
  tasks of ageing as basis for 152–3

stories
  self stories workshop (case example) 250–60
  Stories We Live By 322–3
  see also life stories
structured life review
  characteristics of 305–6
  definition of 305
  duration of 306
  literature review 306–10
  theory underpinning 304–5

Taiwan
  Aged Friendly City program 127–8
  aging population 126–7
  traditional storytelling in 125
  see also life review program (Taiwan)
Talking About Life Experiences (TALE) measure 44
technology *see* information technology
telling own story
  importance of 154–5, 189, 220–1
  narrative care-partners 219–21
theatre, reminiscence
  Across the Sea (play) 285–6
  European Reminiscence Network 292–4
  founding professional company 283–4
  published stories 284, 286
  Remembering Yesterday, Caring Today (RYCT) program 50–2, 71–82, 294–7, 300–2
  Reminiscence Centre Blackheath 286–8
  speaking style retained in 284
  The Good Companions 290–2
  training by 288–90
theory development 59
time
  and meaning 215–7
  present moment as pivotal point 216–7
training
  from theatre company staff 288–90
  Train the Leaders program (Taiwan) 133–7
  see also Certificate in Reminiscence and Life Story Work
trauma, reminiscence therapy for 56–8

unwillingness to reminisce 79–80, 106–7

war veterans 57–8
willingness/unwillingness to reminisce
    79–80, 106–7
women, loss of self-identity (Taiwan
    study) 139–41

writing
    expressive 184–5
    self stories workshop (case example)
        250–60
    see also Memoirs, Inc. (life story
        publishing)

Author Index

Abraham, R. 220
Adam, S. 118
Adler, J.M. 109, 201, 315, 318, 319, 320
Affleck, G. 166
Affonso, D.D. 314
Afonso, R.M. 49
Age UK 276
Aguirre, E. 353
Alea, N. 21, 44, 45, 162, 170, 172, 173, 174, 175, 227, 237, 239, 240
Ali, S. 239
Allé, M.C. 43
Allen, R.S. 170
Alm, N. 345, 350, 355
Alwin, D.F. 128
Alzheimer's Disease International 214
Alzheimer's Research UK 353
Amano, K. 179
Ancient, C. 356
Anderson, R.J. 232
Ando, M. 47, 308
Andrews, J. 111
Antoine, P. 239
Archbold, P.G. 352
Asberg, M. 87
Astell, A.J. 341, 342, 344, 345, 347, 349, 350, 353, 354, 355, 356
Attig, T. 168
Ayduk, O. 241

Ba, Amadou Hampaté 189
Baars, J. 216, 217, 219
Bachem, R. 308
Baddeley, A. 164, 176
Baddeley, J.L. 165, 171, 173, 174, 175
Bailey-Addison, K. 230
Baker, J.E. 171
Baldwin, C. 217, 221
Baldwin, S.A. 164

Balk, D.E. 165
Baltes, P.B. 59
Bangor, A. 346
Barker, T.H. 25
Bassett, H.H. 116
Basting, A. 25
Bauer, I. 319
Baumeister, R.F. 122, 245, 246, 247, 248, 261
BBC 285
Beall, S. 184
Bear-Lehman, J. 54
Bech, P. 352
Beck, A. 53
Beekman, A.T. 230, 231
Bell, G. 43
Bennett, K.M. 172, 175, 176
Bergsma, A. 347
Bernard, M. 275
Berntsen, D. 44, 167, 238
Berry, E. 43
Billieux, J. 233
Billitteri, J. 244, 249
Binder, B. 308, 309
Bird, A. 118
Birren Center for Autobiographical Studies 194
Birren, J.E. 23, 38, 48, 128, 129, 132, 137, 165, 170, 172, 180, 185, 190, 191, 192, 193, 194, 196, 244, 321
Bjorn, A. 65
Black, J. 321
Bluck, S. 21, 44, 45, 119, 162, 163, 165, 166, 168, 170, 171, 172, 173, 174, 175, 177, 178, 190, 201, 227, 237, 238, 239, 240, 242, 249, 314, 317, 319
Blustein, J. 219
Boehnlein, J.K. 322

Boerner, K. 164, 167
Bohanek, J.G. 111, 112, 120, 121, 122
Bohlmeijer, E.T. 21, 23, 24, 40, 44, 48, 52, 61, 193, 201, 202, 203, 225, 241, 244, 305, 314, 315, 318, 319, 320, 322, 324, 325
Bonanno, G.A. 164
Booker, J.A. 22, 119, 120, 121
Borkan, J. 368
Bornat, J. 20
Bowlby, J. 59
Boyd, H.D. 354
Brankaert, R. 345
Brassai, L. 202
Breen, A.V. 111
Brewer, W.F. 247
Briggs, P. 42
Brinker, J. K. 232
Broadbent, K. 50
Brockmeier, J. 317
Brooker, D. 77, 244
Brown-Shaw, M. 193
Bruce, D. 172
Bruce, E. 50, 66, 69, 71, 72, 296, 297
Bruner, J. 110
Bryan, J. 213, 214, 215, 216, 217, 220, 223
Bryden, C. 212, 217, 218, 220, 224
Buchanan, K. 282
Buchsbaum, B.C. 167
Burns, C.M. 347
Burns, R. 160
Burnside, I. 17, 18, 70, 244, 321
Burton, N. 143
Butler, R.N. 18, 38, 43, 45, 48, 87, 109, 122, 146, 201, 225, 244, 246, 248, 270, 304, 312
Butow, P.N. 52
Byrne, L. 154

Caldwell, R.L. 122
Calhoun, L.G. 164, 165, 166, 175, 176
Camic, P.M. 29
Campbell, J. 365
Cappeliez, P. 21, 23, 43, 44, 46, 52, 59, 128, 130, 173, 200, 208, 226, 227, 228, 232, 233, 234, 235, 236, 237, 238, 239, 240, 242, 244, 246, 270, 320, 321, 322
Carbine, M. 157
Carers UK 342

Carnahan, H. 276
Carroll, J.M. 345
Carstensen, L.L. 240, 313
Cartwright, J. 270
Caserta, M. 166
Chambers Coxsey, A. 167
Chan, C.L. 325
Chao, S.Y. 143
Charlesworth, G. 51, 52, 69, 81, 353
Chaudhury, H. 173
Chen, Y. 119, 322, 325
Chiang, K. 128
Chippendale, T. 54
Chittenden, M. 275
Chochinov, H.M. 169
Chonody, J. 122
Chou, Y. 139
Chow, A.Y. 325
Choy, J.C. 45, 54, 202, 230
Chung, C.K. 109, 320
Clandinin, D.J. 213, 215, 222
Claxton, A. 21
Clayton, J.M. 52
Cochran, K. 23, 48, 128, 129, 132, 137, 180, 321
Cohen, D.G. 25
Cohen, G.D. 325
Cohler, B.J. 216, 244, 249
Cole, T.R. 244, 249
Coleman, P.G. 20, 79, 87, 107, 226, 271, 272, 313, 321
Collins, J.B. 191
Connelly, D.M. 276
Conway, M.A. 246, 315, 318
Cooney, A. 49
Corbett, L. 157
Cosley, D. 42, 343
Coyle, S.M. 220, 221, 222
Craig, C. 25
Crites, S. 214, 216, 217
Cross, L.H. 19, 313
Cuijpers, P. 324
Culang, M.E. 314
Cully, J.A. 229, 232, 239
Cumberland, A. 116
Cummins, R.A. 56
Currier, J.M. 167

Damasio, A.R. 218
Dambrun, M. 241
Daniels, L.R. 322

Davis, C.G. 165, 173
Davison, E.H. 58
de Lange, J.J. 347
de Medeiros, K. 38, 201, 245, 246, 249, 250, 251
de Vries, B. 162, 168, 180, 189, 190, 191, 193, 194, 216, 244
Degroot, J.M. 168
Delello, J.A. 344
Demiray, B. 172, 201
Demiris, G. 341
Deng, D. 308
Denham, S.A. 116, 118
Dennis, M.R. 163, 165
Department of Health 343
Deschamps, A. 348
Deutchman, D.E. 23, 170, 180, 185, 244, 321
Devisch, I. 374
Dewhurst, S.A. 232
Dias, J. 61, 304, 305
Dickinson, G. 168, 174
Dickson-Swift, V. 277
Diener, E. 131, 137
Disch, R. 19
Dittmann-Kohli, F. 87, 314
Dobrof, R. 19
Domino, G. 314
Dritschel, B. 234
Duce, L. 77, 244
Duke, M.P. 112, 188
Dumas, J.S. 345
Dunlop, W.L. 111
Dunsmore, J.C. 116, 117, 119
Dutt, A.J. 234

Eisenberg, N. 116, 117
El Haj, M. 239
Elfrink, T.R. 344, 357
Eliot, T.S. 28
Emmerik-de Jong, M. 200
Ennis, E. 230
Erikson, E.H. 18, 59, 87, 119, 147, 150, 160, 173, 201, 225, 248, 304, 305, 312, 313
Erikson, J. 147
Eritz, H. 70
Eschenbruch, N. 123
Estey, J. 217, 221
Evans, G.E. 19
Every-Palmer, E. 374

Fabes, R.A. 117
Fagerstrom, K.M. 193
Farrant, K. 247, 261
Field, N.P. 168, 176
Fiese, B.H. 111
Filippas, T. 322
Fivush, R. 22, 109, 110, 112, 113, 114, 116, 117, 118, 120, 121, 122, 123, 188, 201, 247, 249, 313, 314
Flaskerud, J.H. 171
Folstein, M.F. 67
Folstein, S.E. 67
Ford, D.F. 212
Forstmeier, S. 38, 52, 305, 324, 325
Fortner, B.V. 314
Fox, C. 29
Frank, A. 221, 222, 223, 224
Frankl, V.E. 18, 147, 151, 152, 153, 202
Frattaroli, J. 320
Freeman, G.P. 173, 215, 218, 245
Freeman, M. 318
Freud, S. 164

Gabrian, M. 234
Gallo, E. 110
Garland, C. 87
Garland, J. 87
Garner, P.W. 117
Garrett, C.R. 378
Gemmell, J. 43
Genevro, J.L. 163
Gfeller, J.D. 229
Gibson, A. 345, 346, 347, 351
Gibson, F. 17, 18, 19, 22, 28, 38, 71, 140, 244, 248, 296, 363
Gilhooly, M.L. 167
Gillies, J. 164, 165, 166
Gitlin, L.N. 353
Glover, M. 376
Goffman, E. 245
Gomes, B. 178
Gonzalez, M. 47
Good, A. 343
Gottschall, J. 110
Gould, O. 313
Gowans, G. 354
Grace, L. 232, 237, 239
Graci, M.E. 110, 120
Graff, M.J. 347
Granek, L. 164
Greenberg, M.A. 185

Greenhoot, A.F. 320
Groenewoud, H. 347
Groenewoud, J.H. 347
Gross, E. 171
Grusec, J.E. 117
Gudex, C. 70
Guindon, M. 21, 239
Gulotta, R. 169
Gwynne, G.V. 25

Haber, D. 128
Habermas, T. 119, 120, 201, 202, 314, 317
Haden, C.A. 113, 118, 249
Haesner, M. 344
Hagman, G. 167
Hagstrom, F. 26
Haight, B.K. 17, 18, 22, 48, 50, 61, 66, 70, 226, 244, 304, 305, 306, 307, 308, 309, 310, 321, 363, 364
Haight, B.S. 48, 306, 307, 308, 309, 310, 364
Halberstadt, A.G. 116, 117, 118
Hallford, D.J. 54, 56, 201, 204, 207, 208, 209, 227, 241, 322
Hamel, A.V. 42, 344, 345, 349, 350, 351
Hannah, M. 314
Hannan, R. 275
Hanson, E. 345, 348, 351
Hardy, P. 355
Harris, C.B. 172, 227, 242
Harris, I. 374
Haslam, C. 246
Haug, F. 47
Hecht, A. 340
Heckhausen, J. 167, 319
Heincke, S. G. 314
Heinik, J. 348
Heintzelman, S.J. 202, 240
Hellstrom, I. 348
Help the Aged 18, 20
Hendrix, S. 22
Henkel, L.A. 44, 45, 233
Hepper, E.G. 234
Hewitt, N. 21
Higginson, I.J. 178
History Alive 128
Hodgson, S. 297
Hofer, J. 228, 233

Howick, J. 374
Hsiang Shang Culture and Education Foundation 143
Hsu, H. 127
Hu, Y. 139
Huang, H.C. 70
Hulstijn, W. 348
Hunter, E.G. 169

Igou, E.R. 234
Ingersoll-Dayton, B. 50
Istvandity, L. 52
Ivani-Chalian, C. 87

Jack, F. 119
Jacobs, S.C. 164, 179
James, D.T. 25
James, W. 315
Janoff-Bulman, R. 165
Jenkins, D. 145
Joddrell, P. 347
Johnson, C.W. 47
Johnson, M.L. 18
Jones, T. 347
Jung, C.G. 173

Kadel Taras, S. 365
Kaminsky, M. 19
Karlsson, E. 342, 343, 351
Karn, M.A. 117
Kastenbaum, R.J. 167
Katz, L.F. 116, 118
Keal, R.M. 52
Keck, D. 214
Kelly, F. 356
Kemp, M. 18
Kenyon, G.M. 151, 201, 216, 222, 249
Keren, E. 202
Kerkhof, Y.J. 347, 356
Kerssens, C. 342, 343, 344, 350
Kessels, R.P. 348
Kessler, D. 174
Kevern, P. 213
Killick, J. 25, 29
Kim, Jinsoo J. 195
King, D.B. 44, 46, 227, 228, 230, 233
King, L.A. 202, 240, 319
Kinoshita, H. 178, 179
Kitwood, T. 221, 222, 294

Kivnick, H.Q. 87, 147
Klass, D. 162, 163, 166, 167, 168, 176
Kober, C. 202
Koh, J.B. 116
Korte, J. 53, 55, 209, 228, 229, 233, 237, 240, 322, 325
Kortum, P.T. 346
Koski, P.R. 26
Krause, N. 248
Kretzschmar, F. 349
Krok, D. 202
Kross, E. 241
Kübler-Ross, E. 174
Kuhl, D.R. 193
Kulkofsky, S. 116
Kunz, J. 23, 332
Kuo, T. 133, 137, 195

La Voie, D. 229
Lamers, S.A. 320, 322, 325
Lan, X. 325
Larson, J. 165
Latorre, J.M. 54, 308
Lawrence, A.M. 316
Lawrence, G. 356
Lazar, A. 341, 343, 344, 350, 353, 354
Lazarus, A. 188
Le Guin, U. 198
Legacy Art Work 127
Leming, M.R. 168, 174
Levine, L.J. 21, 163
Lewis, C.N. 18, 346
Lewis, J.R. 346
Lewis, M.I. 109, 122
Liao, H.W. 173, 174, 237, 319, 320
Lilgendahl, J.P. 111, 240
Lim, F.S. 347
Limandri, B. 270
Lin, C. 126
Lindsay, D.S. 172
Lipson, J. 277
Liu, S. 126
Liu-Huang, L. 127
Lopes, T.S. 49
Lord, K. 321
Lorenz, K. 342, 343, 347
Lou, V.W. 45, 54, 202, 230
Lu, P. 127
Luszcz, M.A. 347
Lyubomirsky, S. 232

McAdams, D.P. 110, 111, 119, 173, 201, 249, 314, 317, 320
McCallion, P. 322
McClintock, M. 379
McConkey, J. 20
McCormack, B. 348
McDonnell, E. 353
McElwain, N.L. 117
McHugh, J.E. 351, 353
McHugh, P. 66, 270
MacIntyre, A. 212, 215, 222
Mackay, M.M. 165, 171, 174, 175, 178
McKenna, H. 342
McKeown, J. 274, 353
McKim, A. 201, 318
MacKinlay, E. 21, 145, 147, 148, 149, 151, 152, 153, 154, 155, 156, 157, 158, 159, 160, 212, 217, 219
McLean, K.C. 109, 110, 111, 113, 119, 201, 240, 316, 317, 320
McMahon, A.W. 18
McNally, R.J. 163
McPherson F.C. 165
McWhorter, R.R. 344
Madori, L.L. 136
Maercker, A. 308
Malde, S. 193
Maliken, A.C. 116
Mansfield, C.D. 119
Mansour, E. 316
Martin, M. 201
Marwit, S.J. 162, 168
Mather, M. 240
Mayseless, O. 202
Meléndez, J.C. 54
Mellor, D. 56, 201, 204, 207, 208, 209, 227, 241, 322
Melunsky, N. 51, 52, 81, 353
Menne, H.L. 348
Merriam, S.B. 19, 313
Merrill, N. 109, 110, 120, 121, 122, 123
Metzger, B.M. 220
Mezred, D. 230
Michel, Y. 22
Miller, E.J. 25
Miller, J.T. 346
Miller, W.L. 25, 276
Mischel, W. 241
Mischler, M. 201
Moen, T. 214

Mokel, M. 21
Molinari, V. 19
Montgomery, S.A. 87
Moody, H. 20
Moos, I. 65
Morgan, S. 308
Morita, T. 308
Moules, N.J. 164
Moulin, C.J. 246
Mroz, E.L. 166, 168, 177
Muhlert, N. 43
Mulvenna, M.D. 342, 343, 344, 349, 354
Murphy, B.C. 117
Murphy, R.E. 220
Murray, S. 374
Myers, J.E. 123

National Center for Creative Aging 25
Negru-Subtirica, O. 202
Neimeyer, R.A. 58, 163, 164, 165, 166, 168, 174, 314
Neisser, U. 173
Nelson, K. 112, 113
Neugarten, B.L. 157
Newell, A. 345
Newman, E.J. 172
Nickman, S.L. 166
Niebuhr, H.R. 215, 219
Nijhof, N. 347
Nile, E. 21, 208
Nolen-Hoeksema, S. 165, 232, 235
Northern Health and Social Care Trust 263

O'Connor, S. 308, 345, 347
O'Rourke, N. 21, 23, 43, 44, 46, 173, 200, 202, 226, 227, 228, 230, 232, 233, 234, 235, 237, 238, 239, 240, 242, 341, 350
Orpwood, R. 348
Orrell, M. 51, 76, 80
Orth, K. 195
Osborn, C. 288
O'Shea, E. 49, 342
Ouden, E.D. 345

Palmer, S.B. 356, 357
Pals, J.L. 111, 319
Park, C.L. 202
Parker-Oliver, D. 178

Pasupathi, M. 111, 240, 244, 249, 313, 314, 316
Patterson, M. 25
Pear, T.H. 17, 377
Peisah, C. 356
Pennebaker, J.W. 109, 184, 320
Perlstein, S. 25
Petrie, K.J. 185
Phillips, J. 275
Phinney, A. 341
Pierce, T.W. 42, 47
Piko, B.F. 202
Pillemer, D.B. 175, 320
Pincus, A. 18
Pincus, T. 374
Pinquart, M. 38, 52, 305, 324, 325
Polkinghorne, D.E. 172
Poll, J.B. 224
Pot, A. 322
Poulin, M. J. 319
Price, B. 19
Prigerson, H.G. 164, 179
Pringle, A. 350
Proust, M. 17
Purves, B. 341

Radloff, L.S. 230
Rajaram, S. 247
Randall, W.L. 201, 213, 214, 215, 219, 221, 222, 249, 318
Rappaport, J. 122, 244
Rasmussen, A.S. 44, 238
Rasmussen, L. 293
Rathbone, C.J. 246
Reedy, M. 191, 193
Reese, E. 113, 118, 119, 120, 247, 261
Regier, N.G. 353
Reichlin, R.E. 19
Reker, G.T. 165, 169, 192, 202
Reminiscence Network Northern Ireland 278
Reminiscence Theatre Archive 285
Rengade, C.E. 234
Reutens, S. 356
Rhudick, P.J. 18
Ribeiro, O.M. 49
Ricard, M. 241
Rice, C. 314
Ricoeur, P. 110
Riley, P. 345, 348

Robinaugh, D.J. 163
Robinson, L. 345, 348
Robinson, M. 87
Robitaille, A. 21, 128, 130, 233, 239, 320
Rochat, L. 233
Ros, L. 46, 202, 227, 228, 230, 233
Ross, M. 173
Rossetti, C. 167
Rosson, M.B. 345
Rowles, G.D. 169
Roziek, J. 213
Rubin, S.S. 170
Russell, I. 63, 64, 65
Ruth, J.E. 172, 190
Rutherford, J. 162, 168
Ryan, A.A. 342, 351, 352, 353
Ryff, C.D. 193, 314

Saarni, C. 116
Sabat, S.R. 217, 218, 219, 224
Sabir, M. 47, 54
Sales, J.M. 118
Salmon, K. 118
Salovey, P. 233
Sarne-Fleischmann, V. 343, 351, 354
Sas, C. 168
Sauro, J. 345, 346
Savage, C. 356
Sawin, L. 157
Sayer, A. 314
Scheier, M.F. 319
Schiff, B. 89, 216, 313
Schroots, J.J. 38, 192
Schulz, R. 319
Schut, H. 164, 167
Schwab, R. 162, 174
Schweitzer, P. 24, 50, 51, 66, 69, 72, 284, 285, 286, 288, 291, 292, 297, 299
Scogin, F. 319
Seamark, D.B. 276
Seamon, J.G. 43
Sedikides, C. 234
Sedney, M.A. 171, 172, 176
Segal, Z.V. 241
Segerstrom, S.C. 233
Serrano, J.P. 122, 241, 308
Shadden, B.B. 26, 219, 220, 221
Shair, H. 164

Shakespeare, W. 177
Shand, A.F. 167
Shear, K. 164
Sheikh, J.I. 131, 137
Shellman, J.M. 21, 46, 230, 322
Shenk, D. 354
Sherman, E.A. 246
Shik, A.W. 29
Silverman, P.R. 166
Singer, J.A. 165, 171, 173, 174, 175, 176, 315, 320
Singh, A.A. 47
Skowronski, J.J. 319
Slavney, P.R. 270
Smit, F. 324
Smith, D.L. 270
Smith, E.E. 197
Smith, K.L. 354, 357
Smith, T.B. 224
Sneed, J.R. 314
Sok, S.R. 308
Soltys, F. 23
Somerville, S. 350
Sommer, K.L. 122
Sools, A.M. 322
Southam-Gerrow, M. 117
Span, M. 345, 347, 348
Spector, A. 66, 76
Spielberger, C.D. 236
Spinrad, T.L. 116
Spruytte, N. 76, 352
Srivanas, E. 122
Stahel, P. 365
Staudinger, U.M. 226, 236
Steger, M.F. 202, 203, 205, 208
Steinhauser, K.E. 178
Stenhouse, R. 351, 355
Stettler, N.M. 116
Stone, A.A. 185
Stratford & Associates 265, 278, 279
Stroebe, M. 164, 167
Su, B. 125
Subramaniam, P. 24, 68, 70, 83, 308, 343, 349, 355, 356
Summer, T. 355
Svensson, C.M. 109, 128, 132, 165, 180, 190, 192
Sweeting, H.N. 167
Swinton, J. 217, 220
Syed, M. 111, 113

Taiwan Ministry of Health and Welfare 143
Taiwan National Development Council 126
Tamura, T. 341
Tanaka, K. 308
Tarman, V.I. 29
Taylor, C. 213, 214, 221
Teasdale, J.D. 241
Tedeschi, R.G. 164, 165, 166, 175, 176
Teri, L. 230
Testad, I. 70
Thanasoula, L. 195
Thiry, E. 343
Thomas, L. 42
Thompson, H. 341
Thompson, P. 19
Thorgrimsen, L. 51, 72, 76
Thorne, A. 194, 316
Thornton, J.E 180, 185, 189, 191
Timmer, E. 314
Tischler, V. 29
Tornstam, L. 160
Tõugu, P. 113
Tractinsky, N. 343, 351, 354
Tracy, J.L. 111
Tran, K. 196
Trevitt, C. 21, 145, 148, 151, 154, 155, 160, 219
Triliva, S. 322
Trilling, A. 299
Tripp, G. 118
Tsuda, A. 308
Tyrrell, M. 339, 340

Uehara, I. 112
Upton, D. 347, 349
Upton, P. 347

Valenkamp, M.W. 203
Valentino, K. 56
Van Bergen, P. 21, 208
van den Hoonaard, D.K. 171
van den Hoven, E. 168
Van der Linden, M. 233
van der Velden, A.M. 241
van Dongen, L. 192
van Gemert-Pijnen, J.E. 347
van Tilborg, I.A. 234, 348
van Tilburg, W.A. 234
Vandervoort, A.A. 276
Vidal-Hall, S. 172, 175, 176, 178
Volling, B.L. 117
Vota, R.L. 191
Vowinckel, J.C. 204
Vygotsky, L.S. 112

Wahl, H.W. 234
Walker, W.R. 319
Wallace Consulting 264
Wallace, T. 347
Walter, T. 174
Wang, C.W. 325
Wang, D. 122
Wang, Q. 111, 113, 116
Ward, S.J. 240
Warnock, M. 17, 20
Washington, G. 46
Waters, T.E. 201, 227
Watkins, E. 235
Watson, L.A. 234
Watt, L.M. 43, 52, 59, 61, 164, 169, 270, 271, 321, 322
Wayman, L. 343
Webster, J.D. 20, 22, 23, 40, 41, 42, 43, 46, 48, 58, 59, 123, 130, 172, 173, 175, 200, 202, 204, 208, 209, 226, 230, 244, 246, 313, 314, 315, 363
Weeks, T. 111, 314
Wenborn, J. 276
Werner, P. 348
Westerhof, G.J. 23, 24, 40, 44, 48, 52, 169, 170, 200, 203, 225, 230, 241, 244, 245, 246, 261, 314, 315, 318, 319, 320, 321, 322, 325
Westwood, M.J. 57, 193
Wetzstein, V. 195
Whitaker, C. 68, 168
Whitbourne, S.K. 245, 314
White, N. 119
Whitlatch, C.J. 348
Whittaker, S. 43
Williams, J.G. 320
Williams, J.M. 50, 241
Williams, K. 42
Wilson, A.E. 173
Wink, P. 89, 313
Wisco, B.E. 232

Wong, P.T. 43, 61, 164, 169, 270, 271
Woodhead, D. 301
Woods, B. 23, 24, 49, 51, 52, 66, 68, 69, 70, 72, 78, 83, 343, 349, 353, 355, 356
Woods, R.T 63, 64, 65, 74, 76, 308
World Health Organization 127
Worthington, A. 164
Wortman, C.B. 167
Wright, A.A. 163
Wright, T. 349
Wrosch, C. 319
Wyatt, T. 116

Xiao, H. 308, 322, 325

Yancura, L.A. 42
Yasuda, K. 354
Yesavage, J.A. 131, 137
Yin, R.K. 250
Young, R. 29

Zaman, W. 113, 114, 116, 122
Zeilig, H. 29
Zhang, D. 46
Zhang, X. 322, 325
Zizioulas, J.D. 214